Contemporary Issues with Multidisciplinary Perspectives on Social Sciences

Yusuf Kaderli, Engin Çakır (Eds.)

Contemporary Issues with Multidisciplinary Perspectives on Social Sciences

PETER LANG

Bibliographic Information published by the Deutsche Nationalbibliothek
The Deutsche Nationalbibliothek lists this publication in the Deutsche Nationalbibliografie; detailed bibliographic data is available online at http://dnb.d-nb.de.

Library of Congress Cataloging-in-Publication Data
A CIP catalog record for this book has been applied for at the Library of Congress.

ISBN 978-3-631-81593-9 (Print)
E-ISBN 978-3-631-84843-2 (E-PDF)
E-ISBN 978-3-631-84844-9 (EPUB)
E-ISBN 978-3-631-84845-6 (MOBI)
DOI 10.3726/b18093

Peter Lang – Berlin · Bern · Bruxelles · New York · Oxford · Warszawa · Wien

This publication has been peer reviewed.

www.peterlang.com

Preface

Scientific knowledge, which has a cumulative character, emerges as the product of a mastered point of view as a result of long years of research. Scientific knowledge comprises the result of a rational and public way of thinking from the past to the future. Social sciences are also an area that produces scientific knowledge.

Social sciences are made up of science disciplines that research humanity, society, and the world with a human dimension, therefore its domain of influence is also serious and wide. Naturally, the social scientist has the power to influence society with his research and writing. Philosophers such as Confucius, Socrates, Jean-Jacques Rousseau, Karl Marx, Ibn Khaldun have deeply influenced society with their writings. In other words, they have pioneered the change in history. Because of the importance of Social Sciences, it needs to be supported and to be used for the benefit of society.

For this reason, social sciences require a channel where there are literature and discussions about the field. University literature comes first among these channels. Books, magazines, articles, etc. are platforms in which the academic information is produced and contributes to the cumulative knowledge from which it comes.

In today's world, the studies in the field of social sciences increase its importance and new approaches are emerging. This book, in which we include scientific research on current issues in the field of social sciences, is thought to contribute to the researchers working in the relevant field.

This study aims to add the contributions of academicians from different disciplines to the social sciences fields they specialize in the academic literature and to give an idea about new researches. In this context, scientific articles in the departments of business, economics, public finance, tourism, international relations have been included in the book. The book consists of twenty-five chapters. All scientific writing, ethical and legal responsibilities of the articles published in the chapters of the book belong to their authors. We would like to thank our colleagues, who contributed to the creation of the book both by writing and by refereeing, and Peter Lang Publishing Group.

We hope that it will be useful to all readers, researchers, and the world of science.

Contents

List of Contributors

Melda Akbaba
Asst.Prof.Dr., Kilis 7 Aralık University, Kilis, Turkey, mharbalioglu@kilis.edu.tr, ORCID ID: 0000-0001-8701-017X

Zeynep Aydin
Aydin Adnan Menderes University, Aydin, Turkey, zynpayydin@gmail.com, ORCID ID: 0000-0002-3358-0000

Engin Cakir
Asst.Prof.Dr., Aydin Adnan Menderes University, Aydin, Turkey, engincakir@adu.edu.tr, ORCID ID: 0000-0002-5906-4178

Mesut Cakir
Asst.Prof.Dr., Aydin Adnan Menderes University, Aydin, Turkey, mcakir@adu.edu.tr, ORCID ID: 0000-0003-4980-1047

Yildirim Beyazit Cicen
Asst.Prof.Dr., Gumushane University, Gumushane, Turkey, ybcicen@gumushane.edu.tr, ORCID ID: 0000-0002-3425-280X

Zuhal Cilingir Uk
Asst.Prof.Dr., Ondokuz Mayıs University, Samsun, Turkey, zuhal.cilingir@omu.edu.tr, ORCID ID: 0000-0002-3271-7765

Necmiye Comertler
Prof.Dr., Aydin Adnan Menderes University, Aydin, Turkey, ncomertler@adu.edu.tr, ORCID ID: 0000-0002-0370-843X

Mehmet Metin Dam
Asst.Prof.Dr., Aydin Adnan Menderes University, Aydin, Turkey, metindam@adu.edu.tr, ORCID ID: 0000-0003-3980-7832

Cem Duran
Asst.Prof.Dr., Istinye University, Istanbul, Turkey, cduran@istinye.edu.tr, ORCID ID: 0000-0001-5171-0270

Ramazan Ekinci
Asst.Prof.Dr., Bakircay University, İzmir, Turkey, ramazan.ekinci@bakircay.edu.tr, ORCID-ID: 0000-0001-7420-9841

Mehmet Levent Erdas
Asst.Prof.Dr., Akdeniz University, Antalya, Turkey, leventerdas@gmail.com, ORCID ID: 0000-0001-6594-4262

Zeynep Ezanoglu
PhD student, Suleyman Demirel University, Isparta, Turkey, zeynepezanoglu@gmail.com, ORCID ID: 0000-0002-4601-7567

Sidre Gul Bige Gocekli
Res.Asst., Aydin Adnan Menderes University, Aydin, Turkey, sgb.gocekli@adu.edu.tr, ORCID ID: 0000-0002-5406-4304

Burcu Hicyilmaz
Res.Asst.Dr., Aydin Adnan Menderes University, Aydin, Turkey, burcu.yilmaz@adu.edu.tr, ORCID ID: 0000-0003-3501-2012

İsmail İsler
Asst.Prof.Dr., Pamukkale University, Denizli, Turkey, iisler@pau.edu.tr, ORCID ID: 0000-0002-9666-130X

Hatime Kamilcelebi
Asst. Prof. Dr., Kirklareli University, Kirklareli, Turkey, hatimekamilcelebi@klu.edu.tr, ORCID ID: 0000-0002-1028-7135

Busra Kutlu Karabiyik
Res.Asst.Dr., Aydin Adnan Menderes University, Aydin, Turkey, busra.kutlu@adu.edu.tr, ORCID ID: 0000-0002-6691-2921

Serhat Karaoglan
Res.Asst.Dr., Kirikkale University, Kirikkale, Turkey, serhat@karaoglan.net, ORCID ID: 0000-0002-4120-4013

İbrahim Karatas
Dr., Istinye University, Istanbul, Turkey, ibratas@gmail.com, ORCID ID: 0000-0002-2125-1840

Yusuf Kaya
Asst.Prof.Dr., Pamukkale University, Denizli, Turkey, ykaya@pau.edu.tr, ORCID ID: 0000-0002-2076-9808

Gamze Kayan
Res.Asst., Ondokuz Mayıs University, Samsun, Turkey, gamze.kayan@omu.edu.tr, ORCID ID: 0000-0001-8726-5551

Mustafa Cem Kirankabes
Assoc.Prof.Dr., Balikesir University, Balikesir, Turkey, ckirankabes@balikesir.edu.tr, ORCID ID: 0000-0002-0807-5897

Cagri Koroglu
Assoc.Prof.Dr., Aydin Adnan Menderes University, Aydin, Turkey, cagrikoroglu@hotmail.com, ORCID ID: 0000-0003-4073-1847

Asli Kose
Asst.Prof.Dr., Gumushane University, Gumushane, Turkey, asl_kse@hotmail.com, ORCID ID: 0000-0002-8044-6592

Aslihan Yavuzalp Marangoz
Asst. Prof.Dr., Toros University, Mersin, Turkey, aslihan.marangoz@toros.edu.tr, ORCID ID: 0000-0002-5119-4330

Yakup Soylemez
Asst.Prof.Dr., Zonguldak Bülent Ecevit University, Zonguldak, Turkey, yakup.soylemez@beun.edu.tr, ORCID ID: 0000-0002-6185-3192

Kezban Talak
Dr., Istanbul Medeniyet University, Istanbul, Turkey, ktalak@gmail.com, ORCID ID:0000-0002-7837-5852

Nihat Tavsan
Dr., Piri Reis University, Istanbul, Turkey, antavsan@pirireis.edu.tr, ORCID ID: 0000-0001-7085-0893

Sevgi Eda Tuzcu
Dr., Ankara University, Ankara, Turkey, stuzcu@politics.ankara.edu.tr, ORCID ID: 0000-0002-3658-2546

Mehmet Utku
Asst.Prof.Dr., Pamukkale University, Denizli, Turkey, mutku@pau.edu.tr, ORCID ID: 0000-0002-7076-6891

A. Elif Ay Yalcinkaya
Asst.Prof.Dr., Dokuz Eylul University, İzmir, Turkey, elif.ay@deu.edu.tr, ORCID-ID: 0000-0003-4417-2341

Gulizar Seda Yilmaz
Res.Asst.Dr., Aydin Adnan Menderes University, Aydin, Turkey, seda.corak@adu.edu.tr, ORCID ID: 0000-0003-2430-6808

Murat Yorulmaz
Asst.Prof.Dr., Kocaeli University, Kocaeli, Turkey, murat.yorulmaz@kocaeli.edu.tr, ORCID ID: 0000-0002-5736-9146

Secreteria

Res.Asst. Sidre Gul Bige Gocekli

Referees

DR. AHU YAZICI AYYILDIZ
DR. ALİ PETEK
DR. ARZU ORGAN
DR. ASLI YENİPAZARLI
DR. AYNUR UÇKAÇ
DR. AZİZ BOSTAN
DR. BURCU HİÇYILMAZ
DR. BÜLENT YILDIZ
DR. BÜŞRA KUTLU KARABIYIK
DR. ÇAĞRI KÖROĞLU
DR. DİLEK ELVAN ÇOKİŞLER
DR. E.YASEMİN BOZDAĞLIOĞLU
DR. ECE AKSU ARMAĞAN
DR. ENGİN ÇAKIR
DR. ESİN SAYIN
DR. ESMA DURUKAL
DR. FATMA ÇAKIR
DR. FERİŞTAH SÖNMEZ
DR. FUNDA ÇONDUR
DR. GÖKHAN AKEL
DR. GÖNÜL TEZCAN
DR. GÜLİZAR SEDA YILMAZ
DR. GÜLŞAH SEZEN AKAR
DR. HATİCE EROL
DR. HÜSEYİN ŞENKAYAS
DR. İSMAİL İŞLER
DR. İSMET ATEŞ
DR. KIYMET YAVUZASLAN
DR. MEHMET BÖLÜKBAŞ
DR. MEHMET METİN DAM
DR. NECMİYE CÖMERTLER
DR. OSMAN PEKER
DR. SADULLAH ÇELİK
DR. SEDAT ALATAŞ
DR. SEMA OĞLAK

DR. SERCAN YAVAN
DR. ŞABAN ERTEKİN
DR. ŞANSEL ÖZPINAR
DR. TARIK ILİMAN
DR. TUĞBA AKIN
DR. UMUT EVLİMOĞLU
DR. UMUT TOLGA GÜMÜŞ

İbrahim Karatas

Russian Information Warfare: The Case of the White Helmets in Syria

Abstract Syria's opposition civil-defense network, namely the White Helmets, has been under the military and information warfare of Russia since the Russian army began to fight alongside the Syrian regime against rebel groups in September 2015. Designating the organization as a terrorist group, Russians attacked the White Helmets' operation centers and simultaneously waged an information war to smear the organization and perpetuate confusion among the world audience. This study has analyzed Russian media, affiliated news outlets, social media, pro-Russian reports disseminating Russian claims, the White Helmets' reports and concerning news in the Western media. It also made interviews with top officials of the organization to check the accuracy of Russian accusations. After comparing allegations of both sides, it has concluded that there is massive Russian information warfare on the White Helmets that testifies Russian and the regime crimes on the frontline. The research has also contended that Russian black propaganda has become successful. As a side finding, this study has revealed which tactics the Russian propaganda machine uses during the discrediting campaigns. Methodologically, both quantitative and qualitative researches were used.

Keywords: Information Warfare, Russia, Syria, White Helmets, Security

1 Introduction

The White Helmets (officially the Syrian Civil Defence) has been rescuing victims of the war from rubbles in mainly opposition-held areas of Syria since its establishment in 2013. Consisting of former engineers, bakers, tailors, students, shopkeepers, and people with many other professions, the humanitarian organization with over 3.000 volunteers has saved more than 100.000 lives as of January 2020. The White Helmets are funded, trained and supported by foreign governments particularly the US, the UK, Canada, European countries and some Arab states. They have a so dangerous job that some of the group members lost their lives or got injured while rescuing civilians in war-torn regions that were under continuous bombardment. According to the organization's website, 252 volunteers have been killed and a double of that number was injured (The White Helmets, 2019). Besides deaths emanating from the ongoing Russian and Syrian regime bombardments, they have been the private target of jet fighters due to their humanitarian activities and being the witnesses of war crimes. Thus, their buildings, cars and medical centers have been under deliberate attacks of artillery bombardment, missiles or barrel bombs. However, their efforts went viral thanks to Western media, which culminated in a nomination for Nobel Prize. Besides, a documentary film named 'The White Helmets' streamed at Netflix won 'the Best Documentary' at the 89th Academy Awards.

The White Helmets are now sandwiched between asymmetric warfare and information warfare conducted by Russia. The humanitarian aid group had been operating in areas out of the Syrian regime's control since the civil war erupted. Its efforts got praise from the world governments and audience but things changed when Russia directly got involved in the civil war on the side of the Assad regime. As soon as Russian jets dropped the first bomb on opposition groups on September 30, 2015, Russian media outlets launched a massive anti-White Helmets campaign simultaneously (The Syria Campaign, 2017: 8). Since then, the White Helmets have been hit by bombs and the black propaganda of Russian information warriors. The White Helmets operates in fatal conditions to minimize the number of deaths. Yet, while the group and its volunteers could escape from bombardments, they could not save themselves from the virtual warfare perpetrated by pro-Russian individuals. This study investigates how a humanitarian aid association can be discredited through internet blogs, social media, trolls, and classic media though it saves lives in the combat. To reveal the truth about the White Helmets and the reliability of Russian claims that are regarded as false propaganda by the Western media, accusations of pro-Russian groups and responses of the White Helmets have been analyzed for this study. By this way, this study intends to unveil; (1) how Russian information warfare is influential alongside the real war, (2) how perceptions can be changed negatively even against well-intentioned activities, and (3) why and how information warfare is complementary to ordinary warfare. This research contends from analyzes that Russia uses information as a weapon because Russians want to; (1) create doubt and confusion in the minds of foreign public, (2) do not want to witnesses on the ground that uncover their war crimes, (3) legitimize its attacks and whitewash the Assad regime, and (4) eliminate the White Helmets. In addition, it will also try to reveal how Russian propaganda works by analyzing their methods. In other words, this study plans to unveil Russian information warfare through analyzing its attacks on the White Helmets. The article expects to contribute to the theoretical literature of information warfare, particularly that of Russia.

Methodologically, pro-Russian media disseminating Russian claims, counter reports and allegations of the White Helmets and concerning news in the Western media that aim to disprove Russian evidence have been examined and compared with each other. Further to documentary analysis, telephone and face-to-face interviews were made with the group leader Raed Saleh and some other officials of the organization. No people from Russian and the Syrian regime side could be accessed. While a section was dedicated to Russian information warfare, the White Helmets group is briefly explained in Introduction (see above) due to space problem.

The White Helmets (officially the Syrian Civil Defence) has been rescuing victims of the war from rubbles in mainly opposition-held areas of Syria since its establishment in 2013. Consisting of former engineers, bakers, tailors, students, shopkeepers, and people with many other professions, the humanitarian organization with over 3.000 volunteers has saved more than 100.000 lives as of January 2020. The White Helmets are funded, trained and supported by foreign governments particularly the US, the UK, Canada, European countries and some Arab states. They have a so dangerous job that some of the group members lost their lives or got injured while rescuing civilians in war-torn regions that were under continuous bombardment. According to the organization's website, 252 volunteers have been killed and a double of that number was injured (The White Helmets, 2019). Besides deaths emanating from the ongoing Russian and Syrian regime bombardments, they have been the private target of jet fighters due to their humanitarian activities and being the witnesses of war crimes. Thus, their buildings, cars and medical centers have been under deliberate attacks of artillery bombardment, missiles or barrel bombs. However, their efforts went viral thanks to Western media, which culminated in a nomination for Nobel Prize. Besides, a documentary film named 'The White Helmets' streamed at Netflix won 'the Best Documentary' at the 89th Academy Awards.

The White Helmets are now sandwiched between asymmetric warfare and information warfare conducted by Russia. The humanitarian aid group had been operating in areas out of the Syrian regime's control since the civil war erupted. Its efforts got praise from the world governments and audience but things changed when Russia directly got involved in the civil war on the side of the Assad regime. As soon as Russian jets dropped the first bomb on opposition groups on September 30, 2015, Russian media outlets launched a massive anti-White Helmets campaign simultaneously (The Syria Campaign, 2017: 8). Since then, the White Helmets have been hit by bombs and the black propaganda of Russian information warriors. The White Helmets operates in fatal conditions to minimize the number of deaths. Yet, while the group and its volunteers could escape from bombardments, they could not save themselves from the virtual warfare perpetrated by pro-Russian individuals. This study investigates how a humanitarian aid association can be discredited through internet blogs, social media, trolls, and classic media though it saves lives in the combat. To reveal the truth about the White Helmets and the reliability of Russian claims that are regarded as false propaganda by the Western media, accusations of pro-Russian groups and responses of the White Helmets have been analyzed for this study. By this way, this study intends to unveil; (1) how Russian information warfare is influential alongside the real war, (2) how perceptions can be changed negatively even against well-intentioned activities, and (3) why and how information warfare is complementary to ordinary warfare. This research contends from analyzes that Russia uses information as a weapon because Russians want to; (1) create doubt and confusion in the minds of foreign public, (2) do not want to witnesses on the ground that uncover their war crimes, (3) legitimize its attacks and whitewash the Assad regime, and (4) eliminate the White Helmets. In addition, it will also try to reveal how Russian propaganda works by analyzing their methods. In other words, this study plans to unveil Russian information warfare through analyzing its attacks on the White Helmets. The article expects to contribute to the theoretical literature of information warfare, particularly that of Russia.

Methodologically, pro-Russian media disseminating Russian claims, counter reports and allegations of the White Helmets and concerning news in the Western media that aim to disprove Russian evidence have been examined and compared with each other. Further to documentary analysis, telephone and face-to-face interviews were made with the group leader Raed Saleh and some other officials of the organization. No people from Russian and the Syrian regime side could be accessed. While a section was dedicated to Russian information warfare, the White Helmets group is briefly explained in Introduction (see above) due to space problem.

2 Information Warfare vs. Russia

Information warfare is a concept referring to the use of information and communication technology to obtain a competitive advantage over the adversary. It is secret, bloodless, ambiguous and invisible and there are no doctrines or battlefields for it. Activities include stealing, interdicting, distorting, manipulating or destroying information by using computers, smartphones, internet, social media, classical media, trolls, politicians, celebrities, and so on (Giles,

2016: 4). It aims to disseminate misinformation to polarize, demoralize, discredit, demonize or delegitimize its target (Porotsky, 2018). Such warfare is sustained through fake news/information generated by state institutions, concerning public servants and hired people whose audience are local and foreign public that are addressed to be deceived, got confused, change their perceptions, support the side trolls want them to do, etc. Information warfare and cyber warfare are not the same. While the former targets mind and perceptions of people through misinformation, the latter aims to steal information by hacking computers or destroy both software and the hardware of an IT system. For example, while fake news is a part of information warfare, sending viruses to a computer system that controls the electricity network is in the cyber warfare category. More clearly, in spite of a blurred line between the two, for instance, a hacker is a cyber-warrior while a troll spreading fake news can be called an information-warrior.

Regarding Russia's information warfare (*informatsionnaya voyna*), it is one of the most influential countries wielding information as a weapon in the world. Russia is unique in this area since their understanding of the concept and methods they use are quite different than in other countries. First of all, it is a national (war) policy of the country, which Vladimir Putin expresses as "We must take into account the plans and directions of development of the armed forces of other countries... Our responses must be based on intellectual superiority, they will be asymmetric, and less expensive (Giles, 2016: 3)". Russian former Chief of Staff General Valery G. Gerasimov says that the ratio of non-military to military activities is 4:1 (for Russia). On the other hand, Aleksander Dvornikov, another top commander being well aware of the effect of non-military measures, says that Russia owes its success in Syria to information operations (Tashev, Purcell & McLaughlin, 2019: 133–134). Russians explain their goals as to obtain psychological and ideological superiority, damaging political systems of hostile countries, particularly those in the Western camp, and affect perceptions of foreign populations, which we all know as public diplomacy. Unlike other countries, for the Russian state, it is an ongoing activity both in peacetime and wartime. Generally, countries begin it just before a war to legitimize their attacks but Russians do it even if there is no state of war. Besides, the Russian state has a holistic approach to this issue that all governmental bodies and even Russian people get involved in information warfare while in other countries, conversely, it is the military staff that undertake this duty. For example, almost all Russian embassies use twitter actively, respond to anti-Russian claims and get into polemics with foreign politicians. According to Ajir and Vailliant (2018: 72–81), the Russian regime maintains its warfare over the legacy of the Soviet Union, which began to use information as a weapon from 1919 onwards and dedicated 15,000 personnel and an annual budget of $3–4 billion. Russia utilizes such warfare because it does not have enough resources to confront the United States and its allies. Besides, it is a cheaper way when compared to military solutions and allows gaining superiority in some spheres.

4 The Russian Information Warfare Against the White Helmets

The White Helmets define itself as a neutral organization that focuses only on the humanitarian side of the war. However, they are not impartial politically. Interviewees are particularly furious to Bashar Assad and accuse him of killing his citizens. Therefore, they express that Assad must be held accountable and judged in the court. A top political executive of opposition groups that wanted to remain anonymous argues that not only Assad but his regime formed by his father should also be abolished as the system is the main creator of the current civil war. Yet, despite being anti-Assad, they refuse any allegations that they are working with armed groups or their volunteers are also fighters. On the other hand, the Syrian regime and Russia see the organization as a terrorist group linked with other militant groups (Malsin, 2016). The White Helmets are also accused of lobbying foreign military intervention and working as agents (Samir, 2019).

Before discussing Russia's information warfare against the group, it should be noted that Russians also wage a real war against them. Since the Assad regime and its main supporter Russia have labeled the group as a terrorist organization, they do not discriminate between armed factions and the White Helmets. Interviewees and reports prepared by the group contend that Russians use a 'double-tap' tactic, meaning that they re-bomb a site already bombed a short while before. The aim is to kill the rescue team, harm their equipment and cause more civilian loss (SNHR, 2019). Therefore, while the first strike is conducted to kill a premeditated target, the second is done to kill those running to rescue injured people. In other words, the second strike is exclusive to the White Helmets. In addition, civil-defense centers are specifically pounded by Russian jets to kill volunteers. Another way of eliminating volunteers is assassinations. For example, according to Sanchez (2017), seven members of the White Helmets were assassinated in their operation center located in Salmin, Idlib. Volunteers argue that they encounter such attacks continuously. As a result, 15 % of volunteers have either been killed or injured since the formation of the group.

Regarding the basic subject, Russia's information warfare against the White Helmets, it was launched as soon as Russia began to bomb anti-regime groups in September 2015. RT, Sputnik, blogs, trolls, and journalists close to Russia inaugurated a massive campaign to smear the White Helmets. As will be explained below, Russian black propaganda is systematic, coordinated and carried out by a network that feeds each other in terms of information. The aim looks misinforming and misleading people, distorting and covering facts on the ground, gaining the support of the international audience, and showing their attacks as fighting terrorism. According to Solon (2017) of *The Guardian*, Russians have generally succeeded in changing the perception of the world audience. However, as the claims dominating media are not always correct, this study has selected some basic claims of Russian media and compared it with responses of the White Helmets written in their reports and the Western media.

The first claim is that the White Helmets are an Al-Qaeda-linked terrorist organization and a tool of Western powers used for a regime change in Syria since it receives financial support from Western governments (Lester, 2018: 33). In addition, the group is accused of false flag chemical attacks aiming to force the US-led coalition to attack the regime forces (Nocetti, 2019: 7). Besides, it is blamed for assisting the executions of rebel groups. Operating only in rebel-held regions is also a matter of criticism. Further to the Assad regime, the YPG, Kurdish armed group controlling some parts of northern and eastern Syria, is also a critique of the White Helmets, arguing that it is an organization affiliated with armed groups based in Idlib. In line with such accusations, Russian media and journalists have published many reports claiming that the volunteers of the White Helmets are both rescuers and militants. They also publish and televise testimonies and photos of allegedly former members of the group. For example, Bartlett (2018) argues on RT's website that offices of the White Helmets are always close to Al-Qaeda and other terrorist groups including ISIS. She also claims that the volunteers of the group got involved in executions, cheered killings and disposed remains of Assad's soldiers. To support her arguments, she gives some links of websites containing videos allegedly proving the involvement of the White Helmets in murders. When websites (mintprsessnews.com, threadreaderapp.com, 21stcdenturywire.com, etc.) are analyzed, it can be seen that they are full of Russian propaganda content. What is more, the editor of 21stcdenturywire.com is Vanessa Beeley, another staunch supporter of Russian policies with British origin writing anti-White Helmets articles at Russian media and her blog. Canadian journalist Eva Bartlett introduces herself as a rights activist and an independent writer. Yet, she has photos with a wristband

'I love Bashar' (The Syria Campaign, 2017: 31). She also made a speech at the UN to support the Assad government in 2016.

Maxim Grigoriev's allegations are also worth mentioning. Mr. Grigoriev is the Director of The Foundation for the Study of Democracy. He wrote a book together with his colleague S. Maizel named 'The White Helmets: Fact-Checking By Eyewitnesses and Former Volunteers'. The book is allegedly based on interviews with the current and former White Helmets volunteers and residents living in areas where the organization operates. According to the book, volunteers confessed that they were doing rescue operations due to fear of armed groups, helping executions, getting regular payment, fighting, and so on. Authors also share photos of some volunteers with rifles (papes 9, 16, 19 and 22). They conclude from the interviews that; (1) most of the White Helmets are not volunteers but permanents workers with a monthly salary, (2) armed groups forced them to join the group as an alternative to being imprisoned or fighting, (3) the White Helmets offices were working closely with armed groups, (4) they got combat-training from Al-Nusra, and (5) most of volunteers continued to fight for various terrorist organizations (Grigoriev & Maizel, 2019: 7–10). The aforementioned book can be found in pdf format in almost all pro-Russian websites. In addition to Russians, Kurdish YPG and their supporters claim that the White Helmets are affiliated with Al-Qaeda. Salmo (2020), one of the interviewees, says he was working as the head of the organization in Afrin until 2015 but detained by YPG that accused the White Helmets of having ties with Al-Nusra.

The above accusations were asked to the White Helmets by phone and in face-to-face meetings. Raed Saleh (2020) denies terror links and says that they are an impartial organization with no terror links. He says they offer help to any group regardless of their ideologies. He argues that these are all the regime and Russian propaganda to discredit their organizations. In addition, he adds, had the White Helmets collaborated with terrorist groups, their Western donors would not support them. On the other hand, Salmo (2020) says when a person wants to be a volunteer, he/she has to leave other groups and forget politics. The White Helmets has a 'volunteer agreement', which is compulsory to sign. Besides, volunteers must have no double-profession and a clean past with no crimes. Grigoriev and Maizel's book was shown to three interviewees during the interview. They identified some of their friends but rejected accusations. Salmo said that "Those photos with guns were taken before volunteers joined the organization. Russians find photos and present them as if they are still fighting". He added that he had a gun when the uprising erupted in 2011 to protect himself from the paramilitary forces of Assad. Yet, he left the gun after joining the rescue group. Abdullah (2020) told the story of Abdul Hadi Kamil, a volunteer arrested by the regime forces. While Kamil was accompanying a civilian convoy, the regime's soldiers captured and imprisoned him. Then, he appeared at a Russian TV and said the White Helmets was working with Al-Qaeda. Thus, interviewees claim that the regime gets fake confessions by torture. Salmo (2020) mentioned about another method of Russians to get untrue confessions. He said that when a city is surrendered by regime forces, many volunteers leave the city but some of them stay there since it is their hometown. For example, when the Syrian Arab Army (SAA) entered Aleppo, 30 out of 150 volunteers left there. Hundred volunteers in Homs, 200 out of 500 in Ghouta and 400 in Daraa stayed instead of leaving. When soldiers asked civilians who were working for the organization, volunteers were fingered out by their scared neighbors. Hence, they were arrested and threatened to talk against the White Helmets. Moreover, interviewees claimed that some photos in the book are fake. For example, there are two photos of a volunteer (one with a gun and one with the uniform of the organization) on page 16. They said that photos belong to two different people, claiming that the authors inserted a photo of another person looking like a volunteer. Regarding YPG's hostility to the White Helmets, the Kurdish group criticizes the organization to operate in Afrin currently controlled by Turkey-backed Free Syrian Army but no attacks on volunteers have been reported. Yet, YPG refused the White Helmets' help for extinguishing fires burning wheat and barley crops in the YPG-held area in 2019.

Besides the White Helmets, Western media also found some discrepancies in Russian propaganda. For example, Qui (2017) of *The New York Times* argues that they have found no evidence that the White Helmets are linked to terrorist organizations. On the other hand, France 24 (2018) analyzed a few allegations shared by pro-Russian groups alleging that the White Helmets are undercover Islamist terrorists. The French media outlet, for example, uncovered that a person confessing at a pro-Assad TV was arrested and forced to read a pre-prepared script. In addition, it revealed that the posted video alongside the volunteer's testimony was actually taken in Bahrain in 2011. Moreover, France 24 posts an example of how a photo of suffocating children with no wounds was claimed to be fake propaganda of the White Helmets pretending to treat unwounded children. The photo was spread on Twitter by a person through a tweet tagging pro-Russian bloggers Eva Bartlett and Vanessa Beeley. The tweet was retweeted 12.500 times and liked 13.600 times. Yet, the person twitting the allegation admitted in another tweet that the photo was real, and apologized. That twit was retweeted 45 times and liked 56 times. Furthermore, *Bellingcat* website proved that the photos Rossiya 1 TV broadcasted in a news report supposedly indicating that the White Helmets stage videos for fake evidence are actually from a film called 'Revolution Man' (Bellingcat, 2016). Furthermore, Worrall (2016) of Channel 24 analyzed Eva Bartlett's claims about Syrian children. Bartlett claimed in her blog that 'Al Qaeda/White Helmets rescue the same girl three times in three months' and showed the three photos of allegedly the same girl, arguing that the White Helmets are featuring the same girl in their videos to deceive people. Yet, after contacting photographers and examining photos, Worrall concludes that photos were taken by international news agencies, for example Reuters, and there are three different girls in photos. In fact, the White Helmets indeed staged their 'Mannequin Challenge' video. Yet, as soon as it went viral, Russian trolls used it as evidence that the White Helmets is producing fake videos. The organization accepted its mistake and apologized for it but it had already been misused by Russian media[1].

Another allegation is that the White Helmets use chemical weapons to provoke Western countries to strike the regime. According to Schneider and Lütkefend (2019: 4), there have been 336 chemical weapons attacks since the Syrian Civil war started, of which 98 % are attributed to the regime and 2 % to ISIS. The most conspicuous attacks are the one in Ghouta that killed 1400 civilians on August 21, 2013, Khan Shaykhun attack killing 91 people on April 4, 2017, and Douma attack killing around 50 people in April 7, 2018. Gas attacks are regarded as a collective way of punishing rebel groups and populations in rebel-held areas. While foreign governments and international organizations accused the Assad regime, and the US defined such attacks as its red line that led it to fire tomahawk missiles to punish the Syrian government, Russian information warriors deny that SAA forces used chemical weapons. According to them, it is the White Helmets that spread such fake news.

Russians also blamed the organization for using chemical weapons. For example, right after the Douma attack, stories shared on social media and TVs claimed that there was no chemical attack, testimonies were fake, no patients in hospitals and it was fabricated by the White Helmets. Nocetti (2019: 1) believes that the Russian strategy was to cause confusion in the Western public, divide foreign leaders and sow doubt on the truth. On the contrary, McKeigue et al. (2019: 3–17) cast doubt on the White Helmets' claims about chemical attacks. They claim, for example, that during the sarin attack in Khan Shaykhun,

1 More analyzes about dubious photos and videos made viral by Russian accounts can be found at above media outlets and others.

100 affected patients came to the hospital before the attack. In addition, they argue that gas cylinders were highly likely placed at locations manually rather than dropped from an aircraft. Finally, the authors claim that no regime or Russian aircraft flew over the area. On the other hand, Wikileaks published an email of a member of the investigation team appointed by the Organization for the Prohibition of Chemical Weapons (OPCW). The undisclosed inspector expressed his suspicion about the possibility of the chemical attack made via dropping barrels from an aircraft. As expected, Russians used this email to whitewash the regime. However, Fernando Arias, the head of OPCW, stood by the report contending that the attack was carried out by a regime aircraft. In addition, OPCW inspectors said they were not allowed to enter the site for inspection. Since OPCW insisted on the correctness of its report, Russia threatened not to approve the organization's next year's budget. On the other hand, CBS News (2019) reports that it is not OPCW's duty to state whether cylinders were placed manually or dropped from the air.

Moreover, Schneider and Lütkefend look allegations about chemical attacks from a different but more scientific perspective. First, they argue that munitions used in all chemical attacks in Syria are always the same. The regime uses either Soviet-era munitions or homemade ones produced in Latakia (Schneider & Lütkefend, 2019: 11). Therefore, it is hardly acceptable to blame White Helmets for munitions of the regime. Second, chemical barrels are dropped by SAA's Mi-8/17 transport helicopters fleet. These helicopters are under the command of the Syrian army's elite troops called 'Tiger Forces', whom OPCW accuses of conducting chemical attacks. For example, when they were first deployed in Aleppo in 2015, chemical attacks were begun to be witnessed. When they moved to northern Hama in 2017, this time regime helicopters dropped chemical barrels to that place. Finally, when they were redeployed to Damascus in February 2018, helicopters conducted another gas attack in Eastern Ghouta (Ibid: 19–20). Regarding the reason for why the regime uses chemical gas, the White Helmets attribute it to merciless of Russians and the regime as well as forcing civilians to push militants to surrender. Indeed, civilians protested armed groups after attacks and eventually, militants had to accept an evacuation plan with the Assad forces.

Meanwhile, the Russian side has many other minor allegations about the White Helmets. Among them is whether people of the group are volunteers or paid workers. According to Di Giovanni (2018), full-time working volunteers are paid \$150 per month. Yet, Russians refuse them to be called volunteers. Abdussamed (2020), a volunteer, insists that they are volunteers. He says that he worked for one year without a stipend. In the second year, he got 10\$ per month and then got paid $150 a few years later. According to his explanation, the amount volunteers get paid depends on how much donation the organization receives. The more donations are, the more their salaries are high. If there is no donation, there will be no salary. Russian information warriors also claim that the White Helmets are in the organ trafficking business. When the allegation is tracked, it is seen that Beeley (2019) disseminated it via her article at rt.com. Yet, Beeley's source is a testimony, which the White Helmets argue taken under torture, published in Grigoriev and Maizel's above book. On the other hand, the organization's relations with James Le Mesurier, the late head of Mayday Foundation, are presented as a clue proving that the White Helmets is an agent working for Western states. Le Mesurier, a former British Army officer, was found dead in Istanbul in November 2019. According to the Turkish police, he committed suicide due to psychological problems (Daily Sabah, 2019). While British authorities saw him as a true hero, Russians propagated that he was a spy (MacMillan, 2019; RT, 2019). Regarding his connection with the White Helmets, Salmo (2020) says "We found Le Mesurier before he found us while we were looking for donors". Moreover, the White Helmets point to Russian black propaganda a few days before Le Mesurier died, implying without insisting that Russians might have been behind his death if the reason is not suicide. In one of twits of Russian Foreign Ministry dated November 8, 2019, three days before Le Mesurier's death, ministry's spokesperson Maria Zakharova accuses Le Mesurier of being an agent of Britain's MI6 (Russian MFA, 2019).

In association with information warfare, how Russians disseminate their claims in media is an important issue that needs to be analyzed. In fact, the organization already got a social media report prepared to *Graphika Intelligence* firm and published the details of the report in another report called 'Killing The Truth' (The Syria Campaign, 2017). According to the 48-page report, Russian bots and trolls reached 56 million people with twits that insulted the White Helmets during ten key incidents taking place in 2016 and 2017, particularly to cover up sarin gas attack to Khan Shaykhoun. Besides misinformation, twits also targeted the organization. For example, Vanessa Beeley, a key person in the Russian campaign, went far to say that "White Helmets are not getting it. We know they are terrorists. Makes them a legit target" in a twit dated October 30, 2015. While she deleted her twit later, it can still be found on many websites. Graphika found out that 50 % of those sharing anti-White Helmets twits have been involved in other Russian social media campaigns. The intelligence firm argues that they are well organized, functioning in the same network and act together. For example, on September 28, 2017, 21 accounts shared a video of Russian 'In The Now' website claiming that Khan Shaykhoun was a false flag within 42 seconds. In addition, on the same day, #SyriaHoax hashtag became the number one topic on Twitter with the help of a troll army. Simultaneously, prominent people such as American radio host Alex Jones, Senator Richard Black, and Democrat Congresswoman Tulsi Gabbard stated their doubts about the attack, confusing people's minds.

As cited from Western media above, Russia employs hundreds of trolls, tens of blogs and a few influential state-sponsored media outlets. To test how influential they are in social media, twits with #whitehelmets hashtag shared on January, 30 and 31, 2020 were analyzed for this study and seen that while 32 twits were anti-White Helmets, 18 were supporting the organization. Those twitting against the White Helmets do not use real names and share twits of Eva Bartlett, Vanessa Beeley and Sputnik News. While some accounts twit about the White Helmets twice a day, their main arguments are the organization's being a terrorist organization and staged chemical attacks.

Finally, based on the above analysis, why the Russian government wages information warfare on the White Helmets is a bit clear now. According to the interviewees, since the White Helmets operate frontline, they can supply first-hand evidence showing the real perpetrators of attacks. While Russia and the Assad regime do not want testimonies of their attacks, the White Helmets do not give up operating under the bombardments. Therefore, they target volunteers and affiliate them with terrorist groups to make the organization's evidence null. In addition, the White Helmets are an anti-regime group that wants Assad to be held accountable for his crimes. Thus, even if not physically, the organization is hostile to the regime, a reason that provokes the Syrian regime to attack the volunteers. Moreover, the White Helmets is funded by Western governments, which do not prefer to see Assad in power. In other words, from Assad's point of view, the organization is on the wrong side, thereby deserves attacking. Meanwhile, Jain (2018: 3) criticizes Western states' attitude which he calls 'selective humanitarianism'. He uses this term because 400 volunteers evacuated by the Israeli army on July 21, 2018, were accepted by Western governments to resettle in their countries. Jain argues that these governments remove the most qualified people from the frontline and leave rescue operations to unqualified people. Yet, resettlement of volunteers happened once and there are still thousands of volunteers in Syria. Overall, the White Helmets are struggling to survive from Russian military and information warfare while rescuing civilians from rubbles.

5 Conclusion

Russia's information warfare alongside military warfare has been more conspicuous in the course of the Syrian civil war. While using the information as a weapon during wartime is usual, speeches of top Russian officials disclose that Russia has such activities during peacetime as well. This study analyzed how Russian black propaganda hit the White Helmets, a civil-defense network operating in Syria since the civil war erupted. Reports, news, analysis of social media and interviews have shown that Russian media and affiliated people deliberately attack the White Helmets as it is the only organization that can catch the Syrian regime and Russian army while committing crimes. Russia's vast information army attack the organization through an organized and collective work to distort facts, misinform people and get confusion among the world audience. One aspect this study discovered is that the people got involved in smear campaigns are both evidence producers and disseminators. One can hardly find a source not affiliated to the huge network. Yet, such tactics work, and thanks to them, the White Helmets have been supposed as a terrorist organization by a considerable number of people. Even volunteers of the White Helmets admit that their propaganda has become successful. While the Western media counter-attempt to disclose fake evidence through fact-checking, they do not seem to balance Russian propaganda. However, despite the harming propaganda, the organization continues its humanitarian operations.

Bibliography

Abdullah, I. (2020). Interview, by Author, Istanbul.

Abdussamed, A. (2020). Interview, by Author, Istanbul.

Ajir, M., & Vailliant, B. (2018). Russian Information Warfare: Implications for Deterrence Theory. *Strategic Studies Quarterly*, 2018(Fall), 70–89.

Bartlett, E. (2018, August 10). Decision to Bring White Helmets to Canada Dangerous and Criminal. *Russia Today*. https://www.rt.com/op-ed/435670-white-helmets-canada-syria/, Accessed 02.01.2020.

Beeley, V. (2019, January 22). The White Helmets, Alleged Organ Traders & Child Kidnappers, Should Be Condemned Not Condoned. *Russia Today*. https://www.rt.com/op-ed/449431-syria-white-helmets-organ-traders/, Accessed 10.01.2020.

Bellingcat (2016, November 30). There's No Such Thing as a Good Fake – When Publicity Stunts Go Wrong. https://www.bellingcat.com/resources/articles/2016/11/30/theres-no-thing-good-fake-publicity-stunts-go-wrong/, Accessed 21.12.2019.

CBS News (2019, November 25). Chemical Weapons Watchdog OPCW Defends Syria Report as Whistleblower Claims Bias. https://www.cbsnews.com/news/opcw-chemical-weapons-watchdog-douma-chlorine-gas-wikileaks-russia-syria-claim-bias-today-2019-11-25/, Accessed December 30, 2019.

Daily Sabah (2019, November 20). Officials Reveal White Helmets Founder's Cause of Death. https://www.dailysabah.com/politics/2019/11/20/turkish-officials-reveal-white-helmets-founder-le-mesuriers-cause-of-death, Accessed December 25, 2019.

France 24 (2018, May 14). White Helmets 'Staging Fake Attacks' In Syria? We Sort Fact from Fiction. https://observers.france24.com/en/20180514-white-helmets-allegations-fact-fiction, Accessed December 30, 2019.

Giles, K. (2016). *Handbook of Russian Information Warfare*. Rome: NATO.

Di Giovanni, J. (2018, October 16). Why Assad and Russia Target the White Helmets. *TheNew York Review Daily*. https://www.nybooks.com/daily/2018/10/16/why-assad-and-russia-target-the-white-helmets/, Accessed 10.01.2020.

Grigoriev, M., & Maizel, S. (2019). *The White Helmets: Fact-Checking*. Moscow: The Foundation for the Study of Democracy.

Jain, V. (2018, August 2). Resettling the White Helmets: A Dangerous Foreign Policy Precedent for Health in Syria. *Journal of International Affairs*. https://jia.sipa.columbia.edu/online-articles/resettling-white-helmets-dangerous-foreign-policy-precedent-health-syria, Accessed January 21, 2020.

Lester, N. (2018). Introducing a Trauma-Informed Practice Framework to Provide Support in Conflict-Affected Countries: The Case of the Syrian White Helmets. *The Rusi Journal*, *163*(6), 28–41.

MacMillan, A. (2019, November 11). Former British Officer Who Helped White Helmets Hailed As 'True Hero'. *The National*. https://www.thenational.ae/world/mena/former-british-officer-who-helped-white-helmets-hailed-as-true-hero-1.936165, Accessed 10.01.2020.

Mahmoud, I. (2020). Interview, by Author, Istanbul.

Malsin, J. (2016, October 6). As the War Worsens, Rescue Workers Risk Their Lives on The Front Lines. *Time*. https://time.com/syria-white-helmets/, Accessed 17.01.2020.

McKeigue, P., Miller, D., Mason, J., & Robinson, P. (2019). How the OPCW's Investigation of the Douma Incident Was Nobbled. *Research Gate*. https://www.researchgate.net/publication/334733143_How_the_OPCW%27s_investigation_of_the_Douma_incident_was_nobbled?channel=doi&linkId=5d3dfa7e299bf1995b53c730&showFulltext=true, Accessed 21.01.2020. doi:10.13140/RG.2.2.17223. 85927.

Nocetti, J. (2019). *Dazed and Confused: Russian "Information Warfare" and the Middle East – The Syria Lessons*. Report No. 93. Barcelona: Euro Mesco.

Porotsky, S. (2018, February 8). Analyzing Russian Information Warfare and Influence Operations. *Global Security Review*. https://globalsecurityreview.com/cold-war-2-0-russian-information-warfare/, Accessed 03.01.2020.

Qui, L. (2017, April 10). Syria Conspiracy Theories Flourish, at Both Ends of the Spectrum. *The New York Times*. https://www.nytimes.com/2017/04/10/us/politics/factcheck-syria-strike-conspiracy-theories.html, Accessed December 23, 2019.

RT (2019, November 15). Assad Likens 'Suicide' of White Helmets Founder to Epstein & Other High-Profile Mystery Deaths. https://www.rt.com/news/473579-assad-epstein-white-helmets-deaths/, Accessed 03.01.2020.

Russian MFA (@mfa_russia) (2019, November). Zakharova'a Tweet. *Twitter*. https://twitter.com/mfa_russia/status/1192763676878610432?ref_src=twsrc%5Etfw%7Ctwcamp%5Etweetembed%7Ctwterm%5E1192763676878610432&ref_url=https%3A%2F%2Fwww.thenational.ae%2Fworld%2Fmena%2Fformer-british-officer-who-helped-white-helmets-hailed-as-true-hero-1.936165, Accessed 10.01. 2020.

Saleh, R. (2020). Interview, by Author, Idlib (via phone).

Salmo, A. (2020). Interview, by Author, Istanbul.

Samir, A. (2019, May 28). Who Really Are the Syrian White Helmets?. *Insideover*. https://www.insideover.com/war/who-really-are-the-syrian-white-helmets.html, Accessed 02.01.2020.

Sanchez, R. (2017, August 12). Seven Members of Syria's White Helmets Shot Dead By Unknown Gunmen. *The Telegragh*. https://www.telegraph.co.uk/news/2017/08/12/seven-members-syrias-white-helmets-shot-dead-unknown-gunmen/, Accessed December 17, 2019.

Schneider, T., & Lütkefend, T. (2019). *Nowhere to Hide: The Logic of Chemical Weapons Use in Syria*. Berlin: Global Public Policy Institute.

SNHR (2019). Syrian-Russian Alliance Forces Target 31 Civil Defense Vital Facilities in The Fourth De-Escalation Zone in 11 Weeks. *Relief Web*. https://reliefweb.int/sites/reliefweb.int/files/resources/The_Syrian_Russian_alliance_forces_target_31_vital_centers_of_the_Civil_Defense_Organization_en.pdf, Accessed December 28, 2019.

Solon, O. (2017, December 18). How Syria's White Helmets Became Victims of an Online Propaganda Machine. *The Guardian*. https://www.theguardian.com/world/2017/dec/18/syria-white-helmets-conspiracy-theories, Accessed 05.01.2020.

Tashev, B., Purcell, M., & McLaughlin, B. (2019). Russia's Information Warfare Exploring the Cognitive Dimension. *MCU Journal*, *10*(2), 129–147.

The Syria Campaign (2017). Killing the Truth. https://thesyriacampaign.org/wp-content/uploads/2017/12/KillingtheTruth.pdf, Accessed December 27, 2019.

The White Helmets (2019). Main Page. https://whitehelmets.org/en/, Accessed 23.01.2020.

Worrall, P. (2016, December 20). Eva Bartlett's Claims About Syrian Children. *Channel 4*. https://www.channel4.com/news/factcheck/factcheck-eva-bartletts-claims-about-syrian-children, Accessed 03.01.2020.

Sidre Gul Bige Gocekli and Necmiye Comertler

On "The Human" and Behavioral Economics[1]

Abstract Economics is a social science which has humans as its subjects. Economics investigates human behavior on economic decisions and tries to arrive at a generalized theory about economic situations. However, in the process of time, economics lost its humanity. The human has been left out of the equations of the economic theories. This absurd situation was caused by the endeavor of economics to be accepted as a science. Nevertheless, some economists fortunately realized the peril economics is in and proposed some ways which are now called "behavioral economics" to let the human in economics again. The human should be brought back to economics. Humans in economics can gain "their humanity" only by including the individual and social characteristics that make human beings human to economic models. After this is made possible then economics will be what it should be, and behavioral economics and economics will become the same thing. In this study we first discuss about what the human is and his/her place in economics, and then deliberate on what behavioral economics is and its history shortly.

Keywords: Human, Homo-economicus, Rationality, Economics, Behavioral Economics

1 Introduction

Individuals come together to form the society. On the other hand, they are heavily influenced by the community they create, that is, society in general. While traditional economics examines the individual and society as the mathematical sum of individuals, it ignores the individual-society interaction. There will be those who would argue that examining individuals one by one and studying society as a community is different. The individuals who forming societies determine the general characteristics of society and affect society. In other respects, individuals living in society too are affected by the properties of the society they are in, such as religion, language, culture, etc. while being evolved with the rules and norms of the society. Therefore, it is impossible to dissociate the individual and society. Researching the individual abstracted

1 This paper has been produced from the unpublished ongoing thesis "Gocekli, S. G. B. (2021). *Davranışsal İktisat ve Beklenti Teorisi Üzerine 3 Makale.* (Unpublished Ph.D. Thesis). Aydin Adnan Menderes University Institute of Social Sciences, Aydin."

from society or the society abstracted from the individual will lead to incomplete and incorrect results.

When individuals create communities, they first come together with other individuals who are similar to themselves but also have the characteristics that can complement their shortcomings. Then, within the community that is formed, individuals begin to influence and be influenced by others' characteristics. Thus, a society with common grounds arise. Those born in this society will have similar characteristics to the individuals who raise them. The individual and society are in constant interaction. Therefore, examining only the individual or only the society independent of each other will lead to the failure of the established theories over time in sciences such as economics, the main subject of which is the human and human decisions. What is worse than severing the relationship of man with society in Traditional Economics Doctrine is the expulsion of the human from economics, which is a social science that claims to examine the human being.

Economic theories use mathematical models to make economic analysis, interpret the past, and make predictions. Using mathematics as a tool gives an objective perspective to economics. However, these mathematical models, which were created over time, ceased to be a tool for predicting economic behavior and turned into a goal; and mathematical and economic assumptions were made to give consistency to the results obtained from these models. For instance, the "ceteris paribus" assumption (when everything else is fixed) is one of them. Although there is nothing constant in real life and all the variables change continuously and simultaneously, this is a necessary assumption to simplify the mathematical model to be able to make economic predictions. With this assumption, the mathematical model becomes mostly a linear model with few unknowns and is relatively easier to solve. Otherwise, the model will become nonlinear equations with many unknowns which is hard to get out of. Therefore, "the ceteris paribus" assumption is a productive one to make simple comments. But it is not essential. Models without this assumption should be developed to make more up-to-date and more accurate determinations. Although it was difficult to analyze models without assumptions until the development of supercomputer technologies and technologies that can perform very complex calculations, it has become possible today. Removing the ceteris paribus conjecture over time may be beneficial for developing economic theories that model more realistic economic behavior thanks to these technologies.

How successful can ordinary people be in solving complex economic problems that even their experts have difficulty solving? At this point, the biggest mistake made by traditional economics to facilitate theoretical modeling is "homo economicus" (economic-man) or rationality assumption. Economic-man or rational human assumption, which is one of the most fundamental assumptions of traditional economics, helps economic models to become completely mathematically consistent within themselves. Because the rational individual is a selfish creature, such as an android-robot, who minds his cost-benefit calculations, can make these calculations from the mind, his economic decisions are always consistent within, and his decisions are always the same without an external factor that can mislead him.

Thaler calls economic man "an econ" and describes him as an unusual alien creature. (Thaler & Sunstein, 2009: 7–9; Thaler, 2016: 1577–1578). Since this creature is a constant element and his decisions are unchanging, the creature himself is treated as given and excluded from the model, thus the model works without any problems. As can be seen, economics, whose subject is human, tries to interpret the results caused by the decisions of the subject while leaving its subject out of the model. This situation is similar to holding the wedding of a person without his knowledge and then describing how the wedding went to the person himself.

The human should be brought back to economics. Humans in economics can gain "their humanity" only by including the individual and social characteristics that make human beings human to economic models. For this purpose, economics should benefit from other disciplines of science such as psychology, sociology, anthropology, biology, and neurology. In this context, behavioral economics tries to correct the erroneous rationality assumption of traditional economics by using these science disciplines and to establish models that include real people in economics.

2 The Return of the Human to Economics: The Emergence and Development of Behavioral Economics

Behavioral economics is about developing economic analysis for real people in the real world, making economic models more robust, more accurate, and more practical. Behavioral economics, as in traditional economics, deals with incentives, costs and benefits, impulse-response, and economic efficiency. Behavioral economics enriches the toolbox of traditional economics by utilizing psychology, neurology, sociology, politics, and law (Altman, 2012: 9). Empirical findings from detailed research show that making the model of the economic man at the center of behavioral economics more accurate and realistic will improve the economic understanding and thus make the discipline of economics more functional (Diamond & Vartiainen, 2007).

To explain how people make decisions in real life and to make economic analyzes based on more realistic assumptions about the conditions that affect these decisions are among the goals of behavioral economics. In behavioral economics, people are not calculators. Rather, they are decision-makers who act with passion and reason. This enriched economic theory provides us with a better understanding of the economic behavior of individuals and societies (Altman, 2012: 9).

Throughout the 18th century, philosophers such as David Hume wrote articles about how the mind works. Hume's (1739) "A Treatise of Human Nature" is accepted as the founding document of cognitive science by philosophy historians. This study influenced scientists in many disciplines, especially psychology. I also affected economists of that period like Adam Smith. Scrutinization of the operation of the human mind has led economists to begin to notice the discrepancies between what "rational man" should do and what he does. During the 1800s, economists such as William Stanley Jevons has done studies that would form the basis of traditional economics. These economics was based on hedonic psychology, and therefore they viewed the utility as pleasure and pain. (Angner & Loewenstein, 2006: 7–8).

It is difficult to say exactly when behavioral economics started. However, according to Cartwright (2018a: 5), Adam Smith can be pointed as its founder. In his book "The Theory of Moral Sentiments" published in 1759, Smith mentions that people are not motivated only by their self-interests, but they also have a natural sympathy for others and have a natural sense of virtue. In his book "Wealth of Nations" published in 1776, Adam Smith claimes that economic behavior is motivated by personal interests. However, in 1759, 17 years before this work, he proposed a theory of human behavior that resembles anything but self-interest. In "The Theory of Moral Sentiments", Adam Smith claimes that behavior was determined as a result of the conflict between the terms which he calls "passions" and "impartial spectators". Passions include impulses such as hunger and sexuality, emotions such as fear and anger, and motivational states such as pain. Smith saw behavior as directly under the control of passions but believed that people could suppress their passion-driven behavior by evaluating their behavior as an impartial bystander from an outsider's perspective (Ashraf, Camerer & Loewenstein, 2005: 131).

In the first centuries after Smith, economists focused a lot on emotions, impulses, incentives, morality, and the like. However, as the 20th century began, economists turned away from psychology and behavioral economics. This situation was caused by Vilfredo Pareto. In a letter that dates to 1897, Pareto stated that it would be beneficial for a pure political economy to rely as little as possible on the field of psychology. In his article where he then described a new approach to choice theory, Pareto claimed that the greatest achievement of this approach was that it eliminated all psychological analysis. Psychology can be removed from economics by focusing on choice rather than desire. Inferences can be made on just what people do instead of why they do what. Pareto stated that he is not concerned with why one is indifferent between two things but is concerned with the pure and naked truth. Pareto questioned what happens when people act rationally. Likewise, Adam Smith made the invisible hand argument by asking the question of what would happen when people behave selfishly. Assuming that humans are rational and selfish for mathematical convenience does not mean that they are truly rational and selfish. Smith made this distinction. Even Pareto distinguished when what people do could be represented by rational choice or not (Cartwright, 2018a: 5).

In 1948, Edward Chamberlin published his article "An Experimental Imperfect Market". This article is considered to be the first experimental paper published in the field of economics. In this study, Chamberlin reached the key finding that market results can deviate from the market equilibrium. He emphasized that the findings obtained by conducting experiments in the laboratory of society can be appreciated as scientific results. This approach was a pioneering idea for that period (Cartwright, 2018b).

In the 1950s, Herbert Simon published articles on the concept of "bounded rationality". These studies are particularly important for behavioral economics as they are a direct attack on the belief that "man is rational" which is the dominant view of the time. (Hosseini, 2003).

Considering that behavioral economics is divided into old and new, it can be said that the old behavioral economics started in the 1950s and early 1960s with the studies of George Katona and Herbert Simon. Simon's contributions are well known because of the popularity of the "bounded rationality" and "satisficing[2]" theories and because he won the Nobel Prize in Economics. However, economists do not know the contributions of Katona that well (Hosseini, 2011).

Katona is known as the founding father of the old behavioral economics discipline, which pioneered modern behavioral economics. Katona (1980) mentions three main features of behavioral economics in his work "Essays

---

2 The word satisficing, a combination of the words satisfy and suffice was created by Simon. He explains that bounded rational people make their choices as soon as they find the first option that satisfies their desire levels among various options instead of optimization (Geiger, 2014: 3).

on Behavioral Economics". First of these consists of empirical studies of the behavior of firms and consumers in a particular country at a given time. Generalizations about economic behavior emerge gradually from comparing observed behavior in different situations. Second, behavioral economics focuses on studying the decision-making process of these behaviors rather than analyzing the amounts spent, saved, and invested as a result of spending, saving, investment, and similar behaviors. Third, the study of the human factor has a significant place in behavioral economics. Katona tried to bring realism to the economic analysis with the help of psychological concepts (Hosseini, 2011). For these reasons, Katona and Simon are regarded as the founding fathers of behavioral economics.

While traditional economists assume that the principles of economic behavior, which they infer from the characteristics of human nature, are the same in all times and cultures, Katona and Simon reject this and try to explain the actual behavior of economic actors (Yang & Lester, 1995; Hosseini, 2003; Hosseini, 2011: 978). They wanted to replace the mechanical psychology of traditional economics with its real counterpart to create economics, which "tries to find out what happens when people make decisions as consumers, producers, or policymakers" as Katona (1975: 71) states.

Katona was misunderstood and criticized by the economists of his time for being a psychologist. However, his views should not be denied due to his contributions to the emergence and development of behavioral economics, although he misjudged some economic theories due to his insufficient knowledge in economics.

Simon questioned the rationale for representing people with the Homo-economicus. Simon (1955) first states how the rational person should behave, then expresses there is no evidence that people did or could do these calculations in any of the real choice situations. Therefore Simon suggests examining people's knowledge and computational capacities and that this should be the beginning of economic models. The limitations people face lead Simon to the concept of "bounded rationality" (Cartwright, 2018a: 6–7). Publishing "Models of Man" in 1957, Simon created a model of human concept that is more compatible with the bounded rationality theory (Hosseini, 2003). Simon argued that behavioral economics emerged because it was necessary to enrich the existing traditional economic theory to reach a more realistic picture of the economic process. According to Simon, economists as social scientists should be prepared to describe key characteristics of people. This can only be possible by using behavioral economics (Gilad & Kaish, 1986: xvi). Simon tried to add the bounded rationality of human beings into various economic theories by creating heavy mathematical models and was criticized by the economists of his time. Simon won the Nobel Prize in Economics in 1978 for his pioneering research on the decision-making process within economic institutions. However, the call to replace the Economic Man with a more realistic human being has been ignored (Cartwright, 2018a: 7).

In 1962, Vernon Smith reports on a series of market experiments carried out between 1955 and 1961. These experiments were some of the first experiments carried out in economics. Smith (1962: 134) demonstrated that there are strong tendencies in achieving competitive equilibrium of supply and demand, as long as individuals can prohibit alliances and collusion and maintain absolute openness of all auction bids and transactions, although the numbers are small. Smith won the Nobel Prize in Economics in 2002 for establishing laboratory experiments "as a tool in empirical economic analysis, especially in studies of alternative market mechanisms" (Cartwright, 2018a: 8) and for his contribution which is stated by Nobel Prize Committee (2002) as developing "methods for laboratory experiments in economics, which has helped our understanding of economic behavior". Smith's experiment showed that in some cases, traditional economics gave correct results and which raised the question of the necessity of behavioral economics. However, Smith's study showed that the accuracy, errors, and deficiencies of the economic models can be determined via experiments. The experiments of Smith gave new tools to economists and paved the way for new behavioral economics. Smith's works helped the behavioral economics but he is considered not as a behavioral economist but an experimental economist. New behavioral economics is considered to began in 1970s with the works of Kahneman, Tversky and Thaler.

In economics, the market is understood to direct the behavior toward a competitive equilibrium where all economic actors behave optimally and social welfare is maximized. However, many economists have seen this ideal market picture's shortcomings in limited information, few buyers and sellers, adverse selection, moral hazard, and the like. What psychologists Daniel Kahneman and Amos Tversky brought to economics in the 1980s was the idea that market imperfections could also result from erroneous human behavior (Heukelom, 2014: 1). Kahneman and Tversky published the article "Judgment under Uncertainty: Heuristics and Biases" in 1974 and in 1979 they put forward the "Prospect Theory". Kahneman and Tversky (1979) realized that the Expected Utility Theory did not work in many situations and developed Prospect Theory to show how people perceive the utility. According to this, people perceive utility differently in cases of gain and loss and make different choices than rational economic people.

Tversky and Kahneman (1981: 453) stated that the definition of rationality is controversial, but the consensus is that rational choices must meet some basic requirements of integrity and consistency. Kahneman and Tversky defined decision problems in their studies where people systematically violate the requirements of integrity and consistency. They realized these violations can be explained with the psychological principles of the evaluation options and perception of decision problems. Kahneman won the Nobel Prize in Economics in 2002 for introducing a new approach to economics, particularly in human judgment and decision making under uncertainty (Since Tversky passed away before this date, the award was given only to Kahneman) (Cartwright, 2018a: 8).

Robert Aumann and Thomas Schelling won the Nobel Prize in Economics in 2005 for their contribution to cooperation and conflict. In particular, Schelling's work focused on how people behave rather than how they should behave. This is an important step towards behavioral game theory (Cartwright, 2018b).

Richard Thaler (1985) used the concept of mental accounting in his work "Mental Accounting and Consumer Choice". In his study, he stated that losses and gains pass through hedonic coding in mind. He stated that the decisions of individuals differ in cases such as lottery tickets being free of charge, being a gift, or incurring a cost beforehand. He has also shown that the resulting pleasure is different when the reward is obtained at once or in parts. Richard Thaler and Cass Sunstein (2009) highlighted the importance of framing and context effects in their book "Nudge". They also argued that the targeted results could be achieved more easily by using these, in other words, by nudging people, by policymakers. Thaler won the Nobel Prize in Economics in 2017 for his contributions to the field of behavioral economics and for building a bridge between economics and psychology.

3 Conclusion

Behavioral economics today is classified under microeconomics because it mostly deals with the economic behavior of the individual. The starting point of behavioral economics is to take the human out of the mold that traditional economics has put him. However, this goal makes it difficult to define behavioral economics. Because all studies that serve this purpose can be evaluated within the framework of behavioral economics. That is, any theory that replaces any of the core features of traditional economics with alternatives that have a better empirical basis in human behavior is a potential member of the class of behavioral economic theories (Dhami, 2016: 2).

Although it is difficult to define behavioral economics precisely, it can be said that it is not a hostile theory that aims at the destruction of traditional economics, but rather a discipline of economics that aims to restore the human element that has been forgotten in time and to renew and improve existing economic theories.

Using various psychological factors to better understand the world and make more accurate predictions about economic behavior is no different from using a new data source. Therefore, behavioral economics is not a revolution, but rather a return to the open-minded and intuitively motivated discipline that Adam Smith found. The increasing interest in studies on "humans" instead of econs has started a wave that will make new theoretical developments possible. If the developments in economics continue in this line and everyone adds all the factors that determine economic behavior to the analysis, the term "behavioral economics" will gradually disappear from the dictionaries. Because all economics will be behavioral to the extent the subjects allow and an approach that increases the explanatory power of economic models will be acquired (Thaler, 2016: 1597). In short, economics will be what it should be, and behavioral economics and economics will become the same thing.

Bibliography

Altman, M. (2012). *Behavioral Economics for Dummies.* John Wiley & Sons Canada Ltd., Mississauga.

Angner, E., & Loewenstein, G. (2006). *Behavioral Economics*, To appear vol. 5. Elsevier's Handbook of the Philosophy of Science.

Ashraf, N., Camerer, C. F., & Loewenstein, G. (2005). Adam Smith, behavioral economist. *Journal of Economic Perspectives, 19*(2005), 131–145.

Cartwright, E. (2018a). *Behavioral Economics Third Edition.* Routledge Advanced Texts in Economics and Finance. Routledge, New York.

Cartwright, E. (2018b). *Behavioral Economics Third Edition Web Material, Timeline for Behavioral Economics.* Access date December 2019, https://routledgetextbooks.com/textbooks/9781138097124/students.php

Chamberlin, E. H. (1948). An experimental imperfect market. *The Journal of Political Economy, 56*(2), 95–108.

Dhami, S. (2016). *The Foundations of Behavioral Economic Analysis.* Oxford University Press, Oxford.

Diamond, P., & Vartiainen, H. (Eds.). (2007). *Behavioral Economics and Its Applications.* Princeton University Press, New Jersey.

Geiger, N. (2014). The rise of behavioural economics: A quantitative assessment, *Schriftenreihe des Promotionsschwerpunkts Globalisierung und Beschäftigung, No. 44/2015*, Universität Hohenheim, Stuttgart, http://nbn-resolving.de/urn:nbn:de:bsz:100-opus-10845

Gilad, B., & Kaish, S. (Eds.) (1986). *Handbook of Behavioral Economics*, Vols. A and B. JAI Press, London.

Heukelom, F. (2014). *Behavioral Economics: A History.* Cambridge University Press, New York.

Hosseini, H. (2003). The arrival of behavioral economics: From Michigan, or the Carnegie School in the 1950s and the early 1960s. *Journal of Socio-Economics, 23*(2003), 391–409.

Hosseini, H. (2011). George Katona: A founding father of old behavioral economics. *The Journal of Socio-Economics, 40*(2011), 977–984.

Hume, D. (1739). *İnsanın Doğası Üzerine Bir İnceleme.* Çeviren Aziz Yardımlı, 2016. İdea Yayınevi, İstanbul.

Kahneman, D., & Tversky, A. (1979). Prospect theory: An analysis of decision under risk. *Econometrica, 47*(2), 263–291.

Katona, G. (1975). *Psychological Economics.* Elsevier, London.

Katona, G. (1980). *Essays on Behavioral Economics.* University of Michigan Press, Ann Arbor, MI.

Nobel Prize Committee. (2002). Vernon L. Smith Facts. *The Sveriges Riksbank Prize in Economic Sciences in Memory of Alfred Nobel 2002.* https://www.nobelprize.org/prizes/economic-sciences/2002/smith/facts/

Simon, H. A. (1955). A behavioral model of rational choice. *Quarterly Journal of Economics, 69*(1), 99–118.

Smith, A. (1759). *Ahlaki Duygular Kuramı.* Çeviren Derman Kızılay, 2018. Pinhan Yayıncılık, İstanbul.

Smith, A. (1776). *Milletlerin Zenginliği.* Çeviren Haldun Derin, 8. Basım, 2014. Türkiye İş Bankası Kültür Yayınları, İstanbul.

Smith, V. L. (1962). An experimental study of competitive market behavior. *Journal of Political Economy, 70*(2), 322–322.

Thaler, R. H. (1985). Mental accounting and consumer choice. *Marketing Science, 4*(3), 199–214.

Thaler, R. H. (2016). Behavioral economics: Past, present, and future. *American Economic Review, 106*(7), 1577–1600.

Thaler, R. H., & Sunstein, C. R. (2009). *Nudge: Improving Decisions About Health, Wealth and Happiness,* Penguin Books, London.

Tversky, A., & Kahneman, D. (1981). The framing of decisions and the psychology of choice. *Science, 211*(4481), 453–458.

Yang, B., & Lester, P. (1995). New directions for economics. *Journal of Socio-economics, 24*(1995), 443–456.

A. Elif Ay Yalcinkaya and Ramazan Ekinci

Profitability of Turkish Manufacturing Firms: Efficiency or Market Power?

Abstract The relationship between efficiency, profitability and market power in the literature has developed on the basis of the efficient-structure (ES) hypothesis by Demsetz (1973) and the structure-conduct-performance (SCP or market power) hypothesis by Bain (1951) and Baumol (1982). This paper tests the different hypotheses explaining profitability in the generic framework of hypotheses of collusion versus efficiency, presenting as its main contribution the use of a direct measurement of efficiency. The analysis is performed on 115 firms operating in the Turkish manufacturing industry during the 2010–2019 period. The data is extracted from the Public Disclosure Platform (KAP) and firms balance sheet items. In order to test the hypotheses, the profit efficiency measures within the method of Bayesian Stochastic Frontier Analysis were used. In the empirical section, we perform a static and dynamic panel data approach to estimate the regression equations. The static and dynamic results show that there is a negative and significant relation between concentration and profitability for all industry, while a positive and significant relation between large firms' concentration ratio and profitability. We also find a positive and significant effect of profit efficiency on firm profitability. This supports the ES hypothesis in the Turkish manufacturing industry.

Keywords: Efficient-Structure Hypothesis, Structure-Conduct-Performance Hypothesis, Turkish Manufacturing Industry, Bayesian Stochastic Frontier Analysis, Profitability

1 Introduction

One of the basic assumptions of industrial organization theory is that firms act for profit maximization. To achieve this goal, firms can maximize their profits by maximizing their revenues or minimizing their costs. In general, there are two different channels for companies to increase their profitability. The first of these channels is the power of firms to increase their prices above the market price depending on the market power, and the second is to increase the efficiency level by reducing production costs and thus reach high profitability levels. The condition of profit maximization based on these two conditions is valid under imperfect competition conditions. Under imperfect competition, average costs stay above the market price. Therefore, the firm cannot obtain enough output to minimize its average costs. As a result, there is a loss of welfare in terms of imperfect competition conditions. Therefore, profit rates are considered as a result of the market power that firms can gain due to imperfect competition. However, under perfect competition conditions, profit maximization becomes equivalent to cost minimization and market power disappears. In the long run, the firm can only make normal profit.

The relationship between efficiency, profitability and market power in the literature has developed on the basis of the efficient-structure (ES) hypothesis by Demsetz (1973) and the structure-conduct-performance (SCP or market power) hypothesis by Bain (1951) and Baumol (1982). According to the SCP hypothesis, price determination power of a firm depends on the market structure. For this reason, it is stated that firms' higher market power with collusion between them results in higher price policy and profitability. Therefore, in a market where concentration is high, it is stated that the inefficiency created by low level of competition leads to monopoly pricing and excessive (monopoly) profitability. On the other hand, according to the efficient structure hypothesis that is put forward by Demsetz (1973), competitive market structure creates pressure on firms and forces firms to be effective. As a result, as companies increase their efficiency levels, they gain competitive power. Thus, it is stated that they gradually grow in the market and dominate a larger market share. As a result, it is claimed that the increase in competition created by efficiency increases the profit of the firm.

The question of whether higher concentration is due to market power or efficiency is one of the most controversial issues in the literature. The purpose of this study, in the framework of market power and efficient structure hypothesis, is to analyze the activities that determine the profitability of the manufacturing industry in Turkey. First of all, the relationship between profitability and concentration is estimated within the framework of the SCP hypothesis and the coefficients that explain the basic hypothesis are obtained. Then, within the framework of the ES hypothesis, the relationship between profitability and efficiency is estimated and the coefficients of the efficiency parameters are obtained. Finally, by evaluating the results of these two hypotheses together, it is tried to determine the basic variables explaining the profitability level of the sector and their parameters (market power or efficiency). Market share is generally used as an indicator of efficiency in the literature. In this study, unlike other studies, efficiency scores estimated on profit function are given to. Thus, different from stochastic frontier analysis, the Bayesian stochastic frontier analysis approach is used as a prediction technique. Depending on the technique used, the validity of the hypotheses is demonstrated by static or dynamic panel data analysis with an approach different from the literature. As a result, it is tried to bring an innovation to the literature with the estimation tools and techniques used.

2 Literature

There are many studies in the literature on financial and non-financial sectors analyzing the effect of market concentration on profitability. In theoretical and empirical studies, there is still no consensus on how the relationship between these two variables emerges, and its consequences (Lee & Mahmood, 2009). As a matter of fact, in theoretical studies, it is seen that concentration has positive and negative significant effects as well as no significant effect. The positive effect of concentration on profitability is explained by two different hypotheses that contradict with each other. The first of them is the SCP hypothesis, caused by market concentration and a positive and significant effect on profitability exists (Bain, 1951). The second is the efficiency hypothesis, which suggests that the relationship between profitability and market concentration is determined by the efficiency of dominant firms (Demsetz, 1973). Apart from these, there are also opinions arguing that market concentration has a negative effect on profitability (Leibenstein, 1966; Keil, 2017). Another view states that there is no significant relationship between profitability and market concentration (Brozen, 1971).

The results of empirical studies as well as theoretical studies reveal inconsistent results. Most of the results obtained indicate a positive effect. On the other hand, there are few studies showing that market concentration has a negative effect on profitability (Anderson, Fok, & Scott, 2000; Alhassan Tetteh & Brobbey, 2016; Mukhopadhyay & Chakraborty, 2017). In addition, there are some studies showing that there is no statistically significant relationship between profitability and market concentration after controlling other variables that affect profitability (Clarke, Davies & Waterson, 1984; Khan & Hanif, 2019; Keil, 2018).

The first empirical studies investigating the effect of market concentration on profitability were generally conducted on developed countries. Here, mostly cross section and ordinary least squares methods were used. In most of these studies, it was demonstrated that there is a positive relationship between profitability and market concentration (Collins & Preston, 1969; Strickland & Weiss, 1976). However, the results of the study, conducted by Clarke, Davies and Waterson (1984), show that there is no statistically significant relationship between profitability and market concentration.

On the other hand, as the data becomes accessible more easily and we access to a wider data set, the number of studies on the manufacturing industry increased in both developed and developing countries in recent years. Depending on the increase in the data set, the analysis methods differed. Accordingly, in recent years, there has been an increasing number of studies using panel data methodology and producing mixed results. In this context, McDonald's study (1999) is the first study to reveal the correlation between market concentration and profitability using the dynamic panel data method. McDonald found a positive relationship between profitability and market concentration in Australian manufacturing industries. Gallagher Ignatieva and McCulloch (2015) reached a positive relationship on the Australian example too. Similarly, Bhandari (2010) showed that there is a positive relationship between profitability and market concentration using the static panel data method. In another study, Setiawan and Effendi (2016) revealed a positive relationship between profitability and market concentration in Indonesian manufacturing industry. In the literature, there are also studies showing that there is a negative relationship aside from empirical studies that reveal the positive relationship between profitability and market concentration. For example, Mukhopadhyay and Chakraborty (2017) showed that there is a negative relationship between market concentration and profitability using the dynamic panel data method. In addition to the positive and negative relationships, there are also studies showing that there is no statistically significant relationship between profitability and market concentration. For example, Mishra (2008) could not reach a meaningful relationship between profitability and market concentration on manufacturing industries in Indonesia, by using dynamic panel data method. Similarly, according to Keil (2018), there is no statistically significant relationship between profitability and market concentration in the manufacturing industry in the United States.

3 Model

In order to analyze the impact of concentration on profitability, the model is formed as follows:

$$\Pi_{ijt} = \beta_0 + \beta_1 \cdot Conc_{ijt} + \gamma' Z + \epsilon_{it} \tag{1}$$

Here Π_{ijt} is the profit and $Conc_{jt}$ is the concentration ratio of the firm i in the industry j for the period t. Control variables in the model are represented by the Z vector. The fact that the estimated coefficient β_1 is greater than zero ($\beta_1 > 0$) means that the market structure resulting in higher concentration leads to higher firm profitability. ϵ_{it} is the error term, that changes across the individual firms and time periods. Therefore, it is shown as below:

$$\epsilon_{it} = \lambda_i + \mu_t + \eta_{it}$$

In the equation, λ_i shows the firm effects which is the time invariant component, while μ_t is the time effect which is the firm invariant component. η_{it} is normally distributed random error. In this study, Equation (1) is estimated using two different approaches: static and dynamic models. Although Equation (1) is a static model by its nature, it transforms into a dynamic model by using the lagged value of the rate of profitability as an independent variable. Both models control unobserved factors that differ from one firm to the other, but are constant over time.

The second hypothesis we tried to test in our study is the efficient market hypothesis and is defined as follows:

$$\Pi_{ijt} = \alpha_0 + \alpha_1 \cdot Eff_{it} + \gamma\prime Z + \varepsilon_{it} \quad (2)$$

where Π_{ijt} shows the profit rate of firms as in Equation (1). Eff_{it} is the efficiency level of the firm i for the period t, and it is estimated by stochastic frontier analysis. In the equation, Z is the vector of control variables and ϵ_{it} is the error term. If the coefficient α_1 is positive ($\alpha_1 > 0$) and statistically significant, it can be said that the efficient market hypothesis is valid. On the other hand, when Equations (1) and (2) are evaluated together, if both β_1 and α_1 coefficients are significant and positive ($\beta_1 > 0, \alpha_1 > 0$), it can be said that the source of market power that increases the profitability of firms is efficiency. However, if β_1 is positive ($\beta_1 > 0$) and significant but α_1 is either insignificant or negative, then it can be said that the higher profits are because of market power. In the first case, the efficient-structure (ES) hypothesis, in the second case, the structure-conduct-performance (SCP) hypothesis is valid.

Firm-specific and macroeconomic variables that are thought to have an effect on profitability in the model are as follows:

- age of the firm, which is calculated as the years of the firms in the sector and represents the experience of the firms.
- liquidity ratio, which is current assets divided by short-term liabilities;
- leverage ratio, which is total equity divided by total assets;
- capital intensity, which is fixed assets divided by total assets;
- export intensity, which is export income divided by sales;
- labor cost, which is labor expenses divided by sales;
- annual inflation rate,
- annual growth rate on GDP.

4 Methodology

4.1 The Stochastic Profit Frontier

The stochastic frontier analysis (SFA) was proposed by Meeusen, Van den Broeck (1977) and Aigner, Lovell, Schmidt (1977). SFA allows the composite error, namely a firm may deviate from its optimal frontier because of its own inefficiency and some other changes.

The profit function used in the study is expressed as (Berger and Mester, 1997):

$\pi_{it} = \beta_0 + x'_{it} \cdot \beta + v_{it} - u_{it}$ $\quad i = 1, \ldots, N$ firms; $t = 1, \ldots, T$ time periods,

π_{it} represents *ln* of firm *i*'s profit during period *t*. β_0 is the scalar intercept and β is the vector of parameters to be estimated. x'_{it} is the vector of output and input variables. $v_{it} \sim N(0, \sigma_v^2)$ is identically and independently distributed random error. Last but not least, u_{it} is profit inefficiency. It follows one-sided distribution, confirming that the inefficiency is not negative. We use one output – net sales (y) – and three inputs – financial debt (x_1), labor (x_2) and physical capital (x_3) – as in the studies by Purwanto, Manongga and Pakereng (2014); Kotey and O'Donnell (2002); Assaf and Cvelbar (2011); Pérez-Rodríguez and Acosta-González (2007). The prices of inputs (x_1, x_2, x_3) are as follows: financial debt price (w_1), labor price (w_2) and physical capital price (w_3). All nominal variables are further deflated by the consumer price index with the base year 2010.

The translog profit function to estimate profit efficiency for the panel data is:

$$
\begin{aligned}
\ln \tfrac{\pi}{W_3} = {} & \beta_0 + \beta_1 \ln(y) + \beta_2 \ln\left(\tfrac{W_1}{W_3}\right) + \beta_3 \ln\left(\tfrac{W_2}{W_3}\right) + \beta_4 \ln(Eq) + \beta_5 \ln(Eq^2) \\
& + \beta_6(t) + \beta_7(t^2) + \phi_1 \tfrac{1}{2}(\ln(y))^2 + \phi_2 \tfrac{1}{2}\left(\ln\left(\tfrac{W_1}{W_3}\right)\right)^2 + \phi_3 \cdot \ln\left(\tfrac{W_1}{W_3}\right) \\
& \cdot \ln\left(\tfrac{W_2}{W_3}\right) + \phi_4 \tfrac{1}{2}\left(\ln\left(\tfrac{W_2}{W_3}\right)\right)^2 + \delta_1 \ln(y) \cdot \ln\left(\tfrac{W_1}{W_3}\right) + \delta_2 \ln(y) \cdot \ln\left(\tfrac{W_2}{W_3}\right) \\
& + \kappa_1 t \cdot \ln(y) + \kappa_2 t \cdot \ln\left(\tfrac{W_1}{W_3}\right) + \kappa_3 t \cdot \ln\left(\tfrac{W_2}{W_3}\right) + \xi_1 \ln(Eq) \cdot \ln(y) + \xi_2 \\
& \ln(Eq) \cdot \ln\left(\tfrac{W_1}{W_3}\right) + \xi_3 \ln(Eq) \cdot \ln\left(\tfrac{W_2}{W_3}\right) + \psi_1 t \cdot \ln(Eq) \\
& + \nu_{it} - u_{it}
\end{aligned}
$$

For the linear homogeneity constraint, the dependent variable and input prices in Equation (1) are normalized with the price of capital, W_3. In order to consider the effect of technological change, linear (t) and quadratic time period (t^2)

variables are included in the model. In addition, the equity ratio (equity/total assets, *Eq*) is added to the model as a semi-fixed input to control the differences in risk preferences between firms.

$PE_{it} = exp\,(-u_{it}), 0 < PE_{it} < 1$ is the profit efficiency of the firm *i* during the period *t*. The closer the profit efficiency score of the firms is to 1, the more efficient firms are considered to be with respect to profits.

4.2 Bayesian Estimation

The Bayesian inference in stochastic frontier models are used by Van den Broeck, Koop, Osiewalski and Steel (1994). This includes the prior information about the vector of parameters ($\theta = [\theta_1, \ldots, \theta_k]$) through the probability density function ($p\,[\theta]$). The Bayes' theorem combines two types of information: $p\,(\theta|y) \propto L\,(y|\theta)\; p\,(\theta)$. Here $\propto$ means that "it is proportional to" and $p\,(\theta|y)$ is the posterior probability density function. Also, the information is summarized in the likelihood function ($L\,[y|\theta]$). Therefore, $p\,(\theta|y)$ is proportional to the likelihood function and the prior probability density. In other words, the posterior distribution includes all information about the vector of parameters ($\theta = [\theta_1, \ldots, \theta_k]$). Inferences about the unknown parameters are made by the posterior distribution (Koop, 1994). With different distributions of the error term, the likelihood function of a stochastic frontier model has been provided in various studies (Kumbhakar & Lovell, 2003).

The inefficiency u_{it} follows a one-sided distribution and truncated normal, half normal, gamma and exponential distributions are widely used in the literature. Determining the appropriate distribution for u_{it} is a critical problem to obtain inefficiency (Ehlers, 2011). Because of this, in our study, we compare four models with different distributions and the most appropriate distribution for the term u_{it} is determined. The use of Bayesian techniques involves the evaluation of complex integrals. We estimate by using the Markov Chain Monte Carlo method and the Gibbs sampling algorithm, which is introduced by Koop, Steel and Osiewalski (1995) and widely used in the literature (Tsionas, 2002; Huang, 2004; Kumbhakar & Tsionas, 2005; Griffin & Steel, 2007).

5 Data

In our study, the firm-level data are extracted from the financial statements of 115 firms which operated in Turkey from 2010 to 2019. Since the industry-level data such as the industrial concentration are not available as an official statistic,

Tab. 3.1: Descriptive Statistics of Variables Used in the Efficiency Estimation

Variables	Descriptions	Mean
π (profit)	Defined as earnings before interest and taxes	137,767,429.72 (445,600,310.65)
y (output)	Net sales measured by net revenue from the sale of the company's core products.	2,604,945,279.66 (445,600,310.65)
W_1 (input price 1)	Financial capital price (interest expenses/total debt)	0.577 (9.177)
W_2 (input price 2)	Labor price (personnel expenses/number of employees)	65,253.92 (41,673.39)
W_3 (input price 3)	Physical capital price (depreciation of both tangible and intangible assets/total fixed assets)	0.108 (0.102)
Eq (Equity to total assets)	Capital ratio (total equity/total assets)	0.449 (0.218)

Note: Standard deviation in parenthesis.

the industry level data are aggregated from the firm level data. Namely, for each of the 16 three-digit industries concentration ratio and the Herfindahl–Hirschman index (HHI) are computed separately. All the firm level data are sourced from the Public Disclosure Platform (PDP). Macroeconomic variables are extracted from the Central Bank of the Republic of Turkey (CBRT).

The variables in this study are selected by considering the previous literature and availability of data. Regarding the selected variables, the relationship between input prices, output quantities and profit is represented by the profit function. The dependent variable of the stochastic frontier is profit (π), measured by earnings before interest and taxes. The input prices are estimated through proxy variables, since they are not directly observable. Tab. 3.1 shows the descriptive statistics for all these variables.

6 Results

Determining the most suitable distribution of the inefficiency term (u_{it}) is necessary to estimate the stochastic profit frontier. The Lewis and Raftery values, which are obtained for truncated normal, half normal, exponential and gamma distributions, are compared in Tab. 3.2:

The Lewis and Raftery approximation of the log-marginal likelihood is -812.52, which is larger than what the half normal, truncated normal and gamma models produced. Also, the posterior model probability is considerably

Tab. 3.2: Model Comparison for Different Distributions of the Term Inefficiency

Model	Log-Marginal Likelihood	Type of log-ML Approximation	Prior Model Probability	Posterior Model Probability
Half normal	-1043.38	Lewis & Raftery	0.25	5.46234e-101
Truncated normal	-892.73	Lewis & Raftery	0.25	1.46138e-035
Gamma	-1557.00	Lewis & Raftery	0.25	4.94066e-324
Exponential	-812.52	Lewis & Raftery	0.25	1

higher for the exponential model. Therefore, the data clearly favor the exponential stochastic-frontier model.

Tab. 3.3 gives the results of estimating the translog profit function. After the stochastic frontier is determined, Gibbs sampling are used to estimate posterior means and posterior standard deviations. A total of 50,000 interactions are created to achieve convergence and avoid sensitivity of initial values (5,000 of these interactions are dropped). The standard deviations of most of the parameters are low and this supports the model convergence (Assaf & Magnini, 2012). Except for labor, the sign on posterior expected value of other input elasticities assessed in the sample mean is positive. This means that, an increase in the use of each input would increase output, ceteris paribus, The coefficient of labor is unexpectedly negative, which provides a reflection of the capital-intensive nature of manufacturing industry in Turkey.

Tab. 3.4 shows descriptive statistics of profit efficiency scores estimated by Bayesian Stochastic Frontier Model (BSFA) with exponential distribution. Profit efficiency changes from 78.04 % in 2010 to 74.09 % in 2019, with a mean efficiency of 76.38 %. The real sector is therefore wasting 23.62 % of its potential profits.

Tab. 3.5 represents the estimation results of the profitability function. Columns (A), (B) and (C) present fixed-effects (FE), random effect (RE) and system GMM estimations of Equation (1), respectively. In Equation (1), the main variable is concentration rate which is calculated separately for each year by Herfindahl-Hirschman index (HHI). Since the concentration ratio is an industry measure, it changes between years and industries.

Then the regression model specified in Equation (2) is estimated, which incorporates profit efficiency as an explanatory variable. Fixed effect, random effect and GMM results are reported in Columns (D), (E) and (F), respectively.

Tab. 3.3: The Stochastic Frontier Model's Posterior Statistics

	Posterior M	**SD**	**MCMC sd. error**	**Inefficiency factor**
α	29.507***	1.412	0.021	4.524
β_1 (*lny*)	0.401***	0.113	0.001	3.281
β_2 ($ln\ w_1$)	1.754***	0.156	0.002	5.368
β_3 ($ln\ w_2$)	-2.337***	0.248	0.003	4.387
β_4 ($ln\ Eq$)	-0.237	0.358	0.004	2.971
β_5 ($ln\ Eq^2$)	-0.003	0.014	0.0001	2.120
β_6 (t)	-0.051	0.063	0.0007	2.747
β_7 (t^2)	0.0001	0.003	4.04224e-005	2.517
ϕ_1 ($0.5 \ln y$)	0.033***	0.007	0.0001	5.364
ϕ_2 ($0.5 \ln w_1^2$)	-0.005	0.006	9.37066e-005	4.008
ϕ_3 ($0.5\ lnw_1 \ln w_2$)	-0.093***	0.015	0.0002	5.586
ϕ_4 ($0.5 \ln w_2^2$)	0.340***	0.031	0.0004	4.738
δ_1 ($\ln y \ln w_1$)	-0.059***	0.006	8.70659e-005	3.397
δ_2 ($\ln y \ln w_2$)	-0.009	0.011	0.0001	4.529
κ_1 ($t\ lny$)	-0.0001	0.002	3.09308e-005	2.536
κ_2 ($t\ ln\ w_1$)	-0.004	0.003	4.54487e-005	2.805
κ_3 ($t\ ln\ w_2$)	0.007	0.006	7.48978e-005	2.933
ξ_1 ($ln\ Eq\ lny$)	0.035**	0.014	0.0001	3.144
ξ_2 ($ln\ Eq\ ln\ w_1$)	-0.114***	0.024	0.0003	3.028
ξ_3 ($ln\ Eq\ ln\ w_2$)	-0.032	0.035	0.0004	3.199
ψ_1 ($t\ ln\ Eq$)	0.003	0.003	9.2635e-005	2.328
tau	10.379***	0.830	0.020	12.677
lambda	3.126***	0.192	0.005	15.051
sigma_v	0.311***	0.012	0.0003	12.855
sigma_u	0.321***	0.019	0.0005	14.956

Note: ***, **, and * denote significance at the 1 %, 5 %, and 10 % levels, respectively.

Tab. 3.4: Mean Profit Efficiency

		Obs.			Mean			Std. Dev.		
Efficiency		**1150**			**76.38**			**0.1250**		
Year	**2010**	**2011**	**2012**	**2013**	**2014**	**2015**	**2016**	**2017**	**2018**	**2019**
Avg.Eff.	78.04	77.89	77.76	76.70	76.09	76.60	75.55	76.30	74.82	74.09

According to the dynamic model, a low value of the lagged (ROA (-1)) profitability coefficient (0.28 and 0.23) indicates that the Turkish manufacturing industry is relatively competitive. Many empirical industrial organization studies found a positive relationship between concentration and profits. In this study, the coefficient of the industry concentration has statistically significant negative sign.

Because of this, concentration variable is separated for small and large firms to control different effect of industry concentration on profits of small and large firms and two variables are created. The first variable is created that takes the HHI value for large firm and zero for small firms. Similarly, the second variable is created that takes the HHI value for small firms and zero for large firms. The coefficients of these variables show different effects of industry concentration of small and large firms on their profitability. In our study, the result shows that the coefficient is positively significant for large firm and positive but not statistically significant for small firms. It is indicated that not all firms can benefit and gain superior profits in a concentrated industry. In the concentrated industries, the large firms get benefit and make more profits, while the small firms will lose to these large firms.

The results reported in (D), (E) and (F) of Tab. 3.5 incorporate efficiency variable and control variables. It is observed that efficiency coefficient is positive and significant in all estimated models (FE, RE, GMM). Since there is a significant positive relationship between the profitability indicator and efficiency scores, this supports the efficient structure hypothesis in Turkish real sector.

7 Conclusion

This study examines the determinants of firm profitability within SCP and ES hypotheses. We use the annual data on 115 firm between the years 2010 and 2019. In this study, HHI values are estimated as proxies for the SCP hypothesis, while profit efficiency scores are estimated as proxies for the ES hypothesis from Bayesian stochastic frontier analysis (BSFA).

Tab. 3.5: Estimation Results of Profitability Function

	(A)	(B)	(C)	(D)	(E)	(F)
	Fixed Effect (FE)	**Random Effect (RE)**	**System GMM**	**Fixed Effect (FE)**	**Random Effect (RE)**	**System GMM**
ROA (-1)			0.2839***			0.2396***
			(0.0220			(0.5617)
Concentration	-2.6415**	-0.8451**	-0.4821			
	(0.5299)	(0.3585)	(0.7984)			
Large firm * Concentration	0.9119***	1.0027***	0.5888***			
	(0.0013)	(0.2212)	(0.0804)			
Small firm * Concentration	0.6508	0.1201	-0.0278			
	(0.5501)	(0.3958)	(0.1013)			
Efficiency				0.1046***	0.0917***	0.0560***
				(0.0304)	(0.0278)	(0.0156)
Age	0.0074***	0.0002*	0.0002**	0.0054***	0.0001	0.0001
	(0.0015)	(0.0001)	(0.0001)	(0.0011)	(0.0002)	(0.0001)
Liquidity	0.0029**	0.0036**	0.0018	0.0024	0.0027*	0.0013
	(0.0012)	(0.0018)	(0.0013)	(0.0014)	(0.0016)	(0.0011)
Leverage	-0.1918***	-0.1942***	-0.1564***	-0.2162***	-0.2149***	-0.1587
	(0.0221)	(0.0157)	(0.0104)	(0.0258)	(0.0204)	(0.0130)
Export intensity	0.0375***	0.0252***	0.0150***	0.0307***	0.0234***	0.0141***
	(0.0118)	(0.0084)	(0.0035)	(0.0101)	(0.0084)	(0.0043)
Capital intensity	-0.0314**	-0.0250**	-0.0230***	-0.0332**	-0.0278**	-0.0226***
	(0.0129)	(0.0107)	(0.0040)	(0.0132)	(0.0128)	(0.0052)
Labor cost	-0.2544**	-0.1997***	-0.1320***	-0.2295**	-0.2038***	-0.1419***
	(0.1010)	(0.0581)	(0.0204)	(0.1001)	(0.0695)	(0.0271)
Inflation	0.0002	0.0012*	0.0004	0.0010	0.0018***	0.0003
	(0.0007)	(0.0006)	(0.0002)	(0.0007)	(0.0006)	(0.0003)
Growth	-0.0003	-0.0002	0.0040**	0.0032***	-0.0026**	0.0034***
	(0.0008)	(0.0008)	(0.0020)	(0.0011)	(0.0010)	(0.0005)
Constant	-0.0692	0.1446***	0.1071*	-0.1769***	0.0980***	0.0844***
	(0.0514)	(0.0231)	(0.0580)	(0.0527)	(0.0281)	(0.0164)
Number of observations	1150	1150	1150	1150	1150	1150
Firm fixed effects	Yes	Yes	Yes	Yes	Yes	Yes

Tab. 3.5: Continued

	(A)	(B)	(C)	(D)	(E)	(F)
Time fixed effects	Yes	Yes	Yes	Yes	Yes	Yes
F-test	22.12***			15.49***		
Wald chi2		257.57***	2995.22***		230.83***	1184.38***
Hansen test (p-value)			0.119			0.160
Arellano–Bond (m1) (p-value)			0.000			0.000
Arellano–Bond (m2) (p-value)			0.433			0.160

Notes: (1) Standard deviations in parenthesis. (2) *** shows 1 % significance level, ** shows 5 % significance level.

From the efficiency estimates of the BSFA, we find the average profit efficiency of 76.38 %. This suggests that an estimated 23.62 % of the profit is lost due to a combination of both technical and allocative inefficiency in production.

The results of static (Fixed Effect, Random Effect) and dynamic (GMM) estimations suggest that there is a negative and significant relation between concentration ratio and profitability, while a positive and significant relation between large firms' concentration ratio and profitability. Additionally, we find insignificant relationship between small firms' concentration ratio and profitability. Hence, the SCP hypothesis are rejected. This suggests the absence of collusive behavior in all industries, which reflects a competitive behavior among small firms. In other words, the ability of large firms to harness the market power can be limited by competition of small firms. Hence it is possible for these small firms to exit from the industry and concentrate the industry. As a result, large firms will grow even more and become industry leaders and have the power to set their products' prices above their marginal cost and make super normal profits. We also find a positive and significant effect of profit efficiency on firm profitability. This supports the ES hypothesis in the Turkish manufacturing industry.

Bibliography

Aigner, D. J., Lovell, C. A. K., & Schmidt, P. (1977). Formulation and estimation of stochastic frontier production function models. *Journal of Econometrics*, 6, 21–37.

Alhassan, A. L., Tetteh, M. L., & Brobbey, F. O. (2016). Market power, efficiency and bank profitability: Evidence from Ghana. *Econ Change Restruct, 49*, 71–93.

Anderson, R. I., Fok, R., & Scott, J. (2000). Hotel industry efficiency: An advanced linear programming examination. *American Business Review, 18*, 40–48.

Assaf, A. G., & Cvelbar, K. L. (2011). Privatization, market competition, international attractiveness, management tenure and hotel performance: Evidence from Slovenia. *International Journal of Hospitality Management, 30*(2), 391–397.

Assaf, A. G., & Magnini, V. (2012). Accounting for customer satisfaction in measuring hotel efficiency: Evidence from the US hotel industry. *International Journal of Hospitality Management, 31*, 642–647.

Bain, J. S. (1951). Relation of profit rate to industry concentration: American manufacturing 1936–1940. *The Quarterly Journal of Economics, 65*(3), 293–324.

Baumol, W. J. (1982). Contestable markets: An uprising in the theory of industry structure. *American Economic Review, 72*(1), 1–15.

Berger, A. N., & Mester, L. J. (1997). Inside the black box: What explains differences in the efficiencies of financial institutions?. *Journal of Banking & Finance, 21*, 895–947.

Bhandari, A. K. (2010). Concentration, entry barriers and profitability in the Indian industries: An empirical analysis. *Journal of Quantitative Economics, 8*(2), 61–80.

Brozen, Y. (1971). Concentration and structural and market disequilibria. *Antitrust Bulletin, 16*, 241–248.

Clarke, R., Davies, S., & Waterson, M. (1984). The profitability-concentration relation: Market power or efficiency? *The Journal of Industrial Economics, 32*(4), 435–450.

Coelli, T. J., Rao, D. S. P., O'Donnell, C. J., & Battese, G. E. (2005). *An introduction to efficiency and productivity analysis*. Boston, MA: Springer.

Collins, N. R., & Preston, L. E. (1969). Price-cost margins and industry structure. *The Review of Economics and Statistics, 51*(3), 271–286.

Demsetz, H. (1973). Industry structure, market rivalry and public policy. *The Journal of Law and Economics, 16*(1), 1–9.

Ehlers, R. S. (2011). Comparison of Bayesian models for production efficiency. *Journal of Applied Statistics, 38*, 2433–2443.

Gallagher, D. R., Ignatieva, K., & McCulloch, J. (2015). Industry concentration, excess returns and innovation in Australia. *Accounting and Finance, 55*(2), 443–466.

Griffin, J. E., & Steel, M. F. (2007). Bayesian stochastic frontier analysis using WinBUGS. *Journal of Productivity Analysis, 27*, 163–176.

Huang, H. C. (2004). Estimation of technical inefficiencies with heterogeneous technologies. *Journal of Productivity Analysis, 21*, 277–296.

Keil, J. (2017). Explaining the concentration-profitability paradox. *Review of Political Economy, 29*(2), 209–231.

Keil, J. (2018). Is there a causal effect of concentration on persistent profitability differentials? *Industrial and Corporate Change, 28*(2), 241–257.

Khan, M. H., & Hanif, M. N. (2019). Empirical evaluation of 'structure-conduct-performance' and 'efficient-structure' paradigms in banking sector of Pakistan. *International Review of Applied Economics, 33*(5), 682–696.

Koop, G. (1994). Recent progress in applied Bayesian econometrics. *Journal of Economic Surveys, 8*(1), 1–34.

Koop, G., Steel, M., & Osiewalski, J. (1995). Posterior analysis of stochastic frontier models using Gibbs sampling. *Computational Statistics, 10*, 353–373.

Kotey, B., & O'Donnell, C. J., (2002). Data envelopment analysis in small and medium enterprises: A study of the Australian food, beverages and tobacco manufacturing Industry. *Small Enterprise Research, 10*(2), 3–22.

Kumbhakar, S. C., & Lovell, C. K. (2003). *Stochastic frontier analysis*. Cambridge, UK: Cambridge University Press.

Kumbhakar, S. C., & Tsionas, E. G. (2005). Measuring technical and allocative inefficiency in the translog cost system: A Bayesian approach. *Journal of Econometrics, 126*, 355–384.

Lee, C. Y., & Mahmood, I. P. (2009). Inter-industry differences in profitability: The legacy of the structure-efficiency debate revisited. *Industrial and Corporate Change, 18*(3), 351–380.

Leibenstein, H. (1966). Allocative efficiency vs. X-efficiency. *The American Economic Review, 56*(3), 392–415.

Meeusen, W., & Van Den Broeck, J. (1977). Efficiency estimation from Cobb-Douglas production functions with composed error. *International Economic Review, 18*(2), 435–444.

McDonald, J. T. (1999). The determinants of firm profitability in Australian manufacturing. *The Economic Record, 75*(229), 115–26.

Mishra, P. (2008). Concentration-markup relationship in Indian manufacturing sector. *Economic and Political Weekly, 43*(39), 75–81.

Mukhopadhyay, J., & Chakraborty, I. (2017). Competition and industry performance: A panel VAR analysis in Indian manufacturing sector. *Journal of Quantitative Economics, 15*, 343–366.

Pérez-Rodríguez, J. V., & Acosta-González, E. (2007). Cost efficiency of the lodging industry in the tourist destination of Gran Canaria (Spain). *Tourism Management, 28*(4), 993–1005.

Purwanto, N., Manongga, D., & Pakereng, M. A. I. (2014). Efficiency of small, and medium-sized Tofu enterprises (SME) in Salatiga using data envelopment analysis (DEA). *International Journal of Computer Applications, 91*(12), 44–50.

Setiawan, M., & Effendi, N. (2016). Survey of the industrial concentration and price-cost margin of the Indonesian manufacturing industry. *International Economic Journal, 30*(1), 123–146.

Strickland, A. D., & Weiss, L. W. (1976). Advertising, concentration, and price-cost margins. *Journal of Political Economy, 84*(5), 1109–1121.

Tsionas, E. G. (2002). Stochastic frontier models with random coefficients. *Journal of Applied Econometrics, 17*, 127–147.

Van den Broeck, J., Koop, G., Osiewalski, J., & Steel, M. F. (1994). Stochastic frontier models: A Bayesian perspective. *Journal of Econometrics, 61*, 273–303.

Burcu Hicyilmaz and Mesut Cakir

The Relationship Between the Vertical Specialization of Exports and Employment[1]

Abstract In the globalization process, as well as the increasing trade of final goods and services, the intermediate goods trade used in the production of the goods subject to trade increased. So trade has become characterized by global value chains increasingly. It caused great changes in the production and trade process and required different calculations and approaches to analyze the structure and effects of international trade. The aim of this study is to investigate the effect of vertical specialization rate of exports of intermediate goods and services on employment in seven countries consisting of Turkey and the most important trade partners of Turkey which is Germany, England, France, Italy, USA, and Russia. The data of ten sectors for seven countries are used in the study and analysis is carried out for the five-year periods of 2000–2004, 2005–2009 and 2010–2014 with the Two-Stage OLS (2SLS) method. According to the results of analysis, while vertical specialization has no effect on employment in 2000–2004 period, it has a statistically significant and negative effect in 2005–2009 and 2010–2014 periods. This effect of the vertical specialization rate, which is the indicator of the backward participation in the global value chain, has shown that this new fact creates an employment-reducing structure in the countries discussed and also creates a process that shifts the employment potential towards foreign countries.

Keywords: Global Value Chains, Vertical Specialization, Employment, Two-Stage OLS

1 Introduction

The developments in globalization and the increasingly intertwined structure of production among economies have led to the emergence of new concepts and the change of existing ones in to explain the current situations. According to Chang, Bayhaqi &Yuhua (2012: 2–3), the main concepts that are considered based on globalization in production can be grouped under three terms: Global supply chains (GSC), global value chain (GVC) and global production chain (GPC). GSC refers to the system of people, information, organization, activities and resources responsible for moving a product or service from the supplier to

1 This article is extracted from my PhD thesis entitled "The Relationship of the Vertical Specialization and Employment" (Yılmaz, 2019).

the buyers. GVC refers to all the value added activities such as raw materials and intermediate inputs, design, marketing and distribution that are required to ensure that a product or service is supplied to end consumers. GPC refers to the links between a group of firms in a certain global value chain to produce a particular product.

In the globalization process, as well as the increasing trade of final goods and services, the intermediate goods trade used in the production of the goods subject to trade increased. So trade has become increasingly characterized by global value chains. It caused great changes in the production and trade process and required different calculations and approaches to analyze the structure and effects of international trade.

The global value chain has changed international trade by affecting countries' interdependence and the structure of competition among countries. Horizontal competition enables firms to compete in the same sector for the same consumer-base; vertical competition, on the other hand, means that firms in the same value chain compete to perform specific and specialized tasks or steps in the manufacturing process (The World Bank, 2014: 37). The fact that countries tend to specialize in different stages of manufacturing in the global value chain is called "vertical specialization" by Balassa (1967) and Findlay (1978), "slicing up of the value chain" by Krugman (1995), and "fragmentation" by Jones and Kierzkowski (1990). In this study, it will be preferred to use the vertical specialization concept from here on.

According to the traditional theories, the impact of the increase in exports on employment is considered positive, while that of the increase in imports is considered negative. For example, in the Heckscher-Ohlin-Samuelson model, international trade affects employment in two channels. First, what is called "the scale effect", is that the increase in international trade integration creates an increase in the output of export sectors and this means an increase in labor demand. Secondly, "the substitution effect" shows that the effect of international trade, which increased in parallel with the increasing import competition, means a decrease in employment in the import sector by substituting domestic production (Van Ha & Tran, 2017: 532).

In the context of the global value chain, trade of intermediate goods between countries has increased as a result of the specialization of each country at certain tasks or specific steps in the manufacturing process. Therefore, exports of countries do not consist entirely of domestic value added; it consists of both domestic and foreign value added. Within the framework of this new phenomenon, for example, it can be said that the global value chains, which may be disrupted as a result of important events affecting the whole world, can disrupt the different macroeconomic variables of many countries in this chains. Determining the effect of foreign intermediate input included in exports of countries, that is vertical specialization of exports, on macro variables is important in determining a country's foreign trade policies in the globalizing world.

Conditions such as the introduction of new businesses in the economies or pulling out of the market of existing businesses, moving various production processes abroad for advantages such as cheap labor power and/or using foreign input during the production stage directly are the situations seen in economies during the reallocation of the production factors required to take advantage of comparative advantage. In this respect, that process has the potential to create both employment and unemployment. Therefore, in addition to the analyzes made with total export and import data, the analyzes made with the data of domestic and foreign value added included in exports have gained importance.

Differentiating from the literature examining the effect of international trade on employment using general variables such as exports, imports and total trade, there is a relatively new developing literature that takes into account the intertwined structure of countries' production processes and investigates the impact of value added content of trade on employment. The study of Feenstra and Hanson (1996a) investigates how outsourcing affects employment demand in America for the period 1972–1992. They found that outsourcing for the period 1972–1979 and 1979–1990 correlated positively with relative increase in nonproduction workers, and weakly and negatively with relative average annual incomes. Amiti and Wei (2009) investigated the employment effect of service offshoring for the United States over the period of 1992–2000. The study concluded that the service offshoring process has no significant effect on employment with aggregated data in 96 manufacturing industries. However, the service offshoring process caused unemployment when manufacturing industries are aggregated to 450 industries.

The employment generation potential of Turkey's exports was analyzed with input-output method by Mıhçı, Akkoyunlu-Wigley and Dalgıç (2016). The study, which has calculated domestic value added at sectoral level using the method of Feenstra and Hong (2007), has determined that the employment generation potential of exports has decreased due to the decrease in the domestic value added component of exports for the period of 1995–2008. The firm-level data also has indicated the same results for the period 2003–2012.

Xikang et al. (2012) evaluated the effect of exports on total domestic value added and employment for China in the years 2002 and 2007 with using input-output methodology. The findings have suggested that traditional manufacturing exports generated higher total domestic value added and employment than high-technology manufacturing exports. The study has interpreted the higher decline in the total employment generated from 2002 to 2007 as the large gains in labor productivity. Wei (2016) examines the impact of imports and exports by conventional trade and exports by processing trade on the labor market performance of China for the period of 1981–2012 with using vector error correction model. The results have showed that there is a long run relationship between the variables and labor market effects of vertical specialization have become important increasingly. The study has suggested using a vertically specialized trade strategy for Chinese government to encourage employment for more inclusive growth.

Shen and Silva (2018) focused on the direct effect of the Chinese economy to the U.S. labor market. Increasing in exposure to value added exports from China has effected share of manufacturing employment negatively. The study also showed that this rising exposure of value added exports from China increases U.S.'s dependency on the position of Chinese exporting industry in the global value chain. Another study, Shen, Silva and Wang (2018) found wage polarization among workers caused by U.S. occupational exposure to value added imports. Sasahara (2019) study, which conducts global input-output analysis with a focus on the USA, China and Japan, confirmed that the increase in exports means increasing in employment, but emphasizes that the impact of exports varies across destination countries. The study also underlined that exports with higher domestic value added such as textile and service sectors create a greater employment effect.

In the context of domestic value added of export, the newly developing literature reveals that exports are not a completely employment-creating process. The aim of this study is to investigate the effect of vertical specialization rate of exports of intermediate goods and services on employment in seven countries consisting of Turkey and the most important trade partners of Turkey which is Germany, England, France, Italy, USA, and Russia. The data of ten sectors for seven countries are used in the study and analysis is carried out for the five-year periods of 2000–2004, 2005–2009 and 2010–2014 with the Two-Stage OLS (2SLS) method.

The organization of this chapter is as follows. After the introduction to basic concepts, theories and literature on the subject of our study, in the second section, beside the data and methodology required for the empirical analysis to be carried out, empirical results will be shared. And finally, in the third section, conclusion was presented.

2 Data, Methodology and Results

2.1 Data

There are three different variables to be used in the analysis. These variables can be listed as follows; vertical specialization rate of exports, total output and number of employees.

The vertical specialization rate of exports of intermediate goods and services (VS, %) to be used in the study was calculated by using data for the period from 2000 to 2014 provided from World Input-Output Database (WIOD)[2]. These tables, published in 2016, cover 43 countries and the rest of the world and 56 sectors. Sectoral and regional aggregation of input output table has been applied in order to reduce size of table and provide simplicity. High-level SNA/ISIC aggregation criteria of NACE sections[3] were used for sectoral aggregation. The group of countries to be included in the analysis except Turkey was determined using foreign trade data by country provided by the Turkish Statistical Institute (TurkStat, 2018). Based on 2014 data, Turkey's exports by country (X), imports by country (M) and foreign trade volume by country (X + M) were obtained. The first seven countries that have the highest share in foreign trade volume and whose data are published in WIOD were selected. The ranking from the country with the highest share in foreign trade volume of Turkey to the lowest one is as follows; Germany, Russia, China, Italy, USA, UK and France. Thus, aggregated input-output tables consisting of ten sectors and nine countries[4] were generated. Then, vertical specialization rates of exports of each sector of the countries were calculated. The second variable to be used in the analysis is the total output (TOT, millions of US$) data for the sectors. This data was obtained from the same aggregated input-output tables.

The number of employees (EMPE, thousands) was obtained from the Socio-Economic Accounts (SEA) table, published in WIOD in 2016, with 56 sectors. This table, which includes 56 sectors, has also been aggregated and reduced to 10 sectors. However, in this table, the number of employees of China is not

---

2 For detailed information, please see Timmer, Dietzenbacher, Los, Stehrer & Vries (2015).

3 These 10 sectors consist of high-level SNA/ISIC aggregation of NACE sections into 10 categories. For detailed information and names of sectors please see EUROSTAT (2008:43–44).

4 Turkey, Germany, Russia, China, Italy, USA, UK, France and the rest of the world (ROW).

Tab. 4.1: Descriptive statistics

Variables	Observations	Mean	St. Dev.	Min.	Max.
2000–2004					
EMPE0004	70	4487.32	7194.24	58.76	40019.14
VS0004	70	1.59	3.89	0.001	17.65
TOT0004	70	481062.3	840917.6	7872.63	4778780
TOT2000 (i.v.)	70	434684.5	808220.5	5520.87	4874307
2005–2009					
EMPE0509	70	4617.36	7470.82	65.7	43069.45
VS0509	70	1.82	4.61	0.0016	20.04
TOT0509	70	683643.1	1077604	15955.21	6005920
TOT2005 (i.v.)	70	608284.5	808220.5	5520.87	4874307
2010–2014					
EMPE1014	70	4642.52	7550.04	70.98	45208.59
VS1014	70	2.03	5.09	0.0012	21.47
TOT1014	70	770286.1	1232521	20759.94	6803112
TOT2010 (i.v.)	70	707521.2	1122582	19946.19	5990267

Note: The abbreviation i.v. means "instrumental variable".

available. After excluding ROW and China, analysis has been conducted with the country group consists of Turkey, Germany, UK, France, Italy, USA and Russia.

After obtaining the annual data of 2000–2014 period for all variables, five-year periods were created. The arithmetic averages of the series were taken according to the five-year periods 2000–2004, 2005–2009 and 2010–2014[5]. The fundamental descriptive statistics for these variables are presented in Tab. 4.1.

5 The series for the period 2000–2004 are symbolized as VS0004, TOT0004 and EMPE0004; the series for the period 2005–2009 are symbolized as VS0509, TOT0509 and EMPE0509; the series for the period 2010–2014 are symbolized as VS1014, TOT1014 and EMPE1014.

2.2 Methodology

There are two different methods used in the study. The first is a method used in the measurement of the VS variable. The second is the 2SLS method, which will be used to estimate the equation.

The VS variable was calculated using the Hummels, Ishii and Yi (2001) method. According to the method, the main measure of VS can be shown as in Equation (1) (for more details see page 78–81 in Hummels, Ishii & Yi, 2001)

$$VS\ share\ of\ total\ exports = \frac{VS_k}{X_k} = u.A^M.\ \left[I - A^D\right]^{-1}.X/X_k \tag{1}$$

where u is a 1xn vector of one's, A^M is the n × n imported coefficient matrix, I is the identity matrix, A^D is the nxn domestic coefficient matrix, X is an nx1 vector of exports, X_k is total country exports and n is the number of sectors. Intermediate input values imported from each country (c = 1,2,3,. . .) and sector i for total output production of sector j can be expressed as $A^M{}_C = \frac{M_{IJ}{}^C}{Y_J}$. In this case, VS share of each country in total exports is calculated as in Equation (1.2) (Gündoğdu & Saracoğlu, 2016);

$$VS_C = u\,A_C^M\ \left[I - A^D\right]^{-1}X \tag{2}$$

The aim of the study is to determine the effect of VS on EMPE and to determine whether the relationship is positive or negative if the effect is statistically significant. For this purpose, based on the study of Shen and Silva (2018)[6], while EMPE is taken as dependent variable, VS and TOT are taken as independent variable. The econometric model to be establish within this framework can be expressed as follows;

$$EMPE_i = \alpha_0 + \alpha_1 VS_i + \alpha_2\ TOT_i + \varepsilon \tag{3}$$

In this model, α_0 is the constant term, α_1 and α_2 are slope parameters and ε is the error term.

For the five-year periods of 2000–2004, 2005–2009 and 2010–2014, the coefficients were estimated by using the cross-sectional data generated by

6 In the study of Shen and Silva (2018: 495), while manufacturing industry employment was taken as dependent variable, net value-added export per employee was taken as independent variable and 2SLS method was used.

taking the arithmetic averages of the series and the effects were examined separately by periods. As a result of the ten sectors in the seven selected countries, there are seventy observations in the analysis.

However, in the model to be estimated, the fact that there is a two-way relationship between TOT and EMPE points to the problem of endogeneity. In order to test whether the results obtained from the regression can be interpreted, it is assumed that there is an endogeneity problem in TOT. Instrumental variable will be selected for each period to represent the TOT variable consisting of a five-year arithmetic average. An instrumental variable that can explain EMPE but will minimize the impact of EMPE on TOT and represent TOT for the period should be included in the model. For this reason, TOT data of the beginning year of the five-year period will be used as an instrumental variable instead of the five-year average TOT data of that period. Therefore, the relationship between EMPE variable consisting of the average of five years for each period and TOT will be minimized. For example, instead of TOT0004, the TOT series of 2000 (symbolized as TOT2000) will be used as the instrumental variable.

Stata 11.1 and "ivregress 2sls" command was used for regression estimation. The results are estimated as "robust" in order to eliminate the heteroscedasticity problem. The 2SLS analysis consists of two stages and post-estimation procedures.

In the first stage, it is investigated whether the instrumental variable to be used represents the explanatory variable that is assumed to be have an endogeneity problem. In the model prediction of the first stage, the endogenous variable is taken as dependent variable and the instrumental variable is taken as independent variable. In this model, it is checked whether the coefficient of the instrumental variable is statistically significant or not. If the coefficient is statistically significant, the instrumental variable can be used in the second stage. In the second stage, Equation (3) is estimated using the instrumental variable.

After this two-step estimation, Wooldrige (1995), which is one of the post-estimation procedures, is used for endogeneity testing and weak instruments testing. The null hypothesis of the endogeneity test is that the variables are exogenous. In this test, χ^2 ve F statistics are reported. If the null hypothesis is rejected according to the two statistics, the variable is considered to be endogenous. So the coefficients which is estimated by using the instrumental variables can be interpreted. If the variable is exogenous according to result of χ^2 statistic but the variable is considered endogenous according to result of F test,

Tab. 4.2: The results of the 2000–2004 period

First Stage			
TOT0004	β_0	**VS0004**	**TOT2000**
	29617.71	408.42	1.04
	(2.94)*	(0.16)	(27.76)*
	$\bar{R}^2 = 0.99$	F = 424*	N = 70
Second Stage			
EMPE0004	α_0	**VS0004**	**TOT2000**
	1630.69	-167.46	0.006
	(2.48)*	(-1.20)	(3.42)*
	$\bar{R}^2 = 0.58$	F = 12.22*	N = 70
Endogeneity Test Wooldrige (1995)	χ^2(prob) = 1.84 (0.1744) F (prob) = 9.35 (0.0032)*		
Weak Instrument Test	F (prob) = 770.826 (0.0000)*		

Source: (Yılmaz, 2019)
Note: The critical values of the weak instrument Wald test for the 2SLS at the rates of 10 %, 15 %, 20 % and 25 % are 16.38, 8.96, 6.66, 5.53, respectively. *, **, *** denotes significance at 1 %, 5 % and 10 %, respectively.

this variable is considered to be endogenous and estimated coefficients can be interpreted. If null hypotheses are accepted according to the both two statistics, since there is no endogeneity problem in the model, the coefficients obtained with the OLS estimator should be interpreted.

In the weak instruments test, F statistics are reported and the null hypothesis is that "instruments are weak". If the F statistic is not significant, the instrument used is considered to be a weak variable. Stock, Wright and Yogo (2002) study states that if the 2SLS estimator and an instrument variable are used, the F statistic should exceed 10.

2.3 Empirical Results

The estimation results of the model for the first five-year period are illustrated in Tab. 4.2. The t statistic of TOT2000, which will be used as an instrumental variable instead of TOT0004 in the second stage, is statistically significant as can be seen from the first stage results. Also, when the results of post-estimation procedures are examined, it is seen that the TOT variable is exogenous according to the χ^2 test result, and it is endogenous according to the F test.

Tab. 4.3: The results of the 2005–2009 period

First Stage			
TOT0509	β_0	**VS0509**	**TOT2005**
	25423.72 (4.07)* $\bar{R}^2 = 0.99$	4863.72 (2.17)** F = 3110.16*	1.07 (70.54)* N = 70
Second Stage			
EMPE0509	α_0	**VS0509**	**TOT2005**
	1373.2 (1.86)*** $\bar{R}^2 = 0.60$	-278.12 (-2.09)** F = 11.65*	0.005 (3.41)* N = 70
Endogeneity Test Wooldrige (1995)	χ^2 (prob) = 4.48 (0.0343)** F (prob) = 12.97 (0.0006)*		
Weak Instrument Test	F (prob) = 4976.29 (0.0000)*		

Source: (Yılmaz, 2019)
Note: The critical values of the weak instrument Wald test for the 2SLS at the rates of 10 %, 15 %, 20 % and 25 % are 16.38, 8.96, 6.66, 5.53, respectively. *, **, *** denotes significance at 1 %, 5 % and 10 %, respectively.

Although the χ^2 test reveals that the variable is exogenous, the result of the F test, which gives the result at the level of regression, is accepted. In addition, according to the weak instrument test, the instrumental variable (TOT2000) was found to be not weak. So the regression results of second stage are robust and the coefficients can be interpreted. According to the regression results obtained from the second stage, the effect of VS0004 on EMPE0004 is found statistically insignificant for the 2000–2004 period.

Results for the second five-year period are reported in Tab. 4.3. It was observed that the effect of TOT2005, which will be used as instrumental variable in the second stage, on TOT0509 was positive and statistically significant at the level of 1 %. Considering the post-estimation procedure to determine whether the endogenous regressors in the model are in fact exogenous, it seems that the initially accepted assumption of endogeneity is confirmed by both χ^2 and F test.

Besides the instrumental variable used (TOT2005) was found to be not weak. The results of the model regressed with the robust instrumental variable confirmed to be endogenous indicate that the effect of VS0509 on EMPE0509 is negative and statistically significant at the level of 5 %. Likewise, the effect of TOT2005 on EMPE0509 is positive and statistically significant at 1 %.

Tab. 4.4: The results of the 2010–2014 period

First Stage			
TOT1014	β_0	**VS1014**	**TOT2010**
	-6267.232	511.96	1.10
	(-0.64)	(0.26)	(46.39)*
	$\bar{R}^2 = 0.99$	F = 1526.67*	N = 70
Second Stage			
EMPE1014	α_0	**VS1014**	**TOT2010**
	1268.37	-254.03	0.005
	(1.69)***	(-2.10)**	(3.42)*
	$\bar{R}^2 = 0.62$	F = 11.94*	N = 70
Endogeneity Test Wooldrige (1995)	χ^2 (prob) = 0.506 (0.4771) F (prob) = 0.90 (0.3467)		
Weak Instrument Test	F (prob) = 2151.74 (0.0000)*		

Source: (Yılmaz, 2019)
Note: The critical values of the weak instrument Wald test for the 2SLS at the rates of 10 %, 15 %, 20 % and 25 % are 16.38, 8.96, 6.66, 5.53, respectively. *, **, *** denotes significance at 1 %, 5 % and 10 %, respectively.

The results of the third five-year period are presented in Tab. 4.4. From the first stage results, it is observed that the effect of TOT2010 on TOT1014 is statistically significant at %1. When the post-estimate procedures are examined, although the TOT2010 instrumental variable used is found to be robust, the endogeneity assumption accepted at the beginning of the 2SLS analysis could not be confirmed and TOT2010 is found to be in fact exogenous. Therefore, the model should be estimated using the OLS estimator without interpreting the regression and coefficient estimates obtained from the second stage of 2SLS.

Although the assumption of internality is rejected as a result of empirical analysis, employment and total output are known to affect each other in theory. For this reason, in the new model to be estimated with OLS, the TOT2010 variable that represents the total output values of the 2010 will be used. Tab. 4.5 shows these OLS results.

According to the results of Breusch and Pagan (1979) heteroscedasticity test, the null hypothesis of homoscedasticity was rejected and heteroscedasticity assumed. In order to obtain more robust standard deviation values, the model was estimated as robust. In the period 2010–2014, the effect of VS1014 on EMPE1014 is negative and statistically significant at the level of 5 %.

Tab. 4.5: OLS results of the 2010–2014 period

	α_0	**VS1014**	**TOT2010**	χ^2 **(prob)**
Non-Robust	1236.72	-251.44	0.006	163.55
	(1.84)***	(-2.20)**	(10.67)*	(0.0000)
	$\bar{R}^2 = 0.62$	F = 57.18*	N = 70	
Robust	1236.72	-251.44	0.006	-
	(1.67)***	(-2.10)**	(3.54)*	-
	$\bar{R}^2 = 0.63$	F = 6.39*	N = 70	-

Source: (Yılmaz, 2019)
Note: *, **, *** denotes significance at 1 %, 5 % and 10 %, respectively. The values in parentheses below the coefficient estimates show t statistics.

3 Conclusions

The question of how exports affect employment has been the subject of research for many years. Various studies examining this relationship have concluded that there are positive, negative or no relation between the two variables as a result of their analysis. However, new phenomenon such as the fact that countries, which are part of the global value chain, use foreign intermediate goods in the products they produce to export have changed the structure of this relationship. This fact necessitated the relationship between the two variables to be handled again with a different dimension. For this purpose, the answer to the question of how the vertical specialization rate of exports affects employment was sought in the study. The effect of vertical specialization rate of exports of intermediate goods and services on employment have been investigated for three five-year periods in seven countries consisting of Turkey and Germany, England, France, Italy, USA, Russia by using 2SLS method.

The effect of vertical specialization of exports on the number of employees was found statistically insignificant for the 2000–2004 period. Nevertheless, this effect was found to be negative in the period of 2005–2009 and 2010–2014. This effect of the vertical specialization rate, which is the indicator of the backward participation in the global value chain, has shown that this new fact creates an employment-reducing structure in the countries discussed and also creates a process that shifts the employment potential towards foreign countries.

Bibliography

Amiti, M., & Wei, S. J. (2009). Does service offshoring lead to job losses? Evidence from the United States. In Marshall Reinsford and Mmatthew

J. Slaughter (Eds.), *International Trade in Services and Intangibles in the Era of Globalization*. University of Chicago Press. ISBN 0-226-70959-0.

Balassa, B. (1967). *Trade Liberalization among Industrial Countries*. New York: McGraw Hill.

Breusch, T. S., & Pagan, A. R. (1979). A simple test for heteroscedasticity and random coefficient variation. *Econometrica: Journal of the Econometric Society*, 47(5) 1287–1294.

Chang, P., Bayhaqi, A., & Yuhua, Z. B. (2012). Concepts and trends in global supply, global value and global production chains. *Asia-Pacific Economic Cooperation*, APEC#212-SE-01.4.

EUROSTAT. (2008). *NACE Rev. 2: Statistical Classification of Economic Activities in the European Community*. Luxembourg: Office for Official Publications of the European Communities. ISBN 978-92-79-04741-1.

Feenstra, R. C., & Hanson, G. H. (1996). Globalization, outsourcing and the wage inequality. *American Economic Review*, *86*(2), 240–245.

Feenstra, R. C., & Hong, C. (2007). China's exports and employment. *NBER Working Paper*, Working Paper No: 13552.

Findlay, R. (1978). An Austrian model of international trade and interest rate equalization. *Journal of Political Economy*, *86*, 989–1008.

Gündoğdu, C., & Saracoğlu D. Ş. (2016). Participation of Turkey in global value chains: An analysis based on World input output database. *ERC Working Papers in Economics*, 16/10, Economic Research Center, Middle East Technical University.

Hummels, D., Ishii, J., & Yi, K. M. (2001). The natüre and growth of vertical specialization in world trade. *Journal of International Economics*, *54*, 75–96.

Jones, R. W., & Kierzkowski, H. (1990). The role of services in production and international trade: A theoretical framework. In R. W. Jones & A. Krueger (Eds.), *The Political Economy of International Trade*. Oxford: Basil Blackwell.

Krugman, P. (1995). Growing world trade: Causes and consequences. *Brookings Papers on Economic Activity*, *26*(1), 327–377.

Mıhçı, S., Akkoyunlu-Wigley, A., & Dalgıç, B. (2016). Dynamic analysis of employment and domestic value added generated by foreign demand in Turkey: 1995–2008. *METU Studies in Development*, *43*(1), 289–315.

Sasahara, A. (2019). Explaining the employment effect of exports: Value-added content matters. *Journal of the Japanese and International Economies*, doi:10.1016/j.jjie.2019.02.004.

Shen, L., & Silva, P. (2018). Value-added exports and U.S. local labor markets: Does China really matter?. *European Economic Review*, *101*, 479–504.

Shen, L., Silva, P., & Wang, H. (2018). *Polarization of American Workers: The Big Squeeze from Occupational Exposure to Value-Added Imports*. Kansas State University.

Stock, J. H., Wright, J. H., & Yogo, M. (2002). A survey of weak instruments and weak identification in generalized method of moments. *Journal of Business and Economic Statistics*, *20*, 518–529.

The World Bank (2014). Trading up to high income (Turkey country economic memorandum), Poverty Reduction and Economic Management Unit: The World Bank.

Timmer, M. P., Dietzenbacher, E., Los, B., Stehrer, R., & Vries, G. J. (2015). An illustrated user guide to the world input-output database: The Case of the global automotive production. *Review of International Economics*, *23*, 575–605.

TurkStat (2018). Export and import data by country, Foreign Trade Statistics. https://data.tuik.gov.tr/Kategori/GetKategori?p=Foreign-Trade-104 (available at 12.02.2018).

Van Ha, H., & Tran, T. (2017). International trade and employment: A quantile regression approach. *Journal of Economic Integration*, *32*(3), 531–557.

Wei, W. (2016). Chapter 4: Vertical specialization and increasing productive employment: Comparing impacts of conventional trade and processing trade patterns on labor market in China. In *Achieving Inclusive Growth in China Through Vertical Specialization* (pp. 71–138). Chandos Publishing. doi:10.1016/B978-0-08-100627-6.00004-7.

Wooldridge, J. M. (1995). Score diagnostics for linear models estimated by two stage least squares. *In Advances in Econometrics and Quantitative Economics: Essays in Honor of Professor C. R. Rao, ed. G. S. Maddala, P. C. B. Phillips, and T. N. Srinivasan* (pp. 66–87). Oxford: Blackwell.

Xikang, C., Cheng, L. K., Fung, K. C., Lau, L. J., Sung, Y.-W., Zhu, K., Yang, C., Pei, J., & Duan, Y. (2012). Domestic value added and employment generated by Chinese esports: A quantitative estimation. *China Economic Review*, *23*, 850–864.

Yılmaz, B. (2019). *The Relationship of the Vertical Specialization and Employment*. Doctoral Thesis, Aydın Adnan Menderes University Institute of Social Sciences, Aydın/Turkey.

Yildirim Beyazit Cicen

Is Brexit a Transaction Cost Problem?

Abstract This study analyzes the Brexit transaction cost concept. After the introduction, the transaction cost economics is explained in the first section. This section explains transaction cost progress with the contribution of Coase and Williamson. In the same section, the importance of transaction costs is also explained. This explains from which channels the transaction costs affect the economy. Williamson's Transaction Cost Economy is another subtitle in the same section. The relationship between governance and transaction costs is explained in section two. The third section explains the definition of political transaction costs, their importance and economic impacts. Brexit and political transaction costs are discussed in the last section. With Brexit, Britain is moving toward a new governance structure. The political transaction costs are expected to rise due to Britain's necessity to re-contract with the EU and other countries after Brexit. This rise in costs would impact the growth of Britain and the efficiency of the Brexit preference.

Keywords: Brexit, Transaction Cost Economics, Political Transaction Cost, Governance

1 Introduction

The purpose of this analysis is to analyze the Brexit through transaction costs. The choice of government structure by the United Kingdom (UK) depends on the political transaction cost. In order to minimize transaction costs, the EU states use a single contract. The problem is that there are many decision-makers on the EU Council, and the UK complains about several discrepancies. An additional alternative is to conclude individual contracts with more than 30 countries when the UK leaves the EU and regularly renews such contracts. Under opportunism and limited rationality there will be serious contractual problems and increased costs for political transactions. From this perspective, the decision of a country to leave or stay in the European Union (EU) relies on the level of the costs of political transactions in two different governance structures. The political transaction costs also set EU boundaries.

Contracts in the real world tend to be incomplete because they are created at limited prospects and cost. The transaction cost level largely determined by establishing contracts, concluding agreements, monitoring and implementing contractual provisions. Increasing transaction costs reduce the efficiency of the political and economic market. Low transaction costs make trade easier, increase expertise, reduce production costs and increase manufacturing. If, according to the previous governance structure, political transaction costs rise after the UK leaves the EU, trade with other countries will decrease, exportations will decrease and growth will have negative impacts. Therefore, analyzing the Brexit process with the concept of contract-based political transaction costs is important for the countries' long-term economic performance.

The cost economics of transactions will be explained after introduction. In this section the subheadings of Williamson's transaction cost economy will be discussed. Afterwards, governance and transaction costs and the political transaction costs are explained. The last section discusses the political transaction costs and the Brexit relationship.

2 Transaction Cost Economics

Transaction costs have been discussed significantly since the second half of the 20th century. Basically, the transaction cost starting point is Coase (1937). Williamson (1975, 1985, 1996) made significant contributions to Coase's transaction cost analysis using contract law (Foss and Klein, 2010: 2). Other important studies are Arrow (1969), North (1984, 1990), Williamson (1979) and Mankiw (1985).

Coase asserts firms are established to minimize transaction costs. Because a product is produced in the market or company. If produced on the market, the number of contracts will increase. If the transaction is organized within the firm, the company's owner will not bear most of the contracts. This reduces the transaction costs and encourages firms to grow. The company will continue to grow as long as the cost of performing a new transaction is less than the cost of performing it on the market (or the cost of another entrepreneur within the company). This logic also applies to firms merging (Coase, 1937: 388–398).

Another important work on transaction cost is Coase (1960). In this article, Coase says that the effective competitive solution of neoclassical economics will be achieved in a world without transaction costs. If transaction costs are zero, negotiating power does not change results effectiveness. If transaction costs are positive, result effectiveness will change, and negotiating power will determine the economic results. Coase theorem claims that in the case of full ownership rights (if transaction costs are zero), externality can be internalized between the two parties through negotiation.

Williamson sees the firm and the market as alternative transaction structures. According to these studies, the firm aims to economize transaction costs as an organizational form (Williamson, 1975, 1979, 1981). These studies rely on transaction costs and contract theory. In his contract-focused work, Williamson (2008) defines transaction costs as pre-contract drafting, negotiation, contract maintenance, post-contract negotiation, supervision, and commitment provision. Assuming transaction costs are zero, political and economic markets will be effective. Transaction costs reveal ineffective property rights. Because finding a breach of a contract in a real life is expensive, measuring the breach is even more expensive, it is much more expensive to apprehend and punish the contractor (North, 1990).

2.1 Importance of Transaction Costs

Improving economic performance and a more specific governance mechanism passes through transaction cost economizing (Carter, 2012: 136). The increase in transaction costs affects the economy through different channels. Increasing in transaction costs, creating ineffective property rights (Coase, 1960), deteriorating resource allocation efficiency (Dahlman, 1979), insufficient incentives (Estache & Martimort, 1999), decreasing trade volume and frequency (Constantinides, 1986), decreasing exports (Rodrik, 2008), disrupting productivity and specialization (Coase, 2002). Accordingly, transaction costs negatively affect investment and growth in different countries and industries (Wing, Sheng, and Junior, 2011; Musole, 2009). Reducing transaction costs will increase economic efficiency (Gu and Hitt, 2001), reduce overall costs, boost sales and profits, and increase economic growth and employment (Lindfield, 1997).

For policy analysis, making the transaction cost economics to measure economic inferences can be very valuable (Polski, 2001: 26–29). Similarly, according to Zattler (2002: 213), transaction cost economics emphasizes the necessary policy proposals for economic activities and how a well-defined political approach is appropriate for the legal framework. That's the part that clogs Brexit. Estache and Martimort (1999: 2) state that if the transaction costs are considered, the structures and processes will affect the results and the transaction costs should be considered in the regulatory incentive plan. Accordingly, if transaction costs rise after UK leaves the EU, its trade volume with other countries may fall.

2.2 Williamson's Transaction Cost Economy

Williamson's transaction cost research (1975, 1985, 1996, 1998, 2000) is a school on its own. Transaction costs play a key role in arranging contracts and explaining alternatives of economic organization. The important thing is which organizational or contractual form pushes up the transaction cost more than the other. Ranking the relative transaction costs of various organizational structures becomes important, not absolute transaction costs. In empirical studies, transaction costs are not directly measured, and instead uncertainty, transaction frequency, asset specificity, opportunism, and some other variables expected to affect transaction costs are used as instrumental variable.

Transaction costs are partly related to contract relationships (Williamson, 1979). Transaction costs arise during institutional change's governance (game) phase. The institutional change process consists of 4 stages. Stages are as follows (Williamson, 2000: 596–600):

- First stage is informal institutions. Including traditions, customs, norms and religion.
- Second stage is formal institutions. Specifically, the property-related policy, judiciary and bureaucracy stand out. The tools designed at this stage include various governance structures like legislative, executive, judicial and bureaucracy.
- The third stage is governance institutions. These contractual governance structures usually last between 1–10 years. Contract-based relationships result in transaction costs during the game, where players may have disputes. Governance structures are expected to turn this into mutual gains.
- Fourth stage is neo-classical economics. Market prices and output levels are constantly adjusted through rules introduced in the previous phase.

This analysis also serves governance structures. The transaction costs faced by the UK after leaving the EU will be compared to the transaction costs in the EU. This approach would assess the Brexit.

3 Governance and Transaction Costs

Transaction cost is a form of cost generated by governance structures, according to North (1990, 1997), Wallis and North (1986) and Williamson (1999). EU is a governance structure. When the UK exits this structure, a different governance system will be experienced, and the contracts the country faces will be determined according to the new situation.

Transaction cost is the cost of measuring the exchanged item's characteristics, securing rights, enforcing agreements, and monitoring them. Measuring, enforcing and controlling costs are the basis of social, political and economic structures (North, 1990: 11). Accordingly, because transaction costs are the backbone of social, political, and economic structures, the transaction costs created by the Brexit process will direct the course of the UK and EU institutional transformation.

Williamson's work allows us to see which form of governance is more efficient when comparing different operational characteristics. According to Williamson, the transaction cost approach considers the firm more efficient than the market. Because the firm uses a single contract as opposed to a large number of contracts, it reduces transaction costs within a hierarchical structure. Thus, by minimizing transaction costs, the size of firms and vertical integrations that firms will make with other firms can be analyzed. The EU also uses one contract. However, if the UK leaves the EU, it must conclude individual contracts with over 30 countries and renew them regularly. With opportunism and limited rationality, serious contract issues (incomplete contract problems) will occur and transaction costs will arise at this stage.

When contracts are created, transaction costs will increase if there are many, unfamiliar parties and contradictory opinions between them. Moreover, transaction costs will rise if it is not easy to monitor and observe parties' unexpected behavior when a commodity or service is specific. The EU has many decision-making countries. Similarly, there are several opposition decision-makers in the UK. Also, changing the rules of the game reveals governmental opportunism (Spiller, 2013). Therefore, transaction costs will increase.

4 Political Transaction Costs

Furubotn and Richter (2005: 51–64) examines transaction costs by dividing them into three subheadings, including market, managerial and political transaction costs. Executive and adjustments relevant to the state's governance and institutional structure are classified as "political transaction costs". These are:

- The costs of setting up, maintaining and changing a system's formal or informal political organization
- The costs of running a polity

Political transaction costs are due to information-related issues involving the government. Because different institutions are subject to different levels of transaction costs, the main goal is to examine in detail the optimization issues of comparative and regulatory structures (Estache & Martimort, 1999: 2). Political transaction costs affect optimum selection and policy tools. Repeating the game frequently among the mentioned players in this process will open the door to long-term cooperation by making the commitment credible and

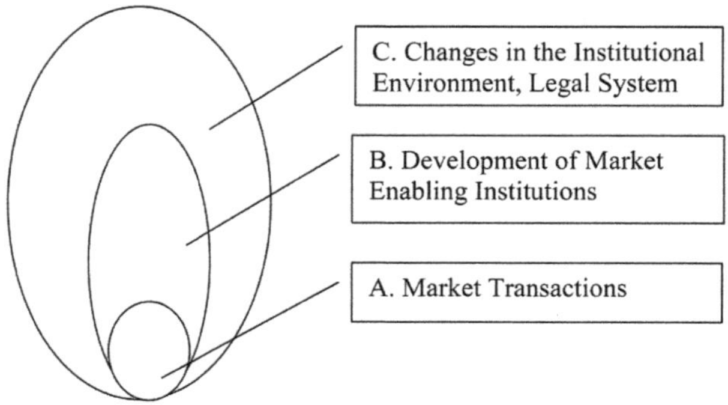

Fig. 5.1: The Magnitude of Political Transaction Cost
Source: (McCann, Colby, Easter, Kasterine, Kuperan, 2005: 530.)

binding, allowing the process to be internalized, reducing information and incentive problems. Consequently, comparing the effectiveness of institutional organizations is sufficient to compare the political transaction costs of these forms (Zattler, 2002: 214–218).

Fig. 5.1 gives us an idea of the extent to which institutional environment will create political transaction costs. Part A shows the magnitude of the market transaction. Part B covers registration, monitoring and implementation costs for public units. Part C can indicate the resulting costs of change in the institutional environment. The parts concerned with political transactions are, therefore, B and C.

Spiller and Tommasi (2003) and Spiller (2013) argue that the process of making policies can be explained from the point of view of transaction costs. Thus, if institutional interaction facilitates political co-operation, the cost of political transactions will be relatively low. A more efficient and adaptive regulatory policy process can be implemented in such an environment.

Laffont (2005) states that the political transaction costs arising from the communication and enforcement of contracts in the policy making process. These contracts relate closely to institutional design. If contracts are incomplete, the policy making process will demonstrate institutional weakness. Obviously, policy processes involve transaction costs, and institutional design structure and quality affect the magnitude of political transaction costs (Levy & Spiller, 1996). When the legal system is problematic and bureaucratic too much formed, the policy is broken and insecure property rights are established

(Moe, 1997: 472). It can therefore be stated that political transaction costs are relatively high even on the most perfect political markets.

As a result, from the economic point of view, political processes are expected to decrease transaction costs as possible. Economic units undoubtedly take political transaction costs into account when making business and investment decisions. Because the flexibility to reduce costs of production is less than increased flexibility in costs of political transactions. Moreover, political transaction costs are one determinant of market transaction costs (Zattler, 2002: 218). It is therefore necessary to examine in detail which institutional structure minimizes the transaction cost. Because the characteristics of the transaction differ in each case.

5 Brexit and Political Transaction Costs

In this section, first of all, what happened in the context of the Brexit process will be explained. The decision of the UK to leave the EU was taken in a referendum held on June 2016. This process is referred to as Brexit. Brexit proponents want to leave the EU due to the inadequacy of the migrant problem, the insufficient integration of refugees within the EU, the failure to use monetary policy instruments efficiently, the increase of racism of Europe, Islamophobia and other thinking movement. According to supporters, if Britain leaves the EU, the bilateral trade agreements could become more entrepreneurial, aggressive and competitive.

Many who oppose Brexit argue that pulling out of the world's largest economic bloc is a major mistake, that Britain can not stand alone in terms of economy, politics or security, and would be struck by a severe crisis. The production side is much more dangerous for the UK. Also, market and economic data support this view. According to 2016 figures, 44 % of the country's overall $465 billion exports directly to the EU. The EU also generates 50 % of its imports[1]. If the British leave the EU, they will have to make individual trade deals with all 32 EU member states while they remain outside the common market. And if these deals are made, these estimates are hard to hit. Since the country doesn't have a significant number of strong companies or brands in the world markets, both in industry and new technologies.

Article 50 of the Treaty of Lisbon gives the EU the right to leave[2]. In the 23 June 2016 referendum, 52 % of voters voted to leave the

1 https://fullfact.org/europe/uk-eu-trade/ – Accessed: 20.03.2020

2 It is not known how the Brexit process will work under article 50 of the Lisbon Treaty.

EU[3]. The 2016 referendum result was supposed to remain in the EU. However, it was mainly accepted as a result of leaving the EU for reasons such as the failure of young people to go to the polls, concerns about the refugee crisis and the inability of the Brussels EU center to be considered administratively sufficient[4]. This surprise result led to several developments. Brexit has sparked a UK political and economic crisis since 2016. After the Brexit referendum, UK Prime Minister David Cameron resigned because he didn't want to take on Brexit's mission. Thus, on July 2016, Theresa May took both the presidency of the Conservative Party and the prime minister's positions. Theresa May's government faced several challenges at this point. There was no political consensus on Brexit. EU Minister David Davis and Foreign Secretary Boris Johnson resigned in May's government on 9 July 2016[5]. Resignations are because Britain made too many concessions to the EU in the negotiations.

Following the Brexit decision, a UK-EU exit agreement has emerged. British Prime Minister May-led government presented the withdrawal agreement to the House of Commons on January 15, 2019, but this draft agreement was rejected by parliamentary majority (202–432 votes). Following this heavy parliamentary rejection, the main opposition party proposed a government vote of confidence. On January 16, 2019, Prime Minister May won this vote against 325 by 306. The second draft withdrawal agreement was re-submitted to the House of Commons on March 12, 2019. This second draft rejected again (202 vs. 412). The third draft Brexit agreement was submitted to the House of Commons on 29 March and rejected again (286 vs. 344). British Parliament postponed Brexit to April 12, 2019 before March 29, 2019 and then to October 31, 2019.

Theresa May, who failed to pass the Brexit withdrawal agreement three times through Parliament, resigned on 24 May due to criticism of the poorly managed process and concessions to the EU. Boris Johnson was elected to the Conservative Party vacated by May on 23 July 2019, and took over the Prime Minister. With resignations and expulsions after the summer break, the Conservative Party lost its parliamentary majority. On September 4, 2019, the House of Commons passed a bill preventing a Brexit no-deal. On October 17, 2019, Prime Minister Johnson succeed in revising the Brexit deal. EU leaders

---

3 Of the 33.2 million voters who voted in the UK referendum, 51.8 % voted for leaving the EU and 48.2 % of the British voted in the direction of "staying in the EU". - https://www.bbc.co.uk/news/politics/eu_referendum/results - Accesses: 23.01.2021.

4 http://www.bbc.com/news/uk-politics-32810887 – Accessed: 26.03.2020.

5 https://www.bbc.com/news/uk-politics-44761056 – Accessed: 24.04.2019.

approved Britain's request to postpone Brexit until January 31 on October 28. Britain voted for an early election on October 29 and Boris Johnson came to power alone on December 12. On January 23, 2020, the Queen approved the Brexit Act[6].

As illustrated, up to this point the Brexit process created many uncertainties. An EU-UK draft is being drafted. But high-level uncertainties and disagreements exists. This entails transaction costs. According to Trebilcock and Leng (2006), weak enforcement of contracts and laws, unsafe property rights, corruption or ineffective bureaucracy will result in increased discouraging norms that would hamper community-specific cooperation and genereate high transaction costs. Therefore, trade, employment and growth will decline.

We can say, based on the illustration of governance, the cost of using the market is the cost UK faces after Brexit. The EU is the hierarchy. In terms of transaction cost analysis, using a single contract, EU countries minimize political transaction costs. UK will make contracts with 32 countries as well as the one it met while in the EU. UK should regularly renews those contracts. This means increased transaction costs. This will negatively reflect UK economic indicators. Another important question is who and at what rate will cover EU-UK contract costs.

As a consequence, institutional structure determines the level of transaction costs. Political institutions are one of the most important factors determining the institutional structure. Political institutions can reduce transaction costs by improving property rights security and ensuring contract execution (Menard & Shirley, 2008). Based on Williamson's approach, the political dynamics and associated risks can be identified as feasible and effective governance structure (Spiller, 2013: 233). The key to opening the black box of policy is the cost analysis of transactions (Spiller, 2010: 147). However, there are no examples in literature of systematic studies on this topic.

6 Conclusion

The UK's choice of governance structure depends on the level of political transaction cost. EU countries use a single contract to minimize transaction costs. The difficulty is the large number of EU Council decision-makers, and the UK complains about several disagreed practices. Another alternative is to make

6 https://www.itv.com/news/2019-10-29/brexit-timeline-from-2013-referendum-promise-to-a-2019-election/ – Accessed: 20.04.2020.

individual contracts with more than 30 countries when UK leaves the EU and renew those contracts regularly. Under opportunism and limited rationality, serious contractual issues will arise, and political transaction costs will rise. To compare the effectiveness of the institutional organizations, it is necessary to compare the political transaction costs generated by these forms. From this perspective, a country's decision to leave or remain in the EU depends on the level of political transaction costs it faces in two different governance structures. Accordingly political transaction costs also determine EU limits.

Considering the political transaction costs in the policy making process, the institutional structure will affect the outcomes. In the real world, contracts tend to be incomplete, as they are created with limited foresight and cost. Creating contracts, concluding agreements, monitoring and implementing contract provisions determine the transaction cost level. Increasing transaction costs reduce political and economic market efficiency. Low transaction costs facilitate trade, increase specialization, reduce production costs and increase production. In this case, if the political transaction costs rise after the UK leaves the EU according to the previous governance structure, trade volume with other countries will decrease, exports will decrease, and growth will be negatively impacted. Therefore, analyzing the Brexit process with the concept of contract-based political transaction costs is important for the countries' long-term economic performance.

The UK's decision to leave the EU was a surprising decision for the member states. Britain's seperation has had a weakening effect on the EU. Since the member countries cannot afford to bear the costs of the disintegration of the EU, it presents the idea of a differentiated Europe. This situation may require revision of both EU governance mechanisms and EU's enlargement policies.

Bibliography

Arrow, K. J. (1969). The Organization of Economic Activity: Issues Pertinent to the Choice of Market versus Nonmarket Allocation. *The Analysis and Evaluation of Public Expenditure: The PPB System, 1*, 59–73.

Carter, R. (2012). Transaction Cost Empirical Work. In *Handbook of the Economics and Theory of the Firm*, eds. Micheal Dietrich and Jackie Kraftt. Edward Elgar Publishing.

Coase, R. H. (1937). The Nature of The Firm. *Economica, 4*, 386–405.

Coase, R. H. (1960). Problem of Social Cost. *The Journal of the Law and Economics, 3*, 1–44.

Coase, R. H. (2002). Interview: Why Economics Will Change?. *International Society for New Institutional Economics, 4*(1), 1–7.

Costantinides, G. M. (1986). Capital Market Equilibrium with Transaction Costs. *The Journal of Political Economy, 94*(4), 842–862.

Dahlman, C. J. (1979). The Problem of Externality. *Journal of Law and Economics, 22*(1), 141–162.

Estache, A., & Martimort D. (1999). *Transaction Costs, Politics and the Design of Regulatory Institutions.* World Bank Policy Research Working Paper, No: 2073.

Foss, N. J., & Klein, P. G. (2010). *Critiques of Transaction Cost Economics: An Overview.* The Elgar Companion to Transaction Cost Economics, ed. Peter G. Klein, Michael E. Sykuta. Edward Elgar Publishing. Chapter 25.

Furubotn, E. G., & Richter R. (2005). *Institutions and Economic Theory: The Contribution of the New Institutional Economics.* Ann Arbor: The University of Michigan Press.

Gu, B., & Hitt, L. (2001). *Transaction Costs and Market Efficiency.* ICIS 2001 Proceedings, Paper 11, 85–96.

Laffont, J. J. (2005). *Regulation and Development.* Cambridge: Cambridge University Press.

Levy, B., & Spiller P. T. (1996). *Regulations, Institutions, and Commitment: Comparative Studies of Telecommunications.* New York: Cambridge University Press.

Lindfield, M. (1997). Planning for the Private Financing of Urban Infrastructure: Transaction Costs and Cross-market Analysis. *Third World Planning Review, 19*(1), 1.

Mankiw, N. G. (1985). Small Menu Costs and Large Business Cycles: A Macroeconomic Model of Monopoly. *The Quarterly Journal of Economics, 100*(2), 529–537.

McCann, L., Colby, B., Easter, K. W., Kasterine, A., & Kuperan, V. K. (2005). Transaction Cost Measurement for Evaluating Environmental Policies. *Ecological Economics, 52*(4), 527–542.

Menard, C., & Shirley, M. M. (2008). *The Handbook of New Institutional Economics*, 2. bs. ed. Claude Menard Claude, Mary M. Shirley (pp. 1–18). US: Springer, New York.

Moe, T. (1997). *The Positive Theory of Public Bureaucracy. Perspectives on Public Choice.* ed. Dennis C. Mueller (pp. 455–480). Cambridge: Cambridge University Press.

Musole, M. (2009). Property Rights, Transaction Costs and Institutional Change: Conceptual Framework and Literature Review. *Progress in Planning, 71*(2), 43–85.

North, D. C. (1984). Transaction Costs, Institutions, and Economic History. *Journal of Institutional and Theoretical Economics, 140*(1), 7–17.

North, D. C. (1990). *Institutions, Institutional Change, and Economic Performance*. Cambridge: Cambridge University Press.

North, D. C. (1997). *The Process of Economic Change. World Institute for Development Economics Research*. Research Paper 128.

Polski, M. M. (2001). *Measuring Transaction Costs and Institutional Change in the US Commercial Banking Industry*. Institute for Development Strategies Discussion Papers, ISSN 01-3. January.

Rodrik, D. (2008). The Real Exchange Rate and Economic Growth. *Brookings Papers on Economic Activity, 39*(2), 365–412.

Spiller, P. T. (2010). Regulation: A Transaction Cost Perspective. *California Management Review, 52*(2), 147–158.

Spiller, P. T. (2013). Transaction Cost Regulation. *Journal of Economic Behavior and Organization, 89*, 232–242.

Spiller, P. T., & Tommasi, M. (2003). The Institutional Foundations of Public Policy: A Transactions Approach with Application to Argentina. *Journal of Law, Economics, and Organization, 19*(2), 281–306.

Trebilcock, M., & Leng, J. (2006). The Role of Formal Contract Law and Enforcement in Economic Development. *Virginia Law Review, 92*, 1517.

Wallis, J. J., & North, D. C. (1986). *Measuring the Transaction Sector in the American Economy, 1870–1970. Long-term Factors in American Economic Growth*. ed. Stanley L. Engerman, Robert E. Gallman (pp. 95–162). Chicago: University of Chicago Press.

Williamson, O. E. (1975). *Markets and Hierarchies: Analysis of Antitrust Implications*. New York: Free Press.

Williamson, O. E. (1979). Transaction-Cost Economics: The Governance of Contractual Relations. *Journal of Law and Economics, 22*(2), 233–261.

Williamson, O. E. (1981). The Economics of Organization: The Transaction Cost Approach. *American Journal of Sociology, 87*(3), 548–577.

Williamson, O. E. (1985). *The Economic Institutions of Capitalism*. New York: Free Press.

Williamson, O. E. (1996). *The Mechanisms of Governance*. New York: Oxford University Press.

Williamson, O. E. (1998). Transaction Cost Economics: How It Works; Where It is Headed. *De Economist, 146*(1), 23–58.

Williamson, O. E. (1999). Public and Private Bureaucracies: A Transaction Cost Economics Perspective. *Journal of Law, Economics, and Organization, 15*(1), 306–342.

Williamson, O. E. (2000). The New Institutional Economics: Taking Stock, Looking Ahead. *Journal of Economic Literature, 38*(3), 595–613.

Williamson, O. E. (2008). Tran*saction Cost Economics. In Handbook of New Institutional Economics* (pp. 41–65). Berlin: Springer.

Wink Junior, M. V., Sheng H. H., & Eid Junior, W. (2011). Transaction Costs: An Empirical Analysis of Their Relationship with Investment and Foreign Direct Investment. *Revista De Administração De Empresas, 51*(2), 175–187.

Zattler, J. K. (2002). Growth Policies in Developing Countries. *Intereconomics, 37*(4), 212–222.

Mustafa Cem Kirankabes

Clustering Approach as a Regional Development Tool and Turkish Automotive Sector Clustering Analysis

Abstract The automotive sector, which is a considered as a strategic sector in almost all developed countries, operates with a fully clustering approach. Clustering is defined as the geographical concentration of firms, specialized suppliers, service providers and related institutions that compete with each other in a particular field of activity, but also cooperate with each other.

In this chapter of the book, first of all, the definition and development of the automotive sector was explained briefly. In the second part, the history and current situation of the Turkish automotive sector was given. In the third part, "Three-star Analysis", which is the most commonly used method in "Cluster Mapping Studies", was performed at the NUTS III (81 provinces) level to cover the entire Turkey. 2019 Compulsory Insured Person data taken from the statistical database of the Social Security Institution of the Republic of Turkey was used in the analysis.

As a result of the three-star analysis conducted within the scope of the study, Bursa, Sakarya and Kocaeli provinces received three-stars. In this sense, it can be said that the heart of the Turkish automotive sector is the East Marmara Region. Izmir province is the only region that receives two stars and shows "potential cluster" characteristics for the automotive sector of Turkey. In terms of the sustainability of mature and potential clusters identified within the scope of the study, it is strongly recommended that they have to integrate into international cluster associations and become able to carry out international joint projects. In the scope of the study, the regions showing "candidate cluster" characteristics by receiving a single star were identified as Aksaray, Istanbul, Konya, Kütahya, Manisa and Eskisehir provinces. In provinces that receive a single star, clustering efforts should be supported under the leadership of public institutions, non-governmental organizations such as Chambers of Commerce and the private sector.

Keywords: Turkish Automotive Sector, Regional Development, Cluster, Three-star Analysis, The European Cluster Observatory

1 Introduction

Clustering is defined as the geographical concentration of firms, specialized suppliers, service providers and related institutions that compete with each other in a particular field of activity, but also cooperate with each other.

The automotive sector is important for the economies due to its relationship with many other sector like "Manufacture of basic metals", "Manufacture of chemicals and chemical products" and "Manufacture of rubber and plastic products", contribution to *Gross Domestic Product* (*GDP*) and the Payment Surplus it generates. In this sense, many developed countries have recognized the automotive sector as one of the important sectors and supported in terms of economic development.

The automotive sector, which is a considered as a strategic sector in almost all developed countries, operates with a fully clustering approach like the Baden-Wuerttemberg automotive cluster in Germany. One of the best examples of automotive clusters is the Baden-Wuerttemberg region in Germany. Baden-Württemberg is the third largest state out of 16 in the Federal Republic of Germany. GDP of Baden-Wuerttemberg is 477 billion euros. This is corresponding to 15.2 % of Germany's GDP. And GDP per capita in the area is 43,700 euros. It is 37,997 euros in Germany. The automotive industry is one of the priority sectors for Germany. According to 2016 data, the automotive sector creates employment for more than 235,000 people in Germany. Around a quarter of the German turnover in the automotive industry is generated in Baden-Württemberg. Moreover, as the center of the German automotive industry, Baden-Württemberg is home to over 1,000 parts suppliers. Throughout the state, there are more than 20 clusters and networks that actively promote innovation and bundle diverse synergies, thus strengthening the international competitiveness of the automotive industry here. With global players such as Daimler, Porsche and Bosch, the Stuttgart region is by far the most important automotive cluster within Europe (Baden-Württemberg International, 2017:2–5)

In this part of the book, the definition and development of the automotive sector is explained briefly. Then, the history and current situation of the Turkish automotive industry is explained. In the third section, a cluster analysis for the Turkish automotive sector is made. In the last part of the study, the cluster analysis results are evaluated.

According to the three-star methodology, if an agglomeration (the geographical concentration of firms) in any sector in the region received three-stars it is called "the mature cluster", if it is received two stars it is called "the potential cluster" and if it is received a single star it is called "the candidate cluster". As a result of the three-star analysis conducted within the scope of the study, Bursa, Sakarya and Kocaeli provinces received three-stars. Izmir province received two stars. İstanbul, Ankara, Eskisehir, Konya, Kütahya, Manisa provinces received one star.

2 Definition and Overview of the Automotive Industry

The automotive sector is a sector that produces motor vehicles and their parts and components. Motor Vehicle is a machine with an engine that is used to take people or things from one place to another, such as a car, bus, or truck (Procter, 1978). The industry that produces these vehicles is the "Main Industry", and the industry that produces parts, modules and systems in accordance with the technical documents determined by the main industry is the "automotive subsidiary industry". Automotive industry covers main industry and automotive subsidiary industry (ISO, 2002:1). According to NACE Rev.2 classification (Statistical *classification of economic activities*) the automotive sector, whose full name is the "Manufacture of motor vehicles, trailers and semi-trailers" is one of the locomotive sectors in all developed economies with its priori and backward connections. The sector is connected with many major sectors such as "Manufacture of basic metals", "Manufacture of chemicals and chemical products" and "Manufacture of rubber and plastic products".

Car production constitutes of approximately 70 % of the total motor vehicles productions in the world. The percentage is almost the same in Turkey (ISO, 2002:3). The automotive sector is a sector where international competition is very intense. The main reason for this is that the automotive sector is one of the sectors where intra-industry trade is quite intensive. As is known *Intra-industry trade* refers to the exchange of similar products belonging to the same *industry.* This is quite natural for the automotive sector. In this sense, the only competitive factor is not selling price. In addition, factors such as quality, technology, safety, product variety, product promotion studies, compliance with environmental norms, alternative fuel use, understanding customer preferences, and creating a brand are the determinants of sales figures. These factors affecting sales are mainly related to the *Research and Development* (R&D) and innovation power of multinational companies of motor vehicle manufacturers.

Competition in the automotive sector is becoming sharper every day. Today, the use of technology in the automotive sector has reached an incredible level. There are some sensors on vehicles that detect situations such as road, traffic and driver fatigue. In addition, Self-driving vehicles are produced by using this sensor, laser camera, GPS and internet. This intensive use of technology forces manufacturers to merge due R&D costs and other factors. For example, Volkswagen, a German company, includes not only the Volkswagen brand, but also English, Italian, French, Spanish and Czech brands such as Bentley, Lamborghini, Bugatti, Seat, and Skoda. Similarly, Opel, a German brand, was recently acquired by the French PSA (Peugeot Société Anonym) group. As can be seen, some multinational companies gather automotive brands regardless of their country of origin.

In order to evaluate the situation of the automotive sector worldwide, it is useful to look at the automotive sector Import and Export data which obtained from the World Trade Organization (WTO) database. Tab. 6.1 shows a list of the most exported regions/countries in the automotive sector prepared with data from the WTO database. The European Union (EU) exported approximately 783 billion dollars of automotive products in 2018. Inside the EU and all over the world, Germany was the most exporting country in the sector with about $ 267 billion in same year. In this sense, automotive exports of Germany, which is a member of the EU, constitute an important part of EU exports. Turkey is ranked 19th on the list. In 2018, Turkey's automotive sector exports just over $ 26 billion dollars. Turkey's share in world automotive sector exports is 1.7 %. Turkey has the potential to increase this rate with its economic strength and sectoral knowledge.

Tab. 6.2 shows the top twenty-five countries/regions with the most import figures in the automotive sector according to WTO data. The most importing region/countries in the sector are EU with 633 billion dollars, USA with 315 billion dollars and Germany with 132 billion dollars, respectively. Turkey is ranked 22th on the list. In 2018, Turkey's automotive sector exports just over 17 billion dollars. Turkey's share in world automotive sector exports is 1.1 %.

Considering the export and import figures given in Tabs. 6.1 and 6.2 above, EU, USA, Germany and People's Republic of China lead the world automotive sector in terms of exports and imports. As can be seen from Tables same countries export and import motor vehicles and their parts each other. Because of that we can say intensive intra-industry trade is carried out in the sector.

The results obtained from a study conducted by Türkcan and Ateş on the USA automotive industry in 2010 support this determination. In this study, it has been analyzed the composition of trade between the USA and it is 37 major trading partners over the period 1989–2006. As a result, it has been determined that there is an inter-sector trade between USA and it is trading partners in the automotive sector (Türkcan & Ateş, 2010:15).

3 Development and Current Situation of Turkish Automotive Sector

Production in the automotive sector in Turkey dates back to 1954. Turk Willys Overland Ltd. began to produce military jeeps and pickup trucks in 1954. This was followed by the truck assembly factory established in Eskişehir in 1960

Tab. 6.1: Top 25 Exporting Countries and Regions in the Automotive Sector

Rank	Country	Export 2017 (Million USD)	Export 2018 (Million USD)	Growth Rate (%)	Country's Share in World Export (%In 2018)
1	European Union (28)	739153	782779	5.90	50.60
2	Germany	261444	266996	2.12	17.26
3	Japan	150080	158416	5.55	10.24
4	USA	135023	135473	0.33	8.76
5	Mexico	109043	123418	13.18	7.98
6	South Korea	64110	63351	-1.18	4.09
7	Canada	63302	60753	-4.03	3.93
8	China	54200	60651	11.90	3.92
9	Spain	57397	60009	4.55	3.88
10	France	54553	59373	8.84	3.84
11	United Kingdom	55195	56277	1.96	3.64
12	Belgium	47927	49595	3.48	3.21
13	Italy	42243	43615	3.25	2.82
14	Czech Republic	40467	43267	6.92	2.80
15	Poland	29804	31603	6.04	2.04
16	Thailand	28728	30900	7.56	2.00
17	Slovak Republic	23638	29421	24.46	1.90
18	Sweden	23234	26420	13.71	1.71
19	Turkey	23851	26279	10.18	1.70
20	Netherlands	23753	25609	7.81	1.66
21	Hungary	22819	23700	3.86	1.53
22	Austria	18349	20714	12.89	1.34
23	United Arab Emirates	12354	17005	37.65	1.10
24	India	13651	15397	12.79	1.00
25	Romanya	12398	15075	21.59	0.97
	World	1466385	1547075	5.50	100.00

Source: (WTO Statistics Database, https://data.wto.org/)

with the partnership of Ford and Koç Holding. Then in 1964, Çiftçiler Holding began its truck assembly operations in Turkey by establishing a production facility. The first bus assembly in Turkey began with Magirus bus assembly which made by İstanbul Otobüs Karöseri Sanayi A.Ş. The first local Turkish

Tab. 6.2: Top 25 Import Countries and Regions in Automotive Sector

Rank	Country	Import 2017 (Million USD)	Import 2018 (Million USD)	Growth Rate (%)	Country's Share in World Import (%In 2018)
1	European Union (28)	588161	632222	7.49	40.80
2	USA	303272	314839	3.81	20.32
3	Germany	124233	131199	5.61	8.47
4	China	83479	86822	4.00	5.60
5	Canada	75987	75982	-0.01	4.90
6	United Kingdom	71697	72813	1.56	4.70
7	France	63786	71668	12.36	4.62
8	Belgium	53511	55915	4.49	3.61
9	Mexico	49830	53130	6.62	3.43
10	Spain	46456	49767	7.13	3.21
11	Italy	47400	49370	4.16	3.19
12	Netherlands	27567	30396	10.26	1.96
13	Australia	28687	29191	1.76	1.88
14	Poland	22928	26249	14.48	1.69
15	Russian Federation	22347	24946	11.63	1.61
16	Japan	22643	24615	8.71	1.59
17	Czech Republic	20249	21448	5.92	1.38
18	United Arab Emirates	22037	20529	-6.84	1.32
19	Austria	18588	20231	8.84	1.31
20	Sweden	18468	18878	2.22	1.22
21	Slovak Republic	13727	17734	29.19	1.14
22	Turkey	20427	17046	-16.55	1.10
23	South Korea	16011	16911	5.62	1.09
24	Brazil	12140	14554	19.88	0.94
25	Switzerland	13641	13980	2.49	0.90
	World	1471736	1549658	5.29	100.00

Source: (WTO Statistics Database, https://data.wto.org/)

automobile (designed and produced in *Turkey*) was produced in 1961 at the Eskişehir State Railways Factory. The name of this car is "Devrim" which was produced only 4 units as a prototype. For reasons still discussed, mass production of the "Devrim" car could not be started. In 1966, the "Anadol" joint venture car was produced in partnership with Ford and Koç Holding.

The production of Anadol continued until 1982. A total of 87 thousand Anadol were produced. A significant increase in production in the Turkish automotive sector has been with the assembly plants established in the late 1960s. Two major manufacturers in the Turkish automotive sector, Tofaş and Oyak-Renault, were established in 1968 and in 1969, respectively. Currently, the share of car production in the Turkish automotive sector is 70 % (TAYSAD, 2020).

With the liberal policies implemented in the economy following the decisions of January 24, 1980, the Turkish automotive sector started to gain a competitive feature in exports in the early 1990s. By the end of the 1990s, the Turkish automotive sector has become an export base after partnerships with international automobile companies. Another milestone that plays a role in the integration of the Turkish automotive sector into the international automotive sector is the "customs union agreement" signed between Turkey and the EU in 1996. The customs union agreement increased the export volume of the Turkish automotive industry. Today, production methods and technologies applied in the Turkish automotive sector are equivalent to the methods and technologies used by multinational main companies (*Republic of Turkey Ministry of Industry and Technology*, 2019: 8–9).

The Turkish automotive industry has evolved, especially in the automotive supplier industry, except for the production of very few engine parts and transmission parts. Eighty-five to ninety percent of the parts used in the vehicles produced in Turkey can be obtained from local suppliers. Local suppliers able to produce lots of vehicle parts like engine and engine parts, transmission parts, brake systems and parts, hydraulic and pneumatic parts, suspension parts, safety parts, rubber and rubber parts, chassis parts and parts, electrical equipment and headlight systems, battery, windows and seats. The Turkish automotive subsidiary industry has gained international competitiveness. Local suppliers produce original and equivalent finished products, semi-finished products and systems in accordance with the technical documents determined by the main industry (*Republic of Turkey Ministry of Industry and Technology*, 2019: 9–10).

In order to accurately assess the place of the Turkish automotive sector in the Turkish economy, it is important to look at the list of the 500 largest industrial enterprises which announced by the İstanbul Chamber of Industry (ISO).

There were five automotive manufacturers in the top ten on 2018 list of ISO 500. These manufacturers are list respectively Ford Otomotiv Sanayi A.Ş., Toyota Otomotiv Sanayi Türkiye A.Ş., Oyak-Renault Otomobil Fabrikaları A.Ş., TOFAŞ Türk Otomobil Fabrikası A.Ş. ve Hyundai Assan Otomotiv San. ve Tic. A.Ş. Five automotive companies in the top ten of the ISO 500 list, clearly show the position of the automotive sector for the Turkish economy (ISO, 2018:98).

Another source that can be looked at to assess the place of the Turkish automotive sector in the Turkish economy is the sectoral export data published by the Turkish Exporters Assembly (TIM). The share of the automotive sector in Turkey's foreign trade is significant. According to the sectoral-based export report prepared by TIM, Turkey's total exports value is $ 165,067,039 in 2019. In the same year, the automotive sector export value is $ 28,051,341. According to this data, the share of the Turkish automotive sector in Turkey's total exports is 16.99 % and it is ranked first in all sectors (TIM, 2020).

Turkey has taken concrete steps for the second time, the domestic automobile production in 2019 with 60 years of experience in the automotive industry. Turkey's Automobile Enterprise Group (TOGG) promoted domestic vehicles for which mass production is planned. The production facility of domestic automobile is being built in Gemlik-Bursa, and it is planned to start mass production in 2023.It is expected that 4,323 people will be employed at the plant, which has a planned fixed investment amount of ₺ 22 billion. When considered together with the supplier industry, it is predicted that the factory will create employment for 20 thousand people. In the first stage, it is planned to produce 5 different models. The investment is expected to contribute 50 billion Euros to Turkey's GDP within 15 years (*Republic of Turkey Ministry of Industry and Technology*, 2020:2).

In terms of international competition, the strength of firms and the sector is very important. However, the overall state of the country's economy determines its international competitiveness. In Tab. 6.3, the world and Turkey's automotive sector export figures are seen. As can be seen from the Tab. 6.3, Turkey's share in world automotive exports in 1990 was 0.048 %, and it was reached 1.699 % in 2018. Despite this increase, according to the World Bank definition, it is still very low for Turkey, which is among the countries of the upper middle income level.

Fig. 6.1 which is below shows a chart drawn using world and Turkey's automotive sector export data taken from the WTO statistical database. The sharpest decline in automotive exports worldwide and in Turkey occurred in 2009, when the effects of the global crisis were most tangible.

Tab. 6.3: World and Turkey's Automotive Sector Export Values (1980–2018 Period)

Year	World Exports (Million US $)	Turkey Exports (Million US $)	Turkey Share (%)	Year	World Exports (Million US $)	Turkey Exports (Million US $)	Turkey Share (%)
1990	318959	153	0.048	2005	921566	9370	1.017
1991	324868	156	0.048	2006	1019891	11689	1.146
1992	361408	229	0.063	2007	1197203	15582	1.302
1993	349220	251	0.072	2008	1236437	17873	1.446
1994	401043	335	0.084	2009	849353	11991	1.412
1995	475668	642	0.135	2010	1094212	13755	1.257
1996	504485	772	0.153	2011	1287202	15677	1.218
1997	527765	667	0.126	2012	1303965	14837	1.138
1998	555757	803	0.144	2013	1348600	16765	1.243
1999	584929	1438	0.246	2014	1405174	17495	1.245
2000	576725	1517	0.263	2015	1329720	16965	1.276
2001	569454	2336	0.410	2016	1365144	19494	1.428
2002	628277	3160	0.503	2017	1466385	23851	1.627
2003	730014	4928	0.675	2018	1547075	26279	1.699
2004	859882	8099	0.942				

Source: (WTO Statistics Database, https://data.wto.org/)

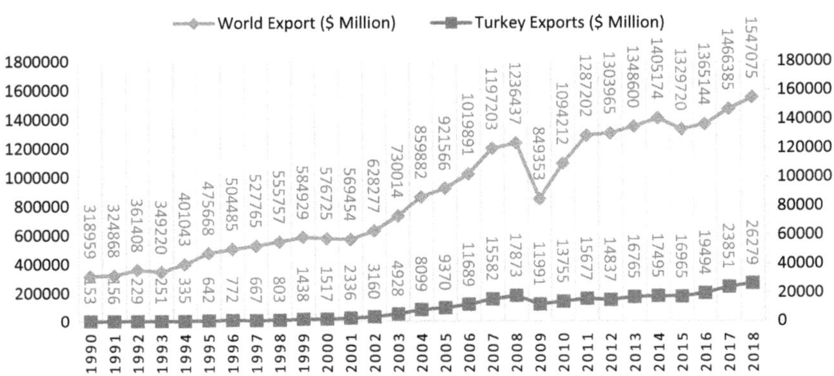

Fig. 6.1: World and Turkey's automotive sector exports ($ Million)

Source: (The Chart Fig. 6.1 was created using data from the WTO statistical database.)

4 Cluster Analysis of Turkish Automotive Sector

Clusters are groups of companies and institutions co-located in a specific geographic region and linked by interdependencies in providing a related group of products and/or services (Ketels, 2003: 3–4). The clustering approach, given a brief definition above, is a policy tool for regional and/or sectoral development that is used in many countries around the world. There are strong clusters in developed countries around the world, especially in the capital intensive sector. One of these sectors is the automotive sector, which is the basis of this chapter. However, clusters do not belong only to developed economies. In all countries, clusters are found in different sectors according to the comparative advantage of the region. Clusters usually begin with the concentration of firms in a certain geography in a sector with a comparative advantage, or they are usually formed under the leadership of public support or a strong private sector business within the framework of a regional development policy.

The regional development approach based on sectoral clustering and creating competitive advantage has become well known especially after Michael Porter's "The Competitive Advantage of Nations" study published in 1990. Porter define cluster as follows "cluster is a geographic concentrations of interconnected companies, specialized suppliers, services providers, firms in related industries, training institutions and support organizations linked around technologies or end product within a local area or region" (Porter, 1990: 210–225).

In this study, a cluster mapping analysis for the Turkish automotive industry at NUTS III level was conducted. The most widely used method in macro level cluster mapping studies worldwide is the three-star analysis method. Three different criteria are used in the evaluation of clusters in the three-star analysis. These are size, dominance and specialization. How these criteria are calculated is explained below.[1] (Sölvell, Ketels & Lindqvist, 2008).

Size: The ratio of sector employment in the analyzed region to the total employment of the sector in the upper region (ex:country)

$$Size = \frac{eir}{Ei}$$

eir: (i) sector employment in the analyzed region.
Ei: Refers to the total employment of the (i) sector in the upper region (ex:country).

---

1 Three-star Analysis was developed by the European Cluster Observatory. http://www.clusterobservatory.eu/

Dominance: the ratio of sector employment in the analyzed region to the total employment in the analyzed region.

$$Dominance = \frac{eir}{enr}$$

eir: (i) sector employment in the analyzed region.
enr: It refers to the total employment of the analyzed region (r).

Specialization (Loction Quotient): LQ shows the ratio of the sector's employment share in the analyzed region to the sector's total employment share in the upper region (ex:country).

$$Specialization\ (LQ) = \frac{\left(\frac{eir}{enr}\right)}{\left(\frac{Ei}{En}\right)}$$

eir: (i) sector employment in the analyzed region.

enr: It refers to the total employment of the analyzed region (r).

Ei: Refers to the total employment of the (i) sector in the upper region (ex:country).
En: It refers to the total employment in the upper region (ex:country).

The most critical point in three-star analysis is the determination of threshold values for size, dominance and specialization criteria. Because according to the threshold values to be determined, the results from the three-star analysis will be different. If the threshold values are set as low, more clustering will be detected in the region than it actually is. On the contrary, it causes an evaluation error. Although the threshold values are taken high, existing clusters cannot be detected. Because of this, it is observed that different threshold values are used in the analysis of three-stars according to the structure of the region in the literature review (Kırankabeş, 2019: 44).

A threshold value for each criterion is determined according to the region to be analyzed, and if the value of the criterion calculated according to the formulas given above exceeds this threshold value, the relevant sector receives a star from this criterion. In the three-star analysis we conducted in this study, threshold value of size and dominance was taken as 0.07. Specialization criteria was taken (LQ) >1. Depends on the analysis result of the sector, if the sector received three-stars we can say there is a mature cluster in this sector in this region. If the sector takes two star we can say there is a potential cluster in this sector in this region. If the sector takes one star, we can say there is a candidate cluster in this sector in this region (Kırankabeş, Özdemir & Özkan, 2014: 558–560).

Tab. 6.4: Automotive Sector Three-Star Cluster Analysis Results

Provinces	Compulsory Insured Persons Employment 2019 [Under Article 4-1/a of Act 5510]	Size	Dominance	Specialization (Location Quotient)	Number of Star Taken from Three-Star Analysis
Bursa	66,019	**0.33**	**0.10**	**6.89**	3 Star
Kocaeli	39,077	**0.19**	**0.08**	**5.56**	3 Star
Sakarya	15,462	**0.08**	**0.09**	**6.13**	3 Star
İzmir	15,392	**0.08**	0.02	**1.23**	2 Star
Aksaray	2,024	0.01	0.04	**2.86**	1 Star
İstanbul	16,533	**0.08**	0.00	0.28	1 Star
Konya	9,121	0.05	0.03	**2.11**	1 Star
Kütahya	3,253	0.02	0.04	**2.80**	1 Star
Manisa	5,314	0.03	0.02	**1.59**	1 Star
Eskişehir	3,219	0.02	0.02	**1.34**	1 Star

When performing cluster analysis 2019 Compulsory Insured Persons Employment Data (Under Article 4-1/a) which taken from Social Security Institution of Turkish Republic were used. The study was conducted at NUTS III (81 provinces) in order to observe all provinces of Turkey. While evaluating the analysis results, provinces with more than 2000 compulsory insured persons in the scope of 4-1/a in the automotive sector were taken into consideration. Tab. 6.4 provides information about the list of provinces with clustering in the automotive sector and the level of clustering in these provinces as a result of the three-star analysis conducted within the scope of the study.

5 Results and Discussions

In the three-star analysis we conducted within the scope of the study, the regions showing "mature cluster" are Bursa, Kocaeli and Sakarya provinces. In this sense, it can be said that the heart of the Turkish automotive sector is the East Marmara Region. Izmir province is the only region that receives two stars and shows "potential cluster" characteristics for the automotive sector of Turkey. In terms of the sustainability of mature and potential clusters identified within the scope of the study, it is strongly recommended that they have to integrate into international cluster associations and become able to carry out international joint projects. In the scope of the study, the regions showing "candidate cluster" characteristics by receiving a single star were identified as

Aksaray, Istanbul, Konya, Kütahya, Manisa and Eskisehir provinces. In provinces that receive a single star, clustering efforts should be supported under the leadership of public institutions, non-governmental organizations such as Chambers of Commerce and the private sector.

It is important to have an innovative perspective in terms of the development and sustainability of the sector in sectors with intense competition such as the automotive sector. In clusters such as automotive clusters with limited information flow in Turkey, competition, price/cost advantage is executed based. Therefore, it will be beneficial to conduct studies that will accelerate the evolution of the East Marmara Automotive Cluster, which should be seen as agglomeration from a different perspective, towards an information/technology-based cluster (T. C. Ministry of Industry and Technology, 2019: 11). For a long time, there has been a very serious international competition in the automotive sector. Therefore, especially small and medium-sized companies do not seem able to cope with this situation. The importance of the clustering approach arises at this point. In order for clusters to become competitive at regional and global levels, stakeholders must work organized and systematically. The joint effort of the private sector, professional organizations, public institutions and educational institutions is required for East Marmara Automotive Cluster. In this sense, it is important that these stakeholders take action to develop the eastern Marmara automotive cluster.

Bibliography

Baden-Württemberg International. (2017, July). Agency for International Economic and Scientific Cooperation. Automotive Industry in Baden-Württemberg. Retrieved from http://bw-i.cn/downfile/Automotive_Industry_en.pdf

European Cluster Observatory. (2020, September 25). Retrieved from http://www.clusterobservatory.eu/

History.com Editors. (2020, September 25). Model T. Retrieved from https://www.history.com/topics/inventions/model-t

ISO. (2002, February). Istanbul Chamber of Industry. Otomotiv Sanayii Sektörü, yayın no:2002/4. Retrieved from http://www.iso.org.tr/file/Otomotiv_Sanayi_Sektoru-382.pdf

ISO. (2018). 500 Büyük Sanayi Kuruluşu. http://www.iso500.org.tr/500-buyuk-sanayi-kurulusu/2018/

ISO. (2019, May). Istanbul Chamber of Industry. Türkiye'nin 500 Büyük Sanayi Kuruluşu. Retrieved from http://www.iso500.org.tr/

Ketels, C. (2003). The development of the cluster concept – present experiences and further developments, NRW conference on clusters, Duisburg, Germany.

Kırankabeş, M. C. (2019). *Kümelenme Yaklaşımı, Teori, Politika ve Uygulama Örnekleri*. Ankara: Gazi Kitabevi.

Kırankabeş, M. C., Özdemir, K., & Özkan, B. (2014). Kümelenme Yaklaşımının Girişimcilik ve Bölgesel Kalkınma Üzerinde Etkisi: Türkiye – Trc1 Bölgesinde Gerçekleştirilen Ampirik Bir Çalışma, *Procedia VI International Congress On Entrepreneurship*. Bishkek, 24–26 April 2014: 555–567.

Porter, M. E. (1990). *The Competitive Advantage of Nations*. New York: The Free Press.

Procter, P. (1978). *Longman Dictionary of Contemporary English*. Harlow, England: Longman.

Republic of Turkey Ministry of Industry and Technology. (2019). Sanayi ve Verimlilik Genel Müdürlüğü, Sektörel Raporlar ve Analizler Serisi, Otomotiv Sektörü Raporu 2019. Retrieved from https://www.sanayi.gov.tr/plan-program-raporlar-ve-yayinlar/sektor-raporlari/mu0203011620

Republic of Turkey Ministry of Trade. (2020, September 25). İhracat Genel Müdürlüğü Makine, Otomotiv, Elektrik-Elektronik Ürünleri Daire Başkanlığı, Otomotiv Sektör Raporu. Retrieved from https://ticaret.gov.tr/data/5b87000813b8761450e18d7b/Oto_Ana-Yan_Sanayi.pdf

Sölvell, Ö., Ketels, C., & Lindqvist, G. (2008). Industrial specialization and regional clusters in the ten new EU member states. *Competitiveness Review, 18*(1/2), 104–130. doi:10.1108/10595420810874637.

TAYSAD. (2020, September 25). *Automotive Suppliers Association of Turkey*. Retrieved from https://taysad.org.tr/tr/turk-otomotiv-sanayi-ve-taysadin-tarihcesi

TIM. (2020, September 25). *Turkish Exporters Assembly. Annual Export Figures December 2018*. Retrieved from https://tim.org.tr/en/export-export-figures

Türkcan, K., & Ateş, A. (2010). Structure and Determinants of Intra-Industry Trade in the U.S. Auto-Industry. *Journal of International and Global Economic Studies, 2*(2), 15–46.

Sevgi Eda Tuzcu

The Use of Spatial Models: Examples from Financial Market Applications

Abstract Spatial econometrics has been used in many areas in the social sciences including financial studies. However, its application is heavily criticized for several reasons. This chapter aims to highlight the common mistakes in the empirical applications of spatial models while providing examples from financial market studies. For this purpose, first, the spatial model selection process and the interpretation of the obtained coefficients are examined. These two issues are often misunderstood and confused with the non-spatial models. Second, the determination of the spatial weight matrices in the spatial models which represent the distance among the units of analysis is investigated. There is no a-priori theory to guide for the determination of spatial weight matrices, so different studies employ different distance definitions. Although this part directly influences the results obtained from the models, many applications overlook the construction process. In this chapter, the use of weight matrices in financial market studies is also explained. By highlighting these issues once more, this study guides the practitioners who want to use spatial models in their analysis.

Keywords: Spatial Model Selection, Coefficient Interpretation, Distance Definitions, Financial Market Studies

1 Introduction

This chapter aims to review the common mistakes in the applications of spatial models while giving examples from the financial market studies. Spatial models differ from the non-spatial techniques in many ways. Yet, its applications are still subject to criticism. Financial market studies with spatial applications are not exceptions. Highlighting once more these errors, I believe, will help practitioners particularly in the finance field. The novelty of this chapter comes from the provided examples from a specific research area.

The spatial interactions are closely related to the concept of neighborhood. Here, the basic understanding depends on Tobler (1970)'s famous analogy: "Everything is related to everything else, but near things are more related than distant things." This statement makes clear why one needs to account for spatial interactions in regional studies. However, this necessity is not crystal clear for financial market studies.

Financial data reflects the individual and institutional decisions as well as the movements in the financial markets. It is very likely to observe a non-random cross-sectional distribution and a dependence across spatial units. However, spatial model applications are rather rare (Bera et al., 2016). Consider the spatial nature of the following research questions: "Does a price change in the real estate investment trust's (REIT) portfolio affect the performance of REITs nearby? How can be the spatial proximity influential on portfolio performance (Zhu & Milcheva, 2018)?" "What is the magnitude and significance of spillovers in the financial risk transmission channel (Chen & Jin, 2020)?" "How does location measured by geographical proximity affect the financial markets (Fernández-Avilés et al., 2012)?" "How strong are the financial relationships across different stock markets? (Asgharian et al., 2013)?" "How do these spillovers affect the debt market (Huyugüzel Kışla & Önder, 2018)?" "Are stock returns influenced by the clustering of corporate headquarters (Moon & LeSage, 2011)?" These questions seek answers for the effects of spatial linkages in financial markets, which is the subject of spatial econometrics.

Gibbons and Overman (2012) criticize the common usage of spatial models for the lack of "economic theory" behind them. They argue that most practitioners begin with a specific spatial model which is assumed to reflect the correct data generation process. Practitioners neglect the economic reasons to expect causation between the dependent and independent variables. Instead, they mostly focus on the spatial process that fits the data best. In this chapter, I review once more the model selection process and different possible departure points that will be useful for the ones who will apply these techniques. Using correct model selection techniques will impede a mere empirical application without economic theory.

Within this scope, first, the spatial spillover types and model selection process will be discussed, and it will be explained why the straight-forward coefficient interpretation can be misleading. Next, the nature of the spatial weight matrix, W, and its construction process will be examined. In spatial econometrics, the distance between observations, peers, or neighbors is added to the analysis with the aid of a spatial matrix, which is represented by W. Geographical distances, such as having a common border (as in Asgharian et al. (2013), queen matrices (as in Golgher & Voss, 2016), or the inverse of the distances between units are common measures of W. Economic W definitions are also welcome in spatial econometrics. The last part of this study provides examples of W matrices employed in financial market studies.

2 Spatial Effects

Spatial econometrics deals with the effects caused by relative locations of agents[1]. According to LeSage (2014), when a characteristic of an agent at location *i* affects the decisions or actions of an agent at location *j*, spatial spillovers occur. Formally, a spatial spillover is the non-zero cross partial derivative representing the effect of an exogenous variable at location *i* on the decision or action at location *j* ($\delta yj/\delta Xi \neq 0$). If all the locations, even the ones that are not immediate neighbors, are affected by a change at location *i*, it is called global spillovers. In this case, when a change occurs at one location, neighbors and neighbors of neighbors are affected. Eventually, a feedback effect occurs across regions and the original location in which the change has started first is affected once more. In other words, endogenous interactions[2] present in the global spillovers. As an example, Asgharian et al. (2013) show that a unit change in return movement in the stock market of country *i* creates an effect on its own stock market through spatial feedback and also an impact on the other countries. Due to the feedback mechanism observed in global spillovers, the stock market *i* experiences more than a unit change in total. The stock markets other than country *i* also experience a change, although no shock in those stock markets is observed. The effect of return movements in all the stock markets will remain until a new equilibrium is settled.

If the impact observed in the cross partial derivatives do not create a feedback effect, instead only affects its immediate neighbors, then local spillovers exist (LeSage, 2014). The non-neighboring locations are not impacted, so no feedback effect is observed in this type of spillover. These spillovers reflect exogenous interactions. Asgharian et al. (2013) note that the changes in the exchange rate in the stock market *i* create stock return movements in the stock markets of immediate neighbors. No change is observed in the neighbors of neighbors.

1 Spatial dependence and spatial heterogeneity are the two effects modeled in spatial analysis (Anselin, 1988). Similar values in the neighboring locations point out the existence of positive spatial dependence. Spatial heterogeneity refers to changing coefficients in a regression model over space. The existence of these leads biased or inconsistent parameter estimations and false significance levels.

2 Manski (1993) defines three types of interactions in a group. These are endogenous interactions that reflect to behave in the same way with others in the group; exogenous interactions that reflect to behave in the a way that depends on independent variables of others; and correlated effects that reflect the same behavior caused by the similar environmental or institutional characteristics.

Non-spatial models ignore both global and local spillovers. LeSage (2014) states that although the spatial models that deal with global spillovers draw more attention, it is more likely to observe local spillovers. Global spillovers are hard to estimate and interpret the obtained results.

The spatial model family provides a large selection of models. Different models include different spillovers. This makes the model selection process particularly important. However, LeSage (2014) notes that many spatial model applications do not use the appropriate model or the coefficient interpretations are not made correctly. Hence, highlighting these issues once more will contribute to the literature.

3 Spatial Model Family and Model Selection Process

The following figure presents a general overview of the spatial models in a general to specific approach. I will explain in turn which type of spillovers these models include briefly.

In all the models shown in Fig. 7.1, y is the dependent variable, X represents the exogenous variables, W is the spatial weight matrix and ρ, λ, and θ are the spatial coefficients for spatial autocorrelation term, error term, and exogeneous variables respectively.

By adding all possible spatial interactions, we obtain the most general spatial model. Besides the endogenous and exogenous interactions, in this model, the error terms show spatial dependence. However, these interactions cannot be separable from one another (Elhorst, 2010; Gibbons et al., 2015). Manski (1993) denotes this issue as "the reflection problem". Therefore, more restricted alternatives must be chosen in empirical applications.

Different from the most general model, in the spatial autoregressive combination (SAC) model, there is no spatial lag for exogenous variables ($\theta = 0$). According to LeSage (2014), the coexistence of a spatial lag and spatial error term brings difficulties in estimation and interpretation, so this model is not recommended either.

When the spatial coefficient in the error term ($\lambda = 0$) equals zero, the SAC model becomes the Spatial Durbin Model (SDM). Here, ρ, the spatial lag parameter shows the endogenous interactions, so the spatial feedback mechanism – the global spillovers. θ shows the local spillovers. Containing both of these effects causes larger coefficient estimations with SDM in comparison to the spatial autoregressive (SAR) model or spatial Durbin error model (SDEM).

An example of the SDM application in the financial markets is seen in the study by Asgharian et al. (2013). In their study, the changes in the stock market

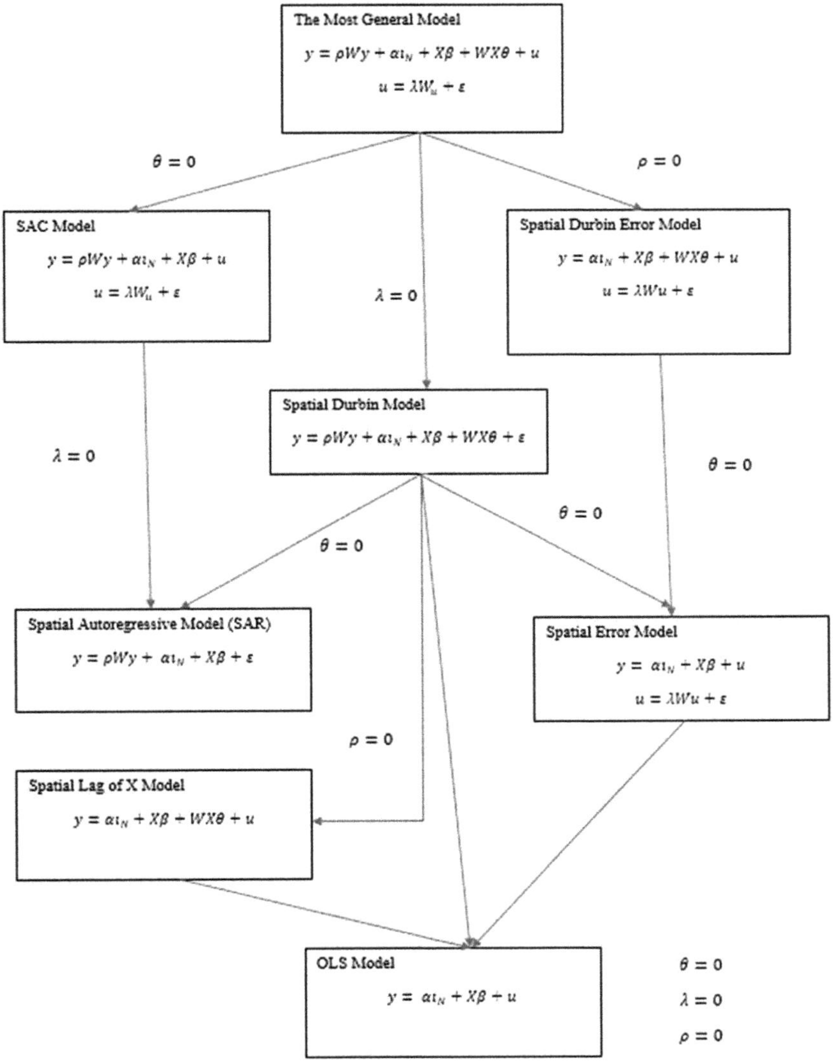

Fig. 7.1: Spatial Model Family

Source: (Elhorst, 2010: 21) and (Golgher &Voss, 2016)

returns are explained by exogenous variables such as exchange rate, unexpected inflation, and interest rates. For the SDM specification, the spatial lag of the stock market returns, and the spatial lag of exogenous variables were also added. In other words, a change in the stock market returns at one location is transmitted to the other stock markets at neighboring locations. Since this indicates a global spillover effect, it transmits to the neighbors of neighbors as well and creates a feedback mechanism. The spatial lag of an exogenous variable, for example, the exchange rate, indicates that a change in the exchange rate in one country creates a change in neighboring countries as well. This is a local spillover effect and only influential on the immediate neighbors.

In SDEM, the spatial lag for the exogenous variables (WX term) shows the existence of local spillovers. It also includes a spatial autoregressive error term which shows the global diffusion in the disturbances. The advantage of this model is that there is a separation of the local spillovers from the global shocks of diffusion (LeSage, 2014). However, there is no global spillover in SDEM, as a result, no feedback effect occurs.

SAR model is among the most popular models in the spatial model family. In these models, only global spillovers are modeled by the spatial term ρ, so they reflect endogenous interactions. ρ is greater than the beta coefficient due to the spillovers caused by the feedback process (Golgher & Voss, 2016).

The spatial lag of X (SLX) model is one of the contributions by LeSage and Pace (2009) to the spatial econometrics literature. This specification only incorporates local spillovers through the θ coefficient. Only the immediate neighbors are affected by a change at location i.

In the spatial error model (SEM), no spatial spillovers are allowed. Instead, this model includes the diffusion of shocks across different locations/observations through the error term (LeSage & Pace, 2014). Interestingly, this diffusion affects all the observations but decreases with the distance among them. In other words, there is a global diffusion in the SEM specifications, so a feedback mechanism.

As an example, Bauer et al. (2018) compare SAR and SEM specifications to explain the herding behavior among institutional investors. The ρ coefficient in their SAR specification represents the magnitude and the direction of the herding behavior among the pension funds.

If no spillover can be detected, OLS can be selected as the appropriate model. Apart from the SLX model, all the spatial models explained above require estimation methods other than OLS. Maximum likelihood and Bayesian estimation methods are among the alternatives. For the SLX model, OLS provides unbiased and correct estimations. Elhorst (2010) and Golgher and Voss (2016) note that the OLS model is mostly used as a benchmark for spatial models.

Model comparison in the spatial models may become particularly complex when there is no prior literature for the research question. The most general model is criticized due to the reflection problem. The SAC model may be considered as a better option because it includes both a spatial lag and spatial error term. LeSage (2014) argues that the SAC model does not include SAR and SEM specifications at the same time. The linear combination of SAR and SEM gives SDM as the data generating process. Therefore, he advises using SDM specification as the departure point.

Elhorst (2010) indicates that SDM provides unbiased estimates even when the true data generation process is another spatial model. SDEM and SAC models, however, may have omitted variable problem if the true model is not described by them. The suggested strategy by Elhorst (2010) is explained in Fig. 7.2.

LeSage and Pace (2014) note that even when a researcher wants to make a model selection between SDEM and SDM, it is not correct to estimate both models and make inferences based on the point estimations of the spatially lagged variables. This would cause the identification problem as discussed by Gibbons and Overman (2012). As an example, in an application of the spatial regressions in the financial markets, Yıldırım and Mert Kantar (2019) investigate the factors affecting the individual pension fund system participation levels while taking the regional dependencies into account. They compare all the models mentioned above and make their choice based on the goodness of criteria. However, as criticized by Gibbons and Overman (2012), in this case, the model selection is made without looking at the underlying theory.

LeSage (2014) states that the selection from the wide range of spatial models must be based on the spillover type. In fact, making the distinction between local and global spillovers is the most important decision in the spatial model applications, which depends on the economic theory itself. If the economic theory indicates global spillovers, it will be enough to estimate SDM, because it includes SAR specification as a more constrained case. Instead, if the economic theory points out local spillovers, then SDEM will be enough. It includes both SLX and SEM specifications. When there is a weak spatial dependence, an SLX specification will be more appropriate.

4 Criticisms Towards Spatial Models

In spatial regression models, there are two issues in which the applications are criticized heavily. The first issue is regarding the interpretation of the

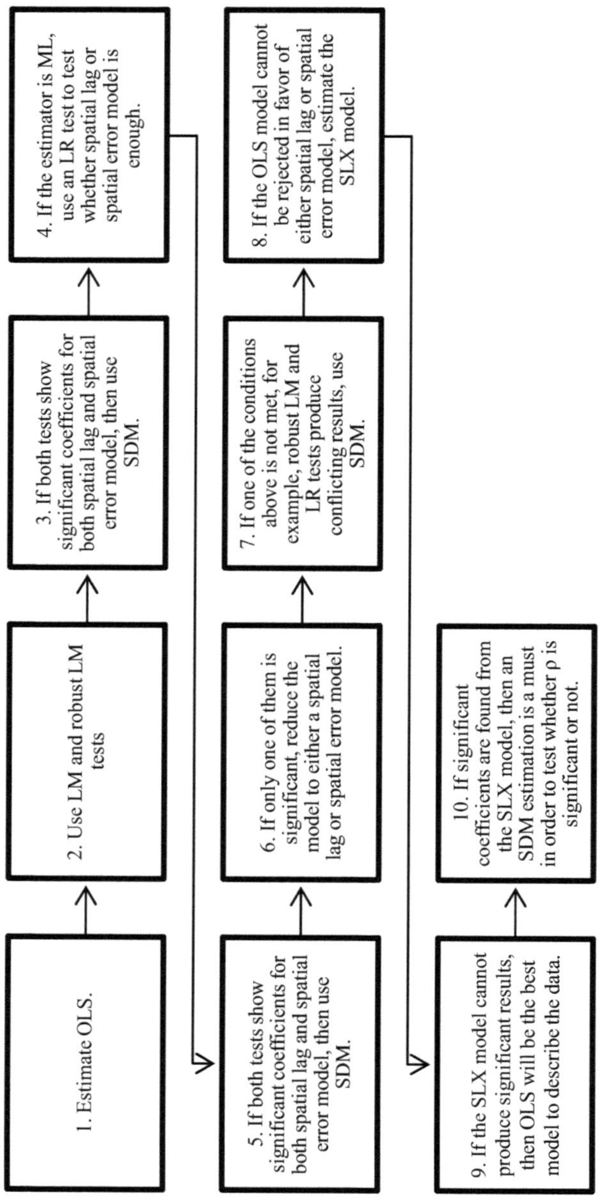

Fig. 7.2: Model Selection Process
Source: (Elhorst, 2010)

Tab. 7.1: Direct and Indirect Effects for Spatial Regression Models

Model Type	**Direct Effect**	**Indirect Effect**
The Most General Model/ SDM	$\frac{(3-\rho^2)}{3(1-\rho^2)}\beta_k + \frac{2\rho}{3(1-\rho^2)}\theta_k$	$\frac{(3+\rho^2)}{3(1-\rho^2)}\beta_k + \frac{3+\rho}{3(1-\rho^2)}\theta_k$
SAR/SAC Model	$\frac{(3-\rho^2)}{3(1-\rho^2)}\beta_k$	$\frac{(3+\rho^2)}{3(1-\rho^2)}\beta_k$
SDEM/SLX Model	β_k	θ_k
SEM/OLS Model	β_k	0

Source: (Elhorst, 2010: 21) and (Golgher & Voss, 2016: 186–187)

coefficients. Although spatial regression models provide a good way to model the spatial spillovers, the model coefficients must be interpreted properly to make correct inferences. The second issue is the construction of the spatial distance matrix, W. The lack of economic theory to determine W is often viewed as a weak point. These issues will be discussed in the next sub-sections.

4.1 Interpretation of the Coefficients

The significance of coefficient estimates is sometimes incorrectly interpreted as the existence or non-existence of the spatial spillovers. Yet, LeSage and Pace (2009) indicate that the correct way to understand the presence of spatial spillovers is to look at the direct, indirect, and total effects and their significance. The coefficient estimates and their significance may lead to misinterpretations about the presence of spatial spillovers. It is because the partial derivatives include not only the direct effects of the variable X on the dependent variable *y* but also indirect effects.

The diagonal elements in the partial derivatives matrix represent the derivatives with respect to exogenous variables, which are the direct effects. The off-diagonals reflect the indirect effects, which are either local or global spillovers. In an OLS model, we expect to observe only diagonal elements, that is, beta coefficients. Since there is no spillover, all off-diagonals are zero. In the spatial regression models, to interpret the coefficients, one must examine each model's partial derivatives matrix. Tab. 7.1 summarizes the properties of partial derivatives and the direct/indirect effects (Elhorst, 2010; Golgher & Voss, 2016).

This table is important for several reasons. First, it shows that each spatial regression model produces different direct and indirect effects. Therefore, model selection is of importance to correctly specify the spatial relations. In this choice, the nature of the spillovers plays a significant role. Second, as seen from Tab. 7.1, for SEM and OLS models, no spillovers exist. Note that in the SEM specification, a global diffusion in the disturbances to other observations are modeled, but not spillovers. Therefore, the indirect effects for these models are zero, and the direct effect contains only the beta coefficient.

A similar interpretation is valid for SDEM and SLX models as well. The local spillovers, represented in the θ coefficient, are not seen in the diagonals of the partial derivatives matrix because there is no feedback effect. As a result, direct effects are only represented by the beta coefficient (Golgher & Voss, 2016; LeSage & Pace, 2014). However, the summation of direct and indirect effects, the total effect, contains both beta and θ coefficients. Different from the OLS model, there only exist local spillovers. LeSage and Pace (2014) indicate that the beta coefficients can be interpreted as in the OLS models. The interpretation for the θ is as such: A change in the exogenous variable X in the neighboring location j generates an impact of θ amount on the dependent variable y at location i where $i \neq j$. In the SDEM specification, besides the local spillovers, there is global spatial diffusion of shocks as well.

Unlike SLX and SDEM, in the SAR model, SAC model, and SDM, the diagonals and off-diagonals of partial derivatives matrix contain both beta and ρ. This makes the straightforward coefficient interpretation invalid. In all of these models, global spillovers exist. Putting it differently, a change in an exogenous variable at location i generates an impact on the dependent variable at location i which is greater than its beta coefficient. It is because the original location i is impacted once more through the feedback effect after the change is observed in the immediate neighbors and neighbors of neighbors. In these models, neither the significance nor the magnitude of the beta coefficient can be used as proof for the presence or non-existence of the spillovers. Instead, as suggested by LeSage and Pace (2009), the direct and indirect effects must be computed and interpreted. The total effect can be higher or lower depending on the signs of each effect.

To observe the coefficient interpretations of models with global spillovers, we may look at two following studies: First, Asgharian et al. (2013) show that a unit stock market shock produces an immediate effect on stock returns by the same amount. However, with the feedback, the effect on the original stock market returns is much larger, around 1.130. The same unit stock market shock creates a mean effect of 0.117 on other markets' stock returns, which is actually the indirect effect.

Huyugüzel Kışla and Önder (2018) investigate the effect of GDP growth rate on the CDS spreads in their SAR specification. They find a coefficient of -4.11

from the SAR model. When this effect is split into direct and indirect effects, it is observed that a unit GDP growth rate change affects the CDS spreads of the same country by the amount of 4.30 bps in the negative direction. However, it produces even a greater spillover effect on the neighborhoods, because the CDS spreads of the neighboring countries alter negatively and by the amount of 4.45 bps. Therefore, considering merely the coefficients could be misleading.

To understand the differences between different spatial models better, one can also look at the direct effect/indirect effect ratio. Tab. 7.1 helps in this comparison as well. In the SAC and SAR models, the spatial lag parameter (ρ) is the only term in the direct effect/indirect effect ratio (Golgher & Voss, 2016). Since this ratio does not include the beta coefficients, it stays the same for different exogenous variables. Elhorst (2010) states that this is an important limitation because, in real-world applications, it is hard to be met. The SDM, however, is free from this constraint (LeSage & Pace, 2014). This is another reason to use the SDM as a departure point if the underlying theory indicates global spillovers.

Last, this table explains why the coefficients obtained from SDM are higher than SAR. SDM contains both exogenous and endogenous interactions. Hence, it produces larger results than the SAR model, which only includes endogenous interactions, and SDEM, which only contains exogenous interactions (Golgher & Voss, 2016).

4.2 The Determination of W

One of the most important and the most criticized parts of spatial econometrics is the determination of the spatial weight matrix (W). The W matrix is a square matrix that shows the neighborhoods/distances among spatial units. It can be designed as a binary matrix which only shows the existence of neighborhood or as a general spatial matrix that demonstrates the distances among the units. In the general W matrix, the impact of neighborhood is inversely related to the distance.

The spatial econometrics depends on the W matrix but it does not specify how to construct one. Anselin (1988) states that the distance definition used in the spatial weight matrix should be meaningful and closely related to the units of analysis. However, there is no underlying theory for its determination. To overcome this criticism, in many empirical applications, the results are checked with different W matrix definitions for robustness. However, LeSage and Pace (2010) argue that the model specification is not very sensitive to the W changes as long as the selected W matrices show a high correlation. They indicate that model selection and spillover specification as global or local are more important to produce robust estimates and inferences.

Anselin (1988) notes that the distance among spatial units can include definitions other than geographical proximity. These are called economic distance measures. Yet, LeSage (2014) states that an important problem regarding the economic distance matrices is that these W matrices can be dynamic in nature. The geographical distances are the same throughout time and always exogenous. However, in the case of economic distance matrices, the spillover effects depending on the proximity across regions must be predicted as well while the new equilibrium is set.

When the financial market studies with a spatial regression application are analyzed, both geographical and economic distance definitions can be seen. For example, Asgharian et al. (2013) use 8 spatial weight matrices based on economic distances as well as using the distance between the capitals of each country while examining the stock market movements among countries. They define the economic distances according to the bilateral linkages that can play a role in the stock market integration. Along these lines, Huyugüzel Kışla and Önder (2018) define three different spatial weight matrices including one based on the average bilateral import and export values between countries and another reflecting the financial linkages. To eliminate the endogeneity problem in the economic distance definitions, they take the time averages in the last two weight matrices.

Bera et al. (2016) highlight that geographical proximity may be insufficient in the description of contiguity in finance and economics studies. They compare three different contiguity definitions based on firms' locations as well as three economic distance measures based on the criteria of operating in the same industry, firm size measured by firm equity, and firm size measured by productivity levels to understand which define the spatial relations best.

5 Conclusion

Although frequently used in many areas, applications of spatial econometrics have been subject to many criticisms. These criticisms can be summarized under the following topics: Model selection process, the interpretation of coefficients, and the determination of the spatial weight matrices. This chapter aims to review these challenges of spatial econometrics once more to help the practitioners in this area, particularly from the finance field.

The stock market co-movements, the potential for contagion in the banking crises, and the herding behaviors both in individual and institutional investors open a possibility for spatial model applications in the financial market studies.

Ignoring spatial linkages in those studies may create misleading and even spurious relationships. To inspire future practitioners, this study provides non-exhaustive examples of recent financial market papers with spatial econometrics applications.

While applying spatial econometrics to the associations observed in the financial markets, the practitioners must particularly pay attention to the economic theory- spatial model match. Applying all spatial models and selecting the best fitting model can be criticized for the lack of an underlying theory. For example, such an approach is adopted by Yıldırım and Mert Kantar (2019) in which they examine the factors affecting the participation rates to the individual pension system. Since they find both the existence of local and global spillovers, selecting SDM as a departure point would be more advisable.

Financial market studies are very open to using economic distance definitions while modeling spatial interactions. In fact, these definitions may reflect the financial associations better as stated by Corrado and Fingleton (2016) and Bera et al. (2016). However, while constructing one, practitioners must consider the dynamic nature of those W matrices in time as well as the possible endogeneity problems. Re-constructing the W matrices each period, taking averages as noted by Huyugüzel Kışla and Önder (2018), or disregarding the observations that may create endogeneity (as in Bauer et al., 2018) would be possible solutions.

With the rapid developments of information technology, it has become possible to store, process, and draw inferences from big data. Financial data is no exception. Now, the real-time data for trading behaviors, trade volumes, and stock prices are available in detail more than ever. This will open new avenues for analyzing the spatial linkages in financial markets. As stated by Arbia and Patuelli (2016), the future of spatial models lies in big data. In this sense, it is logical to advise future researches to focus on big data applications with spatial econometrics.

Bibliography

Anselin, L. (1988). *Spatial Econometrics: Methods and Models* (First Edit). Kluwer Academic Publishers, New York.

Arbia, G., & Patuelli, R. (2016). Conclusions: The Future of Spatial Interaction Modelling. In R. Patuelli & G. Arbia (Eds.), *Spatial Econometric Interaction Modelling* (pp. 465–468). Springer. doi:10.1017/CBO9781107415324.004.

Asgharian, H., Hess, W., & Liu, L. (2013). A spatial analysis of international stock market linkages. *Journal of Banking and Finance*, *37*(12), 4738–4754. doi:10.1016/j.jbankfin.2013.08.015.

Bauer, R., Bonneti, M., & Broeders, D. (2018). Pension Funds Interconnections and Herd Behavior. *SSRN Electronic Journal, 612*. doi:10.2139/ssrn.3279390.

Bera, A. K., Er, Ş., & Kececi, N. F. (2016). Spatial Dependence in Financial Data: Importance of the Weights Matrix. *Arthaniti-Journal of Economic Theory and Practice, 15*(2), 29–42. doi:10.1177/0976747920160203.

Chen, N., & Jin, X. (2020). Industry Risk Transmission Channels and the Spillover Effects of Specific Determinants in China's Stock Market: A Spatial Econometrics Approach. *North American Journal of Economics and Finance, 52*. doi:10.1016/j.najef.2019.101137.

Corrado, L., & Fingleton, B. (2016). The W Matrix in Network and Spatial Econometrics: Issues Relating to Specification and Estimation. *Centre for Economic and International Studies, 14*(3), 1–24. doi:10.2139/ssrn.2731652

Elhorst, J. P. (2010). Applied Spatial Econometrics: Raising the Bar. *Spatial Economic Analysis, 5*(1), 9–28. doi:10.1080/17421770903541772.

Fernández-Avilés, G., Montero, J. M., & Orlov, A. G. (2012). Spatial Modeling of Stock Market Comovements. *Finance Research Letters, 9*(4), 202–212. doi:10.1016/j.frl.2012.05.002.

Gibbons, S., & Overman, H. G. (2012). Mostly Pointless Spatial Econometrics? *Journal of Regional Science, 52*(2), 172–191. doi:10.1111/j.1467-9787.2012.00760.x.

Gibbons, S., Overman, H. G., & Patacchini, E. (2015). Spatial Methods. In *Handbook of Regional and Urban Economics* (1st ed., Vol. 5). Elsevier B.V. doi:10.1016/B978-0-444-59517-1.00003-9.

Golgher, A. B., & Voss, P. R. (2016). How to Interpret the Coefficients of Spatial Models: Spillovers, Direct and Indirect Effects. *Spatial Demography, 4*(3), 175–205. doi:10.1007/s40980-015-0016-y.

Huyugüzel Kışla, G., & Önder, Ö. A. (2018). Spatial Analysis of Sovereign Risks: The Case of Emerging Markets. *Finance Research Letters, 26*(May 2017), 47–55. doi:10.1016/j.frl.2017.12.004.

LeSage, J. P. (2014). What Regional Scientists Need to Know about Spatial Econometrics. *The Review of Regional Studies, 44*, 13–32. doi:10.2139/ssrn.2420725.

LeSage, J. P., & Pace, R. K. (2009). *Introduction to Spatial Econometrics*. Chapman and Hall, London.

LeSage, J. P., & Pace, R. K. (2010). The Biggest Myth in Spatial Econometrics. *SSRN Electronic Journal*, 1–40. Working Paper, doi: 10.2139/ssrn.1725503

LeSage, J. P., & Pace, R. K. (2014). Interpreting Spatial Econometric Models. In M. M. Fischer & P. Nijkamp (Eds.), *Handbook of Regional Science* (pp. 1536–1552). Springer. doi:10.1007/978-3-642-23430-9.

Manski, C. F. (1993). Identification of Endogenous Social Effects: The Reflection Problem. *The Review of Economic Studies*, *60*(3), 531–542.

Moon, K. P., & LeSage, J. P. (2011). Revisiting the Question – Does Corporate Headquarters Location Matter for Stock Returns? *Applied Economics Letters*, *18*(6), 505–508. doi:10.1080/13504851003761780.

Yıldırım, M., & Mert Kantar, Y. (2019). Türkiye'nin Bireysel Emeklilik Sistemindeki Katılımcılarının Mekansal İstatistiksel Analizi. *Eskişehir Teknik Üniversitesi Bilim ve Teknoloji Dergisi B – Teorik Bilimler*, *7*(2), 184–194. doi:10.20290/estubtdb.518706.

Zhu, B., & Milcheva, S. (2018). The Pricing of Spatial Linkages in Companies' Underlying Assets. *Journal of Real Estate Finance and Economics*, 1–33. doi:10.1007/s11146-018-9666-z.

İsmail İsler

Measures Securing the Collection of Public Receivablesin Turkey

Abstract Financing of public expenditures is covered by public revenues. The state should act effectively in collecting public receivables in order not to disrupt public services. collection rates of public receivables accrued in Turkey is about 81 %. However, it can be said that the accrual collection rate has declined in recent years. Collection and protection of public receivables is regulated by Law No. 6183 on public receivables collection procedure. In this context, the Law No. 6183 on the collection procedure of Public receivables grants superior rights and powers to the state and other public administrations in relation to the collection of receivables. In addition, law 6183 has some facilities that are also recognized for those who are in public debt. The establishments regulated in the law numbered 6183; Demanding collateral, showing surety, prudential attachment, prudential accrual, priority right, transactions that cannot be made without payment of public receivables and the responsibilities of those who do, swap, action for nullity,liquidation status, termination of partnership, public debt of a limited company, merger, transfer and division in case of legal entities can be listed as.

Keywords: Public Service, Public Receivable, Collection of Public Receivables, Public Funding, Protection of Public Receivables

1 Introduction

While generating income to cover public expenditures is the most important duty of the state, the existence of effective institutions that facilitate the protection and collection of public receivables is also very important for the financial sustainability of the public. In the study, the place of some public receivables in the central government budget has been shown and the accrual collection rates of the tax, which has the largest share in public revenues, by years are presented. Later, the concept of public receivables was discussed, the differences of public receivables from private receivables were explained, and then the methods of protection of public receivables regulated in Law No. 6183 were examined. Law No. 6183 on the method of collection of public receivables has regulated many security measures. Asking for demanding security, showing surety, precautionary lien, precautionary accrual, priority right, Transactions that will not be made before public receivables are paid and the responsibilities of those who do, swap, annulment action, liquidators and the request for termination of the partnership, public debts of limited companies, merger in legal entities, hand over, in case of division and shape change, the status of public receivables is discussed.

2 Accrual-Collection Status in Tax Revenues, Which Is the Most Important of Public Revenues

The importance of public receivables in terms of financing public expenditures and the continuity of public goods and services provided by the state cannot be denied and it can be said that it is a mandatory requirement to implement certain measures in order to collect public receivables on time. For this reason, measures to secure public receivables are more than measures to secure private receivables. Tax offices affiliated to the Revenue Administration, property directorates affiliated to the General Directorate of Accounts and accounting directorates are authorized in the follow-up of public receivables. Collection offices affiliated to the Ministry of Trade are authorized for public receivables received according to customs legislation. Considering the accrual collection rates in tax revenues, which constitute 80 % of the total budget revenues of the central government, it is seen that the total amount of tax accrued in 2019 was 1 quadrillion 12 billion TL, while the collection amount is 820 billion TL and the accrual-collection ratio is% It was realized as 81.04. It is a success that the accrual-collection ratio is 81.04 %. However, it is possible to say that it was 89.66 % in 2008, 87.44 % in 2009 and 84.70 % in 2015, and this rate has decreased to 81 % in the last 10 years (see Tab. 8.1). It is possible to say that the measures contained in law 6183 to ensure the collection of public receivables are vital for the state to collect public revenues.

Follow-up and collection of public receivables is carried out in accordance with the provisions of the Law No. 6183 on the collection procedure of Public receivables (Law No. 6183). The public receivables are the public law receivables of the State (public administrations constituting the state legal entity), special provincial administrations and municipalities. The receivables of these administrations arising from private law contracts are not considered as public receivables. In addition to the provisions that protect the rights of the creditor public administration in the event that the public debt is not paid in the law numbered 6183, there are some facilities in the payment of the debt to the public debtor.

Tab. 8.1: Central Government Budget Revenue, Taxes Accrued and Collected (Thousand TL)

Years	Central Government Budget Revenue	Accrued Tax Amount	Collected	Collection/ Accrual
2008	232.067.897	211.887.600	189.980.827	%89,66
2009	239.778.222	224.504.297	196.313.307	%87,44
2015	541.146.716	549.259.835	465.229.389	%84,70
2016	626.212.964	652.160.684	529.607.901	%81,21
2017	720.852.113	760.632.702	626.082.414	%82,31
2018	876.323.203	906.541.843	738.180.401	%81,43
2019	1.024.165.558	1.012.025.558	820.148.185	%81,04

Source: Prepared by me with data from Muhasebat.gov.tr, Table 47 and Table 71 from Gelir İdaresi Başkanlığı (2020).

2.1 The Concept of Public Receivable

Payables and receivables are divided into different legal categories and some receivables may have priority and superiority over others. The ranking among the receivables is regulated by the Law No. 6183 on the Procedure of Collection of Public Receivables and the Enforcement and Bankruptcy Law No. 2004 (Baylan, 2013: 38). In this context, the State and other public administrations are given superior rights and powers regarding the collection of their receivables in the Law No. 6183 on the Procedure for Collection of Public Receivables.

The state and other public entities have the authority to collect public receivables by using these superior rights and powers, which are the expression of public power. This situation adds existence to public enforcement law as an area of law independent from general enforcement law (Başar, 2015: 4570). As a rule, public expenditures made for the fulfillment of public services are covered by the financial obligations imposed by the State based on the sovereign power. Economic values transferred from the private sector to the public sector by using legal force to be in return for public services are called public revenues or public receivables (Başar, 2015: 4569).

Public receivable is a broad concept that includes tax receivables. Tax receivable is a narrower and more specific concept, but tax receivable is also a public receivable. In a broad sense, "public revenues" arising from public law reach a stage where they can be collected after the accrual stage and become "public receivables". Therefore, it is possible to define public receivables as public revenues arising from the state's public law and provided by administrative transactions based on public power (Şenyüz et al., 2019: 148). The concept of public receivables is clearly stated in article 1 of the law on the method of collecting public receivables.

> *According to this; "The principal receivables such as court expenses, tax penalties and fines related to taxes, duties, criminal investigations and proceedings belonging to the state, special provincial administrations and municipalities are subject to the provisions of this law. In addition, the provisions of this law are also applied to the other public receivables of the same administrations, other than those arising from tort and unfair acquisition, and their follow-up costs".*

In addition to the definition made above, there are many different definitions in the literature regarding the concept of public receivables. In this context, public receivables; It can be defined as public revenues that the state derives from administrative transactions as a result of liability or debt relationship, or as public revenues arising from public law and provided by the state through administrative transactions based on public power. According to Karakoç; public receivable; These are the revenues brought on the basis of public power to finance public services and arising from financial obligations, which can be collected through administrative transactions by taking part in the budgets of public administrations. According to Candan; claims of the state other than those subject to private law are called public claims (Yapar, 2019: 4).

Since public receivables are the financial source of the performance of public services, they are privileged receivables. Because of this feature, public receivables are excluded from general enforcement law. It is possible to examine public receivables under the law numbered 6183 in four parts. The first of these is the primary public receivables. These will receive taxes, duties, fees, court expenses related to criminal proceedings and tax penalties and fines. The second type of public receivable is secondary public receivables. These, on the other hand, consist of interest and price increases such as delay penalty, default interest, unjust penalty due to failure to pay the original of the public receivable on time. Third public receivables are receivables such as the goodwill arising from the public service practice of the state, municipalities and special provincial administrations, except those arising from contract, tort and unfair acquisition. The fourth type of public receivable is follow-up costs. The follow-up costs include expenses such as announcement, attachment, transfer and protection expenses that must be incurred due to the compulsory collection of public receivables within the scope of the law numbered 6183 (Çiftçioğlu et al., 2015: 99).

3 Methods for the Protection of Public Receivable

The consequences of non-payment or non-payment of taxes on time and their collection by using public power are regulated by Law No. 6183 on the Procedure for Collection of Public Claims. According to Law No. 6183, the measures foreseen for securing public receivables can be examined under two headings as measures for the protection of accrued public receivables and measures for the protection of unaccrued public receivables (Ay & Baran, 2014:10).

3.1 Measures for Protection of Accrued Receivables

Methods for protecting accrued receivables can be listed as; demanding security, showing surety, precautionary lien, precautionary accrual.

3.1.1 Demanding Security

In the tax law, a regulation based on guarantee has been made in many issues. The guarantee requested as a condition of benefiting from certain opportunities provided to taxpayers in tax law and the guarantee regulated as a security measure in the law numbered 6183 are different from each other. In tax law, collateral serves the purpose of "convincing and providing security" to the administration in order to benefit from certain opportunities. In the Law No. 6183, the guarantee serves to secure the tax in the sense of "the money given in advance to pay the possible loss" that will occur if the tax is not paid (Karadağ, 2012: 240).

According to the 10th article of the Law on the collection of public receivables numbered 6183; Money, indefinite guarantee letters issued by banks and private finance institutions, State domestic debt securities issued by the Undersecretariat of Treasury, movable and immovable properties shown by the concerned, movable and immovable property shown by third parties in favor of the concerned parties may be counted as guarantee. If the collateral loses its value completely or partially afterwards or the amount of debt increases, the collateral is requested to be completed or to be presented in its place. The borrower may replace the collateral with others of the same value, partially or completely (Law No. 6183).

3.1.2 Showing Surety

Personal surety is established with a notarized contract in accordance with the conditions to be determined. It is the creditor administration to decide whether to accept the personal guarantee and the person shown. A document is given to the guarantor who pays her public receivables (Law No. 6183).

3.1.2 Prudential Attachment

One of the assurance measures foreseen in the collection of public receivables is the "ancillary attachment " institution. Prudential attachment is an institution designed to prevent the debtor from preventing or significantly complicating the future compulsory collection process of the public debtor's movable and immovable properties, receivables and rights. By a general definition, an injunction is the confiscation of certain goods, receivables and rights of the public debtor, in advance and temporarily, by an administrative decision, based on the reasons specified in the law, in order to secure the collection of public receivables (Yılmaz, 2012: 1445). According to Article 13 of Law No. 6183, in the event of any of the following situations, "prudential attachment" is applied with the decision of the highest local official of the creditor public administration;

- 9 of Law No. 6183. if there are cases that require the request of collateral in accordance with the article,
- If the debtor does not have a specific domicile,
- If the debtor has escaped or has the possibility of escaping, stealing his property and deviating to fraudulent ways,
- If the debtor is asked to provide collateral, but has not provided a collateral or surety within the specified period, or his personal bail offer or surety has not been accepted,
- If the debtor who has been called for the declaration of property has not declared the property within a certain period of time or has made incomplete notification,
- If a public lawsuit is filed due to the act requiring a fine,
- If there are situations requiring the application of articles 27, 29 and 30 of this law, if the goods containing the transactions requested to be canceled are disposed of, a precautionary lien is applied for the other property of the person.

Those who are subject to a lien can file a lawsuit at the tax court within 15 days from the date of notification. In cases to be filed against the application of prudential attachment, it can be argued that the application of precautionary attachment is against the procedure and essentially there are no reasons for precautionary attachment. Claims other than these are not considered by the court (Karadağ, 2012: 243). If the debtor provides collateral, except for the securities attached, the lien is lifted by the authority that placed the attachment.

In short, precautionary lien application is one of the main methods of protecting public receivables. The public administration has no power of disposition over the properties confiscated as a result of prudential attachment.

Precautionary attachment becomes invalid with the notification of the payment order and the final attachment application is initiated (Özgün & Andıç, 2018: 17).

3.1.4 Prudential Accrual

The prudential accrual, which is anticipated to be applied only for some of the taxes, duties and fees within the scope of the Tax Procedure Law, refers to the accrual process of the taxpayers' debts that have not yet accrued without following the normal accrual methods. Prudential accrual is a method for the purpose of protecting public receivables and does not create a definite debt. Prudential accrual gains efficiency when applied together with prudential lien (Ünal, 2014: 8).

In order to apply for a preliminary accrual, one of the situations written in the law must be present. In case of any of the following situations, the provincial treasurer or head of the tax office can give an accrual order upon the written request of the tax office manager. these cases;

- Existence of one of the conditions that require a guarantee from the debtor,
- The debtor does not have a certain domicile,
- If there is a possibility that the debtor escapes, smuggles his property or resort to fraudulent means,
- The debtor called to the goods notification does not notify the goods within a certain period of time or has incomplete notification,
- Prosecution of the debtor for taking actions to prevent or make the collection of public receivables difficult,
- Obtaining evidence that the business of the debtor is collusive and actually belongs to someone else.

Article 17 of Law No. 6183 has left the authority to determine which taxes will be subject to prudential accrual to the Ministry of Treasury and Finance. Based on this authority obtained from the law, the ministry determined which taxes may be the subject of precautionary accrual by the decision of the "General communique on collection" published in the official gazette No. 26568. According to this; Income Tax, Corporate Tax, Value Added Tax, Stamp Tax, Special Consumption Tax, Special Communication Tax, Banking and Insurance Transactions Tax, Games of Chance Tax, Inheritance and Gift Tax can be applied with prudential accrual. In addition to these, a precautionary accrual may be applied to the default interest of these taxes and the tax penalties based on the original tax.

Prudential accrual is applied for tax receivables for which there is a prudential accrual decision, whether it is at the judicial stage or not. Prudential accrual is not a final accrual and is realized on the basis calculated by way of discretion. Receivables subject to prudential accrual and their penalties cannot be collected before the due date. However, a precautionary lien is applied immediately for them. Since the prudential accrual is not a final accrual, it is then adjusted for the amount duly accrued (Öner, 2017: 192).

3.2 Measures for Protection of Unaccrued Receivables

The measures regulated in Articles 21 and 36 of Law No. 6183 can be listed as follows;

- Priority right,
- Transactions that cannot be made without paying public receivables,
- Swap,
- Annulment action,
- Liquidators and the request for Termination of the Partnership,
- Public debts of limited liability companies,
- Merger, transfer, division and shape-shifting.

3.2.1 Priority Right

According to Article 21 of Law No. 6183, for a property for which third parties have initiated a foreclosure transaction, the public creditor may participate in the foreclosure if the public creditor also participates in the proceedings. In this case, the income from the sale is shared between the private creditor and the treasury (Ünal, 2014: 16). Other creditors may not participate in the foreclosure, which has been implemented by the public administration.

3.2.2 Transactions That Cannot Be Performed without Paying Public Receivables and the Responsibilities of Those Who Do

In Article 22 of the Law No. 6183, the transactions that cannot be done without paying public receivables and the responsibilities of those who make transactions are regulated. According to this;

- In all kinds of payments to be made by public administrations subject to Public Financial Management and Control Law No. 5018 and revolving fund enterprises affiliated to these administrations,

- Payments to be made to the beneficiaries due to the procurement of goods or services and construction works by the institutions that are within the scope of the Public Procurement Law and the institutions and organizations with public legal personality,
- Payments to be made due to government aids, incentives and supports provided in cash,
- Registration and registration fees from trade registry fees included in the tariffs attached to the Law on Fees, fees collected from notary fees, contracts and papers, fees collected from land registry and cadastre fees, ship and port fees, fees subject to tariff No. 8 and transactions related to traffic fees,
- In the transactions regarding the building construction fee and occupancy permit fee included in the Municipal Revenues Law, the public debtor will have to request a certificate of no debt before performing the transaction or before paying the remuneration.

According to the 22nd article of the law numbered 6183; Except for employee wage receivables, all kinds of payments can be made first, after leaving the portion to cover the overdue debt to the Ministry of Treasury and Finance. In the implementation of this provision, in cases where payment is required against the receivables of other public administrations, the payment amount should be shared in proportion to their shares.

Administrative fines are imposed on those who make payments without seeking a document stating that there is no debt, despite the obligation imposed by the Collection Office, and institutions and organizations that establish transactions. The administrative fine must be paid within one month from the date of notification to the relevant institution. A lawsuit can be filed against the administrative fine within thirty days following the date of notification in the administrative court. In the event of a fine, the relevant institution may recourse to the responsible person who made the transaction without waiting for the relevant document. In addition, the relevant institution has the right to file a lawsuit with the administrative court within thirty days following the notification of the penalty (Law No. 6183)

3.2.3 Swap

According to the 23rd article of the law numbered 6183, it is investigated whether the debtor has an overdue debt to the administration before the repayment of the public receivables that need to be paid back due to legal reasons. The deduction of the money that will be repaid to the muaccel debts to the administration is arranged as a security measure. Thanks to this transaction, public receivables, which are collected and rejected due to some legal reasons, and outstanding debts of public debtors are exchanged (Yapar, 2019: 293).

3.2.4 Annulment Action

Regulations regarding the annulment of savings action, which is one of the measures to secure public receivables, are included in Articles 24 to 31 of Law No. 6183. In this context, transactions deemed invalid in articles 27, 28, 29 and 30 have been regulated. In Articles 24, 25 and 26, there are regulations regarding the lawsuit to be filed for the cancellation of these transactions. In Article 31, the rights and obligations of third parties benefiting from transactions deemed invalid are regulated (Yapar, 2019: 293). According to the 27th article; Some transactions of those who do not pay their public receivables, who do not declare their property on time, and who declare that they do not have property are invalid. Invalid transactions are donations made within two years from the date of commencement of payment.

In the 28th article of the law numbered 6183, the savings considered as donation are counted. According to this;

- Significant dispositions made between blood relatives up to third degree (including 3rd degree), spouses and affinity relatives up to second degree (including 2nd degree).
- Contracts in which the borrower pays a very insufficient price in return according to the value of the goods given by herself at the time of the contract,
- Contracts in which the debtor establishes revenue and usufruct rights for herself or for the benefit of a third party are accepted as donations.

In addition, pledges made by the debtor to provide an existing debt, payments made for the debt other than the money or normal payment instruments, and payments made for an undue debt, except for the cases listed in Article 29 of Law No. 6183, It is counted among the other null savings.

Finally, according to Article 30 of Law No. 6183, unilateral agreements made by the debtor in order not to allow the collection of some or all of the public receivables and all transactions made with persons who know the purpose of the debtor are null and void, regardless of their dates.

3.2.5 Liquidators and the Request for Termination of the Partnership

According to Article 32 and 33 of Law No. 6183, liquidators or those conducting the liquidation are obliged to notify the relevant collection offices within three days of the start of the liquidation. The liquidators or those conducting the liquidation cannot distribute or dispose of what has been obtained as a result of the liquidation before paying any receivables of the public administrations. Otherwise, the liquidators or those conducting the liquidation are personally and severally liable for the accrued or future public receivables. According to Article 34 of Law No. 6183, if there is no property belonging to the debtor or it is not sufficient to cover the public receivables, or if the debtor or the partnership does not provide a guarantee according to this law, the shares in the capital of the debtor may be requested within the framework of general provisions for the collection of public receivables from the shares in the partnership.

3.2.6 Public Debts of Limited Liability Companies

According to Article 35 of Law No. 6183, limited liability company partners are directly responsible for the public receivables that cannot be collected from the company completely or partially, in proportion to their capital shares. In addition; The public receivables that cannot be collected from the assets of legal entities, minors and restricted persons, foundations and communities without legal personality, are collected from the personal assets of legal representatives and those who manage non-legal entities. This article shall also apply to the representatives of foreign individuals or institutions in Turkey.

3.2.7 Merger, Transfer, Division and Shape-Shifting

According to the 36th article of the law numbered 6183; In case of merger of two or more legal entities, the newly established company is found liable like the old company. Likewise, in the event of a transfer, the transferring company will be responsible like the transferring company. In case of division, the company that takes over the assets of the divided company replaces the old company. In case of change, the new company replaces the old company. In this way, the public debt of the old company is completely counted as the debt of the new company.

4 Conclusion

Public debt and debts based on private law relationship are different from each other and are evaluated in different categories. It can be said that the measures for the protection of public receivables have relatively more privileges than private law debts. These privileges are regulated by the law numbered 6183 on the method of collection of public receivables. Public expenditures made for the fulfillment of public services are covered by the financial obligations imposed by the State based on the sovereign power. The economic values transferred from the private sector to the public sector, based on the sovereign power of the state, in return for public services, are called public revenue or public receivables. Public receivable is a broad concept that includes tax receivables. It is possible to define public receivables as public revenues arising from the state's public law and provided by administrative transactions based on public power. It is possible to examine public receivables within the framework of Law No. 6183 in four parts. These; primary public receivables, secondary public receivables, receivables arising from public service implementation and follow-up costs.

In order for the state to maintain its existence, it must generate public revenue and finance public expenditures. Since public receivables are the financial source of the performance of public services, they are privileged receivables. Because of this feature, public receivables are excluded from general enforcement law. It is very important for the state to be able to collect public receivables. For this reason, the "measures that guarantee the collection of public receivables" it organizes facilitate the collection of public receivables. These measures can be listed as follows; Demanding Security, Showing surety, Prudential attachment, Prudential Accrual, priority right, Transactions that cannot be performed without paying public receivables and the responsibilities of those who do, Swap, Annulment Action, Liquidators and the request for Termination of the Partnership, Public debts of limited companies, Merger, Transfer, Division And Shape-Shifting.

It is possible to say that despite these precautions in Law No. 6183, the state has had difficulties in collecting public receivables in recent years. As a matter of fact, it is seen that the accrual collection rate decreased from year to year and was realized as 81 % in 2019. The effectiveness of the measures included in the law numbered 6183 and securing public receivables should be increased and the accrued collection rate should be increased.

Bibliography

Ay, H., & Baran, T. (2014). Kamu Alacaklarının Korunma Yöntemleri ve Bir Değerlendirme. *Sosyoekonomi*, (21), 45–68.

Başar, C. (2015). Kamu İcra Hukukunun Anayasal Temelleri. *Dokuz Eylül Üniversitesi Hukuk Fakültesi Dergisi*, *16*(Özel Sayı), 4567–4611.

Baylan, M. A. (2013). Kamu Alacaklarının Mutlak Önceliğinden Bahsedilebilir Mi? *Gümrük ve Ticaret Dergisi*, *1*(2), 35–39.

Çiftçioğlu, H., Antepli, A., & Polat, Ö. A. (2015). Kamu Alacaklarının Korunmasına Yönelik Tedbirler. *Kahramanmaraş Sütçü İmam Üniversitesi İktisadi ve İdari Bilimler Fakültesi Dergisi*, *5*(1), 95–116.

Gelir İdaresi Başkanlığı. (2020, 10 December). Tablo 47. Retrieved from https://www.gib.gov.tr/fileadmin/user_upload/VI/GBG/Tablo_47.xls.htm.

Gelir İdaresi Başkanlığı. (2020, 10 December). Tablo 71. Retrieved from https://www.gib.gov.tr/fileadmin/user_upload/VI/GBG/Tablo_71.xls.htm.

Karadağ, N. C. (2012). Vergi Alacağının Güvence Altına Alınmasında Teminat, İhtiyati Haciz ve İhtiyati Tahakkuka İlişkin Özellikli Durumlar. *Maliye Dergisi*, (162), 238–255.

Law No. 6183 on the procedure for the collection of public receivables. (1953, 21 July). Resmi Gazete (Sayı: 8469). Retrieved from https://www.mevzuat.gov.tr/MevzuatMetin/1.3.6183.pdf

Öner, E. (2017). *Vergi Hukuku* (5 Bs.). Ankara: Seçkin Yayıncılık.

Özgün M., & Andıç, N. Ö. (2018). Kamu Alacaklarının Korunması Kapsamında Gümrük Vergilerinin Değerlendirilmesi. *Gümrük Ticaret Dergisi*, *5*(13), 10–29.

Şenyüz D., Yüce, M., & Gerçek A. (2019). *Vergi Hukuku*. (10. Baskı), Bursa: Ekin Yayınevi

Ünal, A. O. (2014). *Vergi Alacağının Güvence Altına Alınması*. Ankara Üniversitesi. (2014 Nov. 23). Retrieved from https://www.academia.edu/6680192/AATUHK_Kapsam%C4%B1nda_Vergi_Alaca%C4%9F%C4%B1n%C4%B1n_G%C3%BCvence_Alt%C4%B1na_Al%C4%B1nmas%C4%B1.

Yapar, B. K. (2019). *Türk Hukukunda Kamu Alacaklarını Güvence Altına Alan Önlemler*. (Unpublished Ph.D. Thesis), Marmara University Institute of Social Sciences, İstanbul.

Yılmaz S. (2012). Kamu Alacaklarının Tahsili Hukukunda İhtiyati Haciz Müessesesi ve İhtiyati Hacze Karşı Açılan Davalarda İdari Yargı Yerlerince Verilen Kararların Uygulanması. *Ankara Üniversitesi Hukuk Fakültesi Dergisi*, *61*(4), 1437–1445.

Engin Cakir

Prioritizing the Problems Confronted by Independent Accountant and Financial Advisors with Best – Worst Method

Abstract Today, Independent Accountant and Financial Advisors (IAFA) keep the books of businesses belonging to real and legal persons; editing their documents such as balance sheets, income statements and returns; establishing accounting systems; providing consultancy on business administration, financial legislation, and practices; It has many duties such as examining, analyzing, and auditing the subjects specified and giving written opinion on financial statements and statements. With the globalization, as a result of the complexity of the transactions made by businesses, members of the profession face many problems in business life. In this study, the problems faced by IAFAs were prioritized by Best-Worst method, which is one of the multi-criteria decision-making methods, and solutions for these problems are presented. In the study in question, firstly, as a result of the literature review, seven main problems faced by IAFA professionals were determined, and then five IAFA professionals experienced in their field in the central district of Bartin were determined as decision makers. Finally, five decision-makers were asked to prioritize the seven main problems faced by IAFA professionals with the questionnaire in accordance with the Best-Worst method. As a result of the analysis of the obtained data, it was concluded that the most important problem faced by the members of the profession was "excessive workload", the second most important problem was "Qualified Staff Problem", and the third most important problem was "Making Accounting Transactions Below Normal Wages".

Keywords: Independent Accountant and Financial Advisors, Problem Prioritization, Best – Worst Method, MCDM

1 Introduction

Independent Accountant and Financial Advisors (hereafter abbreviated as "IAFA") face a number of problems while performing their duties. These problems affect the performance of the IAFA in the workplace negatively and reduce the quality of the service that they can provide to the government and its taxpayers. The stress and pressure of these problems faced by the IAFAs, who perform the profession, may have a negative effect on the profession preferences of the candidates who will choose this profession.

The aim of this study is to prioritize the problems experienced by the members of the profession by evaluating them with the Best-Worst method, which is one of the multi-criteria decision-making methods, and presenting solutions.

In the study, firstly, five experienced IAFA professionals in the central district of Bartın province were selected as decision makers. Afterwards, seven problems that can be encountered in the IAFA profession were identified by decision makers, taking the literature into consideration. Finally, it was ensured that the data obtained with the questionnaire in accordance with the Best - Worst method were analyzed and suggestions were made that the priority problems in the findings should be focused on.

2 Independent Accountant and Financial Advisor (IAFA) Profession and The Problems They Encounter

In Turkey, the accounting profession, entered into force with Law No. 3568, in the Official Gazette, published on 13 June 1989 with number 20194 (Law No. *3568*, 1989). With this Law, professional accountants are counted as Independent Accountant and Financial Advisors and Sworn-in Certified Public Accountants.

According to Article 2 of Law No. 3568, those who carry out IAFA profession establish and develop the accounting systems of enterprises and enterprises belonging to real and legal persons, regulate or act as consultancy on business, accounting, finance, financial legislation and their applications. Again, IAFA examines, analyzes and audits the above-mentioned issues, gives written opinion on issues related to financial statements and submit declarations. They prepare reports and equivalents, they do arbitration, expertise and similar works. Those who do all these works independently of a workplace are called Independent Accountant and Financial Advisor (IAFA).

On the other hand, Sworn-in Certified Public Accountants, besides the authorizations of IAFAs except for accounting, they perform the approval works within the framework of the regulation issued according to the 12th article of the law number 3568. Sworn-in Certified Public Accountants cannot keep books related to accounting, they cannot open accounting offices and they cannot be partners in accounting offices. For this reason, Sworn-in Certified Public Accountants do not operate in the field as in IAFAs. In the accountancy profession, it is necessary to focus on these problems, especially due to the problems in the field are much more and cannot be solved. Therefore, prioritizing the problems experienced by IAFAs constitutes the subject of this study.

A summary of the literature review on the problems experienced by IAFAs and the studies offering solutions to these problems is given in Tab. 9.1.

In this study, five IAFAs operating in the central district of Bartın province were determined as decision makers. Considering the literature in Tab. 9.1, the most basic problems determined by decision makers will be named as criteria in this study. Criteria (problems), explanations about the problem, and information on which study the problem was addressed are given in Tab. 9.2.

In this study, the criteria determined in Tab. 9.2 will be prioritized. For this reason, Best-Worst method, which is one of the multi-criteria decision making methods, and also a very new method in the literature, was preferred.

3 Application

In the study, interviews were conducted with five members of profession; three women, two men, one dependent and four independent members, who practice IAFA profession in the central district of Bartın province. In order to prioritize the criteria specified in Tab. 9.2, it has been decided to use multi-criteria decision making methods, different from the literature.

3.1 Method of Study

In the study, Best – Worst method was used to determine the importance (weights) of the criteria. The Best – Worst method is one of the multi-criteria decision making methods that can compare these criteria with other criteria by determining the best and the worst criteria. With this method, it is not necessary for the respondents to make a comparison between all criteria. They only need to compare the best and worst criteria with others (Mou et al., 2016; Rezaei, 2015).

Best – Worst method was first developed by Rezaei (2015). Then, many researchers like Rezaei et al. (2016), Gupta and Barua (2016), Mou et al. (2016), Ren et al. (2017), Ahmadi et al. (2017), Guo and Zhao (2017), Ahmad et al. (2017), Gupta (2018), Çakır and Can (2019), Aşan and Ayçin (2020), Singh and Rajeev (2020) used the Best – Worst method in the weighting studies of the criteria and successful results were obtained.

3.2 Purpose and Importance of the Study

The aim of this study is to prioritize the problems experienced by those who work as Independent Accountant and Financial Advisor by evaluating them with the Best-Worst method, and to offer solutions.

Tab. 9.1: Literature Review

Source	**Summary of the Study**	**Applied Method**
Kalaycı and Tekşen (2006)	The problems of the members of the profession who do the accountancy profession independently in the city center of Isparta have been determined.	Survey Method
Özulucan, Bengü and Özdemir (2010)	The current problems of those practicing accounting profession are examined.	Survey Method
Gökgöz and Zeytin (2012)	In the studies carried out in Bilecik and Yalova provinces, the problems experienced by the accounting professionals were determined.	Survey Method
Tuğay and Tekşen (2014)	It aimed to determine the problems faced by the accounting professionals and their expectations for the solution of these problems.	Survey Method
İbrahimoğlu, Kara and Karaca (2014)	The determination of the managerial problem of accounting professionals and the causes of the problems are examined.	Survey Method
Işık (2014)	In the province of Tekirdağ, solutions are offered to the problem of accounting professionals.	Survey Method
Aydemir (2015)	Problems of the accounting profession in Turkey are stated and expectations for the solution of these problems has been determined.	Survey Method
Gündüz and Özen (2016)	It is aimed to determine the problems of the professional accountants operating in Uşak and their expectations for the solution of these problems.	Survey Method
Deran, Erduru and Keleş (2016)	The problems and expectations of accounting professionals in Ordu province have been determined.	Survey Method
Öztürk and Şimşek (2017)	It was aimed to determine the problems of the accounting profession in Erzurum province and to determine the burnout of the problems.	Survey Method
Katkat Özçelik (2018)	It was ensured that the problems faced by IAFAs were determined and these problems were evaluated in terms of gender.	Survey Method
Kızıl, Aslan and Kızay (2019)	The problems of the members of the profession who carry out the accountancy profession in Kocaeli province were determined and solution suggestions were presented.	Survey Method

Tab. 9.1: Continued

Source	Summary of the Study	Applied Method
Karakaya and Biçer (2020)	The perception of the unfair competition factor which is one of the problems experienced by accounting professionals, in terms of accountants was measured. Analytical hierarchy process (AHP) was used for these measurements.	AHP Method
Akpınar and Küçükgönsel (2020)	Problems faced by IAFAs in business life are presented and solutions are offered.	Survey Method

Source: (compiled by the author)

Although there are many studies on the problems of the accounting profession, there is no study in which evaluation is made with multi-criteria decision-making methods.

3.3 Findings

As a result of the survey conducted with five decision makers in accordance with the Best – Worst method, the importance levels of the criteria in Tab. 9.2 at each decision-maker level are shown in Tab. 9.3, as a result of the evaluation of the data obtained with the Best Worst method.

By finding the arithmetic mean values of the weights of each decision maker on the basis of the criteria in the table, the final criterion weights belonging to each criterion have been reached and the order of the problems faced by IAFAs was created according to these values.

Thus, the most important criterion has been found as the "C7 - Excessive Workload" criterion with a weight value of 0.2461; and the least important criterion has been found as the "C5 - Unfair Distribution of Taxpayers" criterion with a weight value of 0.0613. In addition, the average consistency ratio with a value of $\xi = 0.0933$ shows that it is consistent in the evaluations of decision makers.

4 Conclusion

As a result of the literature review on the problems of the accounting profession, it has been seen that there are many surveys. In this study, an evaluation was made with multi-criteria decision making methods (Best-Worst method)

Tab. 9.2: Determination of Criteria

Criteria (Problem)		Description of the Problem	Source
C1	Non-Payment of Accounting Fees	The fact that taxpayers do not pay the accounting fees on time or at all may leave IAFAs in difficult situations and affect their business motivation.	(Deran & Beller, 2017; Gökgöz & Zeytin, 2012; Öztürk & Şimşek, 2017)
C2	Taxpayers not bringing their documents on time	In terms of reliable accounting, accounting documents and papers are very important. Recording and classification standard, which is one of the basic functions of accounting for a healthy accounting recording system, is realized with timely documents and papers. Each record is based on documents and papers. Since taxpayers do not deliver their documents on time, members of the profession repeatedly request all of the documents (invoice, receipt, delivery note, payment receipt, self-employment receipt, etc.) from the taxpayers or supplier companies and this situation causes job losses.	(Gökgöz & Zeytin, 2012; Kızıl et al., 2019)
C3	Qualified Staff Problem	Difficulty of accounting professionals to find qualified personnel	(Akpınar & Küçükgönsel, 2020; Öztürk & Şimşek, 2017)
C4	Making accounting transactions below normal wages	Members of the profession suggest a fee below the wage tariff, which reflects on the quality of the service and causes unfair competition. This situation negatively affects both members of the profession and taxpayers.	(Gülçin, 2018; Kalaycı & Tekşen, 2006; Tuğay & Tekşen, 2014)
C5	Unfair Distribution of Taxpayers	An unfair distribution of taxpayers may arise due to the taxpayers' choice of members of the profession.	(Deran et al., 2016; Gülçin, 2018; Karakaya & Biçer, 2020; Kılıç & Arslan, 2017)

Tab. 9.2: Continued

Criteria (Problem)	Description of the Problem	Source
C6 Unlawful Requests of Taxpayers	There may also be unlawful tendencies of taxpayers to avoid paying taxes or to pay less taxes. The main ones of these tendencies are accounting tricks in the book and recording environment, to edit and use misleading and incorrect documents in terms of content, (fake invoice), to prepare the original or copies of the documents completely or partially as fake, knowingly using the documents printed by printing houses that do not have an agreement with the Ministry of Finance, hiding and falsifying books, records and documents, engaging in illegal behaviors to record the accounts and transactions that need to be recorded partially or wholly in the books, in other books, documents or other recording media that will result in a decrease in the tax base.	(Deran & Beller, 2017; Özulucan et al., 2010)
C7 Excessive Workload	Legislation and laws that are difficult to understand and change frequently can also increase the risk of mistakes for the professional member. Even the smallest mistake or indifference can cause all the work done to be wrong. The accountancy profession can never admit mistakes and indifference as these mistakes will cause substantial material or moral damage. Therefore, the professional accountants perform their activities under intense stress due to the fact that the information including the book records they have prepared, tax laws, business legislation, financial statements, reports, and the analyzes they make must be accurate.	(Aydemir, 2015; Tuğay & Tekşen, 2014)

Source: (compiled by the author)

and a ranking was made according to weight values in order to prioritize the problems of the accounting profession. According to the findings, the solution suggestions for the first three problems are as follows:

According to the findings obtained with the Best-Worst method which is one of the multi-criteria decision-making methods, it was concluded that the most important problem experienced by IAFA professionals is "excessive workload". It is possible to encounter a similar result in the study of Gökgöz and Zeytin

Tab. 9.3: Criterion Weights and Averages at the Level of Decision Makers

	C1	**C2**	**C3**	**C4**	**C5**	**C6**	**C7**	ξ_k
	Non-Payment of Accounting Fees	Taxpayers not bringing their documents on time.	Qualified Staff Problem	Making accounting transactions below normal wages	Unfair Distribution of Taxpayers	Unlawful Requests of Taxpayers	Excessive Workload	
DM1	0,0920	0,1150	0,1533	0,1533	0,0365	0,0920	0,3578	0,1022
DM2	0,0853	0,0543	0,3488	0,1421	0,0853	0,0711	0,2132	0,0775
DM3	0,0472	0,0964	0,1606	0,4062	0,0602	0,0688	0,1606	0,0756
DM4	0,1185	0,0344	0,1580	0,0790	0,0948	0,1580	0,3573	0,1168
DM5	0,1414	0,3300	0,2122	0,0606	0,0295	0,0849	0,1414	0,0943
Mean	0,0969	0,1260	0,2066	0,1683	0,0613	0,0950	0,2461	0,0933
w_j	w_1	w_2	w_3	w_4	w_5	w_6	w_7	
Rank	5	4	2	3	7	6	1	

(2012). In addition, in the studies of Kalaycı and Tekşen (2006), it was stated that the workload of 90 % of the members of the profession was too high. What needs to be done to solve this problem is to make things simpler and to eliminate unnecessary work. Additional solution offer may be to learn how to use computer softwares more effectively and to make things more practical.

It can be seen that the second important problem in the findings is the "Qualified Staff Problem". In the study of Bilen (2008), it was stated that more than 50 % of the members of the profession had a qualified staff problem. In the study of Biyan (2012), it was stated that 68.2 % of the participants in the questionnaire had a qualified staff problem. Even though the things that the IAFAs can do about the qualified staff problem is limited, they can reduce the negative effects of this problem by acting more rationally in the selection of personnel.

In the findings, it is seen that the problem of "Making Accounting Transactions Below Normal Wages" is the third most important problem. In the study of Biyan (2012), it was informed that the members of the profession could not apply the minimum wage tariff due to their competitors. In addition, in the study of Aydemir (2015), it was stated that the rate of some profession members keeping an accounting book very cheaply was high. It is thought that this problem can be solved by strengthening the communication network between professional associations and professionals, ensuring coordination and preventing bookkeeping below the minimum wage with the necessary legal regulations.

In subsequent studies, it is recommended to use different multi-criteria decision-making methods, to meet with more professionals and to make evaluations by increasing the number of criteria.

Bibliography

3568 Sayılı Serbest Muhasebeci Mali Müşavirlik ve Yeminli Mali Müşavirlik Kanunu (p. 1989). T. C. Resmi Gazete, 20194, 13 Haziran 1989.

Akpınar, T., & Küçükgönsel, N. Ç. (2020). Serbest muhasebeci mali müşavirlerin iş yaşamlarında karşılaştıkları sorunlar ve çözüm önerileri. *Balkan ve Yakın Doğu Sosyal Bilimler Dergisi*, *6*(1), 34–53.

Aşan, H., & Ayçin, E. (2020). Kurumsal kaynak planlama sistemlerinin seçimindeki kriterlerin Best-Worst metodu ile değerlendirilmesi. *Akademik İzdüşüm Dergisi*, *5*(2), 114–124.

Aydemir, O. (2015). Muhasebe meslek mensuplarının karşılaştıkları sorunlar ve beklentiler. *Muhasebe ve Finansman Dergisi*, *67*, 71–84. doi:10.25095/mufad.396577.

Badri Ahmadi, H., Kusi-Sarpong, S., & Rezaei, J. (2017). Assessing the social sustainability of supply chains using Best Worst Method. *Resources, Conservation and Recycling, 126*(July), 99–106. doi:10.1016/j.resconrec.2017.07.020.

Bilen, A. (2008). Doğu anadolu bölgesindeki muhasebe meslek mensuplarının profilleri, etik kurallarına bakışları ve meslek sorunları üzerine bir araştırma. *Mali Çözüm Dergisi, 85*, 27–42.

Biyan, Ö. (2012). Muhasebe meslek mensuplarına yönelik bir çalışma: Meslek mensuplarının demografik durumları, mesleki sorunları ve değerlendirilmesi. *Sosyoekonomi, 17*(17), 105–134.

Çakır, E., & Can, M. (2019). Best - Worst yöntemine dayalı ARAS yöntemi ile dış kaynak kullanım tercihinin belirlenmesi: Turizm sektöründe bir uygulama. *Atatürk Üniversitesi Sosyal Bilimler Enstitüsü Dergisi, 23*(3), 1273–1300.

Deran, A., & Beller, B. (2017). Muhasebe meslek mensuplarının karşılaştıkları sorunlar ve bağlı bulundukları meslek odasından beklentileri üzerine bir araştırma. *Muhasebe ve Denetime Bakış, 50*, 37–56.

Deran, A., Erduru, İ., & Keleş, D. (2016). Muhasebe meslek mensuplarının mesleki sorunları ve meslek odalarından beklentilerinin demografik özellikler ve faaliyet gösterilen ekonomik çevre açısından Değerlendirilmesi: Ordu örneği. *Selçuk Üniversitesi İktisadi ve İdari Bilimler Fakültesi Sosyal Ekonomik Araştırmalar Dergisi, 16*(32), 84–109.

Gökgöz, A., & Zeytin, M. (2012). Muhasebe meslek mensuplarının mesleki faaliyetlerinde karşılaştıkları sorunlar ve beklentileri: Bilecik ve Yalova illeri uygulaması. *Süleyman Demirel Üniversitesi İktisadi ve İdari Bilimler Fakültesi Dergisi, 17*(1), 477–493.

Gülçin, K. (2018). Muhasebe mesleğinin gelişimi ve meslek mensuplarının karşılaştıkları sorunlar ve çözüm önerileri. *Journal of International Social Research, 11*(58), 669–682. doi:10.17719/jisr.2018.2581.

Gündüz, M., & Özen, E. (2016). Muhasebe meslek mensuplarının sorunları ve mesleki memnuniyetlerinin analizi: Uşak ili örneği. *Muhasebe ve Finansman Dergisi, 70*, 67–90. doi:10.25095/mufad.396681.

Guo, S., & Zhao, H. (2017). Fuzzy best-worst multi-criteria decision-making method and its applications. *Knowledge-Based Systems, 121*, 23–31. doi:10.1016/j.knosys.2017.01.010.

Gupta, H. (2018). Evaluating service quality of airline industry using hybrid best worst method and VIKOR. *Journal of Air Transport Management, 68*, 35–47. doi:10.1016/j.jairtraman.2017.06.001.

Gupta, H., & Barua, M. K. (2016). Identifying enablers of technological innovation for Indian MSMEs using best-worst multi criteria decision making method. *Technological Forecasting and Social Change, 107,* 69–79. doi:10.1016/j.techfore.2016.03.028.

İbrahimoğlu, N., Kara, E., & Karaca, C. (2014). Muhasebe meslek mensuplarının yönetimsel sorunları algılamaları üzerine bir araştırma. *Gaziantep University Journal of Social Sciences, 13*(3), 589–605.

Işık, A. (2014). *Tekirdağ'daki muhasebe meslek mensuplarının sorunları ve çözüm önerileri.* NKUBAP.00.13.AR.14.04 numbered project report.

Kalaycı, Ş., & Tekşen, Ö. (2006). Muhasebecilik mesleğinde karşılaşılan sorunlar ve çözüm önerileri: Isparta il merkezi uygulaması. *Muhasebe ve Finansman Dergisi, 31,* 90–101.

Karakaya, G., & Biçer, A. A. (2020). Muhasebe meslek mensuplarının haksız rekabet algılarının analitik hiyerarşi süreci yöntemi ile değerlendirilmesi. *İşletme Araştırmaları Dergisi, 12*(2), 1149–1158. doi:10.20491/isarder.2020.902.

Katkat Özçelik, M. (2018). Serbest muhasebeci mali müşavirlerin sorunları ve bu sorunların cinsiyet boyutu: Artvin ve Rize örnekleri. *Karadeniz Araştırmaları, 15*(58), 99–125.

Kılıç, M., & Arslan, Ü. (2017). Muhasebe meslek örgütü odalarının günümüzde yaşadığı sorunları ve çözüm önerileri: Batı Karadeniz Bölgesi illeri örneği. *International Journal of Management Economics and Business, ICMEB17 Özel Sayısı,* 523–533. doi:10.17130/ijmeb.2017ICMEB1735885.

Kızıl, C., Aslan, T., & Kızay, Ö. (2019). Muhasebe meslek mensuplarının sorunları ilgili çözüm önerileri: Kocaeli örneği. *Ida Academia Muhasebe ve Maliye Dergisi, 2*(1), 23–37. http://www.idaacademia.org/tr/pub/issue/43491/456176

Mou, Q., Xu, Z., & Liao, H. (2016). An intuitionistic fuzzy multiplicative best-worst method for multi-criteria group decision making. *Information Sciences, 374,* 224–239. doi:10.1016/j.ins.2016.08.074.

Öztürk, M., & Şimşek, A. (2017). Erzurum'daki muhasebe meslek mensuplarının yaşadıkları sorunlar ve sorunların tükenmişlikleri üzerine etkisi. *International Journal Of Eurasia Social Sciences, 8*(29), 851–876.

Özulucan, A., Bengü, H., & Özdemir, F. S. (2010). Muhasebe meslek mensuplarının güncel sorunları, uygulamada karşılaştıkları yetersizlikler ve meslek odalarından beklentilerinin unvanları ve mesleki deneyim süreleri yönüyle incelenmesi: Türkiye genelinde bir araştırma. *Muhasebe ve Denetime Bakış, 31,* 41–64.

Ren, J., Liang, H., & Chan, F. T. S. (2017). Urban sewage sludge, sustainability, and transition for Eco-City: Multi-criteria sustainability assessment of technologies based on best-worst method. *Technological Forecasting and Social Change*, *116*, 29–39. doi:10.1016/j.techfore.2016.10.070.

Rezaei, J. (2015). Best-worst multi-criteria decision-making method. *Omega (United Kingdom)*, *53*, 49–57. doi:10.1016/j.omega.2014.11.009.

Rezaei, J., Nispeling, T., Sarkis, J., & Tavasszy, L. (2016). A supplier selection life cycle approach integrating traditional and environmental criteria using the best worst method. *Journal of Cleaner Production*, *135*, 577–588. doi:10.1016/j.jclepro.2016.06.125.

Singh, M., & Rajeev, K. (2020). Investigating the enablers associated with implementation of Green Lean Six Sigma in manufacturing sector using Best Worst Method. *Clean Technologies and Environmental Policy*, *22*(4), 865–876. doi:10.1007/s10098-020-01827-w.

Tuğay, O., & Tekşen, Ö. (2014). Muhasebe meslek mensuplarının sorunları: Burdur ilinde bir araştırma. *Süleyman Demirel Üniversitesi İktisadi ve İdari Bilimler Fakültesi Dergisi*, *19*(1), 223–232.

Wan Ahmad, W. N. K., Rezaei, J., Sadaghiani, S., & Tavasszy, L. A. (2017). Evaluation of the external forces affecting the sustainability of oil and gas supply chain using Best Worst Method. *Journal of Cleaner Production*, *153*, 242–252. doi:10.1016/j.jclepro.2017.03.166.

Kezban Talak

Culture of Innovation as A Management Function

Abstract Every day, innovation and innovation culture by researchers; Studies are carried out on its role in productivity, employment, economy and social development. According to the results of empirical studies in academic literature, it is revealed that there is a meaningful and positive relationship between entrepreneurship and development, innovation and organizational performance. In addition, innovation is seen as one of the most important factors affecting economic growth by providing competitive advantage and wealth accordingly. In addition, the role of culture in the development of innovation appears to be a curious and highly researched subject. In the context of entrepreneurship – innovation, it is seen that more studies are needed to find answers to the questions of why some businesses are more innovative than others and take part in more entrepreneurial projects, what the factors that affect entrepreneurship – innovation behavior and which areas are effective. Because, despite many studies, it is understood that the factors affecting entrepreneurship-innovation behavior and performance are still not fully explained.

The aim of this study is to examine innovation culture as a management function. However, within the scope of the study, the effect of intra-organizational entrepreneurship on innovation culture and innovation culture on innovation ability will be examined. In addition, the mediating role of innovation culture in the impact of intra-organizational entrepreneurship on innovation ability has been investigated.

As a result of the research, it was determined that the innovation culture positively affected the entrepreneurship and innovation ability within the organization. In addition, it has been observed that innovation culture has a partial mediating role in the impact of intra-organizational entrepreneurship on innovation capability.

Keywords: Organizational Entrepreneurship, Innovation Culture, Innovation Capability

1 Introduction

In today's world, businesses can survive and do not disappear, depending on the understanding of competition, creating a competitive advantage. Innovation can generally be thought of as new ideas, new ways of looking at things, new methods or products with value.

In today's business world, companies must constantly innovate in order to compete and survive in the long term. Most practitioners and scientists argue that the ability of any business to continuously apply innovation is linked to the individual innovation of employees. Employees can apply innovation either as part of their job descriptions or by expressing voluntary innovative work behaviors. This can be explained by the existence of innovation culture.

Radical innovations occurring around the world shape major changes in the world, while increasing innovations continually feed economic change. Innovation is one of the few business concepts that can be appreciated by everyone: it is seen as a contributing factor to strengthen an industry's competitiveness, meet customer expectations, create quality jobs, and motivate employees.

In the global age we are in, commercial environments have become a single market, which forces businesses to constantly change and follow innovation. Otherwise, it is not possible for enterprises to continue their continuity or competition race and gain a competitive advantage. Businesses need to have an innovation culture in order to meet these needs and to innovate. In this context, innovation culture can be explained as sustaining by making a difference and differentiating. However, the concept of innovation has evolved significantly over the past 30 years. Again, in this context of development, the Organization for Economic Cooperation and Development (OECD) has published the Oslo Guide to define, characterize and monitor innovation.

Although it is frequently emphasized that the innovation culture should be developed in the literature, it is not possible to talk about a consensus on what characteristics the culture that supports creativity and innovation should have (Judge et al., 1997). The reason for this can be shown that there have not been enough studies on the characteristics of the innovation culture. However, as a result of the examination of these studies, although their number is small, the aim of this study is to determine the conceptual framework of the innovation culture and to determine the characteristics of the innovation culture. In line with this purpose, first of all, studies in the literature will be examined and a conceptual framework of innovation culture will be created. In the continuation of the study, it will be tried to reveal the characteristics of the organizational culture that affect the innovation culture.

The aim of this study is to examine the innovation phenomenon in the context of culture and management function. However, the relationship between organizational entrepreneurship and innovation capability is also on the topics to be discussed.

As a result of the study, it was concluded that the innovation culture has an important role for the continuity of the enterprises. However, it was concluded that intra-organizational entrepreneurship positively affected the innovation culture and talent, and the innovation culture positively affected the innovation ability.

2 The Concept of Culture

When we look at the literature, there are many definitions related to the concept of culture. McCort and Malhotra (1993) define culture as the most abstract concept that affects human behavior. Youngdahl et al. (2003) stated that while explaining culture, it consists of explicit and implicit behavioral patterns.

Herbig and Dunpy (1998) defined culture as "the sum of how life is lived shared by members of a society such as expected behaviors, beliefs, values, and language". Thus, culture can be defined as a pattern of values, characteristics or behaviors shared by people in a region. This pattern will be valid as long as members are satisfied. When a particular standard does not satisfy community members, other standards will emerge to respond to changing needs. Therefore, culture is in a gradual but continuous change according to the needs of the society (Herbig & Dunpy, 1998).

While Hofstede et al. (1991) defines the phenomenon of culture as a set of characteristics that distinguish the members of a group from others, they state that culture is acquired over time, not innate (Hofstede et al., 1991).

The basis of the phenomenon of culture is based on traditional ideas and the values these ideas are associated with. In this respect, culture stands out as the determinant of both today's and future actions.

3 Innovation

Numerous studies have been conducted on the importance of innovation, which is necessary for organizations to have a competitive advantage. Before making the definition of innovation, mentioning its relationship with similar concepts and types will provide a more accurate definition. The first of these concepts is creativity. Creativity, which is defined as the production of new and useful ideas in any field, is a part of the innovation process, and innovation is the application of an idea developed with creativity. Accordingly, it can be said that creativity constitutes the first step of the innovation process (Flynn & Chatman, 2001).

Another concept related to innovation is invention. But the existence of innovation does not depend on an invention. However, an innovation does not have to be an invention for it to exist. Namely, innovation can happen after innovation and multiple inventions can contribute to a single innovation

(Samsonowa, 2012). However, in order for the invention to be considered as innovation, it must be commercialized. In this respect, innovation is an economic concept rather than a technological concept (Rothwell & Wissema, 1986; Drucker, 2001).

Innovation is a word that is used instead of innovation. However, it is possible to say that innovation is much more than a new one, considering that every innovation has no commercial value (it has no value in the eyes of the customer). There are various classifications of innovation types. These classifications are generally based on type, structure and degree of innovation (OECD, 2005).

One of the most internationally accepted sources on the concept of innovation is the Oslo Guide, published jointly by the OECD and Eurostat. According to this guide, the concept of innovation; "Of a new or significantly modified product or process; a new marketing method; or the application of a new organizational method in business practices, workplace organization or external relations" (OECD-Eurostat, 2006).

When we look at the current literature; It is understood that the researchers agreed that innovation is one of the most effective factors that enable businesses to compete with each other in changing competitive conditions. (Afuah, 2009; Betz, 2011; Bessant, 2002) Concerning this issue, Drucker expresses the opinion that not only businesses but also every organization need a single basic skill and that is innovation (Drucker, 2001).

Christenson (2005), on the other hand, handled the concept of innovation differently, and stated that innovation is a state of existence that ranges from destructive to mildly benign environments (Christensen, 1997).

According to West and Farr (1990), innovation is the whole process of applying new ideas, products and procedures to benefit an organization or organization. Hamel (1999), on the other hand, defines innovation as the process and motivation of adapting to the requirements of the age by departing from traditional management principles (Hamel, 1999).

Innovation is the innovations or significant improvements made in production processes, products, marketing methods or managerial activities and that have a commercial value. Innovation is one of the most important resources that businesses will use to increase their competitiveness (Bessant, 2002; Afuah, 2009; Betz, 2011).

Types of innovation in the literature are product and process innovation, organizational innovation, marketing innovation, sustainable innovation, disruptive innovation, discontinuous innovation, paradigm innovation, finding a new raw material or semi-finished product resource (Schumpeter, 1934), repositioning the business in the sector (Schumpeter, 1934), It is classified as incremental innovation (OECD, 2005).

Agencies monitoring innovation worldwide emphasize that the most effective innovation strategy at the moment is the "Need Seeker" strategy, which includes anticipating future needs and uses. This strategy is conducive to generating radical innovations that focus on the uses and functional qualities of products. In addition, businesses' sustainability of innovation depends on many different factors such as R&D expenditures, the sector they operate in, and the quality of human resources. One of the most important of these factors is culture. The culture factor affects innovation in three contexts. These; The relationship between national culture and innovation is in the form of the relationship between national culture and organizational culture, and between organizational culture and innovation (Nakata & Sivakumar, 1996; Hofstede et al. 1990; Schein, 2010; Tushmann & O'Reilly, 1997; Uzkurt & Şen 2012).

Culture and innovation activities are directly related to each other. Herbig and Dunpy (1998) are the leading researchers who have expressed an opinion on this issue. According to these two researchers, the values of a society directly affect the formation and emergence of innovation. Cultures that have a positive impact on innovation show features such as encouraging creativity, rewarding technical ability and higher education, and supporting entrepreneurship (Herbig & Dunpy, 1998).

According to Mokry (1991), the value attached to education, past experiences, openness to new information, and tendency to take risks are factors that positively affect innovation (Mokry, 1991).

In studies examining the relationship between culture and innovation, dimensions developed by Hofstede (1980) are generally used. One of these studies was conducted by Nakata and Sivakumar (1996). According to Nakata and Sivakumar (1996); Power distance, masculinity and uncertainty avoidance should be low in the initial phase of new product development and high in the implementation phase. In individuality, the situation is the opposite. It should be high in the initial phase and low in the application phase.

However, because it is unthinkable that all cultural features have a relationship with innovation, another concept emerges. This is the innovation culture that can be defined as the sum of cultural characteristics that affect innovation as a sub-dimension of culture.

4 Innovation Culture

The term "innovation culture" is also difficult to define because it is a versatile term. According to Wieland (2004), innovation culture constitutes the innovation culture, the way the actors in an innovation process perceive economic and technical difficulties and the struggle strategies they have developed in the context of norms and values against these difficulties (Wieland, 2004).

Dobni is one of the researchers defining the innovation culture. Dobni (2008) describes the innovation culture; defined as a multidimensional context that includes an organization's intention to innovate, the infrastructure that supports innovation, the operational-level behaviors required to influence a market and drive value, and an environment to implement innovation (Dobni, 2008).

Nagesh (2016) defines the phenomenon of innovation culture as a core value shared in the organizational structure that supports innovations in the structure of the organization and supports perceived practices towards innovation (Nagesh, 2016).

In a study in which O'Reilly examined the norms that develop innovation, it was observed that he frequently emphasized the factors of risk taking, rewarding change and being open to innovation (O'Reilly, 1989).

According to Prabhu, focusing on the future, the competitive environment within the enterprise, supporting all employees for innovation, going beyond existing successful products and turning to new products are among the factors that affect the innovation culture (Prabhu, 2010).

When we make a general evaluation about the factors that affect the innovation culture, these factors can be listed as follows: Being creativity-oriented, realizing organizational learning, ensuring participatory decision-making process, being open-minded by managers, being able to express the leader's vision easily, encouraging taking risks and accepting uncertainty, competitive, Creating a performance-oriented culture, attaching importance to group and team work, learning from failure, realizing the strategic orientation focused on innovation, business goals, goals, mission and vision being innovation-oriented, rewarding, providing individual support to employees (Sharifirad & Ataei, 2012).

5 The Effect of Intra-organizational Entrepreneurship and Innovation Ability on Innovation Culture

Entrepreneurship and intra-organizational entrepreneurship phenomena have been investigated by many researchers on the axis of the disciplines they affect.

Especially the phenomenon of intra-organizational entrepreneurship stands out as an important factor in terms of institutional and economic development of enterprises, In line with this importance, it has been investigated by researchers and practitioners in recent years.

Intra-organizational entrepreneurship stands out as an important factor in terms of institutional and economic development of enterprises, and in line with this importance, it has been investigated by researchers and practitioners in recent years. Intra-organizational entrepreneurship is important not only for large-scale businesses but also for small and medium-sized businesses. Accordingly, a culture that supports and develops entrepreneurship is needed in order to understand the value of intra-organizational entrepreneurship. In the context of this need, the relationship between intra-organizational entrepreneurship and innovation culture comes to the fore (Gürsoy & Güven, 2016).

Entrepreneurship is an important factor to ensure and increase the economic efficiency of businesses. The main reason for this is that entrepreneurship brings innovation to the market, creates new jobs and supports employment levels (Zhao et al., 2005).

Özkul and Dulupçu (2007), among the authors who conducted research on this subject; He argues that entrepreneurship does not only determine the income level of a society, but is also a force that drives change in society or businesses (Özkul & Dulupçu, 2007). This situation can be directly explained by the relationship between innovation culture and intra-organizational entrepreneurship.

Innovative businesses can adapt to market change and develop a strong market focus that can achieve customer loyalty. The engine of a business to be innovative is internal entrepreneurship. Sustainable innovation created through products, processes, systems and technologies that result from entrepreneurial activities can bring businesses to an advantageous position over their competitors (Thornhill, 2006). Innovation is an opportunity for entrepreneurial businesses and continuous innovation practices are the key to success in long-term entrepreneurship (Akın & Reyhanoğlu, 2014).

Innovation is a certain function of entrepreneurship. Innovation is the entrepreneur's creation of prosperity by creating new resources or increasing the use potential ofexisting resources (Drucker, 2001).

Miller and Friesen (1982) state that entrepreneurial and non-entrepreneurial enterprises differ in terms of the strategies they put into practice. Namely; While enterprises with entrepreneurial characteristics make innovation sustainable by constantly resorting to innovative activities, businesses that do not have entrepreneurial characteristics adopt an attitude that put innovation into practice when needed.

Schumpeter (1942) explains the entrepreneur's function as: "... an untested technological possibility to reform or revolutionize the production model using an invention or, more generally, to produce a new commodity or production". In this sense, the entrepreneur goes further than the coordinator and changes the productivity model.

6 Conclusion

When we make a general evaluation, it is understood that innovation comes to the fore as an important factor for businesses to ensure sustainable competitive advantage and survive in today's competitive environment. The way for companies operating in sectors where change and dynamism is experienced rapidly to respond to customer expectations is through continuous innovation. It is essential for companies to have an innovation-oriented innovation culture in order to engage in innovation activities. Companies that do not put innovation in their strategies and do not have an innovation culture cannot be expected to engage in product, process and management innovation activities. First of all, senior management should have a belief in this. Then, an innovation culture should be created in companies with the support of senior management. Without establishing an innovation culture in the company, the money to be spent on innovation studies will be considered as an unnecessary cost, the long-term benefits of innovation will not be seen, and as a result, there will be no growth and competitiveness capability. Another factor as important as management in creating an innovation culture in companies is employees. In order for employees to adapt to the innovation culture, they must be innovation-oriented.

One of the results obtained as a result of the study is that there is a positive relationship between intra-organizational entrepreneurship and innovation culture. In addition, it has been determined that innovation culture has a partial mediating role in the effect of intra-organizational entrepreneurship on innovation ability. One of the most important factors affecting innovation-oriented entrepreneurship is in-house entrepreneurship. Intra-organizational change in entrepreneurship affects innovation and the risk-taking skills required for them. Keeping abreast of the opportunities required for innovation is directly linked to intra-organizational entrepreneurship. The ability of intra-organizational entrepreneurship to become effective in an organization depends on the employment of entrepreneur employees. If the company employees increase their level of entrepreneurship within the organization, they will take an important step in providing the culture of innovation directly. Making the corporate structure focused on intra-organizational entrepreneurship and determining the corporate strategy in this direction will play an important role in establishing the innovation culture in companies. Therefore, businesses that want to establish the innovation culture in their companies should primarily attach importance to intra-organizational entrepreneurship. Intra-organizational entrepreneurship will also affect innovation capability as well as innovation culture. Entrepreneurial employees will have a significant contribution to the development of new products and processes.

If the employees have an entrepreneurial spirit, they will be able to see and express the innovations that need to be made in the products without being under pressure. Intra-organizational entrepreneurs who take initiatives to carry out innovation activities in companies emphasize that they can create new products, processes and services. For this reason, the ability of employees working in the production line to see the deficiencies and innovation needs in the production process and to express their opinions on this subject is directly related to the entrepreneurship characteristics within the organization.

The innovation cultures of the companies will also be effective on their innovation capabilities. Success in product, process and management innovations is directly linked to the innovation culture of companies. It is not an expected situation for a company in which the innovation culture is not established to realize product and process innovation. Herbig and Dunphy (1998: 14) emphasized the great importance of culture in adopting innovation and made the following comment; "Current cultural conditions determine whether a new innovation can be adopted, and if so, when, how and in what way it will be adopted. For this reason, a creative environment in companies where employees can easily convey their new ideas, where internal communication is active and motivating employees with behaviors that stimulate innovation should be the main feature of companies." The impact of intra-organizational entrepreneurship on innovation capability alone is not enough to be innovative. Because companies with strong internal entrepreneurship direction will be successful on product and process innovations, but innovation culture also plays a role in this effect. If the innovation culture in the company is not an established culture, the impact of internal entrepreneurship on innovation will also be low. In other words, internal entrepreneurship alone is not a sufficient factor for success in innovation ability. Innovative organizational culture is also a factor contributing to this success. Companies that will carry out innovative activities should employ entrepreneurial employees within the organization.

Bibliography

Abdullah, N. H., Shamsuddin, A., Wahab, E., & Hamid, N. A. (2013). The Relationship Between Organizational Culture and Product Innovativeness. *International Conference on Innovation, Management and Technology Research*. Malaysia: Elsevier.

Afuah, A. (2009). *Strategic Innovation: New Game Strategies for Competitive Advantage*. New York: Routledge.

Akın, Ö., & Reyhanoğlu, M. (2014). İşletme büyüklükleri bağlamında Türkiye'nin inovasyon portresi. Dokuz Eylül Üniversitesi. *Sosyal Bilimler Enstitüsü Dergisi, 16*(1), 25–31.

Angel, R. (2006). Putting an Innovation Culture into Practice. *Ivey Business Journal*, January-February 2006, 1–5.

Bessant, J. (2002). Developing routines for innovation management within the firm. In J. Sundbo & L. Fuglsang (Eds.), *Innovation as Strategic Reflexivity* (pp. 127–139). New York: Routledge.

Betz, F. (2011). *Managing Technological Innovation: Competitive Advantage from Change* (3rd Edition). New Jersey: John Wiley & Sons.

Boer, H., & During, W. (2001). Innovation, What Innovation? A Comparison Between Product, Process and Organisational Innovation. *International Journal of Technology Management, 22*(1), 83–107.

Chatman, J. A., & Flynn, F. J. (2001). The Influence of Demographic Heterogeneity on the Emergence and Consequences of Cooperative Norms in Work Teams. *Academy of Management Journal, 44*(5), 956–974.

Christensen, C. M. (1997). *The Innovator's Dilemma: When New Technologies Cause Great Firms to Fail.* Boston, MA: Harvard Business School Press.

Christensen, K. S. (2005). Enabling Intrapreneurship: The Case of a Knowledge Intensive Industrial Company. *European Journal of Innovation Management, 8*(3), 305–322.

Damanpour, F. (1991). Organizational Innovation: A MetaAnalysis of Effects of Determinants and Moderators. *The Academy of Management Journal, 34*(3), 555–590.

Dobni, C. B. (2008). Measuring Innovation Culture in Organizations: The Development of a Generalized Innovation Culture Construct Using Exploratory Factor Analysis. *European Journal of Innovation Management, 11*(4), 539–559.

Drucker, P. F. (2001). *The Essential Drucker.* New York: HarperCollins.

Drucker, P. (1985). Innovation and Entrepreneurship: Practices and Principles. *Personnel Strategies and Productivity, 10*(1), 105–109.

Francis, D., & Bessant, J. (2005). Targeting Innovation and Implications for Capability Development. *Technovation*, *25*(3), 171–183.

Gandotra, N. K. (2010). Innovation Culture for Sustainable Competitive Advantage. *APJRBM*, *1*(2), 51–59.

Gürsoy, A., ve Güven, B. (2016). Effect of Innovative Culture on Intrapreneurship. *International Journal of Business and Social Science*, *7*(1), 152–162.

Hamel, G. (1999). Bringing Silicon Valley Inside, From the Magazine (September–October 1999), (20.10.2020) https://hbr.org/1999/09/bringing-silicon-valley-inside

Herbig, P., & Dunphy, S. (1998). Culture and Innovation. *Cross Cultural Management: An International Journal*, *5*(4), 13–21.

Hofstede, Geert H. (1980). *Culture's Consequences: International Differences in Work-RelatedValues*. Newbury Park, CA: Sage.

Hofstede, G. (1991). *Cultures and Organizations: Software of the Mind*. London: McGraw-Hill.

Hofstede, G., Neuijen, B., Ohayv, D. D., & Sanders, G. (1990). Measuring Organizational Cultures: A Qualitative and Quantitative Study across Twenty Cases. *Administrative Science Quarterly*, 35(2), 286-316.

Hurley, R. F., & Hult, G. T. (1998). Innovation, Market Orientation, and Organizational Learning: An Integration and Empirical Examination. *Journal of Marketing*, *62*(3), 42–54.

Judge, W. Q., Fryxell, G. E., & Dooley, R. S. (1997). The New Task of R&D Management: Creating Goal-Directed Communities for Innovation. *In Knowledge and Communities*, *39*(3), 72–85.

McCort, D., & Malhotra, N. K. (1993). Culture and Consumer Behavior: Toward an Understanding of Cross-Cultural Behavior in International Marketing. *Journal of International Consumer Marketing*, *6*(2), 91–127.

Miller, D., & Friesen, P. H. (1982). Innovation in Conservative and Entrepreneurial Firms: Two Models of Strategic Momentum. *Strategic Management Journal*, *3*(1), 1–25.

Mokry, J. (1990). *The Lever of Riches: Technological Creativity and Economic Progress*. Oxford: Oxford University Press.

Nagesh, T. (2016). Linking Knowledge Management and Innovation Culture for Busıness Performance Improvement. *International Journal of Knowledge Management and Practices*, *4*(2), 10–22.

Nakata, C., & Sivakumar, K. (1996). National Culture and New Product Development: An Integrative Review. *Journal of Marketing*, *60*(1), 61–72.

North, D., & Smallbone, D. (2000). The Innovativeness and Growth of Rural SMEs During the 1990s. *Regional Studies, 34*(2), 145–157.

OECD, OSLO Manual. (2005). *The Measurement of Scientific and Technological Activities.* (20.10.2020) https://www.oecd.org/science/inno/2367614.pdf.

OECD (2006). Eurostat-OECD Methodological manual on purchasing power parities, (24.01.2021) https://ec.europa.eu/eurostat/web/products-manuals-and-guidelines/-/KS-BE-06-002

O'Reilly, C. (1989). Corporations, Culture, and Commitment: Motivation and Social Control in Organizations. *California Management Review, 89*(31), 9–25.

Özkul, G., & Dulupçu, M. A. (2007). Kişisel gelişimin girişimci tipleri üzerine etkisi: Antalya, Isparta illerinde bir inceleme. *Çanakkale Onsekiz Mart Üniversitesi Girişimcilik ve Kalkınma Dergisi, 2*(2), 67–92.

Prabhu, J. (2010). The influence of satisfaction, trust and switching barriers on customer retention in a continuous purchasing setting. *International Journal of Service Industry Management, 14*(4), 374–395.

Pun, K. F. (2001). Cultural Influences on Total Quality Management Adoption in Chinese Enterprises: An Empirical Study. *Total Quality Management, 12*(3), 323–342.

Rothwell, R., & Wissema, H. (1986). Technology, Culture and Public Policy. *Technovation, 4*(2), 91–115.

Russell, R. D. (1989). How Organisational Culture Can Help to Institutionalise the Spirit of Innovation in Entrepreneurial Ventures. *Journal of Organizational Change Management, 2*(3), 7–15.

Samsonowa, T. (2012). *Industrial Research Performance Management: Key Performance Indicators in The ICT Industry.* Berlin: Springer-Verlag.

Schein, E. H. (2010). *Organizational culture and leadership*, 4th edition, San Francisco: Jossey-Bass.

Schumpeter, J.A. (1934). The theory of economic development: an inquiry into profits, capital, credit, interest and the business cycle, *Harvard Economic Studies*, Vol. 46, Harvard College, Cambridge, MA.

Schumpeter, J. A. (1942). *Business Cycles: A Theoretical, Historical and Statistical Analysis of the Capitalist Process.* New York: McGraw-Hill Book Company.

Sharifirad, M. S., & Ataei, V. (2012). Organizational Culture and Innovation Culture: Exploring the Relationships between Constructs. *Leadership & Organization Development Journal, 33*(5), 494–517.

Thornhill, S. (2006). Knowledge, Innovation and Firm Performance in High- and Low-technology Regimes. *Journal of Business Venturing, 21*(5), 687–703.

Tushmann, M. L. & O'Reilly, C. A. (1997). Organizational Ambidexterity in Action: How Managers Explore and Exploit, *California Management Review, 53*(4), 5–22

Uzkurt, C., & Şen, R. (2012). Örgüt kültürü ve örgütsel yeniliğin pazarlama yeniliğine etkisi: Gazlı içecek sektöründe bir araştırma. *Anadolu Üniversitesi Sosyal Bilimler Dergisi, 12*(3), 27–50.

West, M. A., & Farr, J. L. (Eds.). (1990). *Innovation and creativity at work: Psychological and organizational strategies.* John Wiley & Sons.

Wieland, T. (2004). *Innovationskultur: Theoretische und empirische Ananäherungen an einen Begriff.* Münchener Zentrumfür Wissenschafts und Technikgeschichte.

Youngdahl, W. E., Kellogg, D. L., Nie, W., & Bowen, D. E. (2003). Revisiting Customer Participation in Service Encounters: Does Culture Matter? *Journal of Operations Management, 21*(1), 109–120.

Zhao, H., Seibert, S. E., & Hills, G. E. (2005). The Mediating Role of Self-Efficacy in the Development of Entrepreneurial Intentions. *Journal of Applied Psychology, 90*(6), 1265–1272.

Cagri Koroglu and Zeynep Aydin

Weighting Cost Calculation Methods by Healthcare Employees Using the SWARA Method

Abstract Along with the various technological developments required by our age, it increases in both national and international area in the competition between enterprises. Along with the difficulties brought by the competition, the businesses had to produce both higher quality products and higher quality services at low cost. In addition to these situations, when added to the economic difficulties in the country and on a global scale, business executives searched for different cost calculation methods. In this study, 11 cost calculation methods determined as criteria were asked to 11 staff working in the health sector and asked to determine in order of importance. In weighting, SWARA method, which is one of the multi-criteria decision-making methods, was used and it was aimed to determine the most important and least important criteria. The study is based on subjective data as a result of personal choices, not on objective data. The people who make the selection of criteria are healthcare professionals who are experts in their fields.

Keywords: Cost, Accounting, Multiple Criteria Decision Making, Swara

1 Introduction

The expenses incurred in the process of any product from production to marketing stage.Reducing these costs is important part for businesses. For that reason, it is necessary to determine the product costs completely, to organize the production processes, to reduce the waste as much as possible, to reveal the basic elements of the cost, to organize the income-expense method and to determine the strategy of the enterprise. Along with globalization, large and small, all the businesses are affected by the advantages and disadvantages which competition brought.

2 Cost Structures in the Health Sector

The increasing need for health among societies and ever-growing technology leaves managers with the problem of providing more health services or financing with less resources.

This problem increases the importance of making realistic decisions about which population regions, what kind of diseases and how to use the resources for interventions (Drummond et al., 2006: 5). To obtain more accurate results than traditional cost methods, strategic cost methods are used to provide both competitive and cost advantage in healthcare organizations. It reaches higher levels and a competitive advantage is achieved by the correct results obtained by the supervision, planning and evaluation of the service provided in hospitals.

3 Cost Calculation Methods

Costing systems are shortly summarized as follows by using the sources in the literature.

3.1 Target Costing

The use of target costing in the new product development process is quite high. This approach is used to determine the costs for a product in the design and planning processes. Besides, industrial marketers clarify the use of cross-functional teams that are risky for design and production decisions required to identify prices and qualities that are less likely to appeal to potential buyers for cost accounting workers (Gagne & Discenza, 1995: 16–18).

3.2 Process Based Activity Based Costing

There is profitability by separating idle capacity costs on customer, product and order basis, in process-based activity-based costing. Activities that do not provide economic value are identified and necessary studies are carried out to increase profitability. While it is aimed to expand the business structure obtained from profitable products and customers, on the other hand, methods that will improve the process for the products that cause loss and for the customers are used (Anderson & Putterman, 2005: 2).

3.3 Product Life Cycle Costing

We can define the life curve costing method as the total of the cash flows starting from the idea process of the product until the end of its useful life. It is clearly seen that how important the life course costing is When it is taken into consideration that in order to increase the profitability of the businesses, it is necessary to provide an income from the manufactured product to meet the expenses of all stages. So it is seen that life cycle costing is very useful both at the product planning stage and at the product pricing stage (Büyükmirza, 2016: 859).

3.4 Activity Based Costing

The changing and developing technology has caused the systems used in many functions such as production, marketing and accounting-finance to change. In manufacturing businesses, Traditional systems have been used for years to calculate product costs but unfortunately it was insufficient. As a result of these deficiencies, Activity Based Costing method has emerged. In the emergence of ABC method, it was thought to determine and control indirect costs, but it has become more detailed in time (Bengü, 2005: 187).

3.5 Traditional Cost Accounting

In the traditional method, quantitative criteria such as labor hours, machine hours and sales amount are used to associate the general production expenses with the product. However, as time passed, technological advances changed the way companies worked, labor expenditures in manufactured products decreased and their effect on traditional costs decreased, and accordingly, deviations occurred in the calculation of product costs (Babayev, 2017: 9).

3.6 Quality Cost System

Quality costs are related to compliance quality. Quality of conformity is the degree where a product meets the technical specifications of its designs. Design quality must necessarily have a high conformity quality of products suitable for customer consumption. In other words, the expenses incurred due to the expenditures made for the production of goods and services that are efficient, effective and capable of meeting the needs of the customers or to produce the quality constitute the quality costs (Kırlıoğlu, 1988: 42).

3.7 Responsibility Accounting

In the accounting system of a company: There should be management features that will determine the goals that will realize the planning, control and objectives, and also present the data correctly. There is a close relationship between business plans. Budgets use the data during planning and budgeting. The accounting which will present these features together in a planned manner is responsibility accounting (Göktürk, 2012: 80–81).

3.8 Centrifugal Management

Centrifugal Management is a management system that transfers the responsibility of making decisions to all management departments in a hierarchical manner from top to bottom in an institution divided into different management levels (Utku, 2009: 14). In businesses with the centrifugal management system, each division of labor is separated as a different responsibility center and each unit is expected to achieve success within its responsibility (Coşkun Arslan, 2006: 47).

3.9 Combined Costing

Combined costs are inextricable due to their nature, since combined products are processed simultaneously with combined costs. The purpose of distributing combined cost in products It is the determination of the appropriate method to distribute this cost to the products and facilitates the process (Hansen et al., 2009: 227).

3.10 Kaizen Cost Method

The main purpose of the Kaizen method is to ensure continuous cost reduction in mature product lines that do not accept innovations by providing continuous improvement in critical processes (Kaplan & Cooper, 1998: 27). As an example, the kaizen cost method of a clockwork company, which has a labor and material-oriented production process, aims to increase the working speed of the machines and to increase the amount of machinery to be used by only one worker (Cooper R., 1994: 25).

3.11 Just in Time Production

The word "just in time" is the philosophy based on the immediate action of the required or requested activities (Şakrak, 1997: 47). For that reason, we can define JITP as a production system in which a product produced in production lines is started to be produced immediately and as required by the following stage. The main purpose of the JITP philosophy is using four elements such as; zero stock, production in a short time, small and at the same time the amount of serial finishing, and high quality and defect-free (Hacırüstemoğlu & Demir, 2002: 15).

4 Literature Review

Yılmaz (2008), in his study focused on determining the costs in hospitals, which have an important place in health institutions The importance of using the activity based costing method has been emphasized. In a study in 2014, it was argued that improvement in health services can only be achieved with quality. A study has been conducted on the sufficiency and costs of expenses in a quality-oriented manner (Arpat et al., 2014). Bekçi and Toraman (2011), it is aimed to highlight the importance of quality costs for companies and to reveal how productivity is affected especially in healthcare institutions, and the benefits that quality costs can provide are revealed in the study of (Bekçi & Toraman, 2011). Kısakürek et al. (2011), in the study, unit cost-volume profit analysis was applied for the data of Cumhuriyet University Faculty of Medicine, Department of Cardiology for 2009. As a result, it has been determined that unit fixed costs are too high. Unit cost-volume profit analysis was applied to the data of the Cardiology Department. As a result, it has been determined that unit fixed costs are too high (Kısakürek et al., 2011). İncesu and Öğüt (2013), in the study conducted in 2013, quality cost calculation was made with the help of PAF (Prevention-Approsial-Failure) model, one of the quality cost calculation models. As a result of the study, it was concluded that at least 25 % of the total costs of the hospital were related to the quality costs. Yeginboy and Yüksel (2015) explained the work order costing system in detail in the study in 2015 and it was applied with the help of a model. The cost of diagnosis and work order cost system of a patient treated in a cardiology outpatient clinic were calculated. Akpınar and Karabay (2017), in the study, the unit costs of an outpatient clinic examination and the hospital's burden were calculated. For expense distribution, simple distribution method is used (Akpınar & Karabay, 2017). Arslan et al. (2015), the structure of the hospital establishments and the importance of the costs incurred in the hospital were explained in the study. In particular, the importance of cost analysis per patient as a branch has been advocated (Arslan et al., 2015). Karademir and Gökberk (2019), in the study, the aim is to determine the service production expense centers. It is within the scope of the study to determine which expenses cause an increase in costs.

5 Material and Method

Decision making process can be defined as choosing only one of several options. In this decision process, several criteria may be involved. MCDM is used in many different fields, such as the scientific point of view or the business world (Zavadskas & Turskis, 2010: 167).

5.1 SWARA Method (Step-Wise Weight Assessment Ratio Analysis)

The SWARA method was revealed by Keršuliene, Zavadskas and Turskis (2010) firstly. When the literature study on the SWARA method is done, we see that it has been used in the solution of many problems. SWARA steps are as follows (Çakır, 2017: 45; Çakır, Akel & Doğaner, 2018):

Step 1: First, a decision team consisting of criteria related to the problem and decision-makers who will be involved in the decision phase should be formed. It is assumed that there are n criteria (C_j, $j = 1,2,\ldots, n$) in the problem and k decision makers (KV_k, $k = 1,2,\ldots, K$) in the decision team.

Step 2: At this stage, each KV involved in the selection process evaluates the criteria based on their knowledge and experience. After this evaluation, KVs are asked to create a common integrated classification to determine the criteria from best to worst. In this integrated ranking, C_1 and C_n show the best and worst criteria.

Step 3: Considering the integrated classification, each KV shows the comparative weight of the criteria, starting from the second rank criterion. In this indicator, KVs give 1.00 points to the most important criterion. Points assigned to other criteria are formed based on the most important criteria. All scores are assigned in multiples of 5 between 0 and 1.

Step 4: A coefficient (*kj*) given in Equation (1) is calculated for each criterias. The most important criteria in the common ranking of the criteria, the kj coefficient is assigned as 1.

$$k_j = \begin{cases} 1 & \text{İf} \quad j = 1 \\ s_j + 1 & \text{İf} \quad j > 1 \end{cases}$$

Step 5: The weight (w_j) for each criteria is calculated with the help of Equation (2). As in the previous stage, the w_j coefficient of the most important criteria in the common ranking of the criteria is 1.

$$w_j = \begin{cases} 1 & \text{İf} \quad j = 1 \\ \dfrac{w_{j-1}}{k_j} & \text{İf} \quad j > 1 \end{cases}$$

Step 6: And finally, each criteria final weights (q_j) are calculated by dividing the criteria weights (w_j) calculated in the previous step by the sum of the criteria weights.

$$q_j = \frac{w_j}{\sum w_j}$$

6 Application

In this application, criteria that can create resistance in the decision stages of health workers were selected and it was aimed to analyze the importance levels of these criteria with the SWARA method. While determining these resistances, health personnel's living in Aydin, İzmir and İstanbul cities were chosen. As a result of the literature review, 11 criteria shown in Tab. 11.1 were created. In determining the criteria used to reach the Cost Calculation resistances, the literature and academicians teaching in the field of Accounting and Finance were used. Criteria codes and criteria are summarized in Tab. 11.1.

The SWARA method, which is one of the MCDM methods, was preferred to determine the significance levels of these criteria. The data obtained as a result of the survey with decision makers were analyzed with Microsoft Office Excel 2010 software.

6.1 Determination of Criteria Weights with the SWARA Method

In the first stage of the SWARA method, each decision-maker was asked to rank the criteria in Tab. 11.1 from the best to the worst. After determining the criteria, the significance ratio among these criteria was ranked in percentage and it was ensured that the order of importance and the weight of the criteria were determined. Tab. 11.2 includes the criteria evaluation survey results of Decision Maker 1.

According to Tab. 11.2, AB = {1,2,10,3,8,9,7,6,5,11,4} vectors and the percentage differences (s_j) between the criteria have been reached. Linear programming model was established and analysis was made by considering all equations starting from Equation (1) up to Equation (11). According to this analysis, criterion weights of KV1 are calculated as C1 = 0,1319; C2 = 0,1256; C3 = 0,1087; C4 = 0,0452; C5 = 0,0712; C6 = 0,0747; C7 = 0,0785; C8 = 0,0906; C9 = 0,0863; C10 = 0,1196; C11 = 0,0678. With the comparisons obtained as a result of the questionnaire made with each decision maker, the linear programming model was analyzed by applying all the SWARA steps and the weights of the criteria were obtained as in Tab. 11.3.

Tab. 11.1: Application Codes of Criteria and Sub-criteria

Criteria Code	Criteria
C1	Target Costing
C2	Process based activity based
C3	Product life cycle
C4	Traditional Cost Accounting
C5	Quality Costing
C6	Responsibility Costing
C7	Centrifugal Management
C8	Combined Costing
C9	Kaizen Costing
C10	Activity Based
C11	Just in Time Production

As a result of the surveys made to decision makers and the averages taken in Excel, the most important – least important criteria were determined according to their weights. According to the order shown in bold, the most important criterion in the research is "C2-Activity Based Costing" and the least important criterion is "C4- Traditional Cost Accounting ". This ranking is completely subjective and determined according to personal prejudices.

7 Conclusion

Control of costs is a very important factor for every businesses. With the developing technology, strategic approaches have emerged and businesses have started to apply this control with the minimum cost principle. In the survey conducted for the health sector personnel, it is seen that the three most important criteria consist of strategic methods. Considering that the financial burden of medical supplies is high, strategic methods are the most logical options in costing. Companies that manage the costing organization well in the health sector, where competition is high and quality is important for individuals, will have an advantage from the competition and will continue to move positively. When the results of decision makers are examined, all of the three most important options consist of strategic methods. The ranking determined according to all subjective decisions met the expectations formed before the research. In addition, the use of knowledge in traditional methods as technology in production environments has caused changes in the cost structures of enterprises and

Tab. 11.2: Criteria Assessments Belong to KV1

Ranked Criteria		s_j	k_j	w_j	q_j	**Criteria**		q_{j1}
C1	Target Costing		1,00	1,000	0,132	C1	Target Costing	0,1319
C2	Process Based Activity Based	0,05	1,05	0,952	0,126	C2	Process Based Activity Based	0,1256
C10	Activity Based	0,05	1,05	0,907	0,120	C3	Product Life Cycle	0,1087
C3	Product Life Cycle	0,10	1,10	0,825	0,109	C4	Traditional Cost Accounting	0,0452
C8	Combined Costing	0,20	1,20	0,687	0,091	C5	Quality Costing	0,0712
C9	Kaizen Costing	0,05	1,05	0,654	0,086	C6	Responsibility Accounting	0,0747
C7	Centrifugal Management	0,10	1,10	0,595	0,078	C7	Centrifugal Management	0,0785
C6	Responsibility Accounting	0,05	1,05	0,567	0,075	C8	Combined Costing	0,0906
C5	Quality Costing	0,05	1,05	0,540	0,071	C9	Kaizen Costing	0,0863
C11	Just in Time production	0,05	1,05	0,514	0,068	C10	Activity Based	0,1196
C4	Traditional Cost Accounting	0,50	1,50	0,343	0,045	C11	Just in Time production	0,0678

while there has been a significant decrease in the labor costs of the enterprises, the general production expenses have increased significantly. In this case, the distribution of the general production expenses to the operating activities and the products produced by the traditional methods of cost accounting may cause the costs not to be calculated exactly. That's why decision makers have turned to the Activity Based Costing option.

Bibliography

Akpınar, S., & Karabay, D. (2017). Sağlık Kurumlarında Birim Maliyetinin Hesaplanması: Fizik Tedavi ve Rehabilitasyon Poliklinik Uygulaması. *İşletme Bilimi Dergisi*, 199–215.

Anderson, S., & Putterman, L. (2005). Building the Profit Focused Supply Chain: A Game Plan for Capturing Real Value. *White Paper*, 1–18.

Arpat, B., Şaşmaz, N., & Yürekli, E. (2014). Sağlık Hizmetlerinde Kalite Maliyetleri. *Süleyman Demirel Üniversitesi İktisadi ve İdari Bilimler Fakültesi Dergisi*, 313–332.

Tab. 11.3: Criteria Weights and Final Weights of Each Decision Maker

Criteria		KV1	KV2	KV3	KV4	KV5	KV6	KV7	KV8	KV9	KV10	KV11	Geometric Average	Average of Results
C1	**Target Costing**	0,1319	0,1249	0,1504	0,1136	0,1068	0,1399	0,1257	0,1089	0,1380	0,1118	0,1458	0,1262	0,1305
C2	**Process based activity**	0,1256	0,1311	0,1432	0,1380	0,1786	0,1469	0,1452	0,1450	0,1200	0,1065	0,1604	0,1388	0,1435
C3	**Product life cycle**	0,1087	0,1189	0,0517	0,1032	0,1624	0,1272	0,0686	0,1038	0,1000	0,1291	0,0580	0,0975	0,1008
C4	**Traditional Cost Accounting**	0,0452	0,0473	0,0369	0,0269	0,0296	0,0419	0,0457	0,0377	0,0283	0,0574	0,0414	0,0389	0,0402
C5	**Quality Costing**	0,0712	0,0896	0,0744	0,1315	0,0198	0,0503	0,0594	0,0785	0,0714	0,0968	0,0739	0,0682	0,0705
C6	**Responsibility Costing**	0,0747	0,0746	0,0819	0,0860	0,1412	0,1106	0,0623	0,1198	0,0649	0,0922	0,0609	0,0850	0,0879
C7	**Centrifugal Management**	0,0785	0,0711	0,0860	0,0662	0,1228	0,0922	0,1093	0,0654	0,1518	0,0663	0,0672	0,0853	0,0882
C8	**Combined Costing**	0,0906	0,1030	0,0620	0,0473	0,0489	0,0694	0,0911	0,0623	0,0589	0,0602	0,0640	0,0669	0,0691
C9	**Kaizen Costing**	0,0863	0,1133	0,0903	0,0430	0,0326	0,0798	0,0792	0,0566	0,0618	0,0838	0,1056	0,0713	0,0737
C10	**Activity Based**	0,1196	0,0646	0,1194	0,1252	0,0890	0,0838	0,1382	0,1318	0,1694	0,1230	0,1268	0,1138	0,1177
C11	**Just in Time Production**	0,0678	0,0615	0,1038	0,1192	0,0684	0,0578	0,0754	0,0902	0,0453	0,0729	0,0960	0,0753	0,0778
													0,9671	1,0000

Arslan, E., Önder, N. T., Kayalı, S., Keskin, Z., & Yiğit, Ö. (2015). Kamu hastanelerinde branş bazında hasta başı maliyet analizi (İstanbul eğitim ve araştırma hastanesi örneği). *Sağlık Akademisyenleri Dergisi*, 40–52.

Babayev, H. (2017). Geleneksel Maliyet Sistemlerine Alternatif olarak Faaliyet Tabanlı Maliyetleme ve Örnek Uygulama. *Lisans Bitirme Tezi*. Bakü, Azerbaycan.

Bekçi, İ., & Toraman, A. (2011). Kalite Maliyetleri ve Bir Hastanede Hesaplanması. *Süleyman Demirel Üniversitesi İktisadi ve İdari Bilimler Fakültesi Dergisi*, 39–57.

Bengü, H. (2005). Faaliyet Tabanlı Maliyetleme Sisteminde Faaliyet Seviyelerinde Maliyet Uygulaması. *Muhasebe ve Finansman Dergisi, 25*, 186–194.

Büyükmirza, K. (2016). *Maliyet ve Yönetim Muhasebesi*. Ankara: Gazi Kitabevi Tic. LTD. ŞTİ.

Çakır, E. (2017). Kriter Ağırlıklarının SWARA-Copeland Yöntemi ile Belirlenmesi: Bir Üretim İşletmesinde Uygulama. *Sosyal Bilimler Enstitüsü Dergisi, 4*(1), 42–56.

Çakır, E., Akel, G., & Doğaner, M. (2018). Türkiye'de Faaliyet Gösteren Özel Alışveriş Sitelerinin Bütünleşik SWARA – WASPAS Yöntemi ile Değerlendirilmesi. *Uluslararası İktisadi ve İdari İncelemeler Dergisi, 2018*(18. EYİ Özel Sayısı), 599–616. doi:10.18092/ulikidince.347658.

Cooper, R. (1994). Japanese Cost Management Practices. *The Management Accounting Magazine*, 25.

Coşkun Arslan, M. (2006). *Merkezkaç Yönetim Açısından Sorumluluk Muhasebesi ve Transfer Fiyatlamanın Üretim İşletmelerinin Performansına Etkisi ve Bir Uygulama*. (Unpublished Master's Thesis), Gaziosmanpaşa Üniversitesi, Sosyal Bilimler Enstitüsü.

Drummond, M. F. (2006). *Methods for the Economic Evaluation of*. New York: Oxford University Press Inc.

Gagne, M. L., & Discenza, R. (1995). Target Costing. *Journal of Business & Industrial Marketing, 10*(1), 16–22.

Göktürk, İ. E. (2012). Sağlık İşletmelerinde Sorumluluk Muhasebesi Sisteminin Uygulanabilirliği: Konya Bölge Hastaneleri Uygulaması. *Doktora Tezi*. Konya.

Hacırüstemoğlu, R., & Demir, V. (2002). Muhasebenin Yönetim Aracı Olarak Kullanımı. *Öneri Dergisi, 5*(19), 15.

Hansen, D. R., Mowen, M. M., & Guan, L. (2009). *Cost Management: Accounting and Control* (6th ed.). Ohio, USA: South-Western College Pub.

İncesu, E., & Öğüt, N. (2013). Hastane İşletmeciliğinde Kalite Maliyet Hesaplaması: Konya Seydişehir Devlet Hastanesinde Bir Uygulama. *Sağlıkta Performans ve Kalite Dergisi*, 113–142.

Kaplan, R. S., & Cooper, R. (1998). *Cost & Effect*. Boston: Harvard Business School Press.

Karademir, R., & Gökberk, C. (2019). Sağlık işletmelerinde maliyetler ve maliyet hesapları. *Anadolu Bil Meslek Yüksekokulu Dergisi*, 125–144.

Kırlıoğlu, H. (1988). *Kalite Maliyetleri Muhasebesi*. Sakarya: Değişim Yayınları.

Kısakürek, M. M., Yılmaz, A., & Kılıç, E. (2011). Cumhuriyet Üniversitesi Hastanesi Anjiyo Ünitesi Maliyet-Hacim-Kâr Analizi. *Elektronik Sosyal Bilimler Dergisi*, 42–59

Şakrak, M. (1997). *Maliyet Yönetimi*. İstanbul: Yasa Yayınları.

Utku, B. D. (2009). *Çağdaş Sorumluluk Muhasebesi*. Ankara: Detay Yayıncılık.

Yeginboy, Y. E., & Yüksel, İ. (2015). Hastane İşletmeleri Kardiyoloji Polikliniğinde Sipariş Maliyet Yöntemiyle Ayaktan Hasta Tanı Maliyetinin Hesaplaması. *Dokuz Eylul University Journal of Graduate School of Social Sciences*, 409–443.

Yılmaz, B. (2008). Hastane İşletmelerinde Rekabet Üstünlüğü Sağlamada Faaliyet Esasına Dayalı Maliyetleme Yönteminin Rolü ve Bir Uygulama. Konya, Türkiye: T.C. Selçuk Üniversitesi.

Zavadskas, E. K., & Turskis, Z. (2010). A New Additive Ratio Assessment (ARAS) Method in Multicriteria Decision-Making. *Technological and Economic Development of Economy*, 159–172.

Mehmet Utku and Yusuf Kaya

Current Developments in the Process of Adoption to the IFRS/IAS in Turkey

Abstract The International Accounting Standards Board (IASB) has published International Financial Reporting Standards (IFRS) in order to ensure confidence, growth and stability in the global economy and to create a common language in international financial markets. Many countries in the world, especially the economies of developed countries, have adopted IFRS in a short time. Turkey, which wants to take a share in international capital movements, is simultaneously trying to harmonize its national accounting policies with these standards with developed economies. Important steps have been taken in this regard since 2005, when the compulsory transition to IFRS began in Turkey. In this study, the aim is to reveal the current developments and their effects in Turkey, especially in recent years, at the point of compliance with the standards intended. Within the scope of the study, the existing accounting system in Turkey is discussed from a historical perspective. Then, the effects of the mandatory transition to IFRS in 2005 for publicly traded companies were revealed by taking into account the studies in the literature. Later, the Financial Reporting Standard for Large and Medium-Sized Enterprises (LME's FRS), which entered into force since 2018, and the effects of transition to this standard on financial statements were examined. Finally, the chart of accounts in accordance with the financial reporting standards and the Financial Reporting Standard for Small and Micro Enterprises (SME's FRS), the draft texts of which have just been published, have been examined and the possible effects are discussed. As a result, Turkey is closely following developments in the world in terms of standardization. It is thought that the current developments since 2017 will have an important effect on the spread of standardization to the whole economy.

Keywords: IFRS Adoption, Current Developments in IFRS, LME's FRS, SME's FRS

1 Introduction

With the removal of borders in world trade, increasing economic activities and international capital movements have caused the need for a common financial language. For global users of accounting knowledge, different accounting policies and regional implementation differences in international markets have increased investment risks and the need for standardization on a global scale has arisen. At this point, the International Accounting Standards Committee (IASC), which was established in 1973 to increase the quality of financial information produced by enterprises, to ensure its understandability and comparability, has published 39 standards until 2000. Founded in 2001, the International Accounting Standards Board (IASB) took over the standard setting task from IASC and the increasing economic and commercial expansion accelerated the accounting standardization process.

With the International Accounting Standards (IAS) and International Financial Reporting Standards (IFRS), a common language has been created in financial reporting worldwide. In this way, more comprehensive, understandable and realistic financial information is produced and efficiency in international markets increases as investors' risks and costs are reduced. The IASB is the board that has developed and published IAS and IFRS as an independent regulatory authority since 2001. The latest updated IFRS standard set, published in 2018, consists of 1 conceptual framework, 17 IFRS and 28 IAS. The Board develops IFRS for the purpose of transparency, accountability and efficiency in financial markets worldwide. Many businesses operating in 166 countries apply these standards in their accounting practices and financial reporting. According to the 2018 report of the IFRS foundation, in 87 % of 166 countries, IFRS implementation is mandatory for the vast majority of businesses. In addition, the same obligation exists in 75 % of G20 countries. The annual GDP of these countries implementing IFRS constitutes 47 % of the total GDP in the world. Financial reporting in accordance with IFRS is made in approximately 27,000 companies traded in 88 major stock exchanges around the world (IFRS Foundation 2018).

Since 2005 many businesses in the world, especially in Europe, started to use international accounting and financial reporting standards instead of national accounting policies. Either being a candidate country for EU membership, or in terms of ensuring integration into the international market IFRS/IAS has been adopted in Turkey. As of January 2005, reporting has been started in accordance with the IFRS set for enterprises subject to Capital Markets Board of Turkey. Parallel to the developments in the world, works in compliance with international standards in Turkey is still continuing from that date to the present. The intended scope of the study, in Turkey IFRS/IAS to reveal the current developments in the integration process is to analyze their actual and likely effects. In this respect, it was examined the historical development of accounting systems in Turkey. What happened in the process of adaptation to international accounting standards in Turkey were revealed. The effects of the 2005 mandatory adoption and current developments were analyzed.

2 Historical Development of Accounting System in Turkey

The settlement of mankind and the commencement of trade made it necessary to record financial information and led to the birth of accounting. Looking at the accounting history, a very wide date range extending to clay tablets in BC periods can be seen (Güvemli, 2000: 8). The development of accounting in Turkey, from the German legal system and entered into force on the Turkish Commercial Law, began in 1926 (Uçma, 2012: 159). Issues such as accounting system and preparing of financial statements are resolved by the law. In the 1950s, Turkey has entered the process of establishing close relations with the US. Independent development policy was abandoned and the transition to a liberal economy started. The process of transforming the administrative structure that started in state institutions, the steps taken by the governments towards the liberalization of trade led to the US influence in the field of accounting as well as commercial life. However, by making a full membership application to the European Union, relations with Europe were preserved. In the 1960s, it is seen that the institutionalization began in the field of accounting in Turkey. Within the framework of reports prepared by various public institutions, improvement studies were carried out by presenting the current situation. These reports and studies can be listed as follows (Akdoğan & Aydın, 1987: 86–94):

- Economic State Organizations Revision Committee Report completed in 1962
- Istanbul University Institute of Business Economics Report, which sets out the accounting principles in 1962.
- The report prepared by the Economic State Enterprises Reorganization Commission, which aims to uniformize the accounting records in 1964.
- The studies that the State Planning Organization (SPO) suggested to use the American Generally Accepted Accounting Principles in the accounting system between 1968 and 1977.

In 1982, the Capital Markets Board (CMB) was established by law. Thanks to Accounting Profession Law in 1989, the accounting profession has been put on a legal ground for the first time in Turkey. As of 01.01.1994, Accounting System Application General Communiqué has been put into effect. With the uniform chart of accounts, standardization has been achieved throughout the country in accounting transactions. In 1994, in order to ensure compliance with international accounting standards, Turkey Accounting and Auditing Standards Board (TAASB) it was established. The organization, which is a member of IASB, has published 19 standards compatible with IFRS until 01.01.2002. In 2002, Turkey Accounting Standards Board (TASB) has initiated activities taking place TAASB. TASB has published a set of accounting standards, consisting of a conceptual framework, 38 accounting standards, and 21 comments, by translating from IFRS. With the publication of the new Turkish Commercial Law in 2011, the Public Oversight Accounting and Auditing Standards Authority (POA) was established and the duty of TASB ended. Since 2011, POA continues its activities as the only institution tasked with setting, developing and publishing standards in line with IFRS.

3 Turkey's Adoption Process of the International Accounting Standards

In Turkey, it has announced a new economic stabilization program including structural transformation in 1980. Transition to liberal economy was aimed with this transformation. Foreign trade was liberalized and decisions were taken to encourage foreign capital investments. However, the economy was not ready to compete in the international markets, the political and economic crises experienced in the process prevented the targeted development. Significant economic crises and capital shortages in 1994, 1997 and 2001 made it necessary to attract foreign investors to the country. For this reason, important economic reforms, especially the banking sector, were implemented after the 2001 crisis. Accounting and financial reporting standards in line with IFRS have been published to ensure integration with international financial markets. The standardization process, which started with companies traded on the stock exchange, was expanded in 2018 to include large and medium size enterprises. Small and micro size enterprises in Turkey is implementing the national accounting system. However, POA plans to include small and micro size enterprises in the standardization process with SME's FRS, for which published its draft plan. Financial reporting framework in Turkey is shown in Fig. 12.1.

3.1 Mandatory Adoption of IFRS and Its Effects

Until 2002, the accounting standards published by TAASB in Turkey has been in more of a recommendation. Unity of implementation could not be achieved due to the fact that the institution does not have the power of sanction and the enterprises are subject to different accounting practices by law. Important steps have been taken in adoption of IFRS with the establishment of TASB, which is the only authorized institution for the formation of accounting standards. The communiqué prepared by the CMB in order to mandatory adoption of

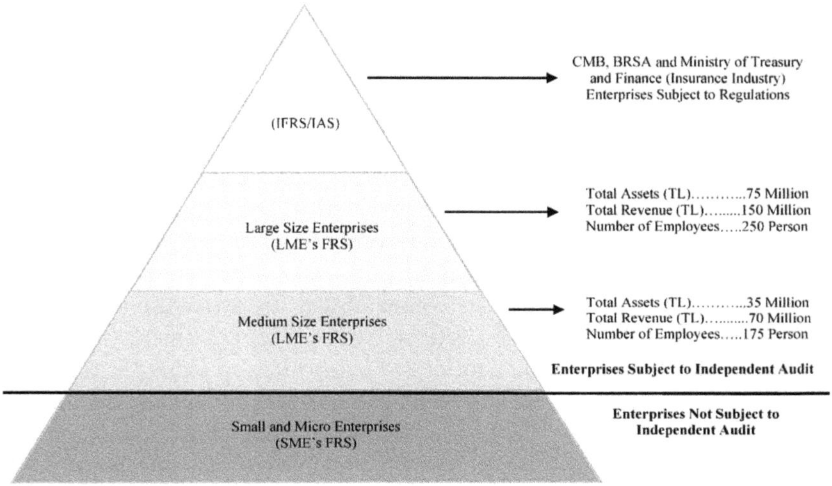

Fig. 12.1: Financial Reporting Framework in Turkey
Source: (www.kgk.gov.tr)

IFRS enter in force in 2003. In 2005, many countries in the world and Turkey, the IFRS/IAS has made it mandatory to use for publicly traded companies. In 2014, IFRS adoption became mandatory for companies subject to Banking Regulation and Supervision Agency (BRSA) and Ministry of Treasury and Finance (Insurance Industry) legislation.

In 2005, the mandatory adoption of IFRS in Turkey, has been important in the short and long term effects on companies. In order to reveal these effects, some of the academic studies in the literature on this subject have been examined.

Ağca and Aktaş (2007) analyzed the impact of IFRS adoption on financial ratios by using the data of 147 companies operating in various sectors in Borsa Istanbul between 2004 and 2005. As a result of the study, they determined that financial ratios have changed in this process, especially in the textile, clothing and leather sector.

Turel (2009), mandatory transition to IFRS in Turkey, the compliance requirements of the financial information presented by the company has found that significantly increase. In the study conducted on 208 companies traded in Borsa Istanbul, it was determined that the transition increased the price explanation degree of the net profit but decreased the equity value.

Abdioğlu and Büyükşalvarcı (2011) conducted analysis on 119 companies from 8 different sectors that are traded on Borsa Istanbul and have implemented IFRS for the first time in 2005. The stock returns of these companies, most of which operate in the manufacturing sector, before and after the transition were analyzed. Except for the first year of transition in companies, statistically significant differences were found in stock returns in all periods until 2010.

Atmaca and Çelenk (2011), conduct a survey on 93 companies traded in Borsa Istanbul. According to the results of the regression analysis; IFRS increases the quality level of financial analysis in companies. In addition, survey participants believe that IFRS positively affects comparability, increases the reliability of financial results and provides accurate performance measurement.

Terzi et al. (2013) used the data of 140 companies operating in the Borsa Istanbul manufacturing sector between 2003 and 2005. They have determined that adoption of IFRS has significant effects on financial reporting and that there is a statistically difference between financial statements prepared in accordance with IFRS and financial statements prepared according to national legislation.

Alkan and Doğan (2012) examined the short and long-term effects of transition to IFRS on financial ratios. In the study, the data of 148 companies traded in Borsa Istanbul between 2000 and 2009 were examined. While there was no significant difference in liquidity ratios during the transition period, an increase was detected in the long term. While there is no significant change in activity ratios in the short term, there are increases in inventory turnover and receivables turnover in the long run. In terms of financial structure, only the long-term debt ratio increased in both short and long terms. Finally, there is no significant difference in profitability ratios between periods.

Akgün (2013), conducted a survey on 35 % of companies traded in Borsa Istanbul. According to the results of the survey, more accurate and reliable financial information is provided to users of financial statements by providing comparability between companies with IFRS. In addition, the quality level in accounting has been positively affected in terms of document and record order.

Terzi, Şen and Üçoğlu (2013) investigated the effect of transition to IFRS on equity. In the study, 121 manufacturing enterprises traded in Borsa Istanbul were analyzed. They found that the transition enabled protection of capital and protected businesses against bankruptcy risk.

Cengiz (2014) analyzed the financial ratios of 84 companies traded in Borsa Istanbul in 6-year periods before and after IFRS adoption. In the study, 15 different ratios were compared and it was concluded that the transition to IFRS caused changes in financial ratios as it affects financial statements.

Aygün et al. (2016) examined the effect of mandatory adoption on the financial rates of 158 companies from different industry traded in Borsa Istanbul. In the study covering the years 1995–2013, only a significant increase in liquidity and activity rates was observed in the post-IFRS period.

Sultanoğlu (2016) analyzed the effects of the transition to IFRS on the relevance of financial information. She has determined that in the five-year period after the transition to IFRS, there has been a significant increase in the relevance of financial information. In the study, it was concluded that financial statements prepared in accordance with IFRS reflect the financial status of the enterprises better and increase the quality of financial information.

Studies in the literature show that the mandatory IFRS adoption in Turkey, has created significant differences in stock returns. Especially in the long run, it caused an increase in liquidity, activity and financial structure ratios. In addition, this transition has increased the quality of accounting recording and financial analysis. As a result, the adoption of IFRS has created positive effects.

3.2 Developments and Effects of Standardization Process in Recent Years

Mandatory adoption of IFRS in 2005, Turkey experienced only a certain number of covered companies. Many companies in the economy have continued to report financially within the framework of the national accounting system. However, studies have continued to spread the standardization in the process and the Financial Reporting Standard for Large and Medium-Sized Enterprises (LME's FRS) was published in 2017. Then, on 26.12.2018, the POA published the draft chart of accounts in accordance with the financial reporting standards and presented it to the public opinion. In 2019, the draft text of SME's FRS was published by POA. The main purpose of these recent developments is to spread the standardization throughout the economy and to ensure full adoption of IFRS.

3.2.1 LME's FRS

LME FRS was published on 29/7/2017 in order to provide fair, relevant and comparable financial statements of large and medium-sized enterprises and entered into force as of 01/01/2018. Fig. 12.1 shows which enterprises are considered as large and medium sized enterprises within the scope of this standard. LME's FRS has been implementing a total of 2663 companies in Turkey as of 11/02/2020. 810 of these companies are large-sized enterprises, 1654 are

Tab. 12.1: Effects of LME's FRS on Financial Statement Elements

Financial Statement Elements	Company Size	Number of Increasing Companies		Number of Decreasing Companies		Average Change	Total LME
		Number	%	Number	%		
Retained Earnings	Large Sized	309	52,02 %	285	47,98 %	-0,75 %	594
	Medium Sized	464	39,29 %	717	60,71 %	-5,86 %	1.181
	Total LME	773	43,55 %	1.002	56,45 %	-2,62 %	1.775
Total Equities	Large Sized	324	51,10 %	310	48,90 %	7,49 %	634
	Medium Sized	523	38,18 %	847	61,82 %	5,41 %	1.370
	Total LME	847	42,32 %	1157	57,68 %	6,61 %	2.004
Net Income	Large Sized	59	45,38 %	71	54,62 %	5,89 %	130
	Medium Sized	60	40,82 %	87	59,18 %	-15,06 %	147
	Total LME	119	42,96 %	158	57,04 %	-1,31 %	277

Source: (POA LME's FRS Report, 2020)

medium-sized enterprises and 199 companies are agricultural producer unions (POA LME's FRS Report, 2020: 4).

LME's FRS is a financial reporting standard introduced for enterprises that are subject to independent audit and do not apply IFRS. This standard, which is in line with IFRS and EU regulations, consists of 27 parts. The topics are written in a unsophisticated and understandable language.

POA conducted a study to examine the impact of the adoption of LME's FRS on the financial statements of enterprises in 2020. In the study, the effects of LME's FRS on retained earnings, total equities and net income according to the previous financial reporting framework were examined. Although there are 2663 enterprises that adopted to LME's FRS, due to lack of data, 1,775 companies in retained earnings, 2,004 companies in total equities and 277 companies in net income were examined. The effects of the adoption are shown in Tab. 12.1.

Accordingly, while the retained earnings in 43.55 % of the enterprises increased, decreased in 56.45 %. It has been determined that with the transition to LME's FRS, a statistically significant decrease by 2.62 % occurred in the retained earnings compared to the previous financial reporting framework.

Then the total equities in 43.55 % of the enterprises increased, decreased in 56.45 %. When the total equities are examined, an increase was observed in 42.32 % of the enterprises and a decrease in 57.68 %. With the transition to LME's FRS, a statistically significant increase of 6.61 % has been detected in the total equities compared to the previous financial reporting framework. Finally, when the net income are examined, an increase was observed in 42.96 % of the enterprises and a decrease in 57.04 %. With the transition to LME's FRS, although there is a 1.31 % decrease in the net income compared to the previous financial reporting framework, it is not a statistically significant difference at 5 % significance level (POA LME's FRS Report, 2020).

The adoption of LME's FRS has created changes in the accounting practices of enterprises. This situation has brought about changes in financial reports and thus financial ratios. It is thought that the effect created by these new standards implemented since 01/01/2018 is mostly based on formal changes, and the economic impact of transition to LME's FRS enterprises can be revealed more clearly in the long term.

3.2.2 Draft Chart of Accounts in Compliance with Financial Reporting Standards

Enterprises in Turkey since 1994, uses the uniform chart of accounts in accounting procedures consistent with the national accounting system and tax laws. However, this chart of accounts falls short of meeting the needs of companies with the adoption of IFRS. Therefore, POA published a draft chart of accounts compliant with IFRS on 26/12/2018 and submitted it to the public opinion.

POA updated the chart of accounts and harmonized the current chart of accounts with IFRS. With this update, the following elements have been added to the draft:

- Financial investments and derivative financial instruments
- Financial assets and liabilities from construction, project or service contracts
- Biological assets and related gains and losses
- Fixed assets and liabilities classified for sale
- Investment properties and related income and expenses
- Deferred tax related to assets and liabilities
- The effect of mergers involving companies subject to joint control
- Accumulated income and expenses in total equities
- Income and expenses related to discontinued operations and taxes related to these income and expenses

Tab. 12.2: Enterprises Size Criteria According to SME's FRS

	EU Directive 2013/34 - Size Criteria	
	Micro Enterprises	**Small Enterprises**
Total Assets	< 350.000 Euro	< 4.000.000 Euro
Sales/Revenue	< 700.000 Euro	< 8.000.000 Euro
Number of Employees	< 10	< 50

Source: (www.kgk.gov.tr)

With the entry into force of this draft prepared by the POA, the inadequacy of the current application will disappear, and the financial statements to be prepared by the enterprises will become more understandable and comparable, compatible with IFRS.

With the draft chart of accounts becoming mandatory for all companies in the economy, the adoption of IFRS will be easier for companies that have not yet implemented IFRS.

3.2.3 SME's FRS

Small and micro enterprises are an important part of Turkish economy. SME's apply national accounting system and tax laws. POA has prepared accounting standards in line with international standards for small and micro enterprises in order to spread standardization throughout the economy and to increase the competitiveness of Turkish companies in international markets. SME's FRS was published as a draft in 12/07/2019. The standard text consists of 22 chapters and 105 pages. Standard has been prepared taking into consideration the current accounting system in Turkey. While it is in line with IFRS provisions, it offers a simpler and more applicable financial reporting framework.

The classification made by POA for small and micro enterprises according to the scales in the EU criteria is shown in Tab. 12.2. Accordingly, the enterprises that meet two of the following criteria are defined as small enterprises and the others as micro enterprises.

These standards enacted, almost all of the enterprises involved in Turkey's economy, will make financial reporting in conformity with IFRS. This will reduce the difficulties faced by SME in obtaining low cost funds. With the SME's FRS, standardization continues expanding day by day in Turkey.

4 Conclusion

In Turkey, IFRS became mandatory in public companies in 2005, within the framework of the standardization studies that continue simultaneously with the world practices.As of 2018, LME's FRS has been implemented for large and medium-sized enterprises that are subject to independent audit and not traded in Borsa Istanbul. For small and micro enterprises, the draft SME's FRS was published in 2019. With this standard, it is aimed to spread financial reporting in compliance with IFRS.

Studies in the literature show that, the mandatory transition to IFRS in 2005, the financial performances of the enterprises have been positively affected, especially the liquidity and activity ratios have increased. In addition, the quality of accounting recording and financial analysis has increased. The economic impact of the transition to LME's FRS and SME's FRS is also considered to be positive in the long-term.

Adoption of IFRS brings along a new accounting process. Fast adaptation to this new mechanism will accelerate the positive effects of the adoption. For this reason, IFRS training for accountants is still continuing both in universities and professional associations. However tax laws in Turkey is enforcing financial reporting duality. Therefore, certain regulations are needed in tax laws for full adoption of IFRS.

As a result, Turkey is closely following developments in the world in terms of standardization. It is thought that most of the enterprises operating in the country will prepare financial statements compatible with IFRS with the standard sets published recently.

Bibliography

Abdioğlu, H., & Büyükşalvarci, A. (2011). Ufrs Uygulamasinin Hisse Senedi Getirileri Üzerine Etkisi: İmkb Şirketleri Üzerine Ampirik Bir Uygulama. *World of IFRS Dergisi*, *10*(2), 1–13.

Ağca, A., & Aktaş, R. (2007). First Time Application of IFRS and Its Impact on Financial Ratios: A Study on Turkish Listed Firms. *Problems and Perspectives in Management*, *5*(2), 99–112.

Akdoğan, N., & Aydın, H. (1987). *Muhasebe Teorileri*. Ankara: Gazi Üniversitesi Yayın No:98.

Akgün, A. İ. (2013). Uluslararası Finansal Raporlama Standartlarının Finansal Analize Etkisi: İMKB'ye Yönelik Bir Araştırma. *Doğuş Üniversitesi Dergisi*, *14*(1), 10–26.

Alkan, G. D., & Doğan, O. (2012). Uluslararası Finansal Raporlama Standartları'nın Finansal Rasyolara Kısa ve Uzun Dönemli Etkileri: İMKB'de Bir Araştırma. *Muhasebe ve Finansman Dergisi*, (54), 87–100.

Atmaca, M., & Çelenk, H. (2011). Uluslararası Muhasebe ve Finansal Raporlama Standartlarının Finansal Analize Etkilerinin Regresyon Analizi İle Ölçülmesine Yönelik Bir Araştırma. *Journal of Accounting & Finance*, (49), 113–125.

Aygün, D., Alpaslan, A., Aslan, Ö., & Çalık, A. (2016). Uluslararasi Finansal Raporlama Standartlarinin Finansal Oranlar Üzerindeki Etkisi: Borsa İstanbul Üzerine Bir İnceleme. *Yüzüncü Yıl Üniversitesi İktisadi ve İdari Bilimler Fakültesi Dergisi*, (1), 126–139.

Cengiz, H. (2014). Effects of International Financial Reporting Standards Application on Financial Ratios in Turkey. *Uluslararası Yönetim İktisat ve İşletme Dergisi*, *10*(21), 163–177.

Güvemli, O. (2000). *Muhasebe Tarihi*. I.Cilt, İstanbul: Süryay Yayınları.

IFRS Foundation. (2018). *Annual Report*. Retrieved from https://www.ifrs.org/news-and-events/2019/05/ifrs-foundation-publishes-2018-annual-report/

POA. (2019). *Küçük ve Mikro İşletmeler İçin Finansal Raporlama Standardı Taslağı*. Retrieved from https://www.kgk.gov.tr.

POA LME's FRS Report. (2020). *BOBİ FRS'nin İlk Geçiş Yılına İlişkin Uygulama Sonuçları*. Retrieved from https://www.kgk.gov.tr/Portalv2Uploads/files/Duyurular/v2/Diger/BOB%C4%B0%20FRS%20UYGULAMA%20SONU%C3%87LARI13_05_2020.pdf.

Sultanoğlu, B. (2016). Borsa İstanbul Şirketlerinde UFRS Etkisi: Finansal Bilginin İhtiyaca Uygunluğu. *World Of Accounting Science*, *18*(2), 369–391.

Terzi, S., Oktem, R., & Şen, İ. K. (2013). Impact of Adopting International Financial Reporting Standards: Empirical Evidence From Turkey. *International Business Research*, *6*(4), 55–66.

Terzi, S., Şen, İ. K., & Üçoğlu, D. (2013). Uluslararası Finansal Raporlama Standartlarına Geçişin Etkilerinin Sermayenin Korunması Açısından Değerlendirilmesi: İstanbul Menkul Kıymetler Borsasında Bir Araştırma. *Muhasebe Bilim Dünyası Dergisi*, *3*, 1–17.

Turel, A. (2009). The Value Relevance of IFRS: The Case of Turkey. *Œconomica*, *5*(1), 119–128.

Uçma, T. (2012). Türkiye'deki Muhasebe Sisteminin Gelişiminin Kurumsal Teori Çerçevesinde Açıklanması. *Muhasebe ve Finans Tarihi Araştırmaları Dergisi*, (2), 145–178.

Aslihan Yavuzalp Marangoz

Entrepreneurial Marketing for a Competitive Advantage

Abstract Companies need to implement strategies other than traditional methods to survive and grow in an intensive competitive environment. Small companies need this more than the big ones because of their lack of resources. They should find a way to achieve more effective strategies with fewer resources. Small companies can use entrepreneurial marketing not only because of their limited resources but also to survive in intensively competitive and changing market environment.

Understanding the importance of the interaction between entrepreneurship and marketing has led to the term entrepreneurial marketing. Entrepreneurial marketing refers the marketing activities with an entrepreneurial perspective. It focuses on proactiveness, innovations, market creation, customer and uses various marketing methods to achieve goals. Recognizing the role and importance of entrepreneurial marketing enables small and medium- size companies to increase their performance and gain a competitive advantage

This chapter examines entrepreneurial marketing theoretically. The purpose of the study is to explain entrepreneurial marketing concepts. Entrepreneurship and marketing are defined, the relationship between these two concepts are explained. Definition, importance, development, dimensions, benefits, types, the process of entrepreneurial marketing and its differences between traditional marketing are identified.

Keywords: Entrepreneurial Marketing, Competitive Advantage, Entrepreneurship

1 Introduction

Companies need to implement strategies other than traditional methods to survive and grow in an intensive competitive environment. Small companies need this more than the big ones because of their lack of resources. Academicians and practitioners both accept that small companies' marketing strategy differ from the big companies (Sole, 2013: 23). So they should find a way to achieve more effective strategies with fewer resources. Small companies can use entrepreneurial marketing not only because of their limited resources but also to survive in intensively competitive and changing market environment (Tekin, 2018: 18).

Understanding the importance of the interaction between entrepreneurship and marketing has led to the term entrepreneurial marketing (Jones & Rowley, 2011: 26). Entrepreneurship and marketing are two different disciplines and especially for small businesses are useful to apply both disciplines principles' to be successful in competitive markets. In this context "entrepreneurial marketing" concept emerged in marketing literature.

Entrepreneurship is the area that consists of opportunities and the process of finding, evaluating and using the opportunities and the people who can manage the process (Shane & Venkataraman, 2000: 218). Marketing is briefly the set of activities of creating value for customers, companies and society (https://www.ama.org/the-definition-of-marketing-what-is-marketing/). And entrepreneurial marketing is a unique research field that combines the information about marketing and entrepreneurship (Tekin, 2018: 16). Marketing and entrepreneurship have key fields of interface. These are; focused on change, opportunity searching and innovativeness (Collinson & Shaw, 2001: 761).

Companies can have a competitive advantage if their consumers perceive that the company presents them with the highest value in the market (Miles & Darroch, 2004: 485). That's why applying entrepreneurial marketing dimensions enables companies to have the advantage.

Recognizing the role and importance of entrepreneurial marketing enables small and medium- size companies to increase their performance and gain a competitive advantage (Azizağaoğlu, 2019: 286).

This chapter examines entrepreneurial marketing theoretically. The purpose of the study is to explain entrepreneurial marketing concepts. Entrepreneurship and marketing are defined, the relationship between these two concepts are explained. Definition, importance, development, dimensions, benefits, types, the process of entrepreneurial marketing and its differences between traditional marketing are identified.

2 Entrepreneurial Marketing Concept

The entrepreneurial marketing concept was occurred in 1982 at a conference. The first empirical research was in 1985, the first research symposium made in 1986, the first article was published in 1987 and the first book was published in 1995. Then articles, books, researches and special issues of journals publications have been going for three decades (Hills, Hultman & Miles, 2008: 103–104).

Entrepreneurial marketing is defined as *proactive identification and exploitation of opportunities for acquiring and retaining profitable customers through innovative approaches to risk management, resource leveraging and value creation* (Morris, Schindehutte & LaForge, 2002: 5). It refers the marketing activities with an entrepreneurial perspective regardless of firm characteristics such as age, size (Kraus, Harms & Fink, 2010:2).

Benefits of entrepreneurial marketing increases in sales and market share, strong company, rising income, prestige, better life standards (Becherer, Helms & McDonald, 2012: 3). With the strategies of entrepreneurial marketing companies can reach more customers and with effective, innovative and value creative methods they can increase their performance and become stronger and more profitable. Entrepreneurial marketing focuses on proactiveness, innovations, market creation, customer and uses various marketing methods to achieve them (Whalen et al., 2016: 8).

3 Entrepreneurial Marketing vs Traditional Marketing

Entrepreneurial marketing and traditional marketing differ in many ways. The table below classifies them. Tab. 13.1 classifies them.

In another study, Stokes (2000) compared the entrepreneurial marketing process with traditional marketing concepts in terms of concept, strategy, methods and market intelligence.

- **Concept**: Traditional marketing is consumer-oriented where entrepreneurial marketing is innovation-oriented.
- **Strategy:** Traditional marketing strategy based on top-down segmentation, targeting, and positioning. In this strategy companies first segment the market according to variables than select the right segment and position their products or services. In entrepreneurial marketing bottom-up strategy is used. Entrepreneurs identify market opportunities, learn target customers' needs and wants than they look for the same profile to expand their markets.
- **Methods:** In traditional marketing mix is used for developing strategy but entrepreneurial marketing uses more interactive methods such as Word- of-mouth marketing (WOMM). The term WOMM refers to the informal communication method between individuals about their evaluations of products or services (Anderson, 1998: 6).
- **Market Intelligence:** Traditional marketing **uses known** research and intelligence systems but informal networking and information gathering are used in entrepreneurial marketing (Stokes, 2000: 7–13).

Tab. 13.1: Comparison of Entrepreneurial Marketing and Traditional Marketing

TRADITIONAL MARKETING	ENTRPRENEURIAL MARKETING
• Basicly reactive behavior to external environment	• - Firms try to effect or redefine external environment
• Marketing attempts to follow customers	• Marketing attempts to guide customers
• Serving current markets	• Creating new markets
• Focuses to manage effective marketing mix	• Focuses to create value for customer relations, resource management and marketing mix
• Tries to minimize the risk	• Tries to manage in calculated risk
• Marketing as an objective, dispassionate science	• With the acknowledging value of science and learning, recognition is given to the roles of passion and commitment in marketing programs
• Trust the proven formulas and rules	• Challenges to common supposition
• Marketing supports the innovation efforts of other functional areas of the firm, mostly R&D	• Marketing is the home of the entrepreneurial process in the organization
• Marketing as a functional silo	• Marketing as a interdisciplinary and interfunctional pursuit
• Most attention is for promotion and customer communication	• The relative investment or resources in different areas of the marketing mix is context specific
• Scarcity mentality	• Opportunity is pursued regardless, or resource controlled; resource leveraging
• Dependency on survey research	• Skeptical use of conventional research
• Marketing facilitates transactions and control	• Marketing facilitates speed, change, adaptability, agility

Source: Adapted from Morris, M. H., Schindehutte, M., & LaForge, R. W. (2001, August). The emergence of entrepreneurial marketing: Nature and meaning. In *15th Annual UIC Research Symposium on Marketing and Entrepreneurship*

4 Dimensions of Entrepreneurial Marketing

Morris et al. suggest seven dimensions for entrepreneurial marketing (Morris, Schindehutte & LaForge, 2002). Four of them (proactiveness, risk- taking, innovativeness and opportunity focus) are the dimensions of entrepreneurship. The others are resource leveraging, customer-driven and value-creating.

- **Proactiveness:** Proactiveness is a perspective to having the insight to see future demand and to shape the environment (Lumpkin & Dess, 2001: 433).

This refers to the behaviors of taking action to satisfy unnoticed potential needs and finding new market or new competition area (Bulut, 2007).

- **Opportunity-focus:** Being opportunity-focused refers to unnoticed and unexplored market or market position (Marangoz & Erboy, 2013: 82) and finding opportunity is one of the basic characteristics of entrepreneurship so it is the basis dimension for entrepreneurial marketing (Morris, Schindehutte & LaForge, 2002: 6).
- **Calculated risk taking:** Risk-taking is a characteristic of entrepreneurship. Calculated risk- taking means obvious efforts to evaluate risk factors and diminish them (Morris, Schindehutte & LaForge, 2002: 7). Entrepreneurs get into new markets and new processes. In risk- taking company uses its resources for projects that its results are unknown (Wiklund & Shepherd, 2005: 75).
- **Innovativeness:** Refers to a firm's tendency to engage in and support new ideas, experiments, and processes that result in new products, services, or technological processes (Lumpkin & Dess 1996: 142). Innovativeness is also an indicator of the financial performance of firms and it enables firms to focus on a new market, new product, or new process (Dal & Dal, 2016: 56).
- **Customer intensity:** Entrepreneurial marketing uses an innovative approach for current customer relations to create new customers or new markets (Azizağaoğlu, 2019: 279) and develops creative approaches for customer retention (Özbölük, 2018: 229).
- **Resource leveraging:** Refers to doing best with low resources. Entrepreneurial marketers can extend the resources that no one did before, can realize new uses of resources, can use others' resources, can combine resources (Morris, Schindehutte & LaForge, 2002: 7–8).
- **Value creation:** The need to offer something to customers and stakeholders more valuable than competitors offer. Companies can increase benefits or decrease costs to achieve (Miles & Darroch, 2004: 494). One of the most important competitive advantage tools of a firm is the process that they take to create competitive customer value in intensive competitive markets (Demir, 2016: 2).

5 Entrepreneurial Marketing Process

Stokes categorized the entrepreneurial marketing process into four stages. He suggests the process starts with entrepreneurs' attention to innovations first in products & services and then in customer issues. In the second stage named

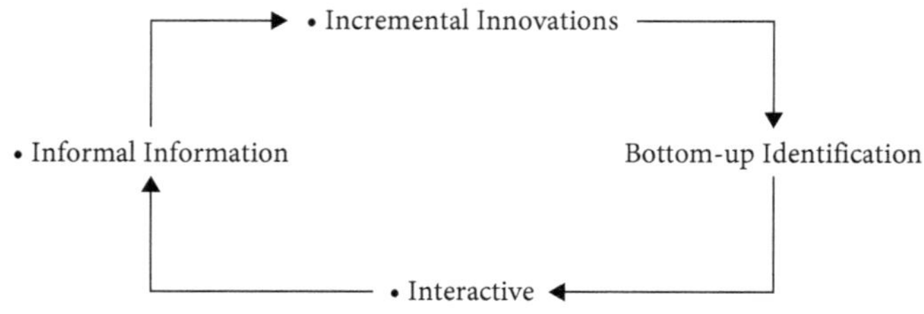

Fig. 13.1: Entrepreneurial Marketing Processes

Source: Stokes, D. (2000a). Entrepreneurial marketing: a conceptualisation from qualitative research. *Qualitative market research: an international journal.*:52.

identification, entrepreneurs identify customers with a bottom-up process of elimination. In the third stage, entrepreneurs communicate to customers in interactive ways such as word of mouth marketing. In the last stage informal information, entrepreneurs collect customers' data from informal networks of the market instead of traditional market research (Stoke, 2000a: 52–53). Figure 13.1 shows the stages.

6 Types of Entrepreneurial Marketing

Different types of entrepreneurial marketing mentioned in the literature such as guerrilla marketing, buzz marketing, viral marketing (Morris, Schindehutte & LaForge, 2002: 3; Kraus, Harms & Fink, 2010: 11; Hisrich & Ramadani, 2017: 92–95) with effective techniques differ from traditional marketing.

- **Guerrilla marketing** is considered as an ancestor of entrepreneurial marketing (Levinson, 1984; Ladokun, 2019: 18). American Marketing Association defines its creative and unique marketing strategy aims maximum results using minimum resources. Guerrilla marketing is, surprising and efficient (Szabo, 2011: 6). So it can achieve its aim with small, attractive, and low-cost actions. Guerrilla marketing strategies are related to promotion more than the other marketing activities.
    - According to Levinson (1993) these are some important principles of guerrilla marketing:
    - Guerrilla marketing provides publicity to small companies easily more than big ones
    - Guerilla marketing is primarily based on human psychology

- o The main requirements for Guerrilla marketing are energy, and imagination more than money.
- o Profit is the primary statistics in guerilla marketing not the sales.
- o Technology is used as a tool to enable a business.
- o Using alternative resources like channels and media.

- **Buzz marketing:** Buzz marketing is a kind of entrepreneurial marketing spreading information about an activity to consumers' surprising and noteworthy way (Hisrich & Ramadani, 2017: 94). It is a communication process between message sender and receiver in online and offline dialogs (Ahuja et al., 2007: 151). Basic principles of buzz marketing are being focused on consumers, choosing the right target, innovation, finding the right message and environment, and implementing word-of-mouth campaigns, and keeping the interest of consumers alive (Taran, 2012: 163–164).
- **Viral marketing:** Viral marketing is the diffusion of product information and its acceptance via the network (Leskovec, Adamic, & Huberman, 2008: 4). It is a new form of entrepreneurial marketing that is closely related to internet development. It involves information transfer between people over the internet (Hisrich & Ramadani, 2017: 95). The elements of viral marketing are enabling transfer to others with lower effort, scaling easily, benefiting from other resources, take advantage of common human motivations (Wilson, 2000: 2).

  It is easy, quick, spreads like a virus, and effective (Morris, Schindehutte & LaForge, 2002: 34).

7 Success in Entrepreneurial Marketing

There are suggested areas for excellence in entrepreneurial marketing. These are (Bjerke & Hultman, 2004: 209–229):

- Entrepreneurs that want to be successful in changing and the intensively competitive area should learn value-creating processes. They should have recognizing and mastering capability important processes and continue it.
- Finding the best resources available for value-creating is another important issue. These resources can be the entrepreneur's abilities, human resources of the firm, or external resources such as technology or cooperation with other firms.
- Enabling vision for the value-creating and managing it. Financial decisions, customer, internal factors, and process issues perspectives can help to

achieve this. The vision should be clear to be understood by both internal and external participants.

- Entrepreneurship -because of its nature- can change the current market's rules. By innovations and true combinations, entrepreneurs can achieve better performance at lower prices than the market situations.
- Leading is also a critical topic in the success of entrepreneurial marketing as managing. Researchers notice that it is important to balance and decide timing to give priority to one of them.
- Being better than consumers' expectations in sales issues such as sales drivers and sale elements.
- Balancing the marketing strategy. Balancing should be done related to the situation, aims, and circumstances. Transactional and relationship marketing and also balancing tangible and intangible elements should be used according to requirements.

8 Conclusion

Competitiveness and consumers' changing need and wants force companies to implement different and effective strategies. Traditional ways may sometimes be insufficient. The concept of "entrepreneurial marketing" is emerged from this perspective. Combining the marketing methods and entrepreneurial perspective enables companies to develop innovative, market, and consumer-focused and value creation strategies.

Entrepreneurial marketing briefly differs from traditional marketing as being more innovative and proactive. It is more customer-focused and focuses on creating value for customers and establish a strong relationship between them. Entrepreneurial marketing has a risk-taking perspective as entrepreneurship. Aims to change the company's environment. And finally, entrepreneurial marketing uses more interactive communication methods than traditional ways.

As mentioned before in the study, entrepreneurial marketing has seven dimensions such as proactiveness, risk-taking, innovativeness, and opportunity focus -like entrepreneurship- and resource leveraging, customer-driven, and value-creating.

To summarize proactiveness refers to foresight the opportunities or changes in a market and take action. Risk-taking means in entrepreneurial marketing to identify risk factors, take them if it's necessary for the potential benefit and try to minimize them.

Being opportunity-focused is one of the main components for entrepreneurship and in entrepreneurial marketing, it refers to evaluate the environment and to explore undiscovered opportunities.

Using resources is the other important dimension of entrepreneurial marketing. Finding the unknown resources, combining them with the current resources or other's resources would be beneficial for companies.

Customer-driven refers to be sensitive to market conditions, consumers' changing needs and expectations. Value creating is offering benefits to consumers more than competitors. This is a crucial success factor to survive in the markets and establish strong and profitable relations with consumers

All these dimensions and characteristics of entrepreneurial marketing provide a competitive advantage. The basic argument of entrepreneurial marketing is gaining a sustainable competitive advantage with innovation and value-creating (Morris, Schindehutte, & LaForge, 2002: 6). And directly and indirectly entrepreneurial marketing increase the sales and company's firm and brings in more income, prestige, stronger company with better performance. To achieve these companies are recommended to create a vision, find the value creation processes and resources to present innovative, effective, and market-driven strategies.

Bibliography

Ahuja, R. D., Michels, T. A., Walker, M. M., & Weissbuch, M. (2007). Teen perceptions of disclosure in buzz marketing. *Journal of Consumer Marketing, 24*(3), 151–159.

Anderson, E. W. (1998). Customer satisfaction and word of mouth. *Journal of Service Research, 1*(1), 5–17.

Azizağaoğlu, A. (2019). Girişimci Pazarlama: Pazarlamaya Proaktif ve İnovatif Bir Yaklaşım. *Uluslararası Yönetim İktisat ve İşletme Dergisi, 15*(1), 276–288.

Becherer, R. C., Helms, M. M., & McDonald, J. P. (2012). The effect of entrepreneurial marketing on outcome goals in SMEs. *New England Journal of Entrepreneurship, 15*(1), 7–18.

Bjerke, B., & Hultman, C. (2004). *Entrepreneurial marketing: The growth of small firms in the new economic era.* Edward Elgar Publishing, Cheltenham.

Bulut, Ç. (2007). *Stratejik oryantasyonlar ve firma performansı.* Yayınlanmamış Doktora Tezi. Gebze Yüksek Teknoloji Enstitüsü, Kocaeli.

Bulut, Ç., Pınar, İ., Halaç, S. D., & Öztürk, A. D. (2013). Girişimsel pazarlamanın firma performansına etkisi. *Dokuz Eylül Üniversitesi Sosyal Bilimler Enstitüsü Dergisi, 15*(2), 209–232.

Collinson, E., & Shaw, E. (2001). Entrepreneurial marketing-a historical perspective on development and practice. *Management Decision*, *39*(9), 761–766.

Dal, N., & Dal, V. (2016). Girişimci Pazarlama: Kavramsal Bir Çalışma-Entrepreneurial Marketing: A Conceptual Study. *Mehmet Akif Ersoy Üniversitesi Sosyal Bilimler Enstitüsü Dergisi*, *8*(14), 42–63.

Demir, D. (2016). Değer Kavramı ve Lojistik Hizmetlerinin Müşteride Yarattığı Değer. *Journal of Current Researches on Business and Economics*, *6*(2), 1–28.

Hills, G. E., Hultman, C. M., & Miles, M. P. (2008). The evolution and development of entrepreneurial marketing. *Journal of Small Business Management*, *46*(1), 99–112.

Hisrich, R. D., & Ramadani, V. (2017). Entrepreneurial marketing mix. In *Effective Entrepreneurial Management* (pp. 75–99). Cham: Springer.

Jones, R., & Rowley, J. (2011). Entrepreneurial marketing in small businesses: A conceptual exploration. *International Small Business Journal*, *29*(1), 25–36.

Kraus, S., Harms, R., & Fink, M. (2010). Entrepreneurial marketing: Moving beyond marketing in new ventures. *International Journal of Entrepreneurship and Innovation Management*, *11*(1), 19–34.

Ladokun, I. O. (2019). Entrepreneurial marketing and performance of medium size hotel businesses in Ibadan, Nigeria. *African Research Review*, *13*(3), 15–26.

Leskovec, J., Adamic, L. A., & Huberman, B. A. (2008). The dynamics of viral marketing. *ACM Transactions on the Web (TWEB)*, *1*(1), 5-es.

Levinson, J.C. (1984). *Guerilla Marketing: How to Make Big Profits in Your Small Business*. 1st Edn., Houghton Mifflin, Boston.

Levinson, J. C. (1993). *Guerrilla marketing excellence: The 50 golden rules for small-business success*. Houghton Mifflin Harcourt, Boston.

Lumpkin, G. T., & Dess, G. G. (1996). Clarifying the entrepreneurial orientation construct and linking it to performance. *Academy of Management Review*, *21*(1), 135–172.

Lumpkin, G. T., & Dess, G. G. (2001). Linking two dimensions of entrepreneurial orientation to firm performance: The moderating role of environment and industry life cycle. *Journal of Business Venturing*, *16*(5), 429–451.

Marangoz, M., & Erboy, N. (2013). Pazarlamada Paradigma Değişimi: Girişimci Pazarlama. *Muğla Sıtkı Koçman Üniversitesi İktisadi ve İdari Bilimler Fakültesi Ekonomi ve Yönetim Araştırmaları Dergisi*, *2*(1), 67–91.

Miles, M. P., & Darroch, J. (2004). Large firms, entrepreneurial marketing processes, and the cycle of competitive advantage. *European Journal of Marketing*, 40(5/6), 485–501.

Morris, M. H., Schindehutte, M., & LaForge, R. W. (2002). Entrepreneurial marketing: A construct for integrating emerging entrepreneurship and marketing perspectives. *Journal of Marketing Theory and Practice, 10*(4), 1–19.

Morrish, S. C. (2011). Entrepreneurial marketing: A strategy for the twenty-first century?. *Journal of Research in Marketing and Entrepreneurship, 13*(2), 110–119.

Morrish, S. C., Miles, M. P., & Deacon, J. H. (2010). Entrepreneurial marketing: Acknowledging the entrepreneur and customer-centric interrelationship. *Journal of Strategic Marketing, 18*(4), 303–316.

Özbölük, T. (2018). Dijital Çağda Girişimci Pazarlama. *Turkish Journal of Marketing, 3*(3), 223–237.

Shane, S., & Venkataraman, S. (2000). The promise of entrepreneurship as a field of research. *Academy of Management Review, 25*(1), 217–226.

Solé, M. (2013). Entrepreneurial marketing: Conceptual exploration and link to performance. *Journal of Research in Marketing and Entrepreneurship,15*(1), 23–38.

Stokes, D. (2000a). Entrepreneurial marketing: A conceptualisation from qualitative research. *Qualitative Market Research: An International Journal, 3*(1), 47–54

Stokes, D. (2000b). Putting entrepreneurship into marketing: The processes of entrepreneurial marketing. *Journal of Research in Marketing and Entrepreneurship, 2*(1), 1–16.

Szabo, R. Z., Hortovanyi, L., Tarody, D. F., Ferincz, A., & Dobak, M. (2011). The role of knowledge in entrepreneurial marketing. *International Journal of Entrepreneurial Venturing, 3*(2), 149–167.

Taran, Z. (2012). The Seven Principles of WOM and Buzz Marketing: Crossing the Tipping Point. *Journal of Consumer Marketing, 29*(2), 163–164.

Tekin, D. (2018). Tekno-girişimlerde girişimci pazarlama, girişimcilik eğilimi ve işletme performansı ilişkisi. (Yayımlanmamış Doktora Tezi). Anadolu University, Eskişehir.

Whalen, P., Uslay, C., Pascal, V. J., Omura, G., McAuley, A., Kasouf, C. J.,. . . & Gilmore, A. (2016). Anatomy of competitive advantage: Towards a contingency theory of entrepreneurial marketing. *Journal of Strategic Marketing, 24*(1), 5–19.

Wiklund, J., & Shepherd, D. (2005). Entrepreneurial orientation and small business performance: A configurational approach. *Journal of Business Venturing, 20*(1), 71–91.

Wilson, R. F. (2000). The six simple principles of viral marketing. *Web Marketing Today, 70*(1), 232.

Zuhal Cilingir Uk and Gamze Kayan

Transition to Multi-sensory Strategies: Sensory Branding

Abstract The senses, not only have a vital role in understanding the outside world, but also have a great influence on consumer decisions. Marketers who understand the effect of senses on consumers frequently use sensory branding approach for reasons, such as strengthening their brands, providing competitive advantage, providing consumers with unique brand experience, brand image, satisfaction and awareness. Sensory branding is based on the idea of using the right combination of five senses in establishing an emotional bond between the consumer and the brand. The aim of this chapter is to theoretically explain sensory branding, described by sensory perception and stimuli. In accordance with this aim, sensory branding with system approach is considered as a flow. Firstly, the concept of branding is described and sense expressions, which are the inputs of the process (sight, sound, taste, smell, touch), are explained with examples. Secondly, the process of sensory branding is introduced. Finally, the results of sensory branding process are mentioned.

Keywords: Brand, Sensory Branding, Senses, Process of Sensory Branding, Outcomes of Sensory Branding

1 Introduction

Marketing strategies are evolving day by day according to changing consumer preferences. Sensory turn-ons are tried to be found by examining consumer behavior more with sensory marketing. Sensory branding, which may prefer five-dimensional communication rather than two-dimensional communication, removes the shortcomings of traditional branding, helping brands to become permanent in the minds of consumers, to be positioned and to achieve consumer satisfaction. When consumers are affected by sensory stimuli, their relationships with the brand are strengthened and their loyalty to the brand strengthens (Suhonen & Tengvall, 2009).

While sensory branding strategies are frequently used in packaged and unpackaged products in the retail sector (Asioli et al., 2011; Ustaahmetoglu, 2015; Gulmez, 2017; Pentz & Gerber, 2013) brands in the subject service sector and retail merchandising areas (Acevedo & Fairbanks, 2017) also uses these strategies. Even, these strategies are now used in the creation process of a destination image (Dițoiu et al., 2014).

In this section, firstly the concept of sensory branding and its purposes will be mentioned. The sensory systems, senses and sensory expressions that are the subject of sensory branding will be explained with examples, the steps that businesses should follow in sensory branding activities will be described and the results of sensory branding will be mentioned.

2 Sensory Branding

Sensory branding is one of the modern marketing approaches that have long been used in various industries. Each of the senses has the power to change simple or important decisions. For this reason, businesses that want to establish stronger bonds with customers are increasingly using stimulants such as scent, music or texture (Yozukmaz & Topaloglu, 2016; Boyle-Brayfield, 2008). The basis of sensory branding is to establish an emotional bond between the consumer and the brand with the right combination of five senses.

Fig. 14.1 reflects the flow of sensory branding considered in the context of the system approach. How the five sensory stimuli are directed to consumers and what sensual experiences consumers encounter (Hulten, Broweus & Dijk, 2009). In other words, sensors are the inputs of the system; the stages that brands will follow in their sensory branding activities are the process of the system and will be explained below.

Sensory branding activities cause a large number of outputs. On the other hand, the highlights of these; brand identity (Cakır, 2010; Hulten, 2011), brand image (Hulten, 2011), brand loyalty (Slatten, Mehmetoglu, Svensson & Svaeri, 2009), brand experience (Agapito, Pinto & Mendes, 2012; Pentz & Gerber, 2013), brand choice (Liegeois & Rivera, 2011; Ustaahmetoglu, 2015), brand equity (Hepola et al., 2017) and brand awareness (Kaplan, 2015; Malhotra et al., 2013; Huang et al., 2015). The aims of sensory branding can be ordered as emotional engagement, an optimized match between perception and reality, creation of a brand platform for product extensions and having a trademark (Lindstrom, 2005).

3 Senses

Although the senses are simply experiences that come together with stimuli in the psychological sense, they contain a biologically complex process (Atkinson et al., 2008). Each of the five senses are elements that help connecting us to the outside world. While sometimes the senses are the guides of our mind,

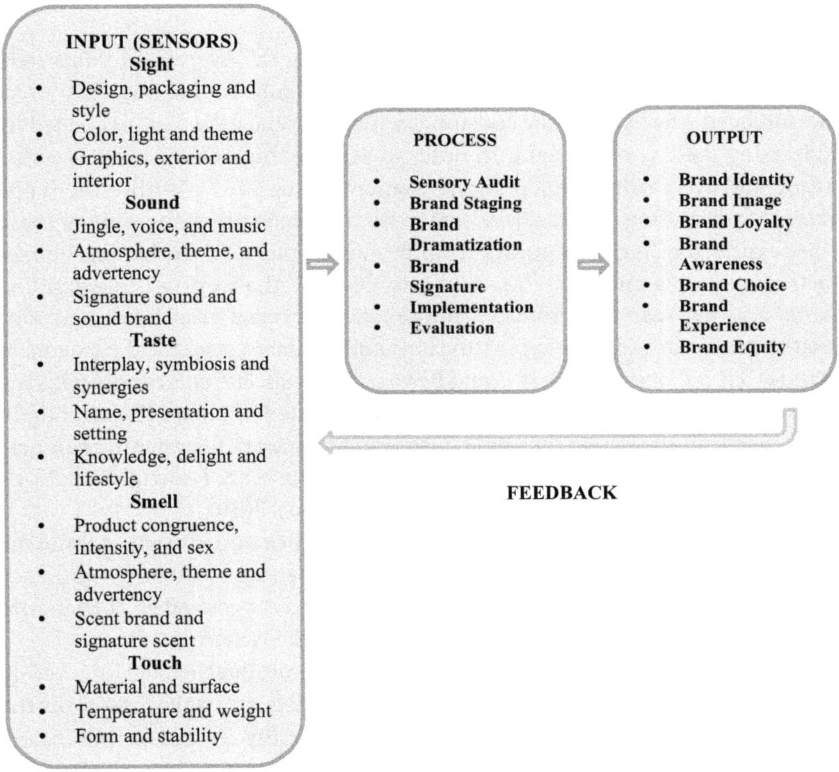

Fig. 14.1: Flow of Sensory Branding

Source: Hulten, Broweus & Dijk, 2009; Lindstrom, 2005

sometimes they can be stronger than our mind (Bati, 2012). By using sensory systems in the best way, marketers try to grab the attention of consumers and then convince them.

Sometimes the scent of a perfume we smell, sometimes a visible picture, a brand emblem, the music we hear, a fabric we touch can lead people to very different emotions (Koc, 2013). Kotler (1973) introduced the concept of atmospheric to explain the effect of environmental stimuli (sight, sound, smell, touch and taste) on purchasing decisions of consumers. In the continuation of the study, the sensors, sensations and sensory expressions that make up the input of sensory marking will be explained.

3.1 Sight

Our sense of sight is the most effective one among the five senses. Marketers primarily try to communicate with consumers visually. In this way, they affect the purchasing decision of the consumer with the brand associations created by addressing their sense of sight. In order to achieve this, brands need to create strong and eye-catching visual brand elements (Bati, 2012). Within the scope of sensory branding, brands have some visual sense expressions. One of these sense expressions is the corporation's or product's colors. Color that symbolizes abstract concepts and thoughts, serves to describe the world of imagination, wants and desires, and produces emotional and visual responses; it is also used to create the identities of institutions and the main structural elements of brands (Icli & Copur, 2008). It would be wrong to associate colors only with the sense of vision. Our five senses are sometimes affected by colors (Yuksekbilgili, 2017). According to researches sight, taste and touch work together in color perception, which is one of the sensory expressions (Simner & Ludwig, 2012; Koch & Koch, 2003; Huang & Lu, 2015; Zampini & Spence, 2010).

Another sense of sight icon is the logo. Well-designed logos should be easily recognized by consumers, have the same meaning by all target audience members, and evoke positive emotions in the mind. Logos reflect the identity and value of the institutions and brands (Odabasi & Oyman, 2013).

Today, packaging has a great importance in product-related marketing processes (Mucuk, 2010). The packaging, which acts as a salesperson on the shelf, is an effective element in consumers, especially in instant purchases, as well as design, color and design. Considering the factors, it contributes to strengthening the brand image (Tek & Ozgul, 2010; Kotler & Keller, 2018).

Typography can be expressed as a whole of letters, numbers, symbols, and punctuation marks that are designed for certain purposes and have similar distinctive designs. Words gain meaning or become ineffective depending on the letter characters they are written in (Bog, 2019). Typography integrated with brands' products make it easier to perceive and remember products.

3.2 Sound

Brands can create distinctive features by completely using sounds and they can convey information about their brands, products or services to their potential consumers (Eroglu, 2003). While voices help to increase the value of customers' customer experiences, they also function as an influential factor in the construction of brand identity in corporate context (Cakir, 2010). When it comes to sense of sound, the first examples of successful brands that come to mind are Nokia's ringing tone, Coca-Cola's opening sound and Intel's world-renowned opening music.

Sounds have an instant power to remind and activate emotions. It is very important that sounds are well designed and organized. Because the sound used by the brands not only engage the consumers but also shape their thoughts (Gobe, 2001). In sensory branding, although the sound sensor is widely used in advertising activities as commercial music, jingle and voice overs, and narrators, its scope is not limited to this. Music used to influence the purchasing decisions of customers, especially in store and service businesses, contributes to the atmosphere (Hulten, Broweus & Dijk, 2009).

The melodies and music chosen should be suitable for the brand and advertisements and unique to that brand in order to increase the brand's recall, reflect the brand identity and facilitate brand recognition (Bati, 2010). Jingles, which are a sense expression used in the sound sensor, are expressed as the transmission of the messages of the services or products offered by the brands to the consumer in the form of verbal music. Jingles are designed to become permanent easily in the consumer mind (Bindea et al., 2009).

3.3 Taste

Although the sense of taste remains in the background compared to the sense of sight and sound, it will provide great advantages for marketers to influence the consumer. Brands often have difficulties in using the sense of taste, but when applied correctly, they leave a lasting experience for consumers (Ilter, 2010). Branding the sense of taste is vital for companies in the food and beverage industry (Moser, 2007). In the literature, sensory marketing studies based on product categories in the food sector are frequently encountered (Ustaahmetoglu, 2015; Gulmez, 2017).

Cultural changes and differences are important factors in the perception of flavors. The sense of taste is a superior differentiation factor in the perception of some products. Being aware of this, businesses want to attract the attention of consumers by developing different flavors according to the types of their products (Akillibas, 2019). By using different flavors, consumers' brand experiences are expanded and brands can contribute to brand image and brand identity by taking advantage of the meanings attributed to certain flavors. For example, the taste of chocolate symbolizes lust and vanilla symbolizes stagnation as well (Post, 2004).

3.4 Smell

The sense of smell can be the main motivating factor in purchasing certain products. According to the researches, the products where the scent is most effective are soft drinks, body care products, dishwasher and washing machine detergents, skin care products, packaging, coffee, etc. such as many food products and cigarettes (Koc, 2013). Every person's perception of smell is different because many factors come into play behind the sense of smell. Age, race and gender can be cited as some of the influencing factors (Lindstrom, 2005; Liegeois & Rivera, 2011; Asioli et al., 2011).

The sensory expressions of the sense of smell are atmosphere and product fragrance. Atmospheric odor occurs only as part of the retail environment, not caused by the product. It can consist of artificial or natural fragrances. Consumer attitudes and behaviors are tried to be influenced by using atmospheric scent technologies. The compatibility of atmospheric scents with the product is associated with gender. While masculine scents are sometimes chosen to impress consumers; sometimes feminine scents are preferred (Hulten, Broweus, & Dijk, 2009).

3.5 Touch

The sense of touch provides many meanings to brands in terms of the values provided by the materials used in products and environmental designs. Features such as the quality of the products, price features, durability level, hardness and weight are conveyed to the consumer with the help of the sense of touch. In addition, the type of materials used in the products can give some ideas about the brand identity (Cakır, 2010). The sense of touch has an important place in consumer perception like the other four senses. The consumer first feels the need to touch the product in the purchasing process. Touch gives confidence to the consumer in the purchasing process.

Tactile stimuli that distinguish a brand from competitors are general design and shape, texture, temperature. Shape designs of products are of great importance in influencing consumer preferences and purchasing behavior (Moser, 2007). Peck (2010) divided touch into four categories in terms of consumer behavior. These are;

- Touch to purchase (by touching without additional information),
- Touch to obtain non-haptic product information (by controlling visual, olfactory, auditory and gustatory senses),

- Touch to obtain haptic product information (by controlling properties such as texture, hardness, weight, temperature)
- Hedonic touch (looking at qualities like sensory experience, entertainment).

4 Process of Sensory Branding

Lindstrom (2005) states that brands using sensory branding in their strategies follow a six-step process. Steps are followed intertwinedly to reveal sensory synergy. The sensory branding steps mentioned are as follows:

Sensory Audit: Sensory audit refers to the knowledge of all stages of the phase from the design of the brand to the presentation to the consumer. It contains information about the consistency and correctness of the senses to be applied to the brand.

Brand Staging: It is the stage that refers to following innovative approaches and activating the brand before the competitors.

Brand Dramatization: The brand dramatization is the stage in which brand personality is intertwined with sensory branding. At this stage, it is important to determine how much the senses play on the brand and to create a synergy between them.

Brand Signature: Brand signature is an expression that distinguishes the brand from its competitors. It can only be created when all sensory components are designed to create a complete sensory graph.

Implementation: It is the stage where a detailed implementation plan is developed for each affected department after a complete plan for sensory branding is prepared.

Evaluation: It expresses the continuity of the evaluation process, which is the last step of the sensory branding stage. It is important to measure the process in a controlled manner and to ensure its continuity.

5 Conclusion

Sensory branding is not a new concept, especially in the consumer goods industry. For years, brands have been working on their logos, jingles and other brand elements in order to gain new customers and create customer loyalty (Genunario, 2007). The important point in sensory branding is the effective use of the five senses together (Bati, 2012). In the traditional branding process, marketers often focused on functionality and the features of products or services and the rational benefit they provide. This process has changed with sensory branding (Hulten, 2011).

In this section, sensory branding has been evaluated as a flow. Sight, sound, taste, smell and touch senses are the inputs of the sensory marketing flow. It can be said that brands have four main purposes in performing sensory branding activities. These are emotional engagement (an optimized match between perception and reality), creation of a brand platform for product extensions, and trademark. In order to achieve these goals, businesses are expected to follow a 6-step process. The stages are respectively; sensory audit, brand staging, brand dramatization, brand signature, implementation, and evaluation.

At the end of this flow, very important outputs for businesses such as building brand identity, positioning the brand, strengthening brand image, developing brand loyalty, brand equity, making customer experiences unique (achieving unique customer experience) and customer satisfaction, preferring the brand to others, creating brand awareness and increasing awareness occur. In addition to these specific outputs, strengthening the bonds between the consumer and the brand with sensory branding, increasing the perceived quality by providing product/brand differentiation (Kaplan, 2015), contributing to competitive advantage, also contributes to the increase in market share (Tan, 2008).

Brands should develop their sensory marketing strategies and follow the relevant steps by deciding which sensory stimuli to use with interaction, considering the outputs they want to achieve. In the future, new studies will be carried out by both academics and brand managers (with eye tracking, functional magnetic resonance imaging (FMRI), electroencephalogram (EEG), etc.) in this field. It is also concluded that brands would include more sensory marketing components in new product development processes and marketing communication activities.

Bibliography

Acevedo, C. R., & Fairbanks, V. (2017). The Effects of Sensory Marketing on Shopping Experience and on Consumer Decision Making. *European Journal of Business and Social Sciences*, *5*(12), 57–69.

Agapito, D., Valle, P. O., & Mendes, J. (2012). Sensory Marketing and Tourist Experiences. *Spatial and Organizational Dynamics Discussions Papers*, *10*, 7–19.

Akillibas, E. (2019). Bes Duyunun Pazarlama Algisindaki Gucu. *Bitlis Eren Universitesi Iktisadi ve Idari Bilimler Fakultesi Akademik Izdusum Dergisi*, *4*(1), 97–124.

Asioli, D., Canavari, M., Castellini, A., de Magistris, T., Gottardi, F., Lombardi, P., Pignatti, E., & Spadoni, R. (2011). The Role of Sensory Attributes in Marketing Organic Food: Findings from a Qualitative Study of Italian Consumers. *Journal of Food Distribution Research*, *42*(1), 16–21.

Atkinson, R. L., Atkinson, R. C., Smith, E. E., Bem, D. J., & Nolen-Hoeksema, S. (2008). Psikolojiye Giris. Y. Alogan (cev.). Ankara: Arkadas Yayinevi.

Bati, U. (2010). Hedef Kitle Davranisini Etkileyen Bir Unsur Olarak Reklamlarda Muzik Kullanimi Konusundaki Yazinin Incelenmesi. *Uluslararasi Insan Bilimleri Dergisi*, *7*(2), 768–808.

Bati, U. (2012). Mark*ethink ya da Farkethink! "Deneyimsel Pazarlama ve Duyusal Markalama"*. Istanbul: Iyi Yayinlari.

Bindea, A., Seserman, A., Bara, M., & Iancu, I. (2009). Tune Your Brand In. The Perfect Jingle Mix. *Journal of Media Research*, *5*, 101–112.

Bog, E. K. (2019). Sehir Kimligi ve Yazi Karakteri Iliskisi. *Dumlupinar Universitesi Sosyal Bilimler Dergisi*, *61*, 109–121.

Boyle-Brayfield, L. (2008). Coming to Their Senses. Multichannel Merchant. 23 October 2020, Retrived from: https://multichannelmerchant.com/marketing/coming-to-their-senses/.

Cakir, S. Y. (2010). Markalarin Duyular Yoluyla Sekillenmesi. *Erciyes Universitesi Iletisim Fakultesi Dergisi*, *1*(4), 39–62.

Diţoiu, M. C., Stăncioiu, A. F., Brătucu, G., Onişor, L. F., & Botos, A. (2014). The Sensory Brand of the Destination Case Study: Transylvania. *Theoretical and Applied Economics*, *21*(5), 37–50.

Eroglu, S. (2003). Soyut Renk, Ses ve Uc Boyutlu Isaretlerin Marka Olarak Tescili. *Dokuz Eylul Universitesi Hukuk Fakultesi Dergisi*, *5*(1), 95–166.

Genunario, L. (2007). Sensory Packaging: Branding That Makes Sense(S). *Brand Packaging*, *9*(7), 12–18.

Gobe, M. (2001). *Emotional Branding; The New Paradigm for Connecting Brands to People*. New York: Allworth Press.

Gulmez, E. (2017). Marka Tercihinde Duyularin Rolu: Starbucks ve Kahve Dunyasi Markalarinin Duyusal Markalama Acisindan Karsilastirilmasi. *Gumushane Universitesi Sosyal Bilimler Enstitusu Elektronik Dergisi*, *5*(1), 58–84.

Hepola, J., Karjaluoto, H., & Hintikka, A. (2017). The Effect of Sensory Brand Experience and Involvement on Brand Equity Directly and Indirectly Through Consumer Brand Engagement. *Journal of Product and Brand Management*, *26*(3), 282–293.

Huang, L., & Lu, J. (2015). Eat with Your Eyes: Package Color Influences the Expectation of Food Taste and Healthiness Moderated by External Eating. *Marketing Management, 25*(2), 71–87.

Huang, R., Lee, S. H., Kim, H., & Evans, L. (2015). The Impact of Brand Experiences on Brand Resonance in Multi-channel Fashion Retailing. *Journal of Research in Interactive Marketing, 9*(2), 129–147.

Hulten, B. (2011). Sensory Marketing: The Multi-sensory Brand-Experience Concept. *European Business Review, 23*(3), 256–273.

Hulten, B., Broweus, N., & Van Dijk, M. (2009). *Sensory Marketing.* London: Palgrave Macmillan.

Icli, G. E., & Copur, M. E. (2008). Pazarlama Iletisiminde Renklerin Rolu. *Trakya Universitesi Sosyal Bilimler Dergisi, 10*(1), 22–33.

Ilter, D. (2010). *Yaratıci Stratejide Duyularla Marka Parcalama.* Yuksek Lisans Tezi. Maltepe Universitesi Sosyal Bilimler Enstitusu. Istanbul.

Kaplan, O. (2015). *Duyularla Marka Parcalama Uzerinden Kavramsal Bir Analiz ve Uygulama Ornekleri.* Yuksek Lisans Tezi, Marmara Universitesi, Sosyal Bilimler Enstitusu, Istanbul.

Koc, E. (2013). *Tuketici Davranisi ve Pazarlama Stratejileri Global ve Yerel Yaklasim.* Ankara: Seckin Yayincilik.

Koch, C., & Koch, E. C. (2003). Preconceptions of Taste Based on Color. *The Journal of Psychology, 137*(3), 233–242.

Kotler, P. (1973). Atmospherics as a Marketing Tool. *Journal of Retailing, 49*(4), 48–64.

Kotler, P., & Keller, K.L. (2018). *Pazarlama Yonetimi.* Istanbul: Beta Yayinlari.

Liegeois, M., & Rivera, C. (2011). *Sensory Marketing on the Natural Cosmetics Market the Impact on Generation X and Generation Y.* Marketing Dissertation, School of Business and Engineering, Halmstad University.

Lindstrom, M. (2005). Duyular ve Marka: 5 Duyuyla Guclu Markalar Yaratmak. U. Sensoy (cev.), Istanbul: Optimist Yayinlari.

Malhotra, N., Dash, S., Kumar, R. S., & Purwar, P. C. (2013). The Nature and Antecedents of Brand Equity and Its Dimensions. *Marketing Intelligence & Planning, 31*(2), 141–159.

Moser, M. (2007). Marka Yaratmanin Bes Adimi, I.B. Kalinyazgan (cev.), Istanbul: MediaCat Kitaplari.

Mucuk, I. (2010). *Pazarlama Ilkeleri.* Istanbul: Turkmen Kitapevi.

Odabasi, Y., & Oyman, M. (2013). *Pazarlama Iletisimi Yonetimi.* Istanbul: MediaCat Yayinları.

Peck, J. (2010). Does Touch Matter? Insights from Haptic Research in Marketing. In Aradhna Krishna (Ed.), *Sensory Marketing: Research on the Sensuality of Products*, (s. 17–33), New York: Routledge.

Pentz, C., & Gerber, C. (2013). The Influence of Selected Senses on Consumer Experience: A Brandy Case. *Acta Commercii*, *13*(1), 1–7.

Post, K. (2004). *Brain Tattoos: Creating Unique Brands That Stick in Your Customers Minds*. New York, USA: Amacom.

Simner, J., & Ludwig, V. U. (2012). The Color of Touch: A Case of Tactile–Visual Synaesthesia. *Neurocase*, *18*(2), 167–180.

Slatten, T., Mehmetoglu, M., Svensson, G. & Sveari, S. (2009). Atmospheric Experiences That Emotionally Touch Customers a Case Study from a Winter Park. *Managing Service Quality*, *19*(6), 721–746.

Suhonen, T., & Tengvall, J. (2009). *Branding in the Air: A Study About the Impact of Sensory Marketing*. Unpublished Master's Thesis, Jönköping International Business School, Jönköping University, Sweden.

Tan, S. C. (2008). Men, Beauty and Senses–A Snapshot of the Effectiveness of Sensory Branding in the Japanese Men's Cosmetics Market. *Journal of Yasar University*, *3*(9), 1047–1060.

Tek, O. B., & Ozgul, E. (2010). *Modern Pazarlama Ilkeleri Uygulamali Yonetimsel Yaklasim*. Izmir: Birlesik Matbaacilik.

Ustaahmetoglu, Y. (2015). Tat Algisi Icin Dilden Daha Fazlası mi Gerekli? Tat Testi Uzerine Bir Uygulama. *Anadolu Universitesi Sosyal Bilimler Dergisi*, *15*(3), 127–134.

Yozukmaz, N., & Topaloglu, C. (2016). Senses in Hospitality: How do Hotel Appeal to Them?. *Journal of Tourism and Hospitality Management*, *4*(2), 51–74.

Yuksekbilgili, N. S. (2017). Renklerin Anlam Algisinda Demografik Ozelliklerin Etkisi Uzerine Bir Arastirma. *Uluslararasi Sosyal Araştirmalar Kongresi*, 77–84.

Zampini, M., & Spence, C. (2010). Assessing the Role of Sound in the Perception of Food and Drink. Chemosensory Perception, *3*(1), 57–67.

Nihat Tavsan and Cem Duran

The Antecedents of Customer Loyalty

Abstract Without a loyal customer base, a business has a significantly less probability of achieving in today's competitive environment. Being aware of the cold fact, businesses try to foster sustainable relationships with their customers and turn them into a loyal clientele. They heavily invest in loyalty programs to retain their customers. Those companies hoping to create customer loyalty in today's global market need to be aware that there are antecedents to customer loyalty. Customers do not suddenly become loyal to a company. Several critical factors need to be in place before committing themselves whole-heartedly to one product, service, brand or company. Research has revealed that perceived value, self-congruity, customer participation, customer brand identification, emotional commitment, customer satisfaction and brand trust must all be present to some degree for the customer's response to be loyal to that brand. Research also shows that companies that take this process seriously have a greater chance of generating a loyal customer base.

Keywords: Customer Loyalty, Self-Congruity, Customer Participation, Customer Brand Identification, Emotional Commitment, Customer Satisfaction, Brand Trust

1 Introduction

We are living in the age of convenience and availability. In today's globalized world, an athlete in Peru can order a pair of shoes from China, or a gardener in Serbia can purchase a lawnmower from Germany. The rules and the nature of commercial competition are becoming more rigid and more challenging. The number of customers in the market is not necessarily increasing; but the number of competitors trying to grab their slice of the pie is increasing exponentially. Because companies are painfully aware of this reality, rather than constantly seeking to acquire new customers, they have begun heavily focusing on keeping their existing ones in hand. In essence, we are talking about "customer loyalty."

Customer loyalty is a behavioral reaction that triggers individuals to make repeated purchases for a product or service (Iriani, 2011). It is about having a willingness to buy products or services from a particular company, give the company feedback if something goes wrong, and share positive recommendations about the brand's products or services with other potential customers (Keller & Kotler, 2007). Predictably, it takes a significant amount of time for companies to build customer loyalty, but customer loyalty leads those customers to become committed partners with the company at the end of the day.

Loyal customers enable companies to reduce consumer turnover costs, reduce marketing costs, and reduce the cost of failure. This is because acquiring a new customer demands more financial investment than keeping an existing customer (Demirgüneş, 2015). Loyal customers who are satisfied give positive feedback to others by word of mouth and organically function as the brand's communication instrument. Customer loyalty does not occur in a vacuum, however. The loyalty bond results from a specific set of variables: (1) Perceived value, (2) Self-congruity, (3) Customer participation, (4) Customer brand identification, (5) Emotional commitment, (6) Customer satisfaction, and (7) Brand trust.

2 Research and Methodology

2.1 Perceived Value

In the contemporary business environment, companies that create value for customers have the opportunity to survive in the cut-throat competition (Slater, 1997). We see that the number of companies understanding this fact increases as they recognize the role of perceived value in strategic management.

Perceived value is fixed by comparing expected value to the delivered value (Demirgüneş, 2015). The perceived value affects the purchase decision of customers (Mayton et al., 1994). Each customer's value expectation is unique and directly affects his or her purchase decisions.

Sheth (1991) suggests that perceived value consists of the emotional value, functional value, conditional value, social value, and epistemic value that customers give to their purchase decisions. On the other hand, other researchers propose emotional, functional, and social values as the components of perceived value (Roing et al., 2006; Izquierdo et al., 2006; Sanchez et al., 2006). An object gains functional value if it includes functional, physical, or utility attributes (Sheth, 1991). Pura (2005) defines functional value as a combination of convenience and monetary value.

Emotional value is linked to sentiments elicited in customers by the brand and should be developed (Sheth, 1991). Emotional sentiment impacts purchase decisions (Pura, 2005) and customer loyalty (Wang et al., 2004). Thus, the emotional value that customers assign to products cannot be ignored if the company is trying to ascertain perceived value. Literature shows that customer loyalty results from perceived customer value (Demirgüneş, 2015; Omar et al., 2011). Therefore, perceived value is an antecedent for repurchase behaviors and customer loyalty (Morar, 2013).

2.2 Self-Congruity

Customers match their self-image with products or services, so that these have specific meaning for them (Sirgy, 1986). Matching self-image and having a special attachment to a product or service is a vehicle of self-expression for customers (Aaker, 1999). The concept of self-congruity is that customers try to find a match between themselves and the brands, products, or services (Sirgy, 1986). One reason that this affects customers' purchase decisions is that the product or the service provides specific meaning to them. Thus, self-congruity is an essential antecedent of customer loyalty (Sidali & Hemmerling, 2014; Line & Hanks, 2016).

Self-image congruity means that customers often identify with a brand, product or service. In other words, they envision it as part of their own self-image or the person they want to be. According to self-concept theory, customers' personalities can be predicted from the brands, products, or services they prefer to purchase (Ross, 1971). There are several dimensions of self-concept: These are ideal self-concept, social self-concept, actual self-concept; and ideal social self-concept. Actual self-concept is how customers see themselves; ideal self-concept is how customers would like to see themselves; social self-concept is how customers think others see them; ideal social self-concept is how customers would like to be perceived by other people. Self-image congruity is related to the actual and ideal self-concept dimensions.

There is an essential impact of self-congruity on customer loyalty. A direct relation between self-congruity and customer loyalty has been confirmed through research studies (Liu et al., 2012).

2.3 Customer Participation

Creating value within customer participation to build loyalty is a competence strategy for companies. Customer participation helps customers to personalize their service or products (Vargo & Lusch, 2008). Active customers affect the formation of new products or services (Prahalad and Ramaswamy, 2000). Creating relevant value for customers requires customer participation (Bharti et al., 2014). Companies create effective value propositions when they interact with their customers (Tanev, 2011). Customer participation generates knowledge for the company to provide superior service (Groonross, 2004).

Customer participation is not only about listening to customers or exchanging views; it requires efficient interaction and engagement (Prahalad and Ramaswamy, 2000). Companies can recognize customers' cultural, emotional, and social backgrounds and point of view through participation (Tanev, 2011). Trust bonds are created within the participation (Ballantyne, 2004).

Loyalty occurs if companies and customers are moving in the same direction and if companies listen to customers and pay attention to their needs when developing a new service or product (Lin et al., 2010). According to Komulainen (2014), the value created with customer participation leads to customer loyalty.

2.4 Customer Brand Identification

Customers often try to create a social identity by exceeding their personal identity (So et al., 2013). Social identity affects customers' perceptions, cognitions, and evaluations. Customers' strong social identification with a product or service can increase loyalty (Huang et al., 2017).

Customer brand identification means that customers match their self-image with the brands' image. It is a kind of psychological state (Lam, 2013). Customer brand identification is an essential variable to develop customer loyalty. Literature suggests that customers who have higher brand identification tend to have loyalty and more satisfaction with the company (Li & He, 2010).

2.5 Emotional Commitment

According to Meyer and Allen (1990), there are three types of commitment: Normative, calculative and emotional. Normative commitment occurs because customers naturally tend to stick with a company that they have a relationship with. Calculative commitment is about customers' tendency to remain with the company's products or services-in other words, they have specific reasons for why they purchased them. When customers feel love or like for a company or brand, they are demonstrating emotional commitment (Fullerton, 2003). Emotional commitment is customers' emotional attachment to the company, which is based on a high level of trust (Fullerton, 2003). Emotional commitment leads customers to have a sense of belongingness (Morgan & Hunt, 1994). Consequently, companies need to develop an emotional commitment to building loyalty bonds with their customers (Sui & Baloglu, 2003).

2.6 Customer Satisfaction

Customers' satisfaction level contributes to their loyalty to the company or the brand (Hennig Thurau et al., 2002). Customers feel satisfaction if their experience with the product or service meets or exceeds their expectations. If companies' products or services do not meet customers' expectations, dissatisfaction occurs (Oliver, 1997).

Customers make their repurchasing decisions after experiencing the company's products or services (Chen, 2010). A high level of satisfaction leads customers to have a continuous relationship with the company (Curth et al., 2014). Satisfied customers will engage in positive word of mouth about the company (Rather & Sharma, 2018)

2.7 Brand Trust

If there is consistency, honesty, benevolence, and credibility in the relationship between the brand and the customer, brand trust occurs (Morgan & Hunt, 1994). In marketing, brand trust leads to loyalty and increases productivity and efficiency (Sui & Baloglu, 2003). If a customer finds a brand credible and trusts the company, that customer believes it will deliver high-quality services. Benevolence trust is about customers' beliefs about the company's competence (Kandampully et al., 2015). Trust is developed over time with repeated interaction of customers with service providers (Shukla et al., 2016). Thus, brand trust affects customer loyalty.

3 Conclusion

Loyal customers support the profitability of companies. A business that aims to build long-term relationships with customers quickly responds to them (Minami & Dawson, 2008). A responsive approach helps companies to develop complementary products as well as better products and services. In sustaining a loyalty relationship, it is imperative to demonstrate kindness and friendliness to customers and to evaluate them without discrimination (Yau et al., 2000).

Trust is a crucial concept in building loyalty bonds (Hapsari, 2018). Mutual trust depends on honesty between customers and producers. The goal of companies should be to turn that trust into commitment, which will lead to customer loyalty. Commitment is about being attached to one company's products or services, having disinterest in other products or services (Tjiptono, 2007). Loyalty is a strong bond between the two parties. As the number of interactions between a customer and the brand increases, the commitment that the customer feels towards the brand grows. Over time, if the company continues to earn that trust, this commitment transforms into customer loyalty. Customers tend to be consistent in their purchases; their self-congruity-seeking patterns push them to be loyal to specific brands. Nonetheless, and at the end of the day, the consumptions are done to fulfill a need. These needs create perceived value, which, if filled, brings customers back to that brand. Consequently, perceived value is a strong antecedent of customer loyalty. Research shows that when customers are permitted to be an active party in value creation, they are more likely to demonstrate loyalty behaviors. By embedding customer participation into their strategies, companies have the potential to expand their loyal customer base.

Customers consume products and services not only to meet their utilitarian values (usefulness) but also for their hedonic (emotional) values. In most cases, their motivation is a combination of utilitarian and hedonic reasons. As part of their hedonistic motivations, customers often see products or services as a way of reflecting themselves; their values, their passions and how they see themselves. Thus, customers frequently show loyalty behavior towards brands that reflect their self-image.

The research shows that emotional attachment is one of the determinants of customer loyalty. Consequently, brands that are trying to build a loyal customer base should focus on emotional attachment. Additionally, emotional attachment shouldn't be evaluated apart from brand identity. Emotional attachment -expressed by customers- should be considered a reflection of brand identity. A relevant brand identity prompts the emotional commitment of the customers and, as a result, the customers express loyalty behavior.

Bibliography

Aaker, J. (1999). The malleable self: The role of self expression in persuasion. *Journal of Marketing Research,36*, 45–57.

Ballantyne, D. (2004). Dialogue and its role in the development of relationship specific knowledge. *Journal of Business & Industrial Marketing, 19*(2), 114–123.

Bharti, K., Agrawal, R., & Sharma, V. (2014). What drives the customer of world's largest market to participate in value co-creation?. *Marketing Intelligence Planning, 32*(4), 413–435.

Chen, C. F., & Chen, F. S. (2010). Experience quality, perceived value, satisfaction and behavioral intentions for heritage tourists. *Tourism Management, 31*(1), 29–35.

Curth, S., Uhrich, S., & Benkenstein, M. (2014). How commitment to fellow customers affects the customer-firm relationship and customer citizenship behavior. *Journal of Services Marketing, 28*(2), 147–158.

Demirgunes, K. (2015). Relative importance of perceived value, satisfaction and perceived risk on willingness to pay more. *International Review of Management and Marketing, 5*(4), 211–220.

Fullerton, G. (2003). When does commitment lead to loyalty?. *Journal of Service Research, 5*(4), 333–344.

Groonroos, C. (2004). The relationship marketing process: Communication, interaction, dialogue, value. *Journal of Business & Industrial Marketing, 19*(2), 99–113.

Hapsari, R. (2018). Enhancing Brand Loyalty Through Online Brand Community: The Role of Value Creation Process, Brand Love, and Trust. The 2018 International Conference of Organizational Innovation, KnE Social Science, 577–586.

Hennig-Thurau, T., Gwinner, K. P., & Gremler, D. D. (2002). Understanding relationship marketing outcomes: An integration of relational benefits and relationship quality. *Journal of Service Research, 4*(3), 230–247.

Huang, M. H., Cheng, Z. H., & Chen, I. C. (2017). The importance of CSR in forming customer-company identification and long-term loyalty. *Journal of Services Marketing, 31*(1), 63–72.

Irani, N. & Hanzaee, K. H. (2011). The Effects of Variety-Seeking Buying Tendency and Price Sensitivity on Utilitarian and Hedonic Value in Apparel Shopping Satisfaction. *International Journal of Marketing Studies, 3*(3), 89–103.

Izquierdo, C. C., Rodrıguez, S., & Jose, R. S. (2006). Customers' perception of value in financial services relationships: A Spanish case. *Journal of International Consumer Marketing, 19*(1), 57–77.

Kandampully, J., Zhang, T., & Bilgihan, A. (2015). Customer loyalty: A review and future directions with a special focus on the hospitality industry. *International Journal of Contemporary Hospitality Management, 27*(3), 379–414.

Komulainen, H. (2014). The role of learning in value co-creation in new technological B2B services. *Journal of Business & Industrial Marketing, 29*(3), 238–252.

Kotler, P., & Keller, K. L. (2007). *Manajemen Pemasaran*. Edisi Kedua Belas. Jakarta: Indeks.

Lam, S. K., Ahearne, M., Mullins, R., Hayati, B., & Schillewaert, N. (2013). Exploring the dynamics of antecedents to customer-Brand identification with a new brand. *Journal of the Academy of Marketing Science, 41*(2), 234–252.

Lee, D., & Hyman, M. R. (2008). Hedonic/functional congruity between stores and private label brands. *Journal of Marketing Theory and Practice,16*(3), 219–232.

Li, Y., & He, H. (2010). CSR and service brand: The mediating effect of brand identification and moderating effect of service quality. *Journal of Business Ethics, 100*(4), 673–688.

Lin, Y., Wang, Y., & Yu, C. (2010). Investigating the drivers of the innovation in channel integration and supply chain performance: A strategy oriented perspective. *International Journal of Production Economics, 127*(2), 320–332.

Line, N. D., & Hanks, L. (2016). The other customer: He impact of self image in restaurant patronage, *Journal of Foodservice Business Research, 8020(August)*, 1–18.

Liu, C. R., Lin, W. R., & Wang, Y. C. (2012). Relationship between self-congruity and destination loyalty: Differences between first time and repeat visitors. *Journal of Destination Marketing Management, 1*(1), 118–123.

Mayton, D. M., Ball-Rokeach, S. J., & Loges, W. E. (1994). Human values and social issues: An introduction. *Journal of Social Issues, 50*(4), 1–8.

Meyer, J. P., & Allen, N. J. (1990). Affective and continuance commitment to the organization: Evaluation of measures and analysis of concurrent and time-lagged relations. *Journal of Applied Psychology, 75*(6), 710–720.

Minami, C., & Dawson, J. (2008). The CRM process in retail and service sector firms in Japan: Loyalty development and financial return. *Journal of Retailing and Consumer Services, 15*(5), 375–385.

Morar, D. D. (2013). *An overview of the consumer value literature perceived value*. International Conference, Marketing from Information to Decision, 6th ed., pp. 69–186.

Morgan, R. M., Hunt, S. D. (1994). The commitment-trust theory of relationship marketing. *Journal of Marketing, 58*(3), 20–38.

Oliver, R. L. (1997). *Satisfaction: A behavioral perspective on the customer.* New York: McGraw Hill.

Omar, N. A., Alam, S. S., Aziz, N. A., & Nazri, M. A. (2011). Retail loyalty programs in Malaysia: The relationship of equity, value, satisfaction, trust and loyalty among cardholders. *Journal of Business Economics and Management, 12*(2), 332–352.

Pura, M. (2005). Linking perceived value and loyalty in location-based mobile services. *Managing Service Quality: An International Journal, 15*(6), 509–538.

Prahalad, C. K., & Ramaswamy, V., (2000). Co-Creation Experiences: The Next Practice in Value Creation. *Journal of Interactive Marketing, 18*(3), 5–14

Rather, R. A., & Sharma, J. (2018). The effects of customer satisfaction and commitment on customer loyalty: Evidence from the hotel industry. *Journal of Hospitality Application &Research, 12*(2), 41–60.

Roig, J. C. F., Garcia, J. S., Tena, M. A. M., & Monzonis, J. L. (2006). Customer perceived value in banking services. *International Journal of Bank Marketing, 24*, 266–283.

Ross, L. (1971). Self concept and brand preferance. *The Journal of Business, 44*(1), 38–50.

Sanchez, J., Callarisa, L. J., Rodriguez, R. M., & Moliner, M. A. (2006). Perceived value of the purchase of a tourism product. *Tourism Management, 27*, 4.

Sheth, J. N., Bruce, I. N., & Gross, B. L. (1991). Why we buy what we buy, a theory of consumption values. *Journal of Business Research, 22*(2), 159–170.

Shukla, P., Banerjee, M., & Singh, J. (2016). Customer commitment to luxury brands: Antecedents and consequences. *Journal of Business Research, 69*(1), 323–331.

Sidali, K. L., & Hemmerling, S. (2014). Developing an authenticity model of traditional food specialities: Does the self concept of consumers matter?. *British Food Journal, 116*(11), 1692–1709.

Sirgy, M. J. (1986). *Self congruity: Toward a theory of personality and cybernetics*. New York: Praeger Publishers.

Slater, S. F. (1997). Developing a customer value-based theory of the firm. *Journal of the Academy of Marketing Science, 25*, 164–169.

So, K. K. F., King, C., Sparks, B., & Wang, Y. (2013). The influence of customer brand identification on hotel brand evaluation and loyalty development. *International Journal of Hospitality Management, 34*, 31–41.

Sui, J. J., & Baloglu, S. (2003). The role of emotional commitment in relationship marketing: An empirical investigation of a loyalty model for casinos. *Journal of Hospitality & Tourism Research, 27*(4), 470–489.

Tanev, S. (2011). How do value co-creation activities relate to the perception of firms' innotiativeness? *Journal of Innovation Economics, 1*(7), 131–159.

Tjiptono, F. (2007). *Pemasaran Jasa Edisi Pertama: Cetakan Ketiga*. Malang: Penerbit Bayumedia Publising.

Vargo, S. L., & Lusch, R. F. (2008). Service dominant logic: Continuing the evolution. *Journal of the Academy of Marketing Science, 36*(1), 1–10.

Wang, Y., Po Lo, H., Chi, R., & Yang, Y. (2004). An integrated framework for customer value and customer-relationship-management performance, a customer-based perspective from China. *Managing Service Quality: An International Journal, 14*(2/3), 169–182.

Yau, H. M. O., McFetridge, R. P., Chow, P. M. R., and Lee, S. Y. J. (2000). Is relationship marketing for everyone? *European Journal of Marketing, 34*(9/10), 1111–11127.

Mehmet Levent Erdas and Zeynep Ezanoglu

Do Research and Development Investments and Financial Development Promote Human Development? Empirical Evidence from Developing Countries

Abstract To determine the welfare levels of countries, indexes are calculated through several financial and macroeconomic variables. However, it is necessary to apply social factors in addition to income to enable development in addition to the application of per capita income for the measurement of development levels. One of the indicators providing development levels considering those factors is the human development index (HDI). It has been applied by the United Nations Development Program as annual development reports since 1990. It measures the development levels of societies not only through the economic indicators but also based on other important aspects of human life such as healthy life, knowledge, and access to information and education. Accordingly, it is necessary to find ways to increase the HDI in developing market economies. To this end, this chapter aims to focus on the financial and macroeconomic factors affecting the HDI were analyzed through the Driscoll and Kraay (1998) standard errors estimators. Analyzes were made using selected developing countries between 2000 and 2017. The results indicate that HDI has a significant positive relationship with research and development investments and financial development. Therefore, human development accumulation is affected by research and development investments and financial development and such kind of policies should be implemented.

Keywords: Research and Development Investments, Financial Development, Human Development Index, Panel Data Analysis, Developing Countries

1 Introduction

Since it is a comprehensive concept, economic welfare cannot be measured by economic growth. Several active factors have a role on the economic development of the countries. The human factor, which is at the center of the world, is considered as an important factor affecting the developments (Caglar & Erdas, 2018: 1067). As a matter of fact, human development was started to be mentioned in the early 1990s after World War II ended, to increase the welfare levels of the underdeveloped countries. It has been indicated that with the human development approach, not only economic growth but also economic activities should be built to develop the human capacity. Monetary criteria were applied to measure the growth and development between the 1950s and 1970s. Per capita income was considered as the most important indicator for the growth and development levels of the countries. However, differences between the economic development levels and welfare levels of the citizens living in the countries with high levels of per capita income were observed. Since the national income increase is not efficient enough on other social components from the 1970s, the indicators reflecting the social characteristics of the countries in addition to the monetary indicators applied for the measurements have started to be mentioned (Sahin & Gokdemir, 2016: 3). Accordingly, an index within which the national income and other social components are evaluated together gained prominence. Human Development Index (HDI) involves the components of earning an income that can provide health, necessary education and minimum living standards which are the main conditions for satisfaction. HDI has been applied by the United Nations Development Program (UNDP) as annual development reports since 1990. HDI is a comprehensive instrument developed by the United Nations in order to measure the social and economic development levels of different countries and sort them accordingly (Shah, 2016: 1). This report is a comparative measure for life expectancy, education, literacy, and living standards. This index, which is applied to compare the countries in the indicated sizes, reflects an average measure of the human development achievements of the countries (UNDP, 2019: 31). HDI can be successfully applied for the future total income and growth literature. The Cobb-Douglas Model, which is known as the total production function in the literature, involves a human capital variable.

Studies conducted under the economic theory emphasize the importance of research and development (R&D) activities as a driving force for growth. Similarly, a strong and developed financial system is considered a driving force for economic growth (McKinnon, 1973; Shaw, 1973). Therefore, several theoretical and applied studies analyzing the relationship between financial development, R&D investments, and economic growth have been conducted since the 19th century. To the best of our knowledge, there is a limited number of studies analyzing the relationship between financial development and HDI, and there is no study analyzing the relationship between R&D investments and HDI. However, financial development and R&D investments may also be related to human capital, as they are related to economic growth. Do the financial development and R&D investments of countries affect education, health, and welfare levels? What is the relationship between financial development, R&D investments and human capital accumulation in selected developing countries?

Based on these questions, this study aims to analyze whether financial development and R&D investments of the developing countries affect HDI. From this point of view, the developing countries were analyzed via panel data analysis through the data from the period between 2000 and 2017.

2 Literature Review

Studies conducted under the economic theory emphasizes the importance of R&D activities as the driving force for growth. Accordingly, internal growth theories indicated that the R&D activities have contributed to the growth processes of the countries in long run. Mankiw et al. (1992) and Romer (1994) revealed in their studies that the human capital and knowledge through R&D and education are the main source for long-term economic growth. Among the indicators applied in order to measure the technological change within the frame of the internal growth models, R&D investments have been applied as an indicator of technical change in several studies since it is easy to compile and is reliable (Sungur et al., 2016: 175). When the studies related to R&D activities are analyzed, it can be observed that the Gross Domestic Product (GDP) is one of the variables, the effects of which are studied the most. In the studies analyzing the causality relationship between the R&D expenses and GDP, it is concluded that there is a bilateral relationship between them (Wu et al., 2007), while there are studies in the literature detecting a unilateral relationship from R&D activities to the economic growth (Altin & Kaya, 2009; Korkmaz, 2010; Genc & Atasoy, 2010; Yaylali et al., 2010). When the literature related to both variables is analyzed, the studies conducted indicate that there is a strong and positive relationship between those two variables in general (Freire-Seren, 1999; Falk, 2007; Sadraoui & Zina, 2009; Horvath, 2011). However, Pessoa (2010) emphasized in his/her study analyzing the relationship between R&D expenses and growth for OECD countries that the relationship between those variables is different for the countries.

Some of the studies analyzing the relationship between the financial development indicators and HDI were included. The studies of De Gregorio and Guidotti (1995), Pagano (1993), De Gregorio (1996), Evans et al. (2002), Papagni (2006), Kendall (2012), Zaman et al. (2012), and Sehrawat and Giri (2017) which focuses on the role of human capital in financial development. Their results indicated that different financial indicators played an important role on increasing human capital. Kuri and Laha (2011) investigated the relationship between financial inclusion and the level of human development in India. The study revealed that the level of human development and financial inclusion are positively correlated. Akhmat et al. (2014) analyzed the relationship between economic growth and financial development for the human development for Bangladesh, India, Nepal, Pakistan and Sri Lanka. The panel cointegration results indicated that there is a long-term relationship between human development and financial development indicators and that the financial development indicators increase human capital development. Azam et al. (2015) analyzed the relationship between direct foreign investment and human capital for the sample consisting of 34 developing countries. They found that there is a positive relationship between direct foreign investments and human capital and that it affects human capital positively. Hatemi-J and Shamsuddin (2016) have examined the causal relationship between financial development and human development. The results indicate that causal relationship running from human development to financial development. Kaya (2017) conducted cointegration and causality tests in order the determine the relationship between financial development and human capital for Turkey. The results of the analysis suggested that the variables are cointegrated and that there is causality from HDI to financial development. Sehrawat and Giri (2017) investigated the relationship between financial development indicators and human capital for Asian countries. Findings support the existence of the long-run relationship among the indicators of financial development and human investments. Arif and Khan (2019) analyzed the relationship between human capital and financial development for Pakistan and found that a strong financial institution enhances human capital development. Similarly, Sethi et al. (2019) concluded that a faster degree of financial sector development increases the development of human capital in South Asia.

3 Data, Model and Results

For econometric researches, panel data analysis provides opportunities to work more data by considering time and section dimensions into consideration. The panel data set is defined as gathering cross-sectional dataset or observations over time periods (Wooldridge, 2002: 9; Tari, 2014: 475; Tatoglu, 2018: 1). For the panel data sets, an increase in the number of observations and degrees of freedom decreases the problem of multicollinearity. Besides, they also increase the reliability of parameter estimations (Baltagi, 2005: 135).

The data related to the period between 2000 and 2017 which are applied in this study analyzing the effects of R&D investments on HDI for the developing countries were obtained from the World Bank's World's Development Indicators and United Nations Development Program Human Development

Tab. 16.1: Variables and Expectations

Variables	Abbreviation	Expected Sign
Human Development Index	HDI	Dependet Variable
Inflation, consumer prices (annual %)	INF	-
Foreign direct investment, net inflows (%of GDP)	FDI	+
Openness (Import + Export) (%of GDP)	Openness	+
GDP (current US$)	GDP	+
Financial system deposits (%of GDP)	FSD	+
Research and development expenditure (%of GDP)	RDE	+

reports. The period was determined between 2000 and 2017 due to the insufficiency of observations related to some variables after 2017. All alternatives related to the dependent and independent variables were included in the models and the most explanatory ones were taken into consideration. A total of six independent variables as macroeconomic and financial performance indicators were subjected to analyze for the study. The independent variables in the research model are inflation, direct foreign investments, openness, GDP, R&D investments, and financial system deposits. The determinants of the HDI in the literature were selected and R&D investments and financial developments of the countries were included as a main independent variable. The abbreviations related to the variables analyzed in the study and expected signs of the coefficients in accordance with the theory are presented in Tab. 16.1.

The hypotheses to be tested and the regression model are presented below;

H0,1: R&D investments do not affect HDI.
H0,2: Financial system deposits do not affect HDI.

$$\begin{aligned} HDI_{i,t-1} = {} & \alpha_0 + \alpha_1 INF_{i,t} + \alpha_2 FDI_{i,t} + \alpha_3 Openness_{i,t} \\ & + \alpha_4 lnGDP_{i,t} + \alpha_5 FSD_{i,t} + \alpha_6 RDE_{i,t} \end{aligned} \tag{1}$$

In the equation, ln represents natural logarithm, i represents country and t represents time. α indicates coefficients to be estimated and e indicates random error term. The independent variables were included in the model after their

Tab. 16.2: Descriptive Analysis of the Variables

Variables	Obs.	Mean	Std. Dev.	Minimum	Maximum
HDI	180	71.23889	7.957389	49.700000	85.700000
INF	162	6.915997	7.352154	-1.124995	54.915370
FDI	180	2.197299	1.489600	-2.577440	8.4963520
Openness	180	50.18827	15.81698	21.852250	96.102630
lnGDP	180	27.36057	0.967871	25.305410	30.141470
FSD	180	37.33282	14.47318	13.316300	66.057600
RDE	123	0.786131	0.428797	0.0423000	2.0460400

Tab. 16.3: Pearson Correlation Analysis

	HDI	*INF*	*FDI*	*Openness*	*lnGDP*	*FSD*	*RDE*
HDI	1						
INF	0.0267	1					
FDI	0.2996	-0.1970	1				
Openness	0.2985	-0.0369	0.1525	1			
lnGDP	0.1997	-0.3182	0.3576	-0.2713	1		
FSD	-0.5305	-0.1684	-0.1367	-0.4439	0.1914	1	
RDE	0.0153	-0.0816	0.1417	-0.4116	0.6730	0.4079	1

logarithms were taken. The variables the logarithms of which were taken were indicated with ln and descriptive statistics related to the variables are presented in Tab. 16.2. While there are 180 observations for the period between 2000 and 2017 for the HDI variable, the lowest variable is related to the RDE variable.

According to the correlation analysis results (see Tab. 16.3), a positive correlation relationship between the HDI, FDI, and the RDE was detected. The highest value of correlation exhibited among explanatory variables is 0.6730 which was found in the case of RDE and GDP. The lowest value of correlation exhibited among explanatory variables is 0.0153 which was found in the case of RDE and HDI. Since there is no high correlation between the variables, all the variables stated are used in the model.

For the flexibility estimations, random effects and fixed effects methods were applied in the study. In order to decide between random effects and fixed effects, the specification test developed by Hausman (1978) was applied. As a result of Hausman tests applied, the null hypothesis indicating that the fixed effects model is the suitable model was rejected. Several tests should be

Tab. 16.4: The Results of Regression Estimations

Variables	(1) POLS	(2) Random Effects	(3) Driscoll-Kraay
INF	0.0435	-0.0186	-0.0151
	(0.0736)	(0.0172)	(0.0177)
FDI	0.4920	-0.0130	0.0187
	(0.3880)	(0.0950)	(0.0841)
Openness	0.0805*	0.0631***	0.0496***
	(0.0445)	(0.0175)	(0.0115)
lnGDP	1.892**	3.779***	3.512***
	(0.950)	(0.380)	(0.325)
FSD	-0.296***	0.0347	0.0602**
	(0.0516)	(0.0293)	(0.0262)
RDE	2.208	4.795***	5.461***
	(1.974)	(0.921)	(0.676)
Constant	20.88	-42.42**	-36.60***
	(25.89)	(9.657)	(8.177)
Observations	108	108	108
R-squared	0.415		0.903
Number of cno		9	9
Wald chi2			886.38
Prob > chi2			0.000
Wooldridge Test			0.000
Wald Test			0.000

Note: Standard errors in parentheses. * $p < 0.10$, ** $p < 0.05$, *** $p < 0.01$. Driscoll-Kraay's approach applies a Newey-West-type correction on the cross-sectional data

conducted in order to test the deviations from the assumptions in the panel data models. Autocorrelation in the indicated model is the existence of a correlation between heteroscedasticity and units. Therefore, Wooldridge sequential dependency (Wooldridge, 2002; Drukker, 2003) and Wald heteroscedasticity (Greene, 2000: 598; Baum, 2001: 101) tests were conducted. The results of the conducted test were presented in Tab. 16.4. The null hypothesis established for the Wooldridge test indicated that a primary autocorrelation does not exist. This hypothesis was rejected. Wald test was conducted to test the heteroscedasticity in the model applied. The null hypothesis related to this test was established to indicate that the variance does not change by units. This hypothesis was rejected. As a result, the autocorrelation and heteroscedasticity tests indicate that those problems exist in the model. Therefore, Driscoll-Kraay (1998) develop a nonparametric covariance matrix estimator that produces heteroskedasticity and autocorrelation robust standard errors for panel regression that are robust to general forms of spatial and temporal dependence (Hoechle, 2007: 282). Thus, Driscoll-Kraay (1998) standard errors regression estimator was applied in this study.

Driscoll-Kraay (1998) estimator was developed to provide estimations related to standard error which are durable against all general forms of spatial and temporal dependencies of covariance matrix estimation techniques which are not standard parametric. The convenience of this approach through Monte Carlo simulations (Driscoll & Kraay 1998: 549). In case even there are heteroskedasticity and correlation and autocorrelation between the units for those estimator units, it is possible to make estimations robust to those deviations (Tatoglu, 2018: 23). Firstly, the panel fixed/random effects method which is applied when autocorrelation and heteroskedasticity do not exist was applied in the study. Due to the existence of unit effects, the pooled ordinary least squares (POLS) method was not applied. The model was decided to be convenient for the dynamic method since it has unit effects and random effects does not exist. However, Driscoll-Kraay (1998) test were deemed suitable since the model has autocorrelation and heteroskedasticity problem.

Note: Standard errors in parentheses. * $p < 0.10$, ** $p < 0.05$, *** $p < 0.01$. Driscoll-Kraay's approach applies a Newey-West-type correction on the cross-sectional data.

In Tab. 16.4, column (1) presents the results of the POLS method, and column (2) presents the results of random effects. In accordance with the results of Driscoll-Kraay (1998) test presented in column (3); it can be observed that the variables of economic openness, GDP, financial system deposit, and R&D investments have positive and significant effects on the HDI. It was concluded that inflation decreases HDI; however, this effect was found statistically insignificant. Besides, it is possible to indicate that the effects of direct foreign investment attempts may increase HDI. The model is considered valid by providing the result of 0.903 for R-square value as a whole. Based on the results of the econometric model, it is possible to mention that the R&D investments and incentives related to them and provision of financial stability are important to increase the welfare level of the society in the recent years where the countries started to mention about economic development in addition to economic growth.

4 Conclusion and Policy Recommendations

In order to determine the welfare levels of countries, indexes are calculated through several financial and macroeconomic variables. However, it is necessary to apply social factors in addition to income in order to enable development in addition to the application of per capita income for the measurement of development levels. One of the indicators providing development levels considering those factors is HDI. Therefore, it is known that HDI is guiding policymakers to determine financial and socio-economic policies. HDI measures the development levels of societies not only through the economic indicators but also based on other important aspects of human life such as healthy life, knowledge, and access to information and education.

The effects of financial development and R&D investments on HDI for the developing countries including Turkey were tried to be determined in this study. For this reason; Driscoll-Kraay (1998) test correcting the autocorrelation and heteroskedasticity problems and making estimation robust from the whole assumption to deviations were applied by considering the data from the period between 2000 and 2017 for the developing countries. With the results of the Driscoll-Kraay (1998) test, it was concluded that R&D investments and financial development have positive and statistically significant effects on HDI. They also show that developing countries need to create policies to increase the level of financial development and R&D investments. The opinion indicating that R&D investments increase growth is the dominant opinion in the mentioned literature. Similarly, it is also widely thought that financial development supports economic growth. It is possible to observe through this study that those variables have significant effects on HDI which includes not only economic growth, but also economic development.

Consequently, it is possible to say that increasing economic growth levels which is one of the main targets of developing countries is not sufficient for competing with other countries. And the human factor, which is the center of today's world, is a factor affecting the developments. Developing human capital in terms of qualification by providing education increases the production capacities of the countries. Especially when the countries switching to the information economy are analyzed, the value-added productions of the citizens of the relevant county gain prominence. In this regard; it is thought that the health, education, and living standards should be increased; and for this purpose, it is necessary to find ways to increase the HDI calculated for this reason. The answer to the question asking how changes on human capital affect countries' economies will enable the countries to apply efficient policies. Therefore;

it is thought that HDI is affected by R&D investments and the financial development level and that it is necessary to develop policies related to this fact. Also, the Covid-19 outbreak has become one of the biggest threats to all countries. Thus, since it will be important to see the powers in the human development Covid-19 period should be evaluated and examined their impact on the human capital accumulation in the future studies.

Bibliography

Akhmat, G., Zaman, K., & Shukui, T. (2014). Impact of financial development on SAARC's human development. *Quality and Quantity*, *48*(5), 2801–2816.

Altin, O., & Kaya, A. (2009). Analysis of the casual relationship between R&D expenditures and economic growth for Turkey. *Ege Akademik Bakış*, *9*(1), 251–259.

Arif, I., & Khan, L. (2019). The role of financial development in human capital development: Evidence from Pakistan. *Pakistan Journal of Commerce and Social Sciences*, *13*(4), 1029–1040.

Azam, M., Khan, S., Zainal, Z., Karuppiah, N., & Khan, F. (2015). Foreign direct investment and human capital: Evidence from developing countries. *Investment Management and Financial Innovations*, *12*(3), 155–162.

Baltagi, H. B. (2005). *Econometric analysis of panel data*. New York: John Wiley & Sons.

Baum, C. F. (2001). Residual diagnostics for cross-section time series regression models. *The Stata Journal*, *1*(1), 101–104.

Caglar, A. E., & Erdas, M. L. (2018). Effects on human capital index of greenhouse gas emission in Turkey. *Innovation and Global Issues Congress IV*, Lara/Antalya, 22–24 November.

De Gregorio, J. (1996). Borrowing constraints, human capital accumulation, and growth. *Journal of Monetary Economics*, *37*(1), 49–71.

De Gregorio, J., & Guidotti, P. (1995). Financial development and economic growth. *World Development*, *23*(3), 433–448.

Driscoll, J., & Kraay, A. (1998). Consistent covariance matrix estimation with spatially dependent panel data. *The Review of Economics and Statistics*, *80*(4), 549–560.

Drukker, D. M. (2003). Testing for serial correlation in linear panel-data models. *The Stata Journal*, *3*(2), 1–10.

Evans, D., Green, C. J., & Murinde, V. (2002). Human capital and financial development in economic growth: The new evidence using the translog production function. *International Journal of Finance and Economics*, (7), 123–140.

Falk, M. (2007). R&D spending in the high-tech sector and economic growth. *Research in Economics, 61*(3), 140–147.

Freire-Seren, M. J. (1999). Aggregate R&D expenditure and endogenous economic growth. *UFAE and IAE Working Papers*, No: WP 436.99.

Genc, M. C., & Atasoy, Y. (2010). The relationship between R&D expenditure and economic growth: Panel data analysis. *The Journal of Knowledge Economy & Knowledge Management, 5*(2), 27–34.

Greene, W. (2000). *Econometric analysis.* Upper Saddle River, New York: Prentice-Hall.

Hatemi, J. A., & Shamsuddin, M. (2016). The causal interaction between financial development and human development in Bangladesh. *Applied Economics Letters, 23*(14), 995–998.

Hausman, J. A. (1978). Specification tests in econometrics. *Econometrica*, (46), 1251–1271.

Hoechle, D. (2007). Robust standard errors for panel regressions with cross-sectional dependence. *Stata Journal, 7*(3), 281–312.

Horvath, R. (2011). Research & development and growth: A Bayesian model averaging analysis. *Economic Modelling, 28*, 2669–2673.

Kaya, A. (2017). Developments in financial markets effect on human development: The case of Turkey. *International Journal of Economics and Administrative Studies, 20*, 169–180.

Kendall, J. (2012). Local financial development and growth. *Journal of Banking and Finance, 36*, 1548–1562.

Korkmaz, S. (2010). Research and development investments in Turkey and the relationship examined between economic development with VAR model. *Journal of Yasar University, 20*(5), 3320–3330.

Kuri, P. K., & Laha, A. (2011). Financial inclusion and human development in India: An inter-state analysis. *Indian Journal of Human Development, 5*(1), 61–77.

Mankiw, N. G., Romer, D., & Weil, D. N. (1992). A contribution to the empirics of economic growth. *The Quarterly Journal of Economics, 107*(2), 407–437.

McKinnon, R. I. (1973). *Money and capital in economic development.* Washington, DC: The Brookings Institution.

Pagano, M. (1993). Financial markets and growth: An overview. *European Economic Review, 37*(2–3), 613–622.

Papagni, E. (2006). Household borrowing constraints, fertility dynamics and economic growth. *Journal of Economic Dynamics and Control, 30*(1), 27–54.

Pessoa, A. (2010). R&D and economic growth: How strong is the link?. *Economics Letters, 107*(2), 152–154.

Romer, P. M. (1994). The origins of endogenous growth. *Journal of Economic Perspectives, 8*(1), 3–22.

Sadraoui, T., & Zina, N. B. (2009). A dynamic panel data analysis for R&D cooperation and economic growth. *International Journal of Foresight and Innovation Policy, 5*(4), 218–233.

Sahin, G., & Gokdemir, L. (2016). Being examined with ARDL limit testing in Turkey scale for human development index components. *The Gazi Journal of Economics and Business, 2*(1), 1–24.

Sehrawat, M., & Giri, A. K. (2017). An empirical relationship between financial development indicators and human capital in some selected Asian countries. *International Journal of Social Economics, 44*(3), 337–349.

Sethi, N., Mishra, B. R., & Bhujabal, P. (2019). Do market size and financial development indicators affect human capital of select South Asian economies?. *International Journal of Social Economics, 46*(7), 887–903.

Shah, S. (2016). Determinant of human development index: A cross-country empirical analysis. *Munich Personal RePEc Archive*, Paper No. 73759. Retrieved September 18, 2020, from https://mpra.ub.uni-muenchen.de/73759/1/MPRA_paper_73759.pdf

Shaw, E. S. (1973). *Financial deepening in economic development.* New York: Oxford University Press.

Sungur, O., Aydin, H., & Eren, M. (2016). The relationship among R&D, innovation, export and economic growth in Turkey: Asymmetric causality analysis. *Suleyman Demirel University, The Journal of Faculty of Economics and Administrative Sciences, 21*(1), 173–192.

Tari, R. (2014). *Ekonometri*. Kocaeli: Umuttepe Publication.

Tatoglu, Y. F. (2018). *İleri panel veri analizi stata uygulamalı*. İstanbul: Beta Basım Publication.

UNDP (2019). Human Development Report 2019, Retrieved September 20, 2020, from http://hdr.undp.org/sites/default/files/hdr_2019_overview_-_turkish.pdf

United Nations Development Programme (UNDP), Retrieved September 15, 2020, from http://hdr.undp.org/en/data

Wooldridge, J. M. (2002). *Econometric analysis of cross section and panel data.* Cambridge, MA: The MIT Press.

World Bank Open Data, World Development Indicators, Retrieved September 15, 2020, from https://databank.worldbank.org/source/world-development-indicators

Wu, Y., Zhou, L., & Li, J. X. (2007). Cointegration and causality between R&D expenditure and economic growth in China: 1953–2004. *International Conference on Public Administration*, *76*, 869–876.

Yaylali, M., Akan, Y., & Isik, C. (2010). Cointegration and causality between R&D investment expenditures and economic growth in Turkey. *The Journal of Knowledge Economy & Knowledge Management*, *5*(2), 13–26.

Zaman, K., Izhar, Z., Mushtag, K. M., & Ahmad, M. (2012). The relationship between financial indicators and human development in Pakistan. *Economic Modeling*, *29*(5), 1515–1523.

Busra Kutlu Karabiyik

Determination of R&D Efficiency Levels of OECD Countries in the Intermediate Innovative Countries Group

Abstract Countries compete for producing technological products in the national and international market. This requires competing countries to constantly update their technology-related capabilities. It is important to use the resources allocated for R&D activities effectively in order to increase technology capabilities. In this study, it is aimed to evaluate the R&D activities of twelve OECD countries, Poland, Portugal, Czech Republic, Slovakia, Cyprus, Malta, Spain, Greece, Lithuania, Latvia, Hungary and Croatia, which are among the moderately innovative countries. Under the assumptions of input oriented constant returns to scale and input oriented variable returns to scale and with the help of the DEAP 2.1. program, data envelopment analysis was carried out. According to the input-oriented CRS model, it was observed that the countries of Poland, Latvia and Hungary are effective and the countries of Portugal, Czech Republic, Slovakia, Cyprus, Malta, Spain, Greece, Lithuania and Croatia are not effecient. Under the VRS assumption, five countries are effective, namely Poland, Czech Republic, Cyprus, Latvia and Hungary and other countries as Portugal, Slovakia, Malta, Spain, Greece, Lithuania and Croatia were found to be inefficient. According to the findings, it was seen that only the Czech Republic has a decreasing return on scale, while Portugal, Slovakia, Cyprus, Malta, Spain, Greece, Lithuania and Croatia countries, which are among the other eight countries, have an increasing return according to the scale.

Keywords: R&D Efficiency, Data Envelopment Analysis (DEAP), CRS, VRS

1 Introduction

Research and Development (R&D) activities increase the stock of information and lead to the use of existing information in new and different fields (Belgin, 2019). For countries that want to pioneer in the field of technology, the development of new and different innovations instead of repetitive technologies has great importance. R&D activities enable the creation, production, dissemination and implementation of information. Therefore, it causes various innovations in technologies, administrations, social and political systems (Wang & Huang, 2007). The size and intensity of R&D investments differ for each country (Guan, Zuo, Chen & Yam, 2016).

Managing the R&D processes of countries efficiently enables countries to create competitive advantages over each other in many respects. The ability to measure efficiency makes it easier to prevent situations that reduce productivity. Therefore, in order to ensure efficiency, the efficiency of R&D processes must first be measurable (Lee & Park, 2005). As countries' investments in R&D increase, their interest in measuring the efficiency of R&D and scientific productivity increases (Thomas, Sharma, & Jain, 2011). Since R&D investments are one of the most important components of scientific and technological processes, countries that cannot use their resources that related to R&D are falling behind than others (Wang & Huang, 2007). In addition, countries that do not use R&D resources efficiently seem to have lower growth rates than those who use them efficiently (Cullmann, Ehmckey & Petra Zloczyst, 2012). R&D activity is expressed as the ratio of R&D outputs to R&D inputs (Thomas et al., 2011). To obtain more outputs than inputs increases the efficiency.

The aim of this study is to evaluate the technical and total activities of the R&D activities of twelve OECD countries; Poland, Portugal, Czech Republic, Slovakia, Cyprus, Malta, Spain, Greece, Lithuania, Latvia, Hungary and Croatia, which are in the group of moderately innovative countries. Thus, to help them use their resources efficiently. In this study, it also aims to determine the degree of improvement of factors affecting R&D efficiency performances.

This study consists of five sections, including introduction, research methodology, research dataset, findings and conclusions and recommendations,

2 Methodology

Data envelopment analysis (DEA) linear programming methodology compares the efficiency of different decision making units with the help of multiple input and output variables (Donthu, Hershberger & Osmonbekov, 2005). It is accepted that DEA method is one of the best options in the event that it is desired to perform efficiency analysis using more than one input and output (Karadayi & Ekinci, 2019).

DEA models make two kinds of measurements: input and output oriented. "While input-oriented models predict the efficiency level of inputs at a given output amount level, output-oriented models estimate the efficiency level of outputs at a given input amount level" (Çınoroğlu, Doruk & Avcı, 2018).

In DEA analysis, decision-making units should have similar characteristics and have a homogeneous structure, since the efficiency of decision-making units in comparison to each other will be discussed. Even a decision making unit, which has a very different structure than others, can change all analysis results (Golany & Roll, 1989).

As the change rate between inputs and outputs can be the same for input-oriented and output-oriented efficiency measurements, this rate can also be different. When the rate of change between inputs and outputs is the same, Constant Return to Scale (CRS) occurs according to the scale. In other words, when inputs are increased, if the outputs increase at the same rate with the inputs, this is called as constant return to scale. In cases where the change rates between inputs and outputs differ from each other, it is formed as a result of Variable Returns of Scale (VRS). If the output increases at a lower rate than inputs when the inputs are increased, the return decreases according to the scale. If the output increases more when the inputs are increased, the return increases according to the scale (Bozkurt & Topçuoğlu, 2019).

In this study, input-oriented data envelopment analysis was preferred because it has more opportunity to control the inputs compared to the outputs that indicate the efficiency of R&D. In this study, DEA was performed separately under constant return on input-oriented scale (CRS) and under variable return on input-oriented scale (VRS). In order to ensure the homogeneity of the decision-making units, the R&D activities of the countries whose innovation performances are close together (intermediate innovative countries) were evaluated. DEAP 2.1 program was used to perform data envelopment analysis.

3 Dataset

The European Union commission publishes innovation scoreboards each year, indicating the innovation status of countries. Countries in this table; they are classified into four groups: leaders in innovation, strong in innovation, intermediate innovators and minimal innovators. Since the input and output variables that are intended to be used in this study cannot be reached for 2020, 2019 and 2018 years, the 2017 years' innovation score table published by the European Union for 2017 was used. In this study, the R&D activities of OECD countries (intermediate innovative countries) whose innovation performances are close to each other and evaluated in the penultimate group (intermediate innovators group) according to the table specified in 2017 were evaluated. These countries are Poland, Portugal, the Czech Republic, Slovakia, Cyprus, Malta, Spain, Greece, Lithuania, Latvia, Hungary and Croatia.

Many studies have suggested that the results of real outputs from R&D input can be seen after a certain period of time. Sharma and Thomas (2008) and Guan and Chen (2010) claimed that the delay time was two years. In this study, we accepted that the delay period was two years. In this context, the data related to the R&D input variables were obtained from the data of 2015 year, while the data on the R&D output variables were obtained from 2017 year.

In this study, as a result of the comprehensive literature review, input and output variables that are frequently used in most of the studies were used. One of the most important parts of DEA analysis is the definition of input and output variables. In this study, while and *"R&D expenditures/gross domestic product" and "number of researchers in R&D"* are considered as input variables, *"patent applications" and "high technology exports/total exports"* and are considered as output variables. A total of two input variables and two output variables were used. The data for the variables were obtained from the website https://stats.oecd.org/. The total number of countries that are decision-making units in this study is 12. Therefore, if the number of inputs is "m (2)" and the output number is "p (2)"; In this case, at least the "m + p + 1 (5)" decision unit is needed.

R&D expenditures; refers to the money spent in the public and private sector to increase knowledge and the use of information systematically (Saljoughian, Ghandehari, Shirouyehzad, Dabestani & Balouei, 2013). Data on R&D spending are mostly meticulously collected by countries. In this study, private sector or public R&D expenditures are discussed together, not separately. R&D expenditures refer to R&D expenditures in all sectors.

Ratio of R&D expenditures to gross domestic product; It is handled in order to clearly see the place of R&D expenditures among countries in all expenditures. This variable is one of the variables that distinguish this study from studies that measure other R&D activities.

Number of researchers in R&D; refers to a person spending one year/full time performance for R&D.

Patent applications; are official documents proving that a new invention, product or process is present. Patents are generally recognized as one of the strongest indicators of innovations and R&D processes. Although it cannot be concluded that all patented innovations are always useful, patents are one of the most important indicators of innovation outputs (Thomas et al., 2011). In this study, patent applications made by people residing in the country are taken into consideration. The applications of people who live in another country but apply in the relevant country are not taken into consideration.

High-tech product export implies to aviation, computers, medicines, scientific instruments, and machinery. In this study, the place of *high technology export/total export variable* and high technology export in total export of the country were taken into consideration. This variable is another variable that distinguishes this study from studies measuring other R&D activities.

Tab. 17.1: Countries' reference sets and reference weights (input oriented crs)

Numbers	Countries	Efficiency value (input oriented crs)	References and reference weights	
1	**Poland**	1.000	1	
2	**Portugal**	0.234	Latvia [0.155]	Poland [0.193]
3	**Czech Republic**	0.891	Hungary [1.202]	Poland [0.042]
4	**Slovakia**	0.724	Latvia [0.486]	Hungary [0.4]
5	**Cyprus**	0.080	Latvia [0.012]	Hungary [0.023]
6	**Malta**	0.446	Latvia [0.353]	Hungary [0.083]
7	**Spain**	0.493	Poland [0.599]	
8	**Greece**	0.224	Latvia [0.164]	Poland [0.113]
9	**Lithuania**	0.536	Latvia [0.695]	Hungary [0.09]
10	**Latvia**	1.000	1	
11	**Hungary**	1.000	1	
12	**Croatia**	0.514	Hungary [0.299]	

Source: (Self Calculation)

4 Findings

Input-oriented DEA under constant return to scale was analyzed and results took part in Tab. 17.1. Considering the reference clusters created for inefficient countries, it was seen that the countries with the highest number of references were two countries, six times Latvia and six times Hungary. According to Tab. 17.2, it is seen that three countries (Poland, Latvia and Hungary) are efficient and the other nine countries (Portugal, Czech Republic, Slovakia, Cyprus, Malta, Spain, Greece, Lithuania, and Croatia) are not.

Tab. 17.1 also includes reference sets and weight values of inactive countries. For example, according to Tab. 17.1, Portugal should take Latvia and Poland as a reference in order to be efficient. Portugal should make improvements based on 15.5 % Latvia and 19.3 % Poland. Similarly, Lithuania should make improvements by taking 69 % Latvia and 9 % Hungary in order to be efficient. Tab. 17.2 shows the input and output improvement rates of the countries under the efficiency limit under the input-oriented CRS assumption.

Tab. 17.2 shows the improvement rates for the input and output variables of the countries. To specify the results above, we will explain three of them that we

Tab. 17.2: The improvement rates of countries that fall into the efficiency limit (Input-oriented CRS)

Countries	Variables	Original Değer (OD)	Target Değer (HD)	Difference (%) $\frac{HD-OD}{OD} \times 100$
Portugal	**Output1:** High technology export/ Total export variable	0.026	0.026	**0**
	Output2: Patent applications	925	925	**0**
	Input1: R&D expenditures/Gross domestic product	1.243	0.291	**-76.5889**
	Input2: Number of researchers in R&D	3711.868	698.973	**-81.1692**
Czech Republic	**Output1:** High technology export/ Total export variable	0.164	0.164	**0**
	Output2: Patent applications	880	880	**0**
	Input1: R&D expenditures/Gross domestic product	1.929	1.682	**-12.8046**
	Input2: Number of researchers in R&D	3591.273	3199.856	**-10.8991**
Slovakia	**Output1:** High technology export/ Total export variable	0.092	0.092	**0**
	Output2: Patent applications	228	293.657	**28.79693**
	Input1: R&D expenditures/Gross domestic product	1.175	0.85	**-27.6596**
	Input2: Number of researchers in R&D	2648.402	1916.405	**-27.6392**
Cyprus	**Output1:** High technology export/ Total export variable	0.004	0.004	**0**
	Output2: Patent applications	6	14.505	**141.75**
	Input1: R&D expenditures/Gross domestic product	0.481	0.039	**-91.8919**
	Input2: Number of researchers in R&D	1009.054	80.816	**-91.9909**
Malta	**Output1:** High technology export/ Total export variable	0.039	0.039	**0**
	Output2: Patent applications	9	95.249	**958.3222**
	Input1: R&D expenditures/Gross domestic product	0.75	0.334	**-55.4667**
	Input2: Number of researchers in R&D	1917.608	854.557	**-55.4363**

Tab. 17.2: Continued

Countries	Variables	Original Değer (OD)	Target Değer (HD)	Difference (%) $\frac{HD-OD}{OD} \times 100$
Spain	**Output1:** High technology export/ Total export variable	0.038	0.042	**10.52632**
	Output2: Patent applications	2799	2799	**0**
	Input1: R&D expenditures/Gross domestic product	1.22	0.601	**-50.7377**
	Input2: Number of researchers in R&D	2638.861	1292.03	**-51.0383**
Greece	**Output1:** High technology export/ Total export variable	0.021	0.021	**0**
	Output2: Patent applications	550	550	**0**
	Input1: R&D expenditures/Gross domestic product	0.966	0.216	**-77.6398**
	Input2: Number of researchers in R&D	3094.011	541.66	**-82.4933**
Lithuania	**Output1:** High technology export/ Total export variable	0.067	0.067	**0**
	Output2: Patent applications	101	145.836	**44.39208**
	Input1: R&D expenditures/Gross domestic product	1.041	0.558	**-46.3977**
	Input2: Number of researchers in R&D	2785.541	1493.753	**-46.3748**
Croatia	**Output1:** High technology export/ Total export variable	0.04	0.04	**0**
	Output2: Patent applications	169	169.851	**0.50355**
	Input1: R&D expenditures/Gross domestic product	0.842	0.407	**-51.6627**
	Input2: Number of researchers in R&D	1503.063	772.391	**-48.6122**

Source: (Self Calculation)

choose accidentally. For example, in order to Portugal to become fully efficient, it must reduce the rate of R&D expenditures/gross domestic product by 76.5 % and decrease the number of researchers in R&D by 81.1 % without changing the high technology export/total export rate and the number of patent applications.

In order for the Czech Republic to become fully efficient, it must reduce the rate of R&D expenditures/gross domestic product by 12.8 % and decrease the

Tab. 17.3: Countries' efficiency values (input oriented VRS)

Countries	CRS (Total efficiency)	VRS (Technical efficiency)	CRS/VRS (Scale efficiency)	Returns by scale (irs or drs)
Poland	1.000	1.000	1.000	-
Portugal	0.234	0.482	0.486	irs
Czech Republic	0.891	1.000	0.891	drs
Slovakia	0.724	0.754	0.960	irs
Cyprus	0.080	1.000	0.080	irs
Malta	0.446	0.732	0.609	irs
Spain	0.493	0.651	0.757	irs
Greece	0.224	0.578	0.387	irs
Lithuania	0.536	0.605	0.887	irs
Latvia	1.000	1.000	1.000	-
Hungary	1.000	1.000	1.000	-
Croatia	0.514	0.934	0.550	irs
Mean	**0.595**	**0.811**	**0.717**	

Source: (Self Calculation)

number of researchers in R&D by 10.8 % without changing the high technology export/total export rate and the number of patent applications.

In order for Spain to become fully efficient, it has to increase the rate of high technology exports/total exports by 10.5 %, must not change the number of patent applications, decrease the rate of R&D expenditures/gross domestic product by 50.7 % and decrease the number of researchers in R&D by 51 %.

After this stage, the efficiency values of the countries will be calculated for the input-oriented VRS. The total, technical and scale efficiency values of the countries are shown in Tab. 17.3.

Under the VRS assumption, five countries (Poland, Czech Republic, Cyprus, Latvia and Hungary) were found to be technically efficient. CRS, VRS and (CRS/VRS) three different efficacy criteria average values used for all countries are 0,595; 0,811 and 0,717 respectively. At the same time, it is seen that only the Czech Republic has a decreasing return on scale compared to the inactive countries, while all other countries have an increasing return on scale.

In Tab. 17.4, reference sets and weight values of inactive countries are given. For example, it is concluded that Portugal should take Cyprus, Poland and Latvia as a reference in order to be efficient. Portugal should make the necessary improvements by modeling 68.6 % Cyprus, 19.3 % Poland and 12.1 % Latvia.

Tab. 17.4: Countries' reference sets and reference weights (Input oriented VRS)

Numbers	Countries	Reference sets and weights		
1	**Poland**	1		
2	**Portugal**	Cyprus [0.686]	Poland [0.193]	Latvia [0.121]
3	**Czech Republic**	1		
4	**Slovakia**	Hungary [0.236]	Latvia [0.764]	
5	**Cyprus**	1		
6	**Malta**	Cyprus [0.533]	Latvia [0.467]	
7	**Spain**	Poland [0.598]	Cyprus [0.402]	
8	**Greece**	Latvia [0.126]	Cyprus [0.761]	Poland [0.113]
9	**Lithuania**	Latvia [0.84]	Cyprus [0.16]	
10	**Latvia**	1		
11	**Hungary**	1		
12	**Croatia**	Poland [0.022]	Cyprus [0.518]	Latvia [0.46]

Source: (Self Calculation)

When the reference sets created for inefficient countries are analyzed, it is seen that the countries with the most reference in terms of frequency are Cyprus and six times Latvia. Tab. 17.5 shows the input and output improvement rates of the countries under the efficiency limit, under the input VRS assumption.

Tab. 17.5 shows the improvement rates for the input and output variables of the countries. To specify the results above, we will explain three of them that we choose accidentally. For example, for Portugal to become fully efficient, it should reduce the rate of R&D expenditures/gross domestic product by 51.7 % and decrease the number of researchers in R&D by 64.2 % without changing the high technology export/total export rate and the number of patent applications.

In order for Greece to become fully efficient, it should reduce the rate of R&D expenditures/gross domestic product by 42.2 % and decrease number of researches in R&D by 59.9 % without changing the number of high technology exports/total exports and patent applications.

In order for Croatia to become fully efficient, it should reduce the rate of R&D expenditures/gross domestic product by 33.6 % and decrease number of researches in R&D 6.6 % without changing the high technology export/total export rate and the number of patent applications.

Tab. 17.5: The improvement rates of countries that fall into the efficiency limit (Input-oriented VRS)

Countries	Variables	Original Değer (OD)	Target Değer (HD)	Difference (%) $\frac{HD-OD}{OD} \times 100$
Portugal	**Output1:** High technology export/Total export variable	0.026	0.026	**0.000**
	Output2: Patent applications	925.000	925.000	**0.000**
	Input1: R&D expenditures/Gross domestic product	1.243	0.600	**-51.730**
	Input2: Number of researchers in R&D	3711.868	1328.308	**-64.215**
Slovakia	**Output1:** High technology export/Total export variable	0.092	0.092	**0.000**
	Output2: Patent applications	228	238.345	**4.537**
	Input1: R&D expenditures/Gross domestic product	1.175	0.801	**-31.830**
	Input2: Number of researchers in R&D	2648.402	1996.182	**-24.627**
Malta	**Output1:** High technology export/Total export variable	0.039	0.039	**0.000**
	Output2: Patent applications	9	66.667	**640.744**
	Input1: R&D expenditures/Gross domestic product	0.75	0.549	**-26.800**
	Input2: Number of researchers in R&D	1917.608	1384.3	**-27.811**
Spain	**Output1:** High technology export/Total export variable	0.038	0.044	**15.789**
	Output2: Patent applications	2799	2799	**0.000**
	Input1: R&D expenditures/Gross domestic product	1.22	0.794	**-34.918**
	Input2: Number of researchers in R&D	2638.861	1696.483	**-35.712**
Greece	**Output1:** High technology export/Total export variable	0.021	0.021	**0.000**
	Output2: Patent applications	550	550	**0.000**
	Input1: R&D expenditures/Gross domestic product	0.966	0.558	**-42.236**
	Input2: Number of researchers in R&D	3094.011	1240.023	**-59.922**

Tab. 17.5: Continued

Countries	Variables	Original Değer (OD)	Target Değer (HD)	Difference (%) $\frac{HD-OD}{OD} \times 100$
Lithuania	**Output1:** High technology export/Total export variable	0.067	0.067	**0.000**
	Output2: Patent applications	101	115.2	**14.059**
	Input1: R&D expenditures/Gross domestic product	1.041	0.603	**-42.075**
	Input2: Number of researchers in R&D	2785.541	1684.496	**-39.527**
Croatia	**Output1:** High technology export/Total export variable	0.04	0.04	**0.000**
	Output2: Patent applications	169	169	**0.000**
	Input1: R&D expenditures/Gross domestic product	0.842	0.559	**-33.610**
	Input2: Number of researchers in R&D	1503.063	1404.544	**-6.555**

Source: (Self Calculation)

5 Conclusions

In this study, it was aimed to evaluate the R&D activities of twelve OECD countries, namely Poland, Portugal, Czech Republic, Slovakia, Cyprus, Malta, Spain, Greece, Lithuania, Latvia, Hungary and Croatia, which were included in the group of moderately innovative countries in 2017. Data envelopment analysis was performed under the assumptions of constant input (CRS) and variable return (VRS) according to the input scale.

According to the input-oriented CRS model, it is seen that three countries (Poland, Latvia and Hungary) are efficient and nine countries (Portugal, Czech Republic, Slovakia, Cyprus, Malta, Spain, Greece, Lithuania and Croatia) are inefficient. Under the VRS assumption, five countries (Poland, Czech Republic, Cyprus, Latvia and Hungary) were active, while seven countries (Portugal, Slovakia, Malta, Spain, Greece, Lithuania and Croatia) were inefficient. According to the results of the analysis, it is seen that the Czech Republic and Cyprus countries, which are not active under the CRS assumption, are active under the VRS assumption. It can be said that the measurements made under the VRS assumption are more flexible than the CRS assumption and therefore the results stated that relatively more countries are efficient are in line with expectations.

In this study, the scale efficiency was calculated for each country and the direction of returns according to the scale was determined for inefficient countries. According to the findings, only the Czech Republic seemed to have a decreasing return on scale, while eight other countries (Portugal, Slovakia, Cyprus, Malta, Spain, Greece, Lithuania and Croatia) had increased returns on a scale. According to this, when the amount of input increases in the Czech Republic, it can be stated that the amount of output increases not at the same rate as the amount of input, but at a lower rate compared to the amount of input. It can be said that 8 countries (Portugal, Slovakia, Cyprus, Malta, Spain, Greece, Lithuania and Croatia), which do not have scale efficiency and have increased return according to the scale, have ability to produce more than one unit with one unit of input, but they produce less than their capacity because of some various factors.

This study evaluates recent R&D performances of countries and suggests various improvements for input and output variables. The results obtained from this study are expected to contribute to increasing the R&D activities of countries. With the input and output variables used in this study, the R&D efficiency performances and progress of the countries can be monitored by years.

Bibliography

Belgin, O. (2019). Analysing R&D efficiency of Turkish regions using data envelopment analysis. *Technology Analysis & Strategic Management*, *31*(11), 1341–1352.

Bozkurt, E., & Topçuoğlu, Ö. (2019). Ar-ge etkinliğinin belirleyicileri üzerine bir tobit model uygulaması. *Trakya Üniversitesi Sosyal Bilimler Dergisi, 21*, 141–163.

Chen, K., & Guan, J. (2012). Measuring the efficiency of China's regional innovation systems: Application of network data envelopment analysis (DEA). *Regional Studies*, *46*(3), 355–377.

Cullmann, A., Schmidt-Ehmcke, J., & Zloczysti, P. (2012). R&D efficiency and barriers to entry: A two stage semi-parametric DEA approach. *Oxford Economic Papers*, *64*(1), 176–196.

Çınaroğlu, E., Doruk, N., & Avcı, T. (2018). Erciyes üniversitesi fakültelerinin veri zarflama analizi yöntemiyle etkinlik analizi. *Uluslararası Yönetim İktisat ve İşletme Dergisi*, *14*(4), 1025–1043.

Donthu, N., Hershberger, E. K., & Osmonbekov, T. (2005). Benchmarking marketing productivity using data envelopment analysis. *Journal of Business Research*, *58*(11), 1474–1482.

Ekinci, Y., & Ön, R. M. (2015). A review on the comparison of EU countries based on research and development efficiencies. *WASET. International Journal of Social, Behavioral, Educational, Economic, Business and Industrial Engineering*, *9*(7), 2368–2371.

Golany, B., & Roll, Y. (1989). An application procedure for DEA. *Omega*, *17*(3), 237–250.

Guan, J., & Chen, K. (2010). Measuring the innovation production process: A cross-region empirical study of China's high-tech innovations. *Technovation*, *30*(5–6), 348–358.

Guan, J., Zuo, K., Chen, K., & Yam, R. C. (2016). Does country-level R&D efficiency benefit from the collaboration network structure?. *Research Policy*, *45*(4), 770–784.

Hu, B., Wang, L., & Yu, X. (2007). R&D and economic growth in China on the basis of data envelopment analysis: Evidence from Hebei Province, PRC. *Journal of Technology Management in China*, *2*(3), 225–236.

Karadayi, M., & Ekinci Y. (2019). Evaluating R&D performance of EU countries using categorical DEA. *Technology Analysis & Strategic Management*, *31*(2), 227–238.

Lee, H.-Y., & Park, Y.-T. (2005). An international comparison of R&D efficiency: DEA approach, *Asian Journal of Technology Innovation*, *13*(2), 207–222.

Saljoughian, M., Ghandehari, M., Shirouyehzad, H., Dabestani, R., & Balouei, H. (2013). Performance evaluation of OECD countries by data envelopment analysis based on science and technology factors. *Journal of Applied Sciences and Engineering Management*, *1*(1), 24–35.

Sharma, S., & Thomas, V. (2008). Inter-country R&D efficiency analysis: An application of data envelopment analysis. *Scientometrics*, *76*(3), 483–501.

Thomas, V. J., Sharma, S., & Jain, S. K. (2011). Using patents and publications to assess R&D efficiency in the states of the USA. *World Patent Information*, *33*(1), 4–10.

Wang, E. C. (2007). R&D efficiency and economic performance: A cross-country analysis using the stochastic frontier approach. *Journal of Policy Modeling*, *29*(2), 345–360.

Wang, E. C., & Huang, W. (2007). Relative efficiency of R&D activities: A cross-country study accounting for environmental factors in the DEA approach. *Research policy*, *36*(2), 260–273.

Yıldırım, İ. (2015). *Avrupa ülkelerinin AR-GE etkinlik analizi.* (Unpublished master's thesis). Ankara University Institute of Social Science, Ankara.

Murat Yorulmaz

Examining the Relationships Between Emotional Labor Behaviour, Burnout and Work Alienation in the Marine Tourism Businesses

Abstract Employees play a key role in ensuring the provision of high-quality services in service businesses as well as customer satisfaction. Marine tourism businesses, which are one of the service businesses, the satisfaction of those in a yacht (yacht passengers who are present in a yacht for travel, sport or recreation) is essential for these businesses to survive and to achieve their objectives and this also depends particularly on the attitudes and behaviors of yacht employees (ship's crew and other service staff) who are in contact with yacht passengers. Thus, this study seeks to reveal the causal relationships between the emotional labor behaviors of employees in commercial yachts operating under marine tourism businesses, and their burnout levels and work alienation. To that end, the data obtained from employees in commercial yachts that operate in the Aegean and Mediterranean Regions were analyzed using SPSS v.22 and AMOS v.22 software package programs by means of the Bootstrap resampling with 5000 replications and structural equation modeling. The findings of this study reveal that emotional labor behaviors among yacht employees have both a direct and an indirect effect on their work alienation, the latter through burnout. As marine tourism is a labor-intensive industry, yacht employees are of pivotal importance for marine tourism sector and they greatly contribute to this sector. For that reason, it is necessary to perform managerial activities to reduce the emotional labor of yacht employees.

Keywords: Maritime, Marine Tourism, Yacht Employees, Emotional Labor, Burnout, Work Alienation

1 Introduction

With the increasing importance of the service sector in the economy in developed economies, businesses in this sector attach importance to the effective management of human capital in order to gain competitive advantage. Because employees are in direct or indirect interaction with customers due to the activities of service businesses. Thus, these businesses need employees with high communication skills, who can demonstrate purposeful behaviors and manage their emotions, rather than muscle power alone. Employees play a key role in ensuring the provision of high-quality services in service businesses as well as customer satisfaction. Marine tourism businesses, which are one of the service businesses, the satisfaction of those in a yacht (yacht passengers who are present in a yacht for travel, sport or recreation) is essential for these businesses to survive and to achieve their objectives and this also depends particularly on the attitudes and behaviors of yacht employees (ship's crew and other service staff) who are in contact with yacht passengers. The concept of emotional labor, defined as the control of an employee's behaviors and attitudes to display the behaviors and attitudes desired by his/her organization and the process of managing his/her emotions in line with the objectives of the organization, is important for the working conditions of the marine tourism industry. Since yacht employees are in face-to-face communication with yacht passengers and provide service for them in the yacht, where sea tourism service is offered and consumed, they spend a lot of emotional labor. Therefore, the individual or organizational consequences of the emotions, emotional labor level and emotional labor of yacht employees in marine tourism businesses should be deemed essential for the success of these businesses. Moreover, the effects of emotional labor on employees and organizations will not be the same in all conditions and sectors. Review of the literature shows that studies on emotional labor generally pertained to tourism (Büyükbeşe & Aslan, 2019; Chu & Murrmann 2006; Gürlek, Tuna & Yeşiltaş, 2020; Kızanlıklı & Ünlüönen, 2016; Lee et al., 2014; Türker, 2016; Yürür & Ünlü, 2011), health (Gök, 2015; Öz & Baykal, 2017; Kıyat, Özgüleş & Günaydın, 2018; Oral & Köse, 2011) and education (Brotheridge & Lee, 2003; Basım & Beğenirbaş, 2012; Çukur, 2009; Karakaş et al., 2016; Naring, Briet & Brouwers, 2006) however, there is no study on emotional labor in marine tourism sector. Thus, this study seeks to reveal the causal relationships between the emotional labor behaviors of employees in commercial yachts operating under marine tourism businesses, and their burnout levels and work alienation. To that end, the data obtained from employees in commercial yachts that operate in the Aegean and Mediterranean Regions were analyzed using SPSS v.22 and AMOS v.22 software package programs by means of the Bootstrap resampling with 5000 replications and structural equation modeling. This study adds new insights to the literature since it is performed with employees in marine tourism sector, examines the emotional labor levels of yacht employees, explores the effect of emotional labor on burnout and work alienation, reveals the intermediary role burnout in the relationship between emotional labor and work alienation and analyzes the abovementioned research variables together.

2 Literature Review

The concept of emotional labor, which indicates the emotions, thoughts and communication skills of the employees that organizations need to manage well in order to achieve their goals and that make up their intellectual capital, is first coined by Hochschild (1983). Hochschild (1983) argued that emotional labor occurs when employees manage their feeling to create a publicly observable facial and bodily display as expected by the organization and according to the requirements of the job, and considered emotional labor as another element of the workforce, just like physical and mental labor. Ashforth and Humphrey (1993), who regarded emotional labor as the process of displaying observable emotional behavior, focused on expressed behaviors rather than emotions. Because these scholars considered emotional labor as exhibiting the expected behaviors in a way to bring out the desired emotions. According to Morris and Feldman (1997), emotional labor refers to the effort of an employee to demonstrate the expected behavior in service delivery and the process whereby s/he controls his/her emotions. Kruml and Geddes (2000) expressed emotional labor as the efforts of employees to increase the service quality of their business and their behaviors to show desired emotions. Whether the focus is on the emotions underlying the behavior or on the exhibited behavior or efforts, it is a known fact that employees who can demonstrate their emotions in line with the organization's expectations contribute more to their organizations (French, Rayner, Rees & Rumbles, 2008). Therefore, service businesses in particular need employees who can manage their emotions well in order to ensure customer satisfaction in the business environment. It can be argued that emotional labor consists of surface-acting and deep-acting dimensions (Hochschild, 1983) as well as the dimension of sincere/genuine behaviors (Ashforth & Humphrey, 1993; Kruml & Geddes, 2000) or the dimensions of emotional deviation and emotional effort (Chu & Murrmann, 2006), or the dimensions of deep acting, hiding emotions and faking emotions (Lee & Brotheridge, 2011). This study addresses the dimension of deep acting as employees' efforts to truly demonstrate and change the required emotions, the dimension of hiding emotions as the effort to hide negative emotions as well as the dimension of faking emotions as the effort to show the desired emotions (Dursun, Aytaç & Bayram, 2014). A case of hiding emotions may occur when a yacht employee covers his/her emotions by hiding the tension s/he experienced due to a work-family conflict and puts a smile on his/her face while serving yacht passengers benefiting from marine tourism services and enjoying their time in the yacht; an example of the dimension of faking emotions may be when a yacht employee who cleans badly-used and dirty cabins shows positive emotions as if everything is fine. An example for deep acting is that such employee believes that his/her duty is to ensure that the yacht passengers enjoy their time in the yacht as a requirement of his/her job, and always puts a smile on his/her face.

Although the literature has mainly focused on the negative consequences of emotional labor, its most important outcome is perhaps customer satisfaction (Oral & Köse, 2011) and customer service performance (Yorulmaz, 2020). On the other hand, as emotional labor requires a certain amount of effort to manage one's feelings, it may have negative consequences on the employee individually and thus on the organization. Because employees who have to exhibit the behaviors desired from them or hide their negative emotions considering the expectations of the organization, may fail in emotion management and experience inconsistencies. The relationship between emotional labor and the organizational attitude and behavior of the employee is based on the emotional conflict theory. This theory posits that inconsistencies between the emotions that the organization wants their employees to show as a requirement of their job and the emotions actually felt and reflected by them affect these employees (Kruml & Geddes, 2000). Such inconsistencies may cause negative outcomes such as work alienation and burnout (Güngör, 2009; Yürür & Ünlü, 2011; Oral & Köse, 2011; Kaya & Serçeoğlu, 2013; Dursun, Aytaç & Bayram, 2014; Tokmak, 2014; Akdu & Akdu, 2016; Güğerçin, 2019; Aslan & Mert, 2019). Based on these insights in the literature, the following hypotheses have been proposed: *Hypothesis 1: Emotional labor behaviors have a positive effect on work alienation. Hypothesis 2: Emotional labor behaviors have a positive effect on burnout.*

People who have to deal with problems in their work life or social life may experience a feeling of burnout when they cannot cope with these problems over time. Particularly, heavy workload, financial difficulties or varying human relations can cause employees to feel burnout. Employees who experience burnout may want to move away from their work environment and be alone, and may become alienated from their jobs over time. Burnout syndrome causes employees to feel inadequate and unsuccessful in the workplace, to be reluctant to their duties and to distance themselves from the workplace and their colleagues. As a result, employees may experience work alienation. Based on the studies in the literature that explore the relationship between burnout and work alienation experienced by employees (Kırıcı & Özkoç, 2017; Moç, 2018; Osin, 2009; O'Donohue & Nelson, 2012; Özler & Dirican, 2014) and reveal the positive correlation between emotional labor behaviors and work alienation, the following hypotheses and research model in Fig. 18.1 have

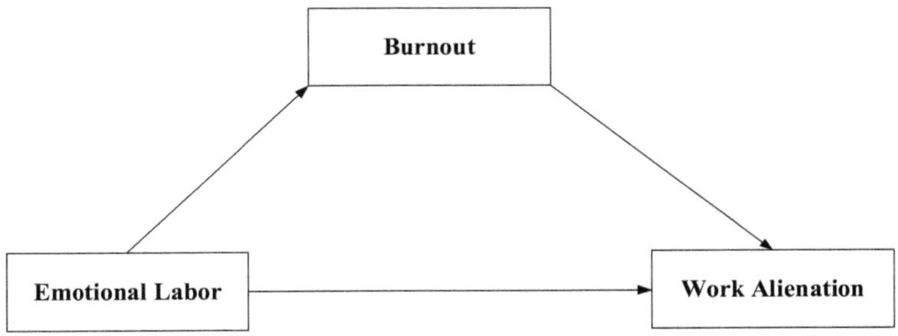

Fig. 18.1: Research model

been proposed: *Hypothesis 3: Burnout has a positive effect on work alienation. Hypothesis 4: Burnout plays an intermediary role in the relationship between emotional labor behaviors and work alienation.*

3 Research Method

3.1 Data Collection and Sampling

This study seeks to analyze the relationship between the emotional labor behaviors, and burnout levels of the crew on commercial yachts and their work alienation based on the data obtained through questionnaire method using Google form between July and September, 2020. The voluntary participation in the questionnaire was encouraged by the yacht enterprises and the human resources departments of the marina enterprises and other enterprises that provide employment for yachts in Turkey. The majority of the participants was male (N = 216, 91.1 %), aged between 30 and 40 (N = 124, 52.3 %), single (N = 122, 51.5 %), high-school graduate (N = 120, 50.6 %) and had experience of 4–7 years in yachting sector (N = 134, 56.5 %). In terms of positions, 110 participants (46.4 %) served as captain, 93 participants (39.2 %) served as deck crew, 24 participants (10.1 %) as service staff and 10 (4.2 %) as engine crew.

3.2 Measures Instruments

The emotional labor scale, developed by Lee & Brotheridge (2011) and consists of 9 items that include the dimensions of in-depth action (3 items), faking emotions (3 items) and hidden emotions (3 items) adapted into Turkish and tested by Dursun, Aytaç and Bayram (2014) (Cronbach's Alpha = 0.81, 0.77 and 0.74). This is a 5-point Likert type scale (1 = never, 5 = always). The results of the explanatory factor analysis (EFA) using the principal components analysis and Varimax rotation, which was performed to determine the consistency and the factor structure of the emotional labor scale, indicated that the scale has a three-dimensional structure with eigenvalues greater than 1 (KMO = 0.717; χ^2 = 864.666; df = 36; $p < 0.001$; factor loads varied between 0.660 and 0.903; total explained variance: 72.4 %). The scale presents items such as "*I pretend to feel the emotions that I do not feel*", "*I hide my feelings*" and "*I really try to feel the emotions that I need to show.*"

To measure the burnout levels of the yacht employees, the 10-item scale with one dimension (Cronbach's Alpha = 0.91) designed by Pines (2005) and translated into Turkish and tested by Tümkaya, Çam and Çavuşoğlu (2009). This is a 5-point Likert type scale (1 = never, 5 = always). The results of the explanatory factor analysis (EFA) using the principal components analysis and Varimax rotation, which was performed to determine the consistency and the factor structure of the burnout scale, indicated that the scale has one dimension with eigenvalue greater than 1 (KMO = 0.717; χ^2 = 864.666; df = 36; $p < 0.001$; factor loads varied between 0.650 and 0.881; total explained variance: 60.5 %). An example of the items in the scale is: "*I feel worthless and like a failure.*"

To measure the work alienation levels of the yacht employees, the 6-item scale with one dimension (Cronbach's Alpha = 0.712) used by Kaya and Serçeoğlu (2013). This is a 5-point Likert type scale (1 = I certainly disagree, 5 = I totally agree). The results of the explanatory factor analysis (EFA) using the principal components analysis and Varimax rotation, which was performed to determine the consistency of the scale, indicated that there were two items with factor loads less than 0.50, which were later removed from the scale. The second EFA showed that the work alienation scale has one dimension with eigenvalue greater than 1 (KMO = 0.749; χ^2 = 321.498; df = 6; $p < 0.001$; factor loads varied between 0.760 and 0.825; total explained variance: 64.2 %). An example of the items in the scale is: "*I am having trouble finding something about myself in my job.*"

3.3 Statistical Analysis

For the purpose of revealing whether the burnout levels of yacht employees has a mediate role in the relationship between their emotional labor behaviors and work alienation, this study performed basic statistical analyzes (frequency analysis, average, explanatory factor analysis, coefficients of skewness and kurtosis and reliability analyzes) by means of SPSS v22, and the validity of the measurement model and the analyzes on the structural model were conducted

Tab. 18.1: Comparison of alternative measurement models

Alternative models	χ^2/sd	CFI	TLI	RMSEA	SRMR	AIC	ECVI
Measurement model (EL_2nd ord.CFA)	1.926	0.929	0.919	0.063	0.077	535.536	2.269
Model 1 (EL_1st ord. CFA)	1.966	0.927	0.916	0.064	0.078	544.551	2.307
Model 2 (Unrelated model)	2.556	0.878	0.864	0.081	0.102	678.870	2.877
Model 3 (Single factored model)	6.482	0.569	0.522	0.152	0.193	1573.835	6.669

using AMOS v22 by Bootstrap resampling with 5000 replications. Further, the Sobel test was carried out to determine the statistical significance of the mediate role.

4 Results

4.1 Validity and Reliability Analysis

Tab. 18.1 presents the results of the confirmatory factor analysis (CFA) to determine the structural validity of the measurement tool. The results showed that the standardized factor loads of the variables observed were greater than 0.60 and statistically significant ($p < 0.001$) as well. As evident in Tab. 18.1, the goodness of fit indices (χ^2/sd = 1.926; CFI = 0.929; TLI = 0.919; RMSEA = 0.063; SRMR = 0.077) in the measurement tool using emotional labor behaviors as the second order CFA and burnout and alienation as the first order CFA (EL_2nd ord.CFA) were more appropriate and acceptable than that in other models (Hu & Bentler, 1999; Hair et al., 2014). Besides, as the AIC and ECVI values of the measurement tool were smaller than that of other models (Browne & Cudeck, 1993), the measurement tool was considered as the most suitable one.

Tab. 18.2 shows the AVE (Average Variance Extracted), CR (Composite Reliability) values of Average Shared Variance (ASV) and Maximum Shared Variance (MSV) of the variables in the measurement tool. The CR values were higher than the AVE values and above 0.70, and the AVE values were above 0.50, which means that the measurement tool has convergent validity (Fornell & Larcker, 1981; Hair et al., 2014).

Moreover, the square root values of the AVE values presented diagonally in Tab. 18.2 were higher than the Pearson correlation coefficients between the variables, and the AVE values were higher than the ASV and MSV values,

Tab. 18.2: Correlations, convergent and discriminant validity and internal consistency reliability

Variables	CA	CR	AVE	MSV	ASV	1	2	3
1.Emotional Labor	0.763	0.780	0.543	0.148	0.092	0.736	0.189**	0.386**
2. Burnout	0.809	0.932	0.580	0.196	0.115		0.716	0.443**
3. Work Alienation	0.922	0.813	0.523	0.196	0.172			0.723

**p < 0,01; values in diagonal are the square root of AVE of each construct.

Tab. 18.3: Means, standard deviations, skewness and kurtosis

Variables	Mean	SD	Skewness	SE	Kurtosis	SE
1. Emotional Labor	2.700	0.734	0.233	0.158	0.258	0.315
2. Burnout	1.810	0.825	1.723	0.158	2.823	0.315
3. Work Alienation	2.112	1.023	0.884	0.158	0.028	0.315

which indicates that the tool has discrimant validity as well. As seen in Tab. 18.2, both CR and Cronbach's Alpha (CA) coefficients of the measurement model were above 0.70, and thus the model was considered as a reliable model (Hair et al., 2014).

Tab. 18.3 presents the coefficients of skewness and kurtosis and means of variables, which were measured to reveal the variables in the measurement model, considered as structurally valid and reliable, were normally distributed or not. The coefficients of skewness and kurtosis of the variables were in the range of ±3 and ± 10 and their critical values were below 10; it follows that the data were normally distributed (Kline, 2016). Also, Tab. 18.3 shows that the burnout and alienation levels of the yacht employees were low whilst their emotional labor levels were moderate.

Furthermore, the Harman's single factor test was conducted to measure common method bias, which may happen when the same participants answer the dependent and independent variables in a questionnaire at the same time, and the order of the scales was modified in order to avoid common method bias. Accordingly, the participants were first asked about the work alienation, which was a dependent variable, and then about burnout and emotional labor behaviors for the order of the scales. Also, the EFA on the 23 items in the tool through non-linear principal component analysis yielded five components with eigenvalues greater than 1, together explaining 57.2 % of the total variance and

Tab. 18.4: Direct and indirect effects

Variables	Work Alienation		Burnout		Work Alienation	
	β	SE	β	SE	β	SE
1. Emotional Labor	0.673***	0.219	0.293***	0.120	0.568***	0.200
2. Burnout	-	-	-	-	0.359***	0.109
R^2	0.453		0.086		0.571	
Bootstrap İndirect Effect	β=0.105*; 95 % CI [0.017; 0.190]					
Model Goodness of Fit İndex	χ^2/sd =1.938; CFI= 0.923; TLI= 0.912; RMSEA= 0.063; SRMR= 0.067					

*p < 0.05; ***p < 0.001

with its first factor explaining 22.3 % of the total variance. In other words, non-linear EFA revealed a number of factors with the first factor failing to explain a significant percentage of the total variance. Besides, the CFA, which was performed by loading 23 items in the tool on a single factor, the goodness of fit indices for the single-factor model remained far below acceptable values, which indicates that there was no common method bias (Podsakoff et al, 2003; Podsakoff et al., 2012).

4.2 Hypothesis Testing

Tab. 18.4 presents the results of the analyzes using AMOS v22 by Bootstrap resampling with 5000 replications to test the research hypotheses. As shown in Tab. 18.4, the goodness of fit indices for the research model (χ^2/sd = 1.938; CFI = 0.923; TLI = 0.912; RMSEA = 0.063; SRMR = 0.067) were within acceptable values (Hu & Bentler, 1999; Hair et al., 2014).

Tab. 18.4 also demonstrates that the total effect of emotional labor on work alienation was positive and statistically significant ($\beta = 0.673$; $R^2 = 0.45$; $p < 0.001$) and the total effect of emotional labor on burnout was also positive and statistically significant ($\beta = 0.293$; $R^2 = 0.09$; $p < 0.001$). The combined effect of emotional labor and burnout on work alienation was also examined and it was found that the effect of emotional labor on work alienation was persistent but decreased ($\beta = 0.568$; $p < 0.001$) whilst that of burnout was positive ($\beta = 0.359$; $p < 0.001$). Further, emotional labor and burnout explained about 57 % ($R^2 = 0.571$) of the change in the levels of work alienation among the yacht employees. Based on these results, *Hypotheses 1, 2* and *3* were all supported.

The indirect effect of emotional labor on work alienation through burnout was determined by considering the confidence intervals obtained by the Bootstrap analysis. The confidence intervals in the Bootstrap analysis were statistically significant and did not include 0 ($\beta = 0.105$; $p < 0.05$; 95 % CI [0.017; 0.190]); from this it follows that burnout is a mediate variable between emotional albor and work alienation (MacKinnon, Lockwood & Williams, 2004). The mediate role of burnout was also analyzed through the Sobel test. The results of the Sobel test point out that its mediate role is statistically significant ($z = 2.356$; $SE = 0.067$; $p < 0.05$). Based on this result, *Hypothesis 4* was supported.

5 Conclusion and Discussion

This is the first study of its kind to analyze the relationship between the emotional labor behaviors and work alienation of commercial yacht employees and the mediate role of burnout in this relationship. The analysis of the data obtained from 237 employees working in commercial yachts through questionnaire method was performed using SPSS v22 and AMOS v22 by Bootstrap resampling with 5000 replications, and the results supported the four research hypotheses.

The findings of this study reveal that emotional labor behaviors among yacht employees have both a direct and an indirect effect on their work alienation, the latter through burnout. That is to say, the burnout levels of the yacht employees, who exhibit emotional labor behaviors as required by their job, are increasing, which results in increased work alienation. The findings of this study indicate that emotional labor increases work alienation (Kaya & Serçeoğlu, 2013; Tokmak, 2014; Aslan & Mert, 2019) and burnout levels (Oral & Köse, 2011; Akdu & Akdu 2016; Güğerçin, 2019) among yacht employees and that burnout causes work alienation (Osin, 2009; O`Donohue & Nelson, 2012; Özler & Dirican, 2014; Kırıcı & Özkoç, 2017; Moç, 2018), which are consistent with the findings in the literature.

In light of these findings, managers in marine tourism businesses need to become aware that yacht employees who make an effort to increase the quality of marine tourism services offered and spend emotional labor will experience burnout and thus work alienation. Therefore, managers should attach importance to the phenomenon of emotional labor and pay attention to emotional labor experienced by their employees. As marine tourism is a labor-intensive industry, yacht employees are of pivotal importance for marine tourism sector and they greatly contribute to this sector. For that reason, it is necessary to perform managerial activities to reduce the emotional labor of yacht employees. For example, the problems faced by yacht employees in providing marine tourism services can be addressed; the opinions of these employees can be taken into consideration, making them feel valuable. In this way, the individual and organizational consequences caused by emotional labor can be reduced.

The major restrictions of this study is that the sample only consists of yacht employees and the study was performed in summer, which is the peak period of the yachting sector. Further studies to follow this research model can include different or larger sample group. Researchers may also include different variables to the model. Moreover, future studies may further explore the intermediary role of burnout in the relationship between emotional labor and work alienation revealed in this study.

Bibliography

Akdu, U., & Akdu, S. (2016). Duygusal Emek ve İş Stresinin Tükenmişlik Üzerindeki Etkileri: Profesyonel Turist Rehberleri Üzerinde Bir Araştirma. *Journal of International Social Research*, *9*(47), 1142–1153.

Ashforth, B., & Humphrey, R. (1993). Emotional Labor in Service Roles: The İnfluence of İdentity. *Academy of Management Review,18*(1), 88–115.

Aslan, H., & Mert, İ. S. (2019). Duygusal Emek ile İşe Yabancılaşma İlişkisinde Psikolojik Sermayenin Düzenleyici Rolü. *OPUS Uluslararası Toplum Araştırmaları Dergisi, 11*(9), 1736–1772.

Basım, H. N., & Beğenirbaş, M. (2012). Emotional Labor in Work Life: A Study of Scale Adaptation. *Journal of Management and Economics, 19*(1), 77–90.

Browne, M. W., & Cudeck, R. (1993). Alternative Ways of Assessing Model Fit. *Sage Focus Editions, 154*, 136–136.

Büyükbeşe, T., & Aslan, H. (2019). Psikolojik Sermaye ve Duygusal Emeğin Örgütsel Bağlılık Üzerindeki Etkisi. *İşletme Araştırmaları Dergisi, 11*(2), 949–963.

Brotheridge, C. M., & Lee, R. T. (2003). Development and Validation of the Emotional Labour Scale. *Journal of Occupational and Organizational Psychology, 76*(3), 365–379.

Chu, K. H. L., & Murrmann, S. K. (2006). Development and Validation of the Hospitality Emotional Labor Scale. *Tourism Management, 27*(6), 1181–1191.

Çukur, C. S. (2009). The Development of the Teacher Emotional Labor Scale (TELS): Validity and Reliability. *Educational Sciences: Theory and Practice, 9*(2), 559–574.

Dursun, S., Aytaç, S., & Bayram, N. (2014). Duygusal Emek Ölçeği Türkçe Formunun Geçerlilik ve Güvenilirlik Çalışması. *İş, Güç Endüstri İlişkileri ve İnsan Kaynakları Dergisi, 16*(2),10–18.

Fornell, C., & Larcker, D. F. (1981). Evaluating Structural Equation Models with Unobservable Variables and Measurement Error. *Journal of Marketing Research*, 1981, 39–50.

French, R., Rayner, C., Rees G., & Rumbles, S. (2008). *Organizational Behaviour* (2th ed.). Chishester, UK: JonhWiley & Sons.

Gök, G. A. (2015). "Presentable" Duygusal Emek: İlaç Mümessillerinde Duygusal Emeğin İşe Bağlılığa Etkisi. *Eskişehir Osmangazi Üniversitesi İktisadi ve İdari Bilimler Dergisi, 10*(3), 277–300.

Güğerçin, U. (2019). Duygusal Emeğin Duygusal Tükenme Üzerindeki Etkisi: Özbenlik Çelişki Teorisi Çerçevesinde Bir Analiz. *Karadeniz Sosyal Bilimler Dergisi, 11*(20), 177–192.

Güngör, M. (2009). Duygusal Emek Kavramı: Süreci ve Sonuçları. *Kamu-İş Dergisi, 11*(1), 167–184.

Gürlek, M., Tuna, A. A., & Yeşiltaş, M. (2020). İşveren Markası İşe Adanmayı Nasıl Etkiler? Duygusal Emeğin Aracılık Rolü. *Afyon Kocatepe Üniversitesi Sosyal Bilimler Dergisi, 22*(2), 593–614.

Hair, J. F., Black, W. C., Babin, B. J., & Anderson, R. E. (2014). *Multivariate Data Analysis* (7th ed.). Upper Saddle River, NJ: Prentice Hall.

Hochschild, A. (1983). *The Managed Heart – Commercialization of Human Feeling.* Berkeley, CA: University of California Press.

Hu, L. T., & Bentler, P. M. (1999). Cut off Criteria for Fit İndexes in Covariance Structure Analysis: Conventional Criteria Versus New Alternatives. *Structural Equation Modeling: A Multidisciplinary Journal, 6*(1), 1–55.

Karakaş, A., Tösten, R., Kansu, V., & Aydın, A. S. (2016). Öğretmenlerin Duygusal Emek Davranışlarının İş Doyumlarına Etkisi. *Elektronik Sosyal Bilimler Bilimler Dergisi,15*(56), 177–188.

Kaya, U., & Serçeoğlu, N. (2013). Duygu İşçilerinde İşe Yabancılaşma: Hizmet Sektöründe Bir Araştırma. *Çalışma ve Toplum, 36*(1), 311–346.

Kırıcı, E., & Özkoç, A. G. (2017). Turist Rehberlerinin Tükenmişlik Düzeylerinin İşe Yabancılaşma Eğilimlerine Etkisi. *Seyahat ve Otel İşletmeciliği Dergisi, 14*(1), 20–32.

Kıyat, G., Özgüleş, B., & Günaydın, S. C. (2018). Algılanan Kurumsal İtibar ve İşe Bağlılığın Duygusal Emek Davranışı Üzerine Etkisi: Sağlık Çalışanları Örneği. *Hacettepe Sağlık İdaresi Dergisi, 21*(3), 473–494.

Kızanlıklı, M., & Ünlüönen, K. (2016). Otel İşletmelerinde Davranış Kuralı Algısı ve İş Doyumun Duygusal Emek Davranışı Üzerindeki Etkisinin Belirlenmesi. *Ege Akademik Bakış, 16*(3), 503–518.

Kline, R. B. (2016). *Principles and Practice of Structural Equation Modeling* (4th ed.). London: The Guilford Publications.

Kruml, S. M., & Geddes, D. (2000). Exploring the Dimensions of Emotional Labor: The Hearth of Hochschild's Work. *Management Communication Quarterly, 14*(1), 8–49.

Lee, R. T., & Brotheridge, C. M. (2011). Words from the Heart Speak to the Heart. *Career Development International, 16*(4), 401–420.

Lee, S. Y., Abdul, A. Y., Md Sidin, S., & Saleh, R. (2014). The İnfluence of Emotional Labour Strategies on Customer Satisfaction and Word of Mouth Recommendations in Group Tours. *International Journal of Economics and Management, 8*(S), 81–96.

MacKinnon, D. P., Lockwood, C. M., & Williams, J. (2004). Confidence Limits for the İndirect Effect: Distribution of The Product and Resampling Methods. *Multivariate Behavioral Research, 39*(1), 99–128.

Moç, T. (2018). *Örgütsel Adalet Algısının Çalışanların İşte Yabancılaşmaya Etkisinde Tükenmişliğin ve Presenteizmin Rolü.* Doktora Tezi, Atatürk Üniversitesi, Erzurum

Morris, J. A., & Feldman, D. C. (1996). The Dimensions, Antecedents, and Consequences of Emotional Labor. *The Academy of Management Review, 21*(4), 986–1010.

Morris, J. A., & Feldman, D. C. (1997). Managing Emotions in the Workplace. *Journal of Managerial İssues*, 257–274.

Naring, G., Briet, M., & Brouwers, A. (2006). Beyond Demand–Control: Emotional Labour and Symptoms of Burnout in Teachers. *Work & Stress, 20*(4), 303–315.

O'Donohue, W., & Nelson, L. (2012). Work Engagement, Burn-Out, and Alienation: Linking New and Old Concepts of Positive and Negative Work Experiences. *2012 BAM Annual Conference*, Australia.

Oral, A., & Köse, S. (2011). Hekimlerin Duygusal Emek Kullanımı ile İş Doyumu ve Tükenmişlik Düzeyleri Arasındaki İlişkiler Üzerine Bir Araştırma. *Süleyman Demirel Üniversitesi İktisadi ve İdari Bilimler Fakültesi Dergisi, 16*(2), 463–492.

Osin, E. (2009). Subjective Experience of Alienation: Measurement and Correlates. *Gesellschaft fur Logotherapie und Existenzanalyse, 1*(26), 16–23.

Öz, S. D., & Baykal, Ü. (2017). Hemşirelerin Duygusal Emek Davranışı. *Sağlık ve Hemşirelik Yönetimi Dergisi, 3*(4), 143–147.

Özler, E. N. D., & Dirican, M. (2014). Örgütlerde Yabancılaşma İle Tükenmişlik Sendromu Arasındaki İlişkiyi Belirlemeye Yönelik Bir Araştırma. *Dumlupınar Üniversitesi Sosyal Bilimler Dergisi, 39*, 291–310.

Peterson, M. F., Smith, P. B., Akande, A., Ayestaran, S., Bochner, S., Callan, V., & Hofmann, K. (1995). Role Conflict, Ambiguity, and Overload: A 21-Nation Study. *Academy of Management Journal, 38*(2),429–452.

Pines, A. M. (2005). The Burnout Measure Short Version (BMS). *International Journal of Stress Management, 12*(1), 78–88.

Podsakoff, P. M., MacKenzie, S. B., Lee, J. Y., & Podsakoff, N. P. (2003). Common Method Biases in Behavioural Research: A Critical Review of the Literature and Recommended Remedies. *Journal of Applied Psychology, 88*(5), 879.

Podsakoff, P. M., MacKenzie, S. B., & Podsakoff, N. P. (2012). Sources of Method Bias in Social Science Research and Recommendations on How to Control İt. *Annual Review of Psychology, 63*, 539–569.

Tokmak, İ. (2014). Duygusal Emek ile İşe Yabancılaşma İlişkisinde Psikolojik Sermayenin Düzenleyici Etkisi. *İşletme Araştırmaları Dergisi, 6*(3), 134–156.

Tümkaya, S., Çam, S., & Çavuşoğlu, I. (2009). Tükenmişlik Ölçeği Kısa Versiyonu'nun Türkçe'ye Uyarlama, Geçerlik ve Güvenirlik Çalışması. *Journal of the Çukurova University Institute of Social Sciences, 18*(1).

Türker, A. (2016). Duygusal Zekâ ve Duygusal Emegin Satis Performansina Etkisi: Acenta Temsilcileri Üzerine Bir Uygulama. *İs, Güç: Endüstri İliskileri ve İnsan Kaynakları Dergisi, 18*(1), 76.

Yorulmaz, M., (2020). Gemi Acentelerinde Duygusal Emek Davranışları İle Müşteri Hizmetleri Performansı ve İş Tatmini Arasındaki İlişkilerin İncelenmesi. *International Social Sciences Studies Journal (SSS Journal), 6*(7), 4378–4386.

Yürür, S., & Ünlü, O. (2011). Duygusal Emek, Duygusal Tükenme ve İşten Ayrılma Niyeti İlişkisi. *İş Güç Endüstri İlişkileri ve İnsan Kaynakları Dergisi, 13*(2), 81–104.

Melda Akbaba

Employees' Perception of Ethical Leadership: A Research on Tourism Establishments

Abstract In this research, it was aimed to determine the level of ethical leadership perception of employees who are employed in tourism sector. For this purpose, questionnaire was applied to 390 employees working in five-star hotel establishments in Antalya. Descriptive statistics, t test and ANOVA analysis were performed using the data obtained from the survey. As a result of the analysis conducted in this study, which aims to determine the level of ethical leadership perceptions of employees in tpurism enterprises, it is seen that the ethical leadership perceptions of employees employed in tourism enterprises are above the average. According to the results of the analysis, no significant difference was found between the gender and the department employees work in and ethical leadership perception. However, a significant difference was found between the age of the employees participating in the study, the duration of employment in the tourism sector, and the perception of ethical leadership.

Keywords: Ethical Leadership, The Hotel Enterprises, Tourism Sector, Tourism Employees

1 Introduction

The most important need of organizations to achieve organizational and personal goals is a leader with ethical values. In the tourism sector, which develops depending on human resources, treating the employees fairly and sincerely, preparing suitable environments for the emergence of the creativity of the employees are the most important factors that increase the productivity, competitiveness and continuity of the enterprises. For this reason, it has become a necessity for organizations to gain the highest level of benefit from their employees by encouraging them with ethical leadership behaviors. In addition, the ethical leadership behaviors perceived by employees employed in tourism enterprises emerge as an important factor in achieving goals in organizations. Although the concept of leadership has a long history, it has always been up to date and has been the focus of attention for researchers. In order to achieve certain goals, people act by forming groups and this situation brings with it the necessity of their management. In this context, the concept of leadership has taken its place among the important issues of management (Bakan & Doğan,

2013: 3). Leadership is the ability to take more harmonious steps outside the business culture to initiate evolutionary change processes (Schein, 1992: 2). In other words, according to Drath and Palus (1994: 4), leadership is defined as the decision-making process by making sense of what can be done together. The concept of ethics is; Although it literally means character, putting all activities and aims in their proper place within the organization; what to do or not to do; what is to be wanted or not; Knowing what to have and what cannot be, "what is good?" or "what should we do?" It can be defined as the branch of philosophy that directs such questions to itself (Şimşek et al., 2011: 474–475). The laws that define the aims and processes of organizations, in a way, determine how managers and other employees should behave and what they should do and what they should not do. However, if the employees are not sufficiently developed in terms of ethical values; laws and policies may not allow employees to demonstrate universally acceptable ethical behavior (Uzunçarşılı, Toprak & Ersun, 2000: 36). Unethical behaviors displayed by employees can have significant costs, directly or indirectly, in organizations. These can be expressed as loss of trust in the organization in general, damage to the organization's image, decrease in group work, decrease in communication within the organization, loss of self-esteem, decrease in sense of commitment, increase in employee turnover, lack of motivation and decrease in performance (Özkalp & Kırel, 2011: 537–538): In this context, an organization with ethical values; Although it is a culture that facilitates mutual respect, trust and honest communication between employees, customers and managers, it has become a new and important tool for organizations to gain competitive advantage (Sökmen & Tarakçıoğlu, 2011: 85). In this sense, the need for ethical leaders who can direct their audiences to ethical behavior and provide a suitable environment for organizations may become a necessity today. Ethical leadership is defined as a type of leadership that exhibits management in normative compliance in personal actions and interpersonal relations and supports the ethical thinking of the audience in two-way communication, empowerment and decision making (Brown, Treviño & Harrison, 2005: 120). In this context, behaviors such as a leader to be honest with his/her employees, rewarding employees' success fairly, not behave selfishly, and creating suitable environments for employees' creativity to emerge can ensure the leader to be perceived as ethical. However, depending on the leader who is ethically perceived, employees will be able to show high performance in achieving the goals of the organization. Therefore, in the study, it was aimed to determine whether the ethical leadership perception levels of the employees employed in tourism enterprises and their ethical leadership perceptions differ according to the demographic characteristics of the employees.

2 The Concept of Ethical Leadership

Ethical leadership is one of the types of leadership that is increasingly important and subject to various studies. Ethical leaders are people, who display ethical behavior, are unbiased, take into account the needs of their objective audience and defend their rights (Teyfur, Beytekin & Yalçınkaya, 2013: 86). Ethical leaders believe in the virtue of honesty and try to apply it daily, both in their private and business lives (Zhu, May & Avolio, 2004: 19). Ethical leadership has an important share for organizations. Because a leader who lacks ethical behavior can harm the organization and its employees, and organizations that do not have an ethical leader can lose their continuity effect and turn out to be a spiritless structure (Erdilek Karabay, 2015: 87). Pickett (2005: 52) defines ethical leadership as a person who serves the business to be synergistic, to expand its living space by growing and to sustain it in the long term. Kanungo and Mendonca (1996) defined ethical leaders as people who display virtuous behaviors that may be beneficial to others and avoid actions that may harm others by drawing attention to the altruistic side of the ethical leader. Similarly, Ciulla (1995) emphasized that the basic characteristic of ethical leadership is to respect the rights and dignities of others. Northouse (2001) proposed five ethical leadership principles based on Aristotel's work. According to these principles, ethical leaders must respect others, serve, have a sense of justice, be honest and act together with employees (cited in Eisenbeiss, 2012: 5). Resick et al. (2006: 346) identified six main characteristics that characterize ethical leadership as a result of their extensive review of the literature. These features are: character and integrity, ethical awareness, community/people focus, motivation, encouragement and empowerment, and ethical responsibility management. Harvey (2004: 23) revealed ten basic characteristics of ethical leadership as a result of his research on ethical leadership. According to these characteristics, ethical leaders;

- By conveying common values and ethical standards to employees regularly, they help them to understand and adopt them.
- They give responsibility to employees to determine whether they and their employees act in accordance with ethical values. In this context, employees who act contrary to ethical values are responsible for this situation.
- He treats employees as he wish to be treated.

- In case of decision making, they keep their ethical values in every decision and behavior by not ignoring their employees and their guiding principles.
- They pay attention that the methods and activities followed are consistent with each other.
- They allocate time and resources for the employees in order to support them in acquiring the necessary confidence and skills to transform their true beliefs into good behavior.
- They pay attention to the feelings, thoughts and behaviors of their employees within their realm of authority.
- Because compliance with ethical rules and values is the result of experience, ethical leaders make many small changes in many areas.
- They take into account the mission, vision and values of the organization as criteria when deciding on employee recruitment or promotion.
- They motivate them within the scope of ethical values by guiding employees in ethical issues.

Because ethical leaders are in a social position intrinsically, they focus on how to use the power they have in their decisions, actions and influencing audiences. Evaluating the dimensions of ethical leadership can provide a more effective understanding of the theory. In this context, Yılmaz (2005) states that ethical leadership consists of four dimensions: communicative ethics, climatic ethics, ethics in decision making and behavioral ethics.

Communicative Ethics: The leader's ethical relationship style in the communication process is valued as a strong unifier of the organizational environment. In this sense, the leader can influence the audience by strengthening the communication networks in order to achieve the organizational goals and by opening it to all employees of the organization and making their expressions understandable (Uğurlu, 2009: 64).

Climatic Ethics: Ethical climate not only helps employees evaluate problems and consider alternatives, but also guides them to make decisions about acceptable and unacceptable behaviors (Barnett & Schubert, 2002: 281). Ethical leaders make many decisions by considering which decision will be ethically correct by rewarding the ethical behavior of the audience and punishing those who do not comply with ethical principles. Concordantly, leaders motivate the audience to make ethical behaviors a part of the organization. In this case, ethical leaders are expected to produce solutions for their audience's problems regarding ethical issues as role models. In this connection, ethical leaders will be able to develop the desired ethical climate in order to achieve the goals of the organization by observing ethical standards (Erdilek Karabay, 2015: 109).

Ethics in Organizational Decision Making: If the decision taken by the leader is likely to cause great harm to the employees, it will be followed by the employees whether the decision of the leader is correct or not within the scope of ethical principles. If the leader makes his/her decisions in an ethical way, he/she will be seen as an ethical leader by the audience (Brown & Trevino, 2006: 602). Ethical leaders must answer six questions before making a decision on a particular issue. These are (Lamberton & Minor, 1995, 333; cited in Aydın, 2006: 32–33); "Is the decision correct?, Is it fair?, Does it hurt others and who will be hurt? Would you tell your close circle about your decision? How do you think the decision will result?" If he/she can answer these questions positively and in accordance with ethical principles, the decision taken by the leader will be seen as ethical and the leader will be evaluated as an ethical leader by the audience.

Behavioral Ethics: The ethical leader needs to take action by calculating how the behavior he/she exhibits will affect others. Because the effect that verbal behaviors will have on the audience is effective in shaping the ethical relationship (Uğurlu, 2009: 68).

According to the studies on ethical leadership, ethical leadership behavior increases the organizational commitment and trust of employees (Ponnu & Tennakoon, 2009), job performance (Walumbwa et al., 2011), job satisfaction (Kim & Brymer, 2011), organizational justice (Yeşiltaş et al., 2012) shows that it positively affects organizational citizenship behavior (Philipp & Lopez, 2013), socialization (Khuong & Nhu, 2015), performance (Park et al., 2015) and ethical leadership behavior negatively affects employees' organizational deviation behaviors (Yeşiltaş et al., 2012) and perception of psychological contract violations (Philipp & Lopez, 2013; Karcıoğlu et al., 2014).

3 Methodology

In this study, it was aimed to determine the level of ethical leadership perception of employees employed in the tourism sector. For this purpose, 390 employees working in 5 star accommodation establishments in Antalya were reached through a questionnaire. Survey questions were prepared beforehand, validity and reliability were tested; It includes the "Ethical Leadership Scale". The survey form of the research consists of two parts. The first part consists of questions about the demographic characteristics of the participants. In the second part of the questionnaire, the Ethical Leadership Scale developed by Yılmaz (2005) was used to determine the ethical leadership perceptions of the participants. The scale consists of 44 items and 4 dimensions: communicative ethics (15), climatic ethics (11), organizational decision making (9) and behavioral ethics (9). The total cronbach's alpha coefficient of the scale in question was determined as α 0.970, the communicative, climatic, ethical and behavioral ethics in organizational decision making from ethical leadership dimensions, and cronbach's alpha coefficients were determined as α 0.974–0.967–0.967 and 0.962, respectively. Since the reliability coefficients as a result of the reliability analysis performed are over 0.70, it can be said that the research scale is quite reliable. Besides, the scale was used by many other researchers (Uğurlu, 2009; Helvacı, 2010; Yıldırım, 2010; Teyfur et al., 2013; Mete, 2013; Ayık et al., 2014; Tombak & Bakan, 2014; Çıraklı et al., 2014).

4 Findings

In this study, which was carried out to determine the level of ethical leadership perceptions of employees in tourism enterprises, the demographic characteristics of the employees participating in the study (Tab. 19.1), descriptive statistics of the employees employed in the tourism enterprises regarding the ethical leadership dimensions of the communicative ethical expressions (Tab. 19.2), climatic ethics descriptive statistics for expressions of ethics (Tab. 19.3), descriptive statistics for ethical expressions in organizational decision making (Tab. 19.4), descriptive statistics for behavioral ethics expressions (Tab. 19.5) were determined with the data obtained through the survey. In addition, in order to determine whether there is any difference in perceptions of ethical leadership according to the demographic characteristics of the employees, t test and ANOVA analysis have been made in Tab. 19.6.

61.3 % of the employees participated in the study were male, 38.7 % were female, the highest rate was between 21 and 30 years with a rate of 35.9 %, the lowest was 51 years and over with a rate of 2.8 % was seen. According to the distribution of the departments they work in, the employees participated in the research were mostly employed in the food and beverage department (39.7 %). The rate of employees working in other departments was less than in the food and beverage department. These were; 18.2 % housekeeping, 17.4 % front office, 11.8 % technical service, 5.4 % accounting, 4.4 % human resources and 3.1 % sales-marketing departments. The experience of the employees participated in the research in the tourism sector was the lowest 2–3 years (29.2 %) and the highest 6–7 years (5.4 %). The highest working time in the same business was

Tab. 19.1: Demographic Characteristics of Employees Participated in the Study

		f	%			f	%
Gender	Male	239	61,3	**Departmants**	Front Office	68	17,4
	Female	151	38,7	**They Work**	Housekeeping	71	18,2
Age	20 years ve under	103	26,4		Technical Service	46	11,8
	21–30 years	140	35,9		Human Resources	17	4,4
	31–40 years	107	27,4		Food and Beverage	155	39,7
	41–50 years	29	7,4		Accounting	21	5,4
	51 years and over	11	2,8		Sales-Marketing	12	3,1
Working Time	0–1 years	80	20,5	**Working**	0–1 years	170	43,6
in Tourism	2–3 years	114	29,2	**Time in**	2–3 years	127	32,6
Sector	4–5 years	59	15,1	**Same**	4–5 years	44	11,3
	6–7 years	21	5,4	**Business**	6–7 years	20	5,1
	8–9 years	27	6,9		8–9 years	15	3,8
	10 years and over	89	22,8		10 years and over	14	3,6
TOTAL		**390**	**100**	**TOTAL**		**390**	**100**

determined as 43.6 % between 0 and 1 year and 32.6 % with 2–3 years. The following groups were; 4–5 years with 11.3 %, 6–7 years with 5.1 %, 8–9 years with 3.8 % and 10 years and over with 3.6 %.

Participation status, arithmetic averages and standard deviations are given in Tab. 19.2 regarding the expressions within the scope of the scale consisting of 15 expressions based on 5-point Likert in order to determine the communicative ethics perceptions of employees employed in tourism enterprises. When the statements regarding the perceptions of communicative ethics, one of the dimensions of ethical leadership, are analyzed according to their average values; Employees stated that the leaders of the hotel mostly feel grateful for the services provided ($\bar{x}$: 3.82). However, they stated that the leader did not judge employees due to their personal characteristics (avg. 3.81). Another communicative ethic statement, with an average value of 3.80, was found to be that the leader was not a mischief-maker among employees. According to the total average value of the communicative ethics perception ($\bar{x}$: 3.76), it can be stated

Tab. 19.2: Participation Status of the Employees Participating in the Statements about Determining the Communicative Ethical Perceptions of the Ethical Leadership Dimensions

Communicative Ethic	**1** (%)	**2** (%)	**3** (%)	**4** (%)	**5** (%)	x̄	**s.d.**
LEADER						**3,76**	**0,90**
Admits his/her mistakes.	2,1	9,2	17,7	53,1	17,9	3,76	0,92
Does not exhibit selfish behavior.	3,1	9,2	17,2	51,5	19	3,74	0,97
Treats employees fairly.	1,8	9,2	19,5	50,5	19	3,76	0,92
Participates in discussions constructively and understandingly.	1,8	9,2	22,3	49	17,7	3,72	0,92
Is patient.	2,6	8,7	17,4	52,6	18,7	3,76	0,94
Is humble.	2,1	7,9	18,7	54,1	17,2	3,76	0,89
Treats people equally.	2,1	10,3	18,7	51,3	17,7	3,72	0,94
Treats all employees affectionately.	2,8	7,9	19,5	53,6	16,2	3,72	0,92
Approaches the employees with compassion.	2,3	9,5	17,9	53,8	16,4	3,73	0,92
Respects the people around him/her.	2,1	8,7	19	53,8	16,4	3,74	0,90
Is not a mediator among employees.	1,0	7,2	19,2	55,6	16,9	3,80	0,83
Is merciful.	1,3	7,4	17,7	58,2	15,4	3,79	0,83
Treats employees sincerely.	1,5	8,7	16,9	55,6	17,2	3,78	0,88
Does not judge employees due to their personal characteristics.	1,5	6,7	17,9	56,9	16,9	3,81	0,84
Gives people a sense of gratitude for the service done.	1,8	6,4	19	54,1	18,7	3,82	0,87

n=390; Scale: 1 = Strongly Disagree 2 = Disagree 3 = Neither Agree nor Disagree 4 = Agree 5 = Strongly Agree

that the employees' level of communicative ethics perception is above average (Tab. 19.2).

Participation status, arithmetic averages and standard deviations are given in Tab. 19.3 regarding the expressions within the scope of the scale consisting of 11 expressions based on 5-point Likert in order to determine the climatic ethics perceptions of employees employed in tourism enterprises. When the statements regarding the climatic ethics perceptions, one of the dimensions of ethical leadership, are analyzed according to their average values; Employees stated that hotel leaders mostly strive to increase the occupational effectiveness of the employees (x̄: 3.79). On the other hand, they stated that the leader created a free environment for the employees for discussions, rewarded the success of

Tab. 19.3: Participation Status of the Employees Participating in the Statements about Determining the Climatic Ethical Perceptions of the Ethical Leadership Dimensions

Climatic Ethic	1 (%)	2 (%)	3 (%)	4 (%)	5 (%)	x̄	s.d.
LEADER						**3,74**	**0,93**
Encourages employees.	4,1	8,7	15,4	56,4	15,4	3,70	0,96
Tries to spread his/her thoughts with an approach based on love.	3,1	8,7	16,4	53,1	18,7	3,76	0,95
Sets concrete goals for the future.	3,8	7,9	19	52,8	16,4	3,70	0,96
Does his/her own work with a sense of responsibility.	2,8	9	17,4	52,1	18,7	3,75	0,95
Prepares a suitable environment for the creativity of employees to emerge.	2,6	8,7	16,4	54,1	18,2	3,77	0,93
Is eager to learn.	1,8	9,2	19,2	50,8	19	3,76	0,92
Accepts that employees can think differently.	1,8	10,8	19,5	50	17,9	3,72	0,94
Rewards employees' success in a fair way.	2,3	8,2	18,2	52,8	18,5	3,77	0,92
Creates the rules of the hotel correctly.	2,3	9,2	18,5	51,8	18,2	3,74	0,93
Creates a free environment for discussions.	2,1	7,2	19,7	53,8	17,2	3,77	0,88
Makes an effort to increase his/her professional effectiveness.	1,0	7,2	19,5	55,9	16,4	3,79	0,83

the employees in a fair way and prepared a suitable environment for their creativity to emerge (x̄: 3.77). On the other hand, it was found that the leader tried to spread his/her own thought with an approach based on love and was willing to learn, with an average value of 3.76 for other climatic ethical expressions. According to the total average value of the climatic ethics perception (x̄: 3.74), it can be stated that the climatic ethics perception levels of the employees are above average.

Participation status, arithmetic averages and standard deviations are given in Tab. 19.4 regarding the expressions within the scope of the scale consisting of 9 expressions based on 5-point Likert in order to determine the ethical perceptions in organizational decision making perceptions of employees employed in tourism enterprises. When the expressions related to ethical perceptions in organizational decision making are analyzed according to their average values, one of the dimensions of ethical leadership; Employees mostly stated that the leader implemented the joint decisions taken in the hotel effectively and determined the measure for the work done (x̄: 3.83). Besides, they stated that the leader did not have bad habits and knew the limits of his/her behavior (x̄: 3.82). In another statement of ethics in organizational decision

Tab. 19.4: Participation Status of the Employees Participating in the Statements about Determining the Ethical Perceptions in Organizational Decision Making of the Ethical Leadership Dimensions

Ethics in Organizational Decision Making	1 (%)	2 (%)	3 (%)	4 (%)	5 (%)	x̄	s.d.
LEADER						**3,79**	**0,89**
Approaches systematically in generating solutions.	2,1	9,2	19,2	50	19,5	3,76	0,94
Does not work to gain profit in political matters.	2,6	7,9	19	53,1	17,4	3,75	0,92
Does not engage in beneficial activities in religious matters.	2,3	6,9	19,7	53,8	17,2	3,77	0,89
Doesn't act in activities that provide personal gain in the economic field	2,1	9	17,9	53,6	17,4	3,75	0,91
Performs his/her professional responsibilities with a sense of honesty.	1,3	8,5	17,9	54,6	17,7	3,79	0,87
Effectively implements the decisions taken jointly in the hotel.	1,5	8,2	16,4	53,3	20,5	3,83	0,90
Determines the size of the work done in the hotel.	1	7,9	16,2	56,9	17,9	3,83	0,85
Does not have bad habits.	1,5	7,4	15,9	57,9	17,2	3,82	0,85
Knows the limits of his/her behavior.	1,8	6,2	18,2	55,9	17,9	3,82	0,86

Tab. 19.5: Participation Status of the Employees Participating in the Statements about Determining the Behavioral Ethical Perceptions of the Ethical Leadership Dimensions

Behavioral Ethic	1 (%)	2 (%)	3 (%)	4 (%)	5 (%)	x̄	s.d.
LEADER						**3,73**	**0,921**
Can evaluate himself/herself.	2,3	9,5	17,7	52,8	17,7	3,74	0,936
Is straightforward.	2,3	10,5	17,7	50	19,5	3,74	0,966
Behaves honestly.	2,1	10	16,7	51,5	19,7	3,77	0,948
Behaves courageously in the face of events.	2,8	8,2	18,7	51,5	18,7	3,75	0,947
Tells the truth in all conditions.	3,1	9,2	17,7	54,1	15,9	3,71	0,947
Has expressions that are close to reality.	1,8	7,7	21,5	53,8	15,1	3,73	0,874
Does his/her activities according to the principle of reality.	1,5	8,7	21	53,3	15,4	3,72	0,881
Protects individual rights.	1,5	9,7	19,7	53,3	15,6	3,72	0,897
Respects the values of the society he/she belongs to.	1,8	9	18,7	54,4	16,2	3,74	0,897

Tab. 19.6: Differences Between Demographic Characteristics and Perception of Ethical Leadership of Employees Participating in the Study

		n		s.d.	F	p
Gender	Male	239	3,72	0,69	3,097	0,245
	Female	151	3,81	0,88		
Age	20 years and under	103	3,54	0,71	6,179	0,000
	21–30 years	140	3,71	0,70		
	31–40 years	107	3,89	0,80		
	41–50 years	29	3,92	0,91		
	51 years and over	11	4,52	0,83		
Departmans They Work	Front Office	68	3,87	0,88	1,664	0,128
	Housekeeping	71	3,80	0,79		
	Technical Service	46	3,83	0,69		
	Human Resources	17	3,97	0,83		
	Food and Beverage	155	3,61	0,70		
	Accounting	21	3,78	0,95		
	Sales-Marketing	12	4,01	0,56		
Working Time in Tourism Sector	0–1 years	80	3,68	0,80	2,518	0,029
	2–3 years	114	3,64	0,68		
	4–5 years	59	3,69	0,73		
	6–7 years	21	3,88	0,65		
	8–9 years	27	3,77	0,83		
	10 years and over	89	3,98	0,77		
Working Time in Same Business	0–1 years	170	3,65	0,74	4,299	0,001
	2–3 years	127	3,81	0,66		
	4–5 years	44	3,64	0,92		
	6–7 years	20	4,18	0,68		
	8–9 years	15	3,65	1,28		
	10 years and over	14	4,39	0,53		

making, it was found that the leader made his/her professional responsibility with a sense of honesty with an average value of 3.79. According to the total average value of ethical perception in organizational decision making ($\bar{x}$: 3.79), it can be stated that the ethical perception levels of employees in organizational decision making are above average.

Participation status, arithmetic averages and standard deviations are given in Tab. 19.5 regarding the expressions within the scope of the scale consisting of 9 expressions based on 5-point Likert in order to determine the ethical perceptions in organizational decision making perceptions of employees employed in tourism enterprises. When the statements about behavioral ethics perceptions, one of the dimensions of ethical leadership, are analyzed according to their average values; Employees stated that their leaders in the hotel behaved honestly the most ($\bar{x}$: 3.77). On the other hand, they stated that the leader was able to evaluate himself/herself, was truthful and respected the values of the society ($\bar{x}$: 3,74). Another behavioral ethics statement, with an average value of 3.75, leader was found to be courageous in the face of events. According to the total average value of behavioral ethics perception ($\bar{x}$: 3.73), it can be stated that the behavioral ethics perception levels of the employees are above the average among ethical leadership dimensions (Tab. 19.5). When the expressions on ethical leadership dimensions were analyzed according to their average values; Employees mostly stated their participation in the ethical dimension in organizational decision making ($\bar{x}$: 3.79). On the other hand, employees stated that the leader effectively implemented the common decisions taken at the hotel, determined the measure in the work done ($\bar{x}$: 3.83), did not have bad habits and knew the limits of his/her behavior ($\bar{x}$: 3.82). Employees expressed their least participation ($\bar{x}$: 3.73) regarding the behavioral ethics dimension.

As seen in Tab. 19.6, no significant difference was found, since the value between the gender and the department they work in and the perception of ethical leadership of the employees participating in the study was $p > 0.05$. On that note, the perception of ethical leadership does not differ according to the gender and the department they work in. However, a significant difference was found between the age of the employees participating in the study, the duration of work in the tourism sector, the duration of work in the enterprise and the value of the perception of ethical leadership with $p < 0.05$. According to this finding, the perception of ethical leadership differs according to the age of employees, working time in the tourism sector and working time in the company. However, according to the average values, it is seen that the highest difference is between the age of 20 and below and over 51 years, and according to the duration of operation, the highest difference is between 0 and 1 years and 10 years and over employees in the tourism sector. According to these findings, it can be stated that as age increases and experience in the tourism sector and business increases, the perception of ethical leadership increases.

5 Conclusion and Recommendations

The most important production factor that ensures the sustainability of tourism enterprises is the employees with a high perception of ethical leadership in the organization. Ethical leadership is important for organizations in terms of employees' identification with the organization, their confidence in the organization and themselves, their focus on cooperation, awareness of their personal competencies and awareness of their rights.

As a result of the analysis conducted in this study, which aims to determine the level of ethical leadership perceptions of employees in tourism enterprises, it is seen that the ethical leadership perceptions of employees employed in tourism enterprises are above the average. However, it was concluded that the highest perceived ethical leadership dimension of the employees participating in the study was ethics in organizational decision making, and the lowest perceived ethical leadership dimension was behavioral ethics. According to this result, it can be said that in the organizational decision-making process, the leader consults the employees' ideas, considers them and performs ethical leadership behaviors by fulfilling his/her responsibilities. In the study, the differentiation of ethical leadership perceptions of the employees employed in tourism enterprises according to the variables of gender, age, working time in the tourism sector, working time in the company and the department they work in were examined. According to the results of the analysis, no significant difference was found between the gender and the department employees work in and ethical leadership perception. However, a significant difference was found between the age of the employees participating in the study, the duration of employment in the tourism sector, and the perception of ethical leadership. According to these findings, the perception of ethical leadership differs according to the age of the employees, working time in the tourism sector and the duration of the business, and does not differ according to gender and the department they work in. At the same time, according to the average values, it is seen that the highest difference is between the age of 20 and below and over 51 years, and according to the duration of operation, the highest difference is between 0–1 years and 10 years and over employees in the tourism sector. Under the light of these findings, it can be stated that the perception of ethical leadership increases as the age and experience in the tourism sector and business increase. The leader's treating employees fairly, equally, compassionately, sincerely and with love, his/her feeling grateful for the services that the employee has provided, his/her encouraging them, setting concrete goals for the future, accepting that employees can think differently, rewarding their achievements in a fair way, protecting their individual rights and telling the truth under all conditions may both increase the perception of ethical leadership in the employee and enable the employee to behave ethically towards other employees. Accordingly, the organizational commitment, trust, work performance, job satisfaction, organizational citizenship behavior and socialization of the employees may increase and the employee may not intend to quit. In this way, the employee turnover rate within the organization may decrease and the resources that the organization will spend for the accustoming or training of the employees will be reduced. In addition, the employees who are employed will be able to make serious contributions to the efficiency and sustainability of the organization with their perceived ethical leadership behavior.

Bibliography

Aydın, İ. (2006). *Eğitim ve öğretimde etik*. 2. Baskı, Ankara: Pegem Yayıncılık.

Ayık, A., Yücel, E., & Savaş, M. (2014). Öğretmenlerin örgütsel bağlılıklarının yordayıcısı olarak okul yöneticilerinin etik liderlik davranışları. *Dumlupınar Üniversitesi Sosyal Bilimler Dergisi, 42,* 27–36.

Bakan, İ., & Doğan, İ. F. (2013). *Liderlik güncel konular ve yaklaşımlar.* Ankara: Gazi Kitabevi.

Barnett, T., & Schubert E. (2002). Perceptions of the ethical work climate and covenanta relationships. *Journal of Business Ethics, 36,* 279–290.

Brown, M. E., & Trevino, L. K. (2006). Ethical leadership: A review and future directions. *The Leadership Quarterly, 17,* 595–616.

Brown, M. E., Treviño, L. K., & Harrison, D. A. (2005). Ethical leadership: A social learning perspective for construct development and testing. *Organizational Behavior and Human Decision Processes, 97,* 117–134.

Ciulla, J. B. (1995). Leadership ethics: Mapping the territory. *Business Ethics Quarterly, 5*(1), 5–24.

Çıraklı, Ü., Uğurluoğlu, Ö., Şantaş, F., & Çelik, Y. (2014). Etik liderlik davranışlarının örgütsel adalet üzerindeki etkisi: Hastanede bir uygulama. *İşletme Bilimi Dergisi 2*(2), 53–69.

Drath, W. R., & Palus, C. J. (1994). *Making common sense: Leadership as meaning-making in a community of practice.* Greensboro, NC: Centerfor Creative Leadership.

Eisenbeiss, S. A. (2012). Re-thinking ethical leadership: An interdisciplinary integrative approach. *Leadership Quarterly, 23,* 791–808.

Erdilek Karabay, M. (2015). *İşletmelerde etik ve etik liderlik: Sigortacılık sektöründe bir araştırma.* İstanbul: Beta Yayınları.

Harvey, E. (2004). Liderlik ve Etik. *Executive Excellence, 8*(87), 13–25.

Helvacı, M. A. (2010). İlköğretim okulu yöneticilerinin etik liderlik davranışı gösterme düzeyleri. *Zeitschrift für die Welt der Türken Journal of World of Turks, 2*(1), 391–410.

Karcıoğlu, F., Aykanat, Z., & Çınar, O. (2014). Psikolojik sözleşmenin ihlali algısında örgütsel adaletin etkisi ve etik liderin aracı değişken olarak rolü: Kalkınma ajanslarında uygulama. *Research Journal of Business and Management, 1*(2), 74–86.

Kanungo, R. N., & Mendoca, M. (1996). *Ethical dimensions of leadership.* Thousand Oaks, CA: Sage.

Khuong, M. N., & Nhu, N. V. Q. (2015). The effects of ethical leadership and organizational culture towards employee's sociability and commitment: A study of tourism sector in Ho Chi Minh City, Vietnam. *Journal of Advanced Management Science, 3*(4), 329–336.

Kim, W. G., & Brymer, R. A. (2011). The effects of ethical leadership on manager job satisfaction, commitment, behavioral outcomes, and firm performance. *International Journal of Hospitality Management, 30*, 1020–1026.

Lamberton, L. H., & Minor, L. (1995). *Human Relations: Strategies For Success* Chicago: Irwin Mirror Press.

Mete, Y. A. (2013). Relationship between organizational cynicism and ethical leadership behaviour: A study at higher education. *2nd Cyprus International Conference on Educational Research, Procedia – Social and Behavioral Sciences, 89*, 476–483.

Northouse, P. G. (2001). *Leadership theory and practice.* Thousand Oaks, CA: Sage.

Özkalp, E., & Kırel, Ç. (2011). *Örgütsel davranış.* 5. Baskı, Bursa: Ekin Yayınevi.

Park, C. H., Kim, W., & Song, J. H. (2015). The impact of ethical leadership on employees' in-role performance: The mediating effect of employees' psychological ownership. *Human Resource Development Quarterly, 26*(4), 385–408.

Philipp B. L. U., & Lopez, P. D. J. (2013). The moderating role of ethical leadership: Investigating relationships among employee psychological contracts, commitment, and citizenship behavior. *Journal of Leadership & Organizational Studies, 20*(3), 304–315.

Pickett, M. C. (2005). Understanding ethical leadership. *ASBBS E-Journal, 1*(1), 44–54.

Ponnu, C. H., & Tennakoon, G. (2009). The association between ethical leadership and employee outcomes: The Malaysian case. *EJBO – Electronic Journal of Business Ethics and Organization Studies, 14*(1), 21–32.

Resick, C. J., Hanges, P. J., Dickson, M. N., & Mitchelsen, J. K. (2006). A cross-cultural examination of the endorsement of ethical leadership. *Journal of Business Ethics, 63,* 346–359.

Schein, E. H. (1992). *Organizational culture and leadership* (2nd ed.). San Francisco: Jossey-Bass.

Şimşek, M. Ş., Akgemci, T., & Çelik, A. (2011). *Davranış bilimlerine giriş ve örgütlerde davranış.* 7. Baskı, İzmir: Gazi Kitapevi.

Sökmen, A., & Tarakçıoğlu, S. (2011). *Mesleki etik.* Ankara: Detay Yayıncılık.

Teyfur, M., Baytekin, O. F., & Yalçınkaya, M. (2013). İlköğretim okul yöneticilerinin etik liderlik özellikleri ile okullardaki örgütsel güven düzeyinin incelenmesi. *Dicle Üniversitesi Ziya Gökalp Eğitim Fakültesi Dergisi, 21,* 84–106.

Tombak, N., & Bakan, H. (2014). İlköğretim okulu yöneticilerinde etik liderlik: Muğla ili örneği. *Muğla Sıtkı Koçman Üniversitesi Sosyal Bilimler Ensitüsü Dergisi, 32,* 95–121.

Uğurlu, C. T. (2009). İlköğretim okulu öğretmenlerinin örgütsel bağlılık düzeylerine yöneticilerinin etik liderlik ve örgütsel adalet davranışlarının etkisi. (Unpublished Ph.D. Thesis), İnönü University Institute of Social Sciences, Malatya.

Uzunçarşılı, Ü., Toprak, M., & Ersun, O. (2000). *Şirket kültürü ve iş prensipleri.* İstanbul Ticaret Odası Yayınları, Yayın No:2000–4, İstanbul.

Walumbwa, F. O., Mayer, D. M., Wang, P., Wang, H., Workman, K., & Christensen, A. L. (2011). Linking ethical leadership to employee performance: The roles of leader-member exchange, self-efficacy, and organizational identification. *Organizational Behavior and Human Decision Processes, 115,* 204–213.

Yeşiltaş, M., Çeken, H., & Sormaz, Ü. (2012). Etik liderlik ve örgütsel adaletin örgütsel sapma davranışları üzerindeki etkisi. *Muğla Üniversitesi, Sosyal Bilimler Enstitüsü Dergisi, 28,* 18–38.

Yıldırım, A. (2010). *Etik liderlik ve örgütsel adalet ilişkisi üzerine bir uygulama,* (Unpublished master's thesis). Karamanoğlu Mehmet Bey University Institute of Social Science, Karaman.

Yılmaz, E. (2005). Etik liderlik ölçeğinin geçerlilik ve güvenirlilik çalışması. *Denizli XIV. Ulusal Eğitim Bilimleri Kongresi, Pamukkale Üniversitesi, Eğitim Fakültesi,* 808–814.

Zhu, W., May, D. R., & Avolio, B. J. (2004). The impact of ethical leadership behavior on employee outcomes: The roles of psychological empowerment and authenticity. *Journal of Leadership and Organizational Studies, 11*(1), 16–26.

Gulizar Seda Yilmaz

A Comparative Analysis of the Health Care Financing Models in the Context of Financing Sources and Health Coverage: Covid-19 Experience

Abstract The primary aim of this study is comparing health financing models in the context of coverage and financing during the pandemic. Because the financing of the healthcare services and population coverage for healthcare services are the main factors affecting the performance of the entire health system including the provision and accessibility of basic health services. Especially between-country differences in the process of combating the pandemic point out the necessity of comparing countries' health systems according to the financing model they adopted. In this regard this study compares three basic models – the Bismarck model, the Beveridge model and the Private Health Insurance model- by using country-specific data such as population coverage for healthcare services, share of the public and out-of-pocket payments in the health expenditures, the measures on financing of the healthcare services and health coverage during the pandemic.

Keywords: Covid-19 Pandemic, Healthcare Financing Models, Health Insurance, Health Expenditures, Access to Health Services, Population Coverage

1 Introduction

With the COVID-19 pandemic developing as a global threat, the provision and organization of health care services has become one of the most important issues in the world since the first quarter of 2020. Even though it is described globally, impact of the pandemic on countries have differed from one another. Differences between countries in access to health care services have become more visible. Covid-19 pandemic has raised questions about whether health systems ensure equitable access to healthcare during the excessive demand on health care services. When health systems are evaluated in terms of service provision and financing, we can see that three basic models stand out, the Bismarck model, the Beveridge Model, and the Private Health Insurance model. These models differ from one another in terms of basic principles on health coverage and financing. The aim of this study is to compare the health financing models through health coverage and health financing which are two remarkable indicators of health systems during the pandemic. In this context, two questions will be tried to answer: (1) Whether health systems ready for a global pandemic, (2) What kind of measures were taken by governments in order to remove the model-based barriers to access to the health care services.

2 Health Care Financing Models

The continuity of health systems is concerned with the supply of human/physical capital and other inputs. Expenditures made for all these inputs refers to the cost of healthcare provision. Financial resources are needed to cover the cost of these inputs. How these resources are obtained, allocated and managed are referred to as the financing of health systems (Mossialos & Dixon, 2002; Ryan, Hill, Solomon, Endy & Aronson, 2019; World Health Organization [WHO], 2020a). There are basically three models for financing health systems: the Beveridge model (public finance model), the Bismarck model (mixed model) and the Private insurance model (private financing model). These models differ in terms of service provision, organization and financing sources (Maynard & Dixon, 2002; Kulesher & Forrestal, 2014; Dastan & Cetinkaya, 2015). Tab. 20.1. shows the characteristics of these models with sample countries. However, this study deals with these models through the financing of health care services rather than the organization of the health system and the provision of services.

One of the main differences of health systems is related to the sources of financing. As can be seen from the table, taxes, out-of-pocket payments and insurance-based payments (social insurance, private insurance) are used for financing health care services. Countries do not use only one resource for financing health services, but a combination of these resources according to the model adopted. For example, while the Beveridge model is mostly tax-based, the Bismarck model is social insurance contributions-based. In countries that adopt the private health insurance model, voluntary health insurance purchasing and out-of-pocket payments are predominant in the financing of the health system. Differences in financing sources may affect health systems' performance in terms of access and equity (Ugurluoglu & Ozgen, 2008).

2.1 The Bismarck Model (Social Insurance Model)

It is a model developed by Otto von Bismarck in the late 1880s to cover the working population for accident, illness, disability and retirement. Since this model is based on an insurance system that aims to collectively cover

Tab. 20.1: Basic Characteristics of Health Care Financing Models

Model	Bismarck Model	Beveridge Model	Private Insurance Model
Share of Public-Private Sector	Mixed	Public	Private
Entitlement	Contribution-based	Citizenship/ residence-based	Based on insurance registration
Funding basis	*Premiums* paid by *employers* and *employees*	Taxes and other public revenues	Predominantly private funds
Insurer	Occupational insurance	Government	Private insurance companies
System	Compulsary insurance	National Health Service	Medicare/Medicaid
Administration	Independent	Governement	Private
Healthcare Provider	Public/*Private healthcare institutions*	Predominantly public healthcare institutions	*Private healthcare institutions*
Sample Countries	Germany, France, Austria, Switzerland, Belgium, Netherlands	UK, Italy, Spain, Denmark	United States of America

Source: (Lameire, Joffe & Wiedemann, 1999; Wild & Gibis, 2003; Kutzin, 2011)

health-related risks, employers, employees, self-employed and the state contribute to the social health insurance fund by paying premiums. Payments by employers and employees are generally related to earnings and wages. The premiums paid by self-employed individuals are usually determined on the basis of estimated income or a fixed price. The state, which mostly performs a regulatory function in the health system, contributes to individuals who cannot afford payment (Ugurluoglu & Ozgen, 2008; Kulesher & Forrestal, 2014). This non-profit model, which aims to cover all citizens is based on a more collective financing and it seems more acceptable to the public in terms of access to health care services (Mossialos & Dixon, 2002; Kutzin, 2011; Dastan & Cetinkaya, 2015).

2.2 The Beveridge Model (National Health Model)

This model was designed by William Beveridge for England's national health system. This model, which is a product of the welfare state, was developed as a model covering all citizens, rather than covering labor force, as in the Bismarck model. Especially in high-income countries, there has been a shift from the understanding that health is seen as an employee right to the understanding that it is a legal right, thus the health coverage has expanded from the working population to all citizens (Kutzin, 2011; Kulesher & Forrestal, 2014). In this model, health services are provided by the state and financed by taxes (Dastan & Cetinkaya, 2015). In the Beveridge model, the entire population is covered and access to services is free, except for legally determined contributions. Who will benefit from health services free of charge is defined by citizenship or other legal rules, regardless of the individual's financial contribution. Funding with taxes is based on the view that a person in need of health care can benefit from whatever health service he or she needs whenever. Although income, which also reflects the ability of individuals to pay, forms a basis for their contribution to the financing of health services, it does not constitute a basis for the right of access to health care services (Ugurluoglu & Ozgen, 2008). In other words, access to health care services is not associated with the ability to pay in this model (Lameire et al., 1999).

As it is understood, the Beveridge and Bismarck models seem common in terms of risk pooling (Delnoij, 2013). However, unlike the Beveridge model, which is financed by taxes, contributions are collected for social security and health care financing in the Bismarck model. In addition, in the Bismarck model, health services are more accessible for those who are registered to insurance (who contribute to the financing of the system), while in the Beveridge model, health services are accessible to all citizens (Ugurluoglu & Ozgen, 2008).

2.3 Private Health Insurance Model

This model is based on private health insurance financed by employer and individual contributions (Kulesher & Forrestal, 2014). In this model, other services, except social care, are financed mainly from private sources (Lameire et al., 1999). Since the premiums are determined according to health risks, individuals with high health risks pay higher premiums. Therefore, it can be said that the private health insurance model works in favor of young and healthy individuals who need less health care (Maynard & Dixon, 2002).

There is an important difference between private insurance and Bismarckian social insurance. The premiums that individuals have to pay in social insurance are directly related to income and are not related to the health status or health risk. However, in private insurance, the premium to be paid by the individual is largely related to health risks or health status (Gungor, 2020). While private insurance is used as the primary health financing model in the USA, it is used as a complementary insurance for services that are not covered in countries that adopt the Beveridge or Bismarck model (Maynard & Dixon 2002; Kulesher & Forrestal, 2014).

3 Comparing Models According to Health Care Coverage and Financing Resources

Covid-19 outbreak did not affect countries or individuals in the same way (Organisation for Economic Co-operation and Development [OECD], 2020b). Although factors such as age, genetics, climate, openness to global mobilization, welfare level, existing health conditions and housing conditions are effective in these asymmetrical effects, financing and coverage, which are a vital elements of the health systems, are also important. Because the social security structure of a country and the financing of health care services are an important determinants in access to health services (Rice, Quentin, Anell, Barnes, Rosenau, Unruh, & Van Ginneken, 2018).

In this section, the differences in financing and coverage of the health financing models discussed in the second section will be compared through the representatives of the models in the context of the Covid-19 outbreak, using comparable data from World Bank and OECD. UK as an example of the Beveridge model, Germany as an example of the Bismarck model, and the USA as an example of the Private insurance model will be examined. Thus, a comparison will be made on the extent to which health systems are prepared for a global pandemic, their incapacities to cover the population and measures taken by governments[1].

3.1 Population Coverage for Health Care

Healthcare demand depends on health dynamics, not on factors such as income. Demand has increased during the global pandemic. But just as demand does not depend on income, access to healthcare should not depend on income, especially during the pandemic (OECD, 2019a). For this reason, one of the most important goals of the World Health Organization is the "universal health coverage", which includes all essential health care services, so that all people can have access to the health care services they need, whenever or wherever they need, without financial barriers (WHO, 2020b). After the Covid-19 outbreak,

1 The study has certain limitations. First, the data belongs to the last year available. Secondly, since the pandemic still continues during the study period, the measures taken by countries within the scope of combating the pandemic may change.

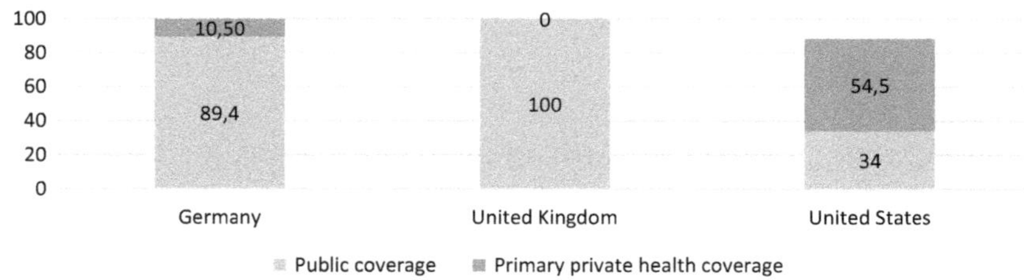

Fig. 20.1: Population coverage for a basic services, 2018 (%of total population)

Source: (OECD Health Statistics, 2020a)

Note: Population coverage for health care refers to the share of the population covered through public + primary private insurance. Services covered vary by country, but generally preventive and curative services are covered. "Public coverage" refers to the share of the population covered through national health insurance/social health insurance. "Primary private health coverage" refers to the share of the population covered through private health insurance which can be voluntary or compulsory (OECD, 2019b).

importance of universal health coverage for health systems has become apparent, especially in terms of access to health care services. Because the gap in health coverage can be a significant financial barrier to access to the services such as testing and treatment, as it will increase out-of-pocket payments for health care services in the event of an unexpected and expensive health demand. This condition can deter people from early diagnosis and treatment and thus increases the transmission rate (Kutzin, 2020; Thomson, Cylus, & Evetovits, 2019; Thomson, Habicht, & Evetovits, 2020; OECD, 2019a). For this reason, health coverage is an important indicator of the health systems of countries during the pandemic. The coverage of the health systems of countries varies according to the basic characteristics of the health models they adopt. In Fig. 20.1, the proportions of the population covered by insurance in 2019 are shown.

In Germany, the representative of the Bismarck model, almost 90 % of the insured population is covered by the social health insurance which based on the combinations of the payroll contributions and taxes. A small portion is covered by primary private health insurance, which may be voluntary or mandatory for primary health care. In UK, the representative of the Beveridge model, the entire population is covered by the National Health Service. In the USA, which is the representative of the private insurance model, there is a relatively large population that is not covered by public or private insurance, and the share of private insurance in the insured population is higher than that of the

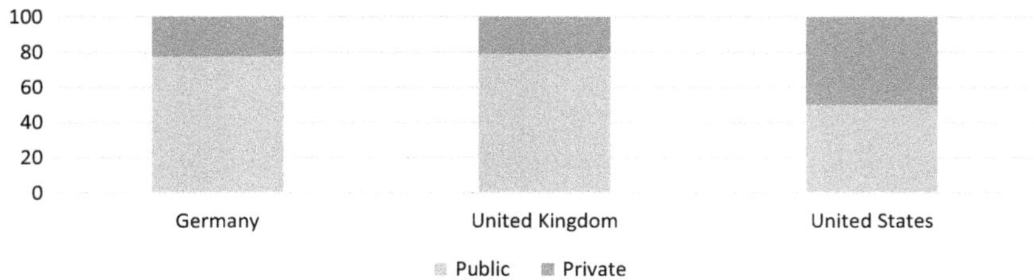

Fig. 20.2: The share of public and private in healthcare financing for 3 countries, 2018

Source: (World Bank Databank, 2020 October)

Note: "Public" includes domestic transfers from government + transfers from abroad distributed by government and social health insurance contributions. "Private" includes compulsory health insurance, voluntary private health insurance, other domestic revenues and direct transfers from abroad (Office for National Statistics, 2019; OECD, 2020c).

public. Public insurance includes Medicaid, State Children's Health Insurance Program (CHIP), Medicare and other government-sponsored health schemes (OECD, 2020c).

3.2 Healthcare Financing

The resources used to finance healthcare services can be categorized as public and private as shown in Fig. 20.2. These resources are used to fund different financing programs that provide access to healthcare, such as government schemes, health insurance schemes and household spending (Office for National Statistics, 2019).

Population coverage for health care provides preliminary information on financial constraints in accessing the services. However, not just the population covered, cost sharing is also important for healthcare services (OECD, 2019b). One of the most discussed elements of the systems, especially in the Covid-19 pandemic, is whether these financing sources create a financial barrier to accessing services (Kutzin, 2020; Banik, Nag, Chowdhury & Chatterjee, 2020). However, just as countries do not implement only single model, the financing of the models does not depend on a single resource. Therefore, the financing resources for the health services of three countries that have adopted different models are listed in Fig. 20.3, Fig. 20.4 and Fig. 20.5.

According to the graphs presenting three examples of different financing structures, following inferences can be made;

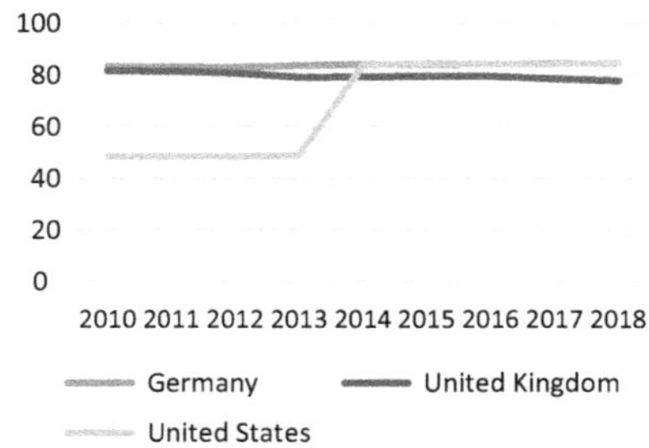

Fig. 20.3: Government/compulsory scheme

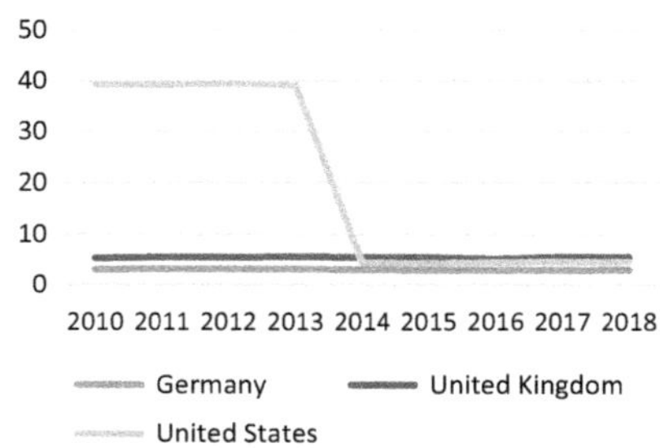

Fig. 20.4: Voluntary health care payments scheme

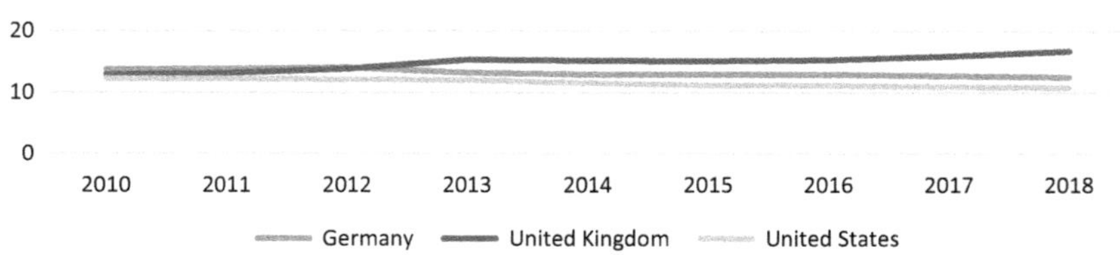

Fig. 20.5: Household out-of-pocket payments (%total health spending)

Source: (OECD Health Statistics, 2020a)

Note: In the data obtained from OECD health statistics, private insurance premiums are not included in out-of-pocket spending. In the US the scope of the Medicaid program was expanded and many poor people were included in the scope of insurance, with the Affordable Care Act (ACA) signed in 2014. Thus, the share of out-of-pocket payments decreased significantly in US, while the share of public/compulsory insurance increased, as people who paid their health services by out of pocket spending because they were uninsured were also covered by insurance (Rice et al., 2018; Office for National Statistics, 2019).

- Public resources have a greater share in the financing of the health care services both in the UK, where the right to access to the healthcare services is based on citizenship and financing scheme is tax-based, and in Germany, where the financing of health services is based on workers and employers' premiums.
- Although there has been a significant decrease in out-of-pocket spending in the US since 2014, the share of the government in the financing structure is lower than in the other two countries.
- Although the population is widely covered in the UK, out-of-pocket expenditures are increasing every year. However, this situation arises from the need for cost sharing due to the increasing burden of the National Health Services (Rice et al., 2018).
- In the USA, although it has a decreasing trend since 2014, the reason for the existence of out-of-pocket payments is due to the lack of universal health coverage. That is, it is an alternative cost sharing that the population not covered by insurance has to bear (Rice et al., 2018; Office for National Statistics, 2019).

3.3 Country-Specific Measures in Response to the Covid-19 Pandemic: Financing and Coverage

The population and services covered by insurance are an important factor in determining the size of out-of-pocket spending. Because in the case of lack of insurance, those who are not covered will have to pay their health services directly. In addition, if the services covered by the insurance are insufficient, cost of the necessary health services will be paid directly (Rice et al., 2018). Increasing share of out-of-pocket payments restricts access to the health care services. The main difference between financing models arises in terms of accessing and affording health care services. For this reason, the World Health Organization proposes to suspend all user fees, including contributions for non-Covid-19 services, to expand the scope of public funding regardless of citizenship or insurance status and to provide income support to households in order to remove barriers to access to the services during the pandemic (Thomson, Habicht, & Evetovits, 2019). In light of these policy proposals, all countries implemented financial measures to support the health systems and economy. However, this study examines only the measures focused on financing of the healthcare services and health coverage. The measures implemented by the three countries during the pandemic are summarized in Tab. 20.2.

Tab. 20.2: Overview of Selected Government Measures on Financing of the Healthcare Services and Health Coverage

	Government Measures on Health Care Financing and Coverage
	Health Insurance Funds provides coverage for all Covid-19 diagnostic tests recommended by a physician (Since February 28th)
	COVID-19 Hospital Relief Act provides financial support for hospitals with lower revenues due to postponed operations. The Act also provides financial support for outpatient care and health care facilities.
	The Law on Prevention and Control of Infectious Disease provides reimbursement of loss of earnings to self-employed workers and freelancers who may not be included in mandatory health insurance.
	Social Protection Package provides increase in short-time work compensation and tax reliefs.
	Government provides stabilization of social security contributions at a maximum of 40 % to keep the insurance system affordable.
Germany	**Government** provides subsidy for statutory health insurance funds and provides additional expenditure for health sector.
	Statutory Health Insurance (SHI) provides health insurance reimbursement for telehealth services and provides coverage for the cost of tests for recovering patients.
	The NHS provides universal coverage for all residents for Covid-19-related services (free of charge), such as for other primary healthcare services.
	The Coronavirus Act 2020 provides measures to fight against the economic effects of the pandemic. Also, it provides special insurance cover for healthcare staff taking on additional responsibilities.
United Kingdom	**The Social Security (Contributions) (Rates, Limits and Thresholds Amendments and National Insurance Funds Payments) Regulations 2020, The Social Security Benefits Up-rating Order 2020, The Tax Credits, Child Benefit and Guardian's Allowance Up-rating Regulations 2020, The Finance Act 2008** provides relief measures about national insurance contributions, benefits and tax liability to employers and employees who affected by pandemic (such as disregardation of the "test and trace support payments" when calculating the contributions).
	The Social Fund Funeral Expenses Payment (Coronavirus) (Amendment) Regulations 2020 provides increase in payments from the Social Fund for arranging a funeral.
	The Coronavirus Preparedness and Response Supplemental Appropriations Act, 2020 provides emergency funding for health system to combat the pandemic.
	The Families First Coronavirus Response Act provides paid sick leave, paid family medical leave. Also provides coverage for goods and services related to COVID-19 diagnostic testing, to all people without cost sharing. The Act provides expansion of unemployment benefits for individuals directly affected by pandemic, food assistance for vulnerable population.

Tab. 20.2: Continued

	Government Measures on Health Care Financing and Coverage
United States	**The Coronavirus Aid, Relief, and Economic Security Act** provides funding to healthcare providers, the medical and hospital industries, medical equipment manufacturers and allocates funding to public health programs. **The Paycheck Protection Program (PPP)** provides business loan program to support employers, employees, self-employed people and non-profit organizations, since income is an important factor to the access to the health care services in US. **Paycheck Protection Program and Health Care Enhancement Act** provides new funding to the Paycheck Protection Program for healthcare providers and COVID-19 testing. **National Disaster Medical System** provides funding for the testing costs of uninsured population.

Source: (Covid-19 Health System Response Monitor, 2020; Desson, Lambertz, Peters, Falkenbach, & Kauer, 2020; European Commission, 2020; Gaffney, Himmelstein, & Woolhandler, 2020; International Monetary Fund [IMF], 2020; KPMG, 2020; Shadmi, Chen, Dourado et al., 2020; Thompson Hine, 2020; OECD, 2020b)

4 Conclusion

The COVID-19 outbreak did not affect every country or every individual in the same way. One of the most important reasons for this difference is the financial barriers to access to the health care services. During the pandemic, the success of health systems in accessing healthcare services has been tested. Even in developed countries with high welfare level and health expenditures, inequalities based on the financing model have become more visible. These inequalities are mainly due to lack of insurance and out-of-pocket spending as both of them make it hard for individuals to access health services in case of an unexpected health demand. With the emergence of the importance of universal health coverage and ability to pay the healthcare services, countries have taken governmental measures such as expanding coverage for testing and treatment or removing out-of-pocket payments. All these measures have been taken regardless of the model adopted by countries. Because pandemic forced countries to respond independent from the characteristics of the models adobted by themselves. For example, although the US has a system financed by private resources, the share of public finance and insurance coverage was increased during the pandemic. In the face of all these developments, it can be said that differences in the implementation of the models are decreasing and models are converging with each other. Typical aspects of the models have been eroded due to the health risks and it becomes increasingly difficult to make a significant distinction between models in terms of financing. However, countries' pre-pandemic situations according to the adopted health model and the measures taken during the pandemic (such as the insurance coverage of the tests) will shed light on the future approaches in the field of health.

Bibliography

Banik, A., Nag, T., Chowdhury, S. R., & Chatterjee, R. (2020). Why do Covid-19 fatality rates differ across countries? An explorative cross-country study based on select indicators. *Global Business Review, 21*(3), 607–625.

Covid-19 Health System Response Monitor. (2020, October 15). *Policy responses for Germany.* Retrieved from https://www.covid19healthsystem.org/countries/germany/livinghit.aspx?Section=4.1%20Health%20financing&Type=Section.

Dastan, I., & Cetinkaya, V. (2015). OECD ülkeleri ve Türkiye'nin sağlık sistemleri, sağlık harcamaları ve sağlık göstergeleri karşılaştırması. *Sosyal Güvenlik Dergisi, 5*(1), 104–134.

Delnoij, D. M. J. (2013). Bismarck or Beveridge: Primary care matters. *European Journal of Public Health, 23*(3), 349.

Desson, Z., Lambertz, L., Peters, J. W., Falkenbach, M., & Kauer, L. (2020). Europe's Covid-19 outliers: German, Austrian and Swiss policy responses during the early stages of the 2020 pandemic. *Health Policy and Technology, 9*(4), 405–418. doi:10.1016/j.hlpt.2020.09.003.

European Commission, Directorate General Economic and Financial Affairs. (2020). Policy measures taken against the spread and impact of the Coronavirus. Retrieved from https://ec.europa.eu/info/sites/info/files/coronovirus_policy_measures_20_august.pdf.

Gaffney, A., Himmelstein, D. U., & Woolhandler, S. (2020). Covid-19 and US health financing: Perils and possibilities. *International Journal of Health Services, 50*(4), 396–407. doi:10.1177/0020731420931431.

Gungor, M. (2020). Sağlık hizmetlerinin finansmanı. In E. Islamoğlu, S. Yıldırımalp (Eds.), *Sosyal bilimlerde yeni araştırmalar - III* (pp. 325–343). Berikan Yayınevi.

International Monetary Fund. (2020). *Policy responses to the Covid-19 pandemic.* Retrieved from https://www.imf.org/en/Topics/imf-and-covid19/Policy-Responses-to-COVID-19

KPMG. (2020). *Government and institution measures in response to COVID-19.* Retrieved from https://home.kpmg/bg/en/home/insights/2020/05/government-and-institution-measures-in-response-to-covid-19.html.

Kulesher, R. R., & Forrestal, E. (2014). International models of health systems financing. *Journal of Hospital Administration*, *3*(4), 127–139.

Kutzin, J. (2011). *Bismarck vs. Beveridge: Is there increasing convergence between health financing systems?*. 1st Annual Meeting of SBO Network on Health Expenditure. 21–22 November 2011. Paris: Oecd.

Kutzin, J. (2020, April 2). *Priorities for the health financing response to COVID-19.* Retrieved from https://p4h.world/en/who-priorities-health-financing-response-covid19

Lameire, N., Joffe, P., & Wiedemann, M. (1999). Healthcare systems – an international review: An overview. *Nephrology Dialysis Transplantation, 14*(6), 3–9.

Maynard, A., & Dixon, A. (2002). Private health insurance and medical savings accounts: Theory and experience. In E. Mossialos, A. Dixon, J. Figueras, & J. Kutzin (Eds.), *Funding health care: Options for Europe* (pp. 80–109). Open University Press, Philadelphia.

Mossialos, E., & Dixon, A. (2002). Funding health care: An introduction. In E. Mossialos, A. Dixon, J. Figueras, & J. Kutzin (Eds.), *Funding health care: Options for Europe* (pp. 1–30). Open University Press, Philadelphia.

Office for National Statistics. (2019). *How does UK healthcare spending compare with other countries? An analysis of UK healthcare spending relative to comparable countries, using data produced to the international definitions of the System of Health Accounts (SHA 2011).* Retrieved from: https://www.ons.gov.uk/peoplepopulationandcommunity/healthandsocialcare/healthcaresystem/articles/howdoesukhealthcarespendingcomparewithothercountries/2019-08-29

Organisation for Economic Co-operation and Development. (2019a). *Out-of-pocket spending: Access to care and financial protection,* April 2019. Retrieved from https://www.oecd.org/health/health-systems/OECD-Focus-on-Out-of-Pocket-Spending-April-2019.pdf

Organisation for Economic Co-operation and Development. (2019b). *Health at a glance 2019: OECD indicators.* Paris: OECD Publishing. doi:10.1787/4dd50c09-en.

Organisation for Economic Co-operation and Development. (2020a, October 10). *Health statistics.* Retrieved from https://stats.oecd.org/Index.aspx?ThemeTreeId=9

Organisation for Economic Co-operation and Development. (2020b). *OECD policy responses to Coronavirus (COVID-19) The territorial impact of COVID-19: Managing the crisis across levels of government.* 16 June 2020. Retrieved from https://www.oecd.org/coronavirus/policy-responses/the-territorial-impact-of-covid-19-managing-the-crisis-across-levels-of-government-d3e314e1/

Organisation for Economic Co-operation and Development. (2020c). *Health statistics definitions, sources and methods*. Retrieved from https://www.oecd.org/els/health-systems/Table-of-Content-Metadata-OECD-Health-Statistics-2020.pdf

Rice, T., Quentin, W., Anell, A., Barnes, A. J., Rosenau, P., Unruh, L. Y., & Van Ginneken, E. (2018). Revisiting out-of-pocket requirements: Trends in spending, financial access barriers, and policy in ten high-income countries. *BMC Health Serv Res*, *18*, 371(2018).

Ryan, E. T., Hill, D. R., Solomon, T., Endy, T. P., & Aronson, N. (2019). *Hunter's tropical medicine and emerging infectious diseases*, 10th ed. Elsevier. doi:10.1016/C2016-0-01879-X.

Shadmi, E., Chen, Y., Dourado, I., Faran-Perach, I., Furler, J., Hangoma, P., Hanvoravongchai, P., Obando, C., Petrosyan, V., Rao, K. D., Ruano, A. L., Shi, L., De Souza, L. E., Spitzer-Shohat, S., Sturgiss, E., Suphanchaimat, R., Uribe, M. V., & Willems, S. (2020). Health equity and COVID-19: Global perspectives. *International Journal for Equity in Health*, *19*(1), [104]. doi:10.1186/s12939-020-01218-z.

Thompson Hine. (2020). *Covid-19 government measures guide*. Retrieved from https://www.thompsonhine.com/uploads/1345/doc/Country-by-Country_Guide_-_Government_Measures_Taken_in_Response_to_COVID-19.pdf

Thomson, S., Cylus, J., & Evetovits, T. (2019). *Can people afford to pay for health care? New evidence on financial protection in Europe*. Copenhagen: WHO Regional Office for Europe; 2019. Licence: CC BY-NC-SA 3.0 IGO.

Thomson, S., Habicht, T., & Evetovits, T. (2020). *Covid-19 health system response monitor cross-country analysis how are countries removing financial barriers to accessing health services in the context of Covid-19.* https://analysis.covid19healthsystem.org/index.php/2020/04/27/how-are-countries-removing-financial-barriers-to-accessing-health-services-in-the-context-of-covid-19/

Ugurluoglu, E., & Ozgen, H. (2008). Sağlık hizmetleri finansmanı ve hakkaniyet. *Hacettepe Sağlık İdaresi Dergisi, 11*(2), 1999–2026.

Wild, C., & Gibis, B. (2003). Evaluations of health interventions in social insurance-based countries: Germany, the Netherlands, and Austria. *Health Policy*, *63*, 187–196.

World Bank. (2020, October 10). *World development indicators*. Retrieved from https://databank.worldbank.org/source/world-development-indicators

World Health Organization. (2020a, October 20). *Health systems financing.* Retrieved from https://www.who.int/healthsystems/topics/financing/en/.

World Health Organization. (2020b, October 20). *Universal health coverage.* Retrieved from https://www.who.int/health-topics/universal-health-coverage#tab=tab_1.

Mehmet Metin Dam

Environmental Benefits of the COVID-19 Pandemic

Abstract The health crisis caused by the COVID-19 virus has led many countries to implement strict social distance rules. In these practices, there were restrictions such as curfew, restriction/suspension of transportation, closing of schools, closing of workplaces or opening them part-time. Although it is aimed to save human life by maintaining social distance and slowing down the spread of the virus with such restrictions, it has created many negative social and economic effects. However, this lockdown also has some positive effects on the natural environment. According to the scientific reports of various international institutions and organizations, it is seen that environmental pollution has decreased in the lockdown caused by the COVID-19 pandemic. Recent data released by NASA (National Aeronautics and Space Administration) and ESA (European Space Agency) show that pollution of COVID-19 has decreased by up to 30 % in some epicenters such as China, Europe and the USA. The International Energy Agency (IEA) emphasized that global emissions decreased by 2.6 Gt CO2 in 2020 compared to the previous year. In addition, according to Japan's Greenhouse Gases Observing Satellite (GOSAT) data, it has been observed that the 2020 carbon emissions in Beijing have decreased significantly compared to the previous years. In this study, the impact of the COVID-19 pandemic on environmental pollution was examined with environmental data published by NASA, ESA and GOSAT, and its impact on environmental quality was discussed.

Keywords: Pandemics, COVID-19, Environmental Pollution, Emission, Environmental Benefits

1 Introduction

Coronaviruses (CoV's) consist of several viruses that pass from animals to humans. The new type of coronavirus (COVID-19) is the third coronavirus after severe acute respiratory syndrome (SARS) and Middle East Respiratory Syndrome (MERS) (Zhong et al., 2003; Ramadan & Shaib, 2019; Bashir et al., 2020). A new infectious disease of the coronavirus family was detected in Wuhan, China, and later named the virus COVID-19 in December 2019 (Chen et al., 2020). The Chinese government closed public transport, educational institutions, business centers, parks and other social interaction points to prevent the transmission of COVID-19 (Muhammad et al., 2020). The World Health Organization (WHO) declared COVID-19 a global pandemic in early

March. After this date, the COVID-19 pandemic spread swiftly to many countries of the world.

The COVID-19 pandemic is having an unprecedented impact on societies around the world. The global health crisis caused by the COVID-19 pandemic has led many countries to implement harsh measures of social distance after China. Among these practices, there were restrictions such as curfew, restriction/suspension of transportation, closing of schools, closing or opening of workplaces part-time. With such restrictions, it is aimed to save human life by maintaining social distance and slowing down the spread of virus (Barrot et al., 2020).

There have been many epidemics in the history of the world, resulting in the death of millions of people. Of these epidemics, about 1 million people died in the Hong Kong flu (H3N2), most of them over the age of 65. It is estimated that between 151,700 and 575,400 people worldwide died in the 2009 Avian flu (N1H1), mostly in the US, Mexico, Canada and UK. SARS, (Severe Acute Respiratory Syndrome) emerged in China at the end of 2002. SARS had a high mortality rate as 9.6 % but was much less contagious than previous pandemics. Most of the cases are in China (5,327) and Hong Kong (1,755), with death rates of 7 % and 17 %, respectively. In addition, the International Air Transport Association (IATA) has announced that economic impact of SARS on air travel is approximately 29 billion USD (di Mauro, 2020).

MERS, Middle East Respiratory Syndrome is a respiratory disease caused by MERS-CoV coronavirus. The first outbreak was detected in Saudi Arabia in 2012 and then spread to many countries. In the WHO report, it was emphasized that the mortality rate of this disease was 35 % (Baldwin and di Mario, 2020).

In addition to the many damages brought about by these epidemic diseases, it has also brought some advantageous situations. As the number of COVID-19 cases and deaths increased in countries, industrial activities decreased/stopped globally and accordingly, a decrease in greenhouse gases that cause global warming has been observed. In this study, the positive impact of the COVID-19 pandemic on the environment is discussed.

2 Global Warming and Environmental Degradation

Based on the comprehensive and extensive scientific evidence made by geologists, it has been determined that the age of the Earth is approximately 4.5 billion. Until the last century, although various deteriorations in the balance of the world occurred in certain periods, there were no major changes in the atmosphere density and global warming (Dam, 2014). Swedish Svante

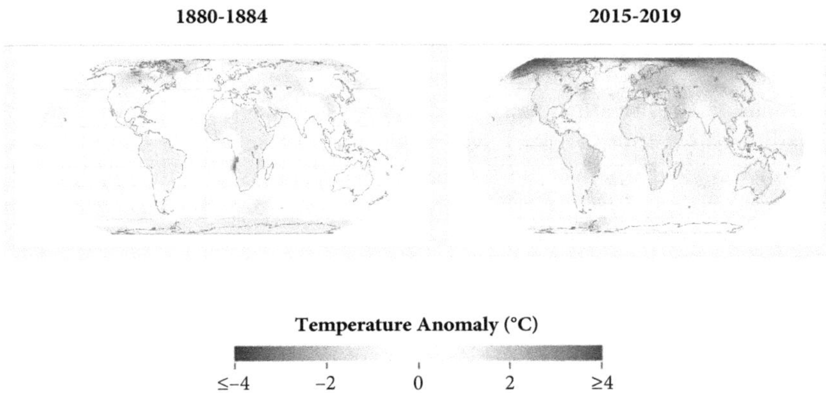

Fig. 21.1: Temperature increases from the industrial revolution to the present
Source: NASA, 2020.

Arrhennius, who received the Nobel Prize in chemistry, made calculations for the first time in the late 19th century that the amount of carbon dioxide in the atmosphere changed, which would affect seasonal temperatures and cause global warming (Madra, 2007). After these calculations, scientists, especially climate scientists, have revealed many scientific studies that the greenhouse gas emissions in the atmosphere are increasing day by day. Greenhouse gas emissions (GHG), especially carbon dioxide (CO2) emissions, are considered to be the main causes of global warming (Soytas et al., 2007). In this context, the Intergovernmental Panel on Climate Change (IPCC) prepares assessment reports on global warming and environmental problems every 5–7 years. According to the IPCC 5th Assessment Report, it was emphasized that global warming was human-induced and that the temperatures increased 0.9°C during the 1901–2011 period, and surface temperatures were 2°C higher than before the industrial revolution. In Fig. 21.1, the temperature difference between the period 1880–1884 and 2015–2019 is given.

The increasing threat of global warming and climate change has been the biggest continuing concern around the world over the past two decades. The impact of global warming on the world economy has been extensively evaluated by researchers since the 1990s (Halicioglu, 2009). Increasing carbon dioxide emissions around the world with each passing day brings about global warming and environmental problems. Since emissions mainly result from fossil fuel consumption, reducing energy consumption is a direct solution to solving the emission problem (Soytas & Sari, 2009). One of the significant effect of increasing environment problem is common usage of fossil fuels which is benificial for economic growth and industry (Ertekin, 2019: 54).

Studies in the literature generally discussed the effects of energy consumption and economic growth on environmental pollution. In this context, it has been investigated whether the Environmental Kuznets Curve (EKC) is valid or not. The EKC hypothesis analyzes the relationship between per capita income and environmental pollution. If there is an inverse U-shaped relationship between these two variables, the EKC hypothesis is assumed to be valid (Acaravci & Ozturk, 2010).

3 Effects of the COVID-19 Pandemic

The year 2020 started with an event that could be one of the turning points in world history. The COVID-19 pandemic, which started in Wuhan, China and spread all over the world within months, infected 46,591,622 people in 219 countries as of August 2020 and caused the death of 1.201.200 people (WHO, 2020). New cases and deaths from COVID-19 are reported by countries every day. The easy and fast contagiousness of the virus has caused a rapid increase in the number of infected people in all countries and caused anxiety and panic all over the world with the subsequent death cases (Remuzzi and Remuzzi, 2020). The SARS-CoV-2 virus caused the COVID-19 epidemic (2019-nCoV in initial studies). This epidemic occurred in Wuhan, China's Hubie province, in December 2019. The COVID-19 virus continues to spread around the world (McKibbin and Fernando, 2020).

Increasing transportation facilities, operating of multinational companies all over the world, growing trade volume between countries with each passing day and the country's economies becoming more dependent on each other are undoubtedly the results of the world becoming a more global village compared to the past. In this process, the phenomenon of globalization has accelerated the growth and spread of the emerging COVID-19 pandemic to the whole world. For countries, this new COVID-19 threat, which has not yet had a vaccine and treatment, has turned into an uncontrollable nightmare and has started to affect every aspect of life. COVID-19 caused significant damage to the economies of the country (Baldwin and di Mario, 2020), triggered the collapse in the stock markets, businesses in many sectors either became unable to do business or were closed within the scope of the measures taken; production has been damaged, the supply chain has begun to deteriorate, and the delivery of health services has started to be discussed.

During the pandemic, instead of waiting for the completion of the event such as the moment of the earthquake and trying to revive life economically after it is over, trying to maintain the normal life without forgetting the fact that the epidemic continues and ensuring that businesses carry out this process will minimize the serious economic damages that may occur. The biggest risks faced by countries in this process are; intensive outflow of foreign capital, contraction in exports and declines in raw material prices, especially oil prices. As a matter of fact, there has been an outflow of approximately 83.3 billion dollars from developing countries as of March 2020 with the sales of bonds and bills and as a result of this, the exchange rates of these countries, especially Brazil, Mexico, Russia and South Africa, depreciated significantly against the dollar (Diaz-Bonilla, 2020). However, in this period, when the COVID-19 pandemic restricted life and reduced production, the fall in demand for energy caused oil prices to fall. However, while this decrease in oil prices creates negative effects for the economies of oil producing countries, it positively affects the economies of countries that are dependent on foreign oil in terms of oil. Because the decrease in the oil price will reduce the production costs and cause the production and output to be positively affected. Countries or international organizations that predicted relatively low economic losses at the beginning of the COVID-19 pandemic have made updates that the economic damage will be higher day by day. In this context, information about the economic losses incurred by the researchers is shown in Tab. 21.1.

COVID-19 has been not just a health crisis, but a global crisis with the potential to change the world. The world, especially the developing countries, is under the threat of economic contraction and leap in unemployment. The crisis is not expected to enter a solution process until a solution is reached on health and the cases are completely eliminated. In this period when the world breathes together, the COVID 19 health crisis has the opportunity to provide an environment for different studies with its experiences.

With the COVID-19 epidemic, which reveals more severe consequences than the previous crises with its dynamics, the insecurity that has emerged all over the world has become visible not only in financial terms, but in every stage of life. In this process, it is seen that countries took unusual attitudes and measures and implemented more nationalist and introverted policies. (TUBA, 2020). Humanity's war against COVID-19 is a worldwide struggle and success in this regard will bring security and peace to the world.

Humans have so far not been able to develop any promising clinical treatment or prevention strategy against coronaviruses. However, researchers are

Tab. 21.1: The impact of the COVID-19 pandemic on the economies of the country

Authors	Countries	Descriptive statistics of key variables	Findings (%deviation from baseline)
Baldwin and di Mario, (2020)	G7 and China	world supply and demand (GDP) world manufacturing world manufacturing exports.	-60 -65 -41
Baker et al. (2020)	USA	total consumption	-35
Barrot et al. (2020)	France	GDP	-5.6
Boone, (2020)	World	Export	-3.7
del Rio-Chanona et al. (2020)	USA	GDP total wage income	-22 -17
McKibbin and Fernando, (2020)	China France Italy Japan Russia Turkey USA	GDP	-6.2 -8.0 -8.3 -9.9 -8.0 -5.5 -8.4
Wren-Lewis, (2020)	UK	GDP	-6

making efforts to develop effective treatment strategies to deal with new types of coronaviruses (Shereen et al., 2020).

4 Emission Effects of the COVID-19 Pandemic

At the end of 2019, a new human-to-human infectious disease (COVID-19) was detected in Wuhan, China, which turned into a global epidemic. Although all countries in the world have mobilized to slow down and alleviate the infection, many sectors, especially health and economy, have been deadlocked and devastated by COVID-19. However, the impact of this lockdown on the natural environment has been positive. Recent data released by NASA (National Aeronautics and Space Administration) and ESA (European Space Agency) indicate that COVID-19 has reduced pollution by up to 30 % in some epicenters such as Wuhan, Italy, Spain and the USA (Muhammad et al., 2020).

Yao et al. (2020), in his study for China, examined the relationship between people who died due to the COVID-19 pandemic and environmental pollution and concluded that environmental pollution has a positive effect on deaths caused by COVID-19.

Bashir et al. (2020), in his study for California, concluded that there is a relationship between the COVID-19 pandemic and the environment, and that the prohibitions and restrictions imposed due to the COVID-19 pandemic reduce human-caused environmental pollution.

Mahato et al. (2020) obtained the following results in his research on the air quality of the Indian city of Delhi during the COVID-19 pandemic. PM10 and PM2.5 concentrations were approximately halved compared to pre-pandemic. There was a significant decrease in NO2 and CO gases.

Berman and Ebisu (2020) examined the comparison of air pollution in the USA during the COVID-19 pandemic compared to the pre-pandemic and they emphasized that nitrogen dioxide (NO2) decreased by 25.5 % compared to the previous years during the COVID-19 pandemic. Regulatory networks have confirmed that air pollution has dropped during the COVID-19 pandemic.

Lal et al. (2020) observed a significant reduction in NO2 and a low reduction in CO due to the COVID-19 pandemic. In addition, COVID-19 pandemic cases in tropical regions are relatively lower than in Europe and America regions.

Mandal and Pal (2020) in a study comparing the COVID-19 pandemic period and before in the region, where the Dwarka river of East India is located, in the middle basin, which is polluted due to quarrying, it was observed that the surface temperature in the region decreased by 3–5 ° C. And the level of noise during contamination has been found to drop from 85dBA to b65dBA and it has been observed that the total dissolved solids concentration in the river water is reduced by a factor of two.

The emission reduction that the Paris Climate Agreement could not/did not do against global warming was realized as a result of the COVID-19 pandemic. As seen in Fig. 21.2, it is emphasized that global emissions will decrease by 2.6 Gt CO2 in 2020 compared to the previous year (IEA, 2020). This emission reduction also reveals the magnitude of the impact of the COVID-19 pandemic in terms of being the biggest reduction of the last 120 years.

Policies and restrictions implemented during the COVID-19 pandemic reduced the consumption of human-made fossil fuels and the emission of many toxic gases, especially carbon dioxide, into the atmosphere temporarily decreased.

To monitor atmospheric CO2 changes from lockdowns of the COVID-19 pandemic, observations collected by the NASA Orbiting Carbon Observatory-2 (OCO-2) satellite and Japan's Greenhouse Gas Monitoring SATellit (GOSAT)

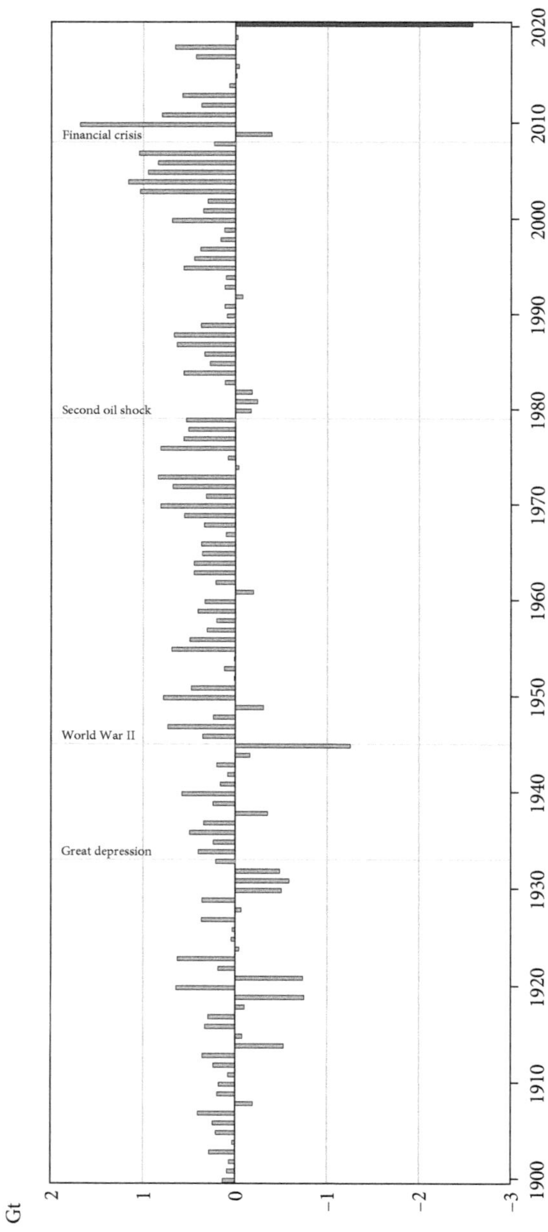

Fig. 21.2: Annual change in global energy sourced CO_2 emissions

Source: IEA, 2020.

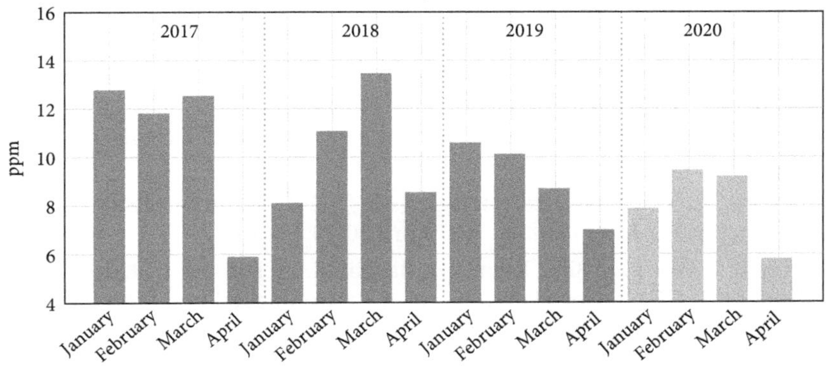

Fig. 21.3: Beijing CO_2 concentration 2017, 2018, 2019, 2020
Source: Japan's Greenhouse gases Observing SATellite (GOSAT) and compiled by ESA/JAXA, 2020.

in the first few months of 2020 are compared with the results collected in previous years.

Targeted observations from GOSAT have been used to monitor changes in major urban areas such as Beijing, Tokyo, Mumbai and New York. In the observations made for Beijing in Fig. 21.3, it was observed that there were significant decreases in carbon emissions in 2020 due to the COVID-19 pandemic.

4 Conclusion

During the COVID-19 pandemic, many sectors, especially health and economy, have experienced deadlocks and as a result, great damage has occurred. However, these lockdowns have reduced fossil fuel consumption, which causes global warming. This decrease in demand for fossil fuels has reflected positively on environmental pollution. During the COVID-19 pandemic process, it is important that this temporary effect is sustainable. In addition, governments and individuals must learn how to reduce pollution in the long run from this deadlock.

Bibliography

Acaravci, A., & Ozturk, I. (2010). On the relationship between energy consumption, CO2 emissions and economic growth in Europe. *Energy, 35*(12), 5412–5420. doi:10.1016/j.energy.2010.07.009.

Baker, S. R., Farrokhnia, R., Meyer, S., Pagel, M., & Yannelis, C. (2020). *How does household spending respond to an epidemic? Consumption during the covid-19 pandemic*, NBER WP 26949.

Baldwin, R., & Weder di Mauro, B. (2020). Introduction. In R. Baldwin & B. Weder di Mauro (Eds.), *Economics in the Time of COVID-19*. CEPR, London, chapter 1, pp. 1–30.

Barrot, J. N., Grassi, B., & Sauvagnat, J. (2020). Sectoral effects of social distancing. *Covid Economics, 3*(10 April 2020), 85–102.

Bashir, M. F., Ma, B. J., Bilal, Komal, B., Bashir, M. A., Farooq, T. H., Iqbal, N., & Bashir, M. (2020). Correlation between environmental pollution indicators and COVID-19 pandemic: A brief study in Californian context. *Environmental Research, 187*, 109652. doi:10.1016/j.envres.2020.109652.

Berman, J. D., & Ebisu, K. (2020). Changes in US air pollution during the COVID-19 pandemic. *Science of the Total Environment, 739*, 139864. doi:10.1016/j.scitotenv.2020.139864.

Boone, L. (2020). 2 Tackling the fallout from COVID-19. In R. Baldwin & B. Weder di Mauro (Eds.), *Economics in the Time of COVID-19*. CEPR, London, chapter 2, pp. 37–44.

Chen, H., Guo, J., Wang, C., Luo, F., Yu, X., Zhang, W., Li, J., Zhao, D., Xu, D., Gong, Q., Liao, J., Yang, H., Hou, W., & Zhang, Y. (2020). Clinical characteristics and intrauterine vertical transmission potential of COVID-19 infection in nine pregnant women: A retrospective review of medical records. *Lancet (London, England), 395*(10226), 809–815. doi:10.1016/S0140-6736(20)30360-3.

Dam, M. M. (2014). Sera *Gazı Emisyonlarının Makro Ekonomik Değişkenlerle İlişkisi*: OECD *Ülkeleri için Panel Veri Analizi*. (Published pHD Thesis). Aydin Adnan Menderes University Institute of Social Sciences, Aydin.

del Rio-Chanona, R. M., Mealy, P., Pichler, A., Lafond, F., & Farmer, D. (2020). Supply and demand shocks in the COVID-19 pandemic: An industry and occupation perspective. *Oxford Review of Economic Policy, 36*(1), 94–137. doi:10.1093/oxrep/graa033.

Diaz-Bonilla, E. (2020). Fiscal and monetary responses to the COVID-19 pandemic: Some thoughts for developing countries and the international community. *IFPRI book chapters*, 98–101.

di Mauro, B. W. (2020). Macroeconomics of the flu. In R. Baldwin & B. Weder di Mauro (Eds.), *Economics in the Time of COVID-19*, CEPR, London, chapter 1, pp. 31–36.

Ertekin, Ş. (2019). Environmental Taxes in Struggle Agaınst Envıronmental Pollution. In M. M. Dam (Ed.), *Agenda Environment An Interdisciplinary Overview*. Alter Publishing, Ankara, pp. 54–80.

ESA/JAXA. (2020). https://eodashboard.org/?country=CN&poi=W5-N2

Halicioglu, F. (2009). An econometric study of CO2 emissions, energy consumption, income and foreign trade in Turkey. *Energy Policy, 37*(3), 1156–1164.

Lal, P., Kumar, A., Kumar, S., Kumari, S., Saikia, P., Dayanandan, A.,. . . & Khan, M. L. (2020). The dark cloud with a silver lining: Assessing the impact of the SARS COVID-19 pandemic on the global environment. *Science of the Total Environment, 732*, 139297. doi:10.1016/j.scitotenv.2020.139297.

Madra, Ö. (2007). *Küresel Isınma ve İklim Krizi*. İstanbul: İdil Yayıncılık.

Mahato, S., Pal, S., & Ghosh, K. G. (2020). Effect of lockdown amid COVID-19 pandemic on air quality of the megacity Delhi, India. *Science of the Total Environment, 730,* 139086. doi:10.1016/j.scitotenv.2020.139086.

Mandal, I., & Pal, S. (2020). COVID-19 pandemic persuaded lockdown effects on environment over stone quarrying and crushing areas. *Science of The Total Environment, 732*, 139281. doi:10.1016/j.scitotenv.2020.139281.

McKibbin, W., & Fernando, R. (2020). *The global macroeconomic impacts of COVID-19: Seven scenarios* (CAMA Working paper 19/2020). Australian National University.

Muhammad, S., Long, X., & Salman, M. (2020). COVID-19 pandemic and environmental pollution: A blessing in disguise? *Science of the Total Environment, 728*. doi:10.1016/j.scitotenv.2020.138820.

Ramadan, N., & Shaib, H. (2019). Middle East respiratory syndrome coronavirus (MERS-CoV): A review. *Germs, 9*(1), 35–42. doi:10.18683/germs.2019.1155.

Remuzzi, A., & Remuzzi, G. (2020). COVID-19 and Italy: What next?. *Lancet, 395*, 1225–1228. doi:10.1016/S0140-6736(20)30627-9.

Shereen, M. A., Khan, S., Kazmi, A., Bashir, N., & Siddique, R. (2020). COVID-19 infection: Origin, transmission, and characteristics of human coronaviruses. *Journal of Advanced Research*, 24, 91–98. doi:10.1016/j.jare.2020.03.005.

Soytas, U., & Sari, R. (2009). Energy consumption, economic growth, and carbon emissions: Challenges faced by an EU candidate member. *Ecological economics*, *68*(6), 1667–1675. doi:10.1016/j.ecolecon.2007.06.014.

Soytas, U., Sari, R., & Ewing, B. T. (2007). Energy consumption, income, and carbon emissions in the United States. *Ecological Economics*, *62*(3–4), 482–489. doi:10.1016/j.ecolecon.2006.07.009.

TUBA. (2020). *COVID-19 Pandemi Değerlendirme Raporu*. Retrieved from http://www.tuba.gov.tr

WHO. (2020). WHO. Retrieved from https://www.who.int/emergencies/diseases/novel-coronavirus-2019

Wren-Lewis, S. (2020). The economic effects of a pandemic. In R. Baldwin & B. Weder di Mauro (Eds.), *Economics in the Time of COVID-19.* CEPR, London, chapter 13, pp. 109–112.

Yao, Y., Pan, J., Wang, W., Liu, Z., Kan, H., Meng, X., & Wang, W. (2020). *Spatial Correlation of Particulate Matter Pollution and Death Rate of COVID-19.* medRxiv, doi:10.1101/2020.04.07.20052142.

Zhong, N. S., Zheng, B. J., Li, Y. M., Poon, L. L. M., Xie, Z. H., Chan, K. H., Li, P. H., Tan, S. Y., Chang, Q., Xie, J. P., Liu, X. Q., Xu, J., Li, D. X., Yuen, K. Y., Peiris, J. S. M., & Xie, J. (2003). Epidemiology and cause of severe acute respiratory syndrome (SARS) in Guangdong, People's Republic of China, in February, 2003. *Lancet, 362*, 1353–1358.

Serhat Karaoglan

The Challenges of the Turkish Music-Entertainment Industry During the Covid-19 Pandemic

Abstract The Covid-19 pandemic has affected almost all industries at the global level. When this effect is viewed from an economic point of view, it is seen as stopping of production, disruption of services, and changing consumption habits. The music industry is also one of the sectors most affected during the extraordinary crisis.

In this chapter, it is tried to shed light on the current situation of the music industry through media, social media, and observations. In addition, a detailed analysis of the current situation is made through interviews with musicians and audiences. Interviews could not be conducted face to face due to the pandemic. Virtual forms have been replied by 21 musicians.

At first, general information about the arts marketing and consumption of arts is given. Then, the subject of music and listeners has been discussed with audience segmentation and music industry and musicians. Under the general problems of music industry title, legitimacy crisis over the musical industry, high prices of musical instruments and equipment and the issue of stopping the music-entertainment sector due to social sensitivities is discussed. The music-entertainment industry, like many other industries, was deeply affected due to the covid-19 pandemic that emerged in the last period of 2019 and subsequently affected the whole world. That's why, at the last section, pandemic and music industry subject is examined.

Keywords: Arts Marketing, Covid-19, Music Industry, Music Audiences, Musicians

1 Introduction

The Covid-19 pandemic has affected almost all industries at the global level. When this effect is viewed from an economic point of view, it is seen as stopping of production, disruption of services, and changing consumption habits. The music industry is also one of the sectors most affected during the extraordinary crisis.

Due to social sensitivities, the entertainment industry has to react first to anything such as terrorist incident or a natural disaster etc. General economic stagnation also causes consumers to withdraw from expenditures that they consider not necessary. With the pandemic effect and health risk added to all of these, the music industry and musicians have started to have hard times with the contribution of legal regulations.

In this chapter, it is tried to shed light on the current situation of the music industry through media, social media, and observations. In addition, a detailed analysis of the current situation is made through interviews with musicians and audiences. Interviews could not be conducted face to face due to the pandemic. Virtual forms have been replied by 21 musicians.

2 Arts Marketing

Even though arts marketing is mostly considered within the scope of non-profit business in the literature, it is possible to be considered as services, due to an important individual and institutional audience that tries to generate income by making art. For this reason, the basic marketing mix elements should not be ignored within the scope of art marketing. In short, price, product, promotion, place, people, physical evidence and process elements called 7P must be taken into consideration.

However, art and especially music should not seem like just part of the entertainment industry. Music is an important element in creating culture and creating local differences in a globalizing world. In addition to this popular culture suppresses and exploits individuals. Cultural imperialism also puts pressure on the artistic activities of individuals. In the current social structure, the artist has to carry the aim of appealing to the society rather than artistic production. Thus, the craftsman emerges as a defined individual instead of the artist as a free individual. It is necessary to accept that cultural differentiation is a challenge to the uniformity of globalization and cultural management should be addressed in this respect.

If it is necessary to define art, it can be said that it is a creative process. There may be slight differences in different management and marketing approaches in different branches of art, but it is still possible to evaluate art under a single roof. For this reason, it is necessary to try to determine the sub-branches of art first. Clancy (1994) described four categories of arts as Hiart (plays, operas, concerts and musicals), Pop (film and rock/pop/jazz music), Exper (art exhibitions, contemporary dance, literature/poetry readings) and Trod (traditional folk dance/music). O'Reilly (2011) showed the branches of art as Fine art, music, performing art, visual arts, literature and festivals in her comprehensive art marketing literature review. It is possible to evaluate music both live and recorded in the field of performing arts. Besides, it is necessary to consider popular music as a commercial activity.

2.1 Consumption of Arts

Due to the demographic homogeneity of art audiences, arts managers tend to see only one audience, but there are significant demographic differences between subscribers, occasional subscribers, and single ticket buyers in terms of age, education level, and income. In performing arts marketing, the focus is on target audiences, but the main goal should be to establish long-term relationships with this audience (Rentschler et al., 2002). The importance of customer satisfaction and the importance of developing stronger relationships offers many opportunities for art to build more loyal audiences. (Johnson & Garbarino, 2001). It is not possible to manage and market art without focusing on differences in attitude, perception, and preferences.

Art consumption is highly motivated and shaped by emotions, for example, the driving role of nostalgia in art consumption has an impact on consumer experiences (Colbert & St-James, 2014). Especially in performance arts, the effect of socialization cannot be ignored. According to Pitts & Burland (2013) research on jazz music, listening to live music has a strong social component. Listeners enjoy attending with others or meeting like-minded enthusiasts in the audience, and they welcome opportunities to chat and relax in venues that help facilitate this. More generally, cultural experiences provide a rich context to develop our understanding of the role of emotions in consumption (Colbert & St-James, 2014).

However, there are few applications on inductive, consumer-oriented methodologies that investigate such experiences. This may be the result of a cultural mindset on behalf of curators or managers, especially if they come from an art or historical background that naturally has their own particular methodology (Goulding & Saren, 2010). The challenge in art marketing is to recognize that organizations sell an experience, whether purely aesthetic, social or embodied (Joy & Sherry, 2003).

3 Music and Audiences

Music takes place in every moment of human life. Both the increase in online music listening possibilities and portable devices make it easier to listen to music. In addition, listening to music takes place in our lives simultaneously with activities such as reading books, traveling, and even working. Fernández-Blanco, Prieto-Rodríguez and Suarez-Pandiello (2017) study also shows similar findings, while it is seen that popular music, along with cinema, is the art products that attract the most attention of consumers.

The music listened from the recording can be listened to at any time and place without any limits, but live music reflects the current situation. Live music can also be recorded and consumed online or offline, but unfortunately, the benefits of music such as socializing and getting away from the environment do not occur.

Reputation and image are extremely important in selling live music, as no audience knows fully the personal benefit of a concert experience until they attend the event (Krueger, 2005). A live concert is not only a temporary experience, but also symbolizes what it means to be admired (Frith, 2007). Live music experience is an environment where musicians and fans are together, a synergy is formed, a meeting is held, and a common feeling is experienced together like a religious ceremony (Duffett, 2012).

In this social context, live listening is an intense, sometimes tiring experience for some viewers; for others it offers a source of relaxation and absorption, with the opportunity to focus on playing well and preferred repertoire. Therefore, live listening is both an individual and a social action, with unpredictable risks and tastes that depend on both elements and vary between listeners, places, and situations (Pitts & Burland, 2013).

Packages offered to the audience (discount for the next concert, drinks, backstage experience, pre-performance interviews) increase customer satisfaction. Loyalty can be increased by adding value and providing satisfaction, and thus increase the likelihood of selling and repurchase (Hall & Binney, 2016). However, it should not be overlooked that customers are price sensitive.

3.1 Audience Segmentation

It will be beneficial to divide the audience into segments, to identify behavioral patterns and to try to target, in short, it is necessary to understand the target audience (Henderson, 2013). After the target audience is understood and determined, it will be good to determine the behaviors accordingly.

People who are hierarchically at the lower levels do not have an interest in performing arts due to their lifestyle and the problems surrounding it. Huntington (2007) suggests that we see the consumption of performing arts as a process of diffusion, in contrast to Andreasen's (1992) hierarchical model of consumer readiness. This approach assumes a different structural model that tries to understand the way consumers are exposed to a product, service or idea and shows how they adopt it. Spread takes place in the market and the rate of adoption of products, services and ideas depends on both the consumer and

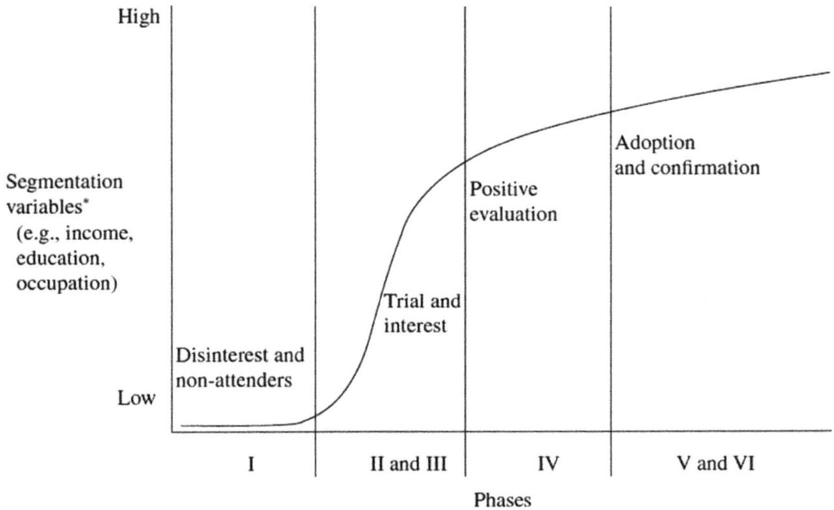

Fig. 22.1: Stages in the performing arts adoption process
Source: Huntington, 2007.

the product. A reinterpretation of Andreasen's hierarchy for performing arts by Huntington (2007) is shown in Fig. 22.1.

Performing arts management has tended to offer artistic value and content, often minimizing the importance of service and venue quality. It shows that it is a strategic imperative for performing arts managers to better segment and understand customer perceptions of service delivery and appreciate the complexity of the repurchase equation. This will ensure that appropriate emphasis is given to the service delivery and venue quality in strategic development and implementation as artistic content (Hume, Mort & Winzar, 2007).

There is a legitimacy crisis (Holden, 2006) because of art organizations cannot attract audiences that differ in age, social or ethnic origin. The public may feel uncomfortable with the contribution to art. People's priorities are changing due to changing economic conditions in Turkey. While young people are closer to more popular music genres, as the age progresses, the tendency towards music genres such as classical music and blues begins to increase. Noticeable changes can be seen in the genre of music made in live music venues.

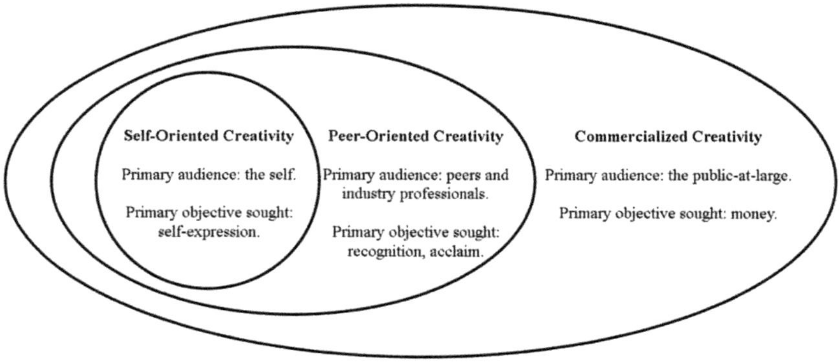

Fig. 22.2: Levels of oriented creativity
Source: Hirschman, E.C. 1983.

3.2 Music Industry and Musicians

The music industry and its associated entertainment industry include not only musicians and managers but also many people working in the background. Therefore, any fluctuations in the music industry not only affect business owners and musicians. In fact, the silence of the music and the closure of the places where music can be listened affect the audience on a psychological level. In arts organizations such as theaters and orchestras, a play or a concert is produced and consumed with actors and audiences. The same happens when music is played, and people dance (Ropo, 2009). Therefore, listeners can be considered as an indispensable part of the music industry. Contemporary discussions indicate that there is a relationship between the production and consumption of music. (Cluley, 2013). From this point of view, it will be possible to say that everyone who takes part in the journey from the production of music to its consumption either through recording or live is involved in the music industry. Thus, it is possible to say that it is a much larger source of employment and economic income than appears. It is not possible to ignore their cultural contributions as in other art branches.

The audience was described above. Some statements were made about performing arts managers. Next, the artists involved in the creative process should be defined. First step of the creative process is central self-oriented creativity (see Fig. 22.2). The primary audience is the creator, and the main target is themself. In other words, the creator has to satisfy and express themselves first

(Rodner & Kerrigan, 2014). Also, cultural producers use culture consumption to make sense of their activities and continue their production (Cluley, 2013). It will not be possible to call these people as prosumers since they do not produce for their own consumption.

3.3 General Problems of Music Industry

Since the last century, only narrow segments of the society have participated, threatening the quality of art forms, and even the younger generation does not keep performing arts at the desired levels culturally or economically (Askegaard, 1999). For this reason, there is a legitimacy crisis over the musical industry. Low level of participation causes music industry managers and musicians to produce non-creative and consumption-oriented products. This is killing musician's creativity and this situation also eliminates cultural production and differences which are one of the main purposes of music.

Cultural production approaches are divided into four as managerial-orientation, consumption-orientation, everyday life-orientation, and cultural product-orientation (Venkatesh & Meamber, 2006). Making cultural production focused on the market and profit creates troublesome situations especially for the artists involved in this production. Some participants of this research are agreed with this statement. For example, 39-year-old professional male musician who plays clavier for 20 years expressed *"Our favorite style and market style don't match"*. Similarly, one other participant who is a DJ for 22 years expressed *"If you want to make your own art, you cannot make money. To make money, you have to meet the expectations of companies rather than the audience"*.

Another problem is that the prices of musical instruments and equipment are high. Exchange rate fluctuations and tax increases on imported products also make it difficult for musicians to own equipment. A musician living in economically developed countries can have equipment at much lower prices. An example illustrating this situation is presented in Fig. 22.3.

The interpretation of the 15-year-old professional singer on this subject is *"Musical instruments and accessories are very expensive and maintenance is very expensive. However, the venues pay very low (It would not be wrong if I say some want money) and the musicians cannot get the income to fully perform their profession. This creates the perception that musicianship is a temporary job, and the subjects such as artistic satisfaction and creativity are avoided"*.

As seen in the figure, when make a price comparison for same intermediate level electric guitar, equipment is about 50 % more expensive in Turkey. Therefore, in Turkey about 3.5 minimum wage can buy that guitar besides 35 %

Fig. 22.3: Price comparison of an intermediate level electric guitar (Left one from Zuhal Music, Turkey; right one from Musikia, France)

of minimum wage can buy the same guitar in France. So, it is possible to say the same guitar that is about 9 times more expensive in Turkey than in France.

One more problem is that in any event that occurs, the music-entertainment sector stops first due to social sensitivities, affecting everyone working in this field. Because musicians are paid when they perform. In addition, there are service personnel working temporarily and daily on-stage days in the sector. The silence of the music affects a large segment. 46 years old 28-year guitarist/singer says *"Everything affects us first. Weather, natural disaster, season, economy, war... We work informally. We can make money when we play. Most of the time we can't get our money right away either"*. Similarly, 33-year drummer says *"Weddings do not stop, other entertainments do not stop. There is a perception that everything related to art has to stop in any situation. Most of the time preparations are made, even the city is changed. You bear a lot of expenses. There are viewers who bought tickets. Why the music is silent? Whenas, we can have a commemoration and relief together. Moreover, entertainment on television continues constantly"*.

3.4 Pandemic and Music Industry

The music-entertainment industry, like many other industries, was deeply affected due to the covid-19 pandemic that emerged in the last period of 2019 and subsequently affected the whole world. As of 31 October 2020, more than 45 million cases were seen, and more than 1,200,000 deaths occurred due to the virus. For this reason, governments have had to take some precautions for activities where people can participate collectively. However, while some sectors were supported, employees in the arts branch remained away from such aids. During this process, the musicians not only suffered financial difficulties, but also spiritual and psychological problems.

In the interviews, it was seen that 11 musicians had income other than music. While music is a secondary source of income for some, others have had to turn to various businesses (for example online commerce) due to the pandemic. After that participants were asked "If the stagnation of the music-entertainment industry continues during the epidemic period, how long could you last without any financial support/credit/debt?". To this question, 2 musicians answered that I have no problem, 4 musicians be good for a year or more, 9 for a few months, 3 musicians for a few weeks, 3 musicians for a few days. Musicians stated that they overcame psychological problems by reading books, doing sports, getting together with friends to play and sing songs, and by recording for publication on social media. While some of them stated that they could not overcome financial problems, some of them stated that they tried to overcome by moving to another line of business, selling their musical instruments, taking the stage for half price and with single instrument or with a vocalist and single instrumentalist, getting financial support from family and friends, and using their savings. Thirty years old 15-year-guitarist expressed his difficulties as *"Live music activities have completely stopped in the city where I live. For this reason, I sold my equipment that I do not use very often. Then I had to sell my car and buy a cheaper car. I had to go to tourism regions and work for very low wages like I have never done in my life. I do not know how to get through the winter, although I have cut a lot of my expenses. If I find any job, I will have to enter and work"*.

In the interviews with the listeners, they stated that listening to live music provides socialization and psychological relaxation. They stated that listening to music live is very different from listening to recorded music. They interact with the artists on the stage and say that they are a part of the stage. Although the epidemic is scary, they think that the music should continue with some precautions and arrangements like in the form of open-air concerts. They argue that they follow live music broadcasts on the Internet, but this situation creates an effect like listening to recorded music. While music companies can make money with online businesses, it seems unlikely for musicians. It has been seen that some of the audience intend to support artists and groups for instance they perform online.

4 Conclusion

Culture is the strategic variable of nations and has the power to differentiate, provide identity and social networking within nations (Calpe & Velez B, 2005). Music is also an important part of culture. Music, which is a part of culture and art, also needs a management philosophy as a business. For this reason, customer/audience environment analysis should be done at first. The following questions should be asked to determine this. Who are the customers? What they want and consume? When, where, why, and how they consume? A final question can be added as why not.

In addition, managers in the music industry (which may also apply to musicians), have to consider elements of the marketing mix. Price should be set correctly, and more audience participation should be ensured. It should not be forgotten that there are different segments who are interested in different types of music and services should be developed. With some discounts, promotions, and memberships, it should be tried to create loyal customer profiles. Areas where audiences listen to music should be arranged considering the health of consumers due to the pandemic. In addition, attention should be paid to factors such as the ease of transportation. It is necessary to pay attention to both the employees and the audiences participating in the activities as the people element. At cultural events, customers prefer to be together and socialize with people like themselves. The processes should be managed well, paying attention to keeping the audience's pleasure from physical elements.

Music associations should do more to protect the rights of musicians. Organized musicians will be able to obtain their rights comfortably. In addition, studies should be carried out before the state and the problems of the artists should be expressed. It is important for the state to support the artist and the industry for the protection and development of the cultural structure.

Bibliography

Andreasen, A. (1992). *Expanding the Audience for the Performing Arts.* Cabin John, MD: Seven Locks Press.

Askegaard, S. (1999). Marketing, The Performing Arts and Social Change: Beyond the Legitimacy Crisis. *Consumption Markets & Culture*, *3*(1), 1–25,

Calpe, W. L., & Velez B., R. (2005). The Cultural Management Philosophy, *8th International Conference on Arts & Cultural Management*, Montreal, Canada.

Clancy, P. (1994). *Managing the Cultural Sector: Essential Competencies for Managers in Arts, Culture and Heritage in Ireland*. Dublin: Oak Tree Press.

Cluley, R. (2013). Why Producers of Music Use Discourses of Consumption (And Why We Shouldn't Think That Makes Them Prosumers). *Arts Marketing: An International Journal*, *3*(2), 117–130.

Colbert, F., & St-James, Y. (2014). Research in Arts Marketing: Evolution and Future Directions. *Psychology and Marketing*, *31*(8), 566–575.

Duffett, M. (2012). Why Promote Sold-Out Concerts? A Durkheimian Analysis. *Arts Marketing: An International Journal*, *2*(1), 21–34.

Fernández-Blanco, V., Prieto-Rodríguez, J., & Suarez-Pandiello, J. (2017). A Quantitative Analysis of Reading Habits in Spain. *International Journal of Arts Management*, *19*(3), 19–32.

Frith, S. (2007). Live Music Matters. *Scottish Music Review*, *1*(1), 1–27.

Goulding, C., & Saren, M. (2010). Immersion, Emergence and Reflexivity: Grounded Theory and Aesthetic Consumption. *International Journal of Culture, Tourism and Hospitality Research*, *4*(1), 70–82.

Hall, E., & Binney, W. (2016). Increasing Loyalty in the Arts by Bundling Consumer Benefits. *Arts and the Market*, *6*(2), 141–165.

Henderson, S. (2013). Sustainable Touring: Exploring Value Creation Through Social Marketing. *Arts Marketing: An International Journal*, *3*(2), 154–167.

Hirschman, E. C. (1983). Aesthetics, Ideologies and the Limits of the Marketing Concept. *Journal of Marketing*, *47*(3), 45–55.

Holden, J. (2006). *Cultural Value and the Crisis in Legitimacy*. London: Demos.

Hume, M., Mort, G. S., & Winzar, H. (2007). Exploring Repurchase Intention in a Performing Arts Context: Who Comes? And Why Do They Come Back. *International Journal of Nonprofit and Voluntary Sector Marketing*, *12*, 135–148.

Huntington, C. S. (2007). Reevaluating Segmentation Practices and Public Policy in Classical Performing Arts Marketing: A Macro Approach. *The Journal of Arts Management, Law, and Society*, *37*(2), 127–141.

Johnson, M. S., & Garbarino, E. (2001). Customers of Performing Arts Organisations: Are Subscribers Different From Nonsubscribers?.

International Journal of Nonprofit and Voluntary Sector Marketing, *6*(1), 61–77.

Joy, A., & Sherry, Jr., J. F. (2003). Speaking of Art as Embodied Imagination: A Multisensory Approach to Understanding Aesthetic Experience. *Journal of Consumer Research*, *30*(2), 259–282.

Krueger, A. (2005). The Economics of Real Superstars: The Market for Rock Concerts in The Material World. *Journal of Labour Economics*, *23*(1), 1–30.

O'Reilly, D. (2011). Mapping the Arts Marketing Literature. *Arts Marketing: An International Journal*, *1*(1), 26–38.

Pitts, S. E., & Burland, K. (2013). Listening to Live Jazz: An Individual or Social Act?. *Arts Marketing: An International Journal*, *3*(1), 7–20.

Rentschler, R., Radbourne, J., Carr, R., & Rickard, J. (2002). Relationship Marketing, Audience Retention and Performing Arts Organisation Viability. *International Journal of Nonprofit and Voluntary Sector Marketing*, *7*(2), 118–130.

Rodner, V. L., & Kerrigan, F. (2014). The Art of Branding– Lessons from Visual Artists. *Arts Marketing: An International Journal*, *4*(1/2), 101–118.

Ropo, A. (2009). Performing Arts as a Source of Aesthetic Bodily Leadership Knowledge, *10th International Conference on Arts & Cultural Management*, Dallas, United States.

Venkatesh, A., & Meamber, L. A. (2006). Arts and Aesthetics: Marketing and Cultural Production. *Marketing Theory*, *6*(1), 11–39.

Yakup Soylemez

Analysis of Causality Relationships Among COVID-19 and Sector Returns: Evidence from Turkey

Abstract The COVID-19 epidemic, which has turned into a global pandemic, has affected the whole world. In addition to the effects of the epidemic threatening human health, it has been observed that the economic effects are also severe. The epidemic has turned into a "sudden stop" crisis, affecting all areas of the economy. Therefore, the economic impact of the epidemic on financial markets needs to be determined. Studies to be carried out especially on the effects on the sectors can be a guide for the measures to be taken against similar crises that may arise in the future. In this context, the direction and degree of the relationship between COVID-19 and sector returns should be investigated. While the study examines the direction and severity of the relationship between COVID-19 and selected sector returns, it adds some financial variables to the data set. Thus, the emergence of false relationships between the epidemic and sector returns are prevented, the direction and degree of the relationship between the epidemic and some other financial variables are also determined. These financial variables are selected as CDS premium, VIX index, gold and oil prices. Autoregressive Distributed Lag Model (ARDL) bounds testing was used to determine the direction of the relationship between variables. Thus, the direction of the relationship among the COVID-19 epidemic and sector returns and some financial variables has been identified with evidence from Turkey. It is thought that the study will contribute to the literature in determining the sectoral effects of sudden stop crises.

Keywords: COVID-19, Pandemic, Sector Returns, Causality, ARDL Bound Test, Turkey

1 Introduction

According to Sharpe, a financial crisis can be defined as the perception of a decline in a basic economic variable as a major movement in the market (Markowitz et al., 2009). Reinhart and Rogoff (2009) separate financial crises as money, sudden stop, debt, and banking. The sudden stop crisis indicates the sudden decrease in the net capital flow entering an economy. In this case, it can be seen decreases in production and consumption and serious volatilities in asset prices. This is clearly demonstrated in the "COVID-19 and Global

Capital Flows" report published by the OECD. While global GDP is expected to contract by 6 %, trade is expected to decrease from 32 % to 12 %.

The restriction decisions taken in Turkey until the end of May 2020 brought the sectoral activities to a halt. The government has started to take some measures in order to reduce the effects of sectoral losses on the economy since June 2020. In this context, measures such as sectoral incentives, increasing liquidity and tax incentives have been taken. Especially, the central bank increased its emission volume by lowering interest rates. However, the effects of both COVID-19 and economic measures under COVID-19 are not clear. However, the impact of the global economic recession caused by COVID-19 on the sectors is still not fully determined. Therefore, it is very important to analyze the effects of COVID-19 on sector returns.

Within the scope of this study, it is tried to reveal whether there is a causality relationship between COVID-19 and the returns of selected sectors traded on Borsa İstanbul (BİST). The selected indices are determined as banking, informatics, food, trade, tourism, and transportation. This study, to analyze the effect of COVID-19 are used the number of cases and deaths in Turkey and the world. Other independent variables used in the study are oil prices, gold prices, CDS Premium, and VIX index values. The dates of 01.09–07.10.2020 have been chosen as the research period. In the study, the ARDL (Autoregressive Distributed Lag Bound Test) method was used to analyze the causality relationship between variables. The study contributes to the literature in terms of analyzing the effect of COVID-19 on sectors. In the study, first of all, the literature was reviewed and detailed information about previous studies was presented. In the third part of the study, the model used in the research is introduced. Afterward, empirical findings were presented and discussed. Finally, the results of the study were analyzed.

2 Literature Review

COVID-19, which turned into a global epidemic in a short time, did not only threaten human health. COVID-19 causes great damage to the economies and industries of countries. For this reason, there are many studies in the literature investigating the economic and sectoral effects of COVID-19. In this section, the main studies in the literature are given.

Goodell (2020) analyzed the global effects of the epidemic, taking into account the effects of similar past events. The study claims that COVID-19 has a more devastating impact economically than nuclear war, climate change and local disasters. Ali et al. (2020) analyzed the response of financial markets to

COVID-19 in terms of decline and volatility in their study. The research has found that the globalization of the epidemic caused a sharp decline in financial markets. In a similar study, He et al. (2020) made an empirical analysis of the response of the Chinese markets to the epidemic. The study found that transport, mining, electricity, and environmental sectors responded negatively to the pandemic; on the other hand, it found that manufacturing, information technology, education, and healthcare sectors are resistant to the pandemic. Al-Awadhi et al. (2020) investigated the outbreak in the Chinese market using probability panel data on stocks. The study has found that all companies are negatively affected by COVID-19. In another study, Anh and Gan (2020) investigated the impact of the epidemic and the subsequent lockdown on Vietnamese markets. The study revealed the negative impact of an increasing number of cases on stock returns. In addition, there are findings that the impact of the epidemic in the financial sector is higher than in other sectors. In another study, Liu et al. (2020) investigated the relationship of the epidemic with 21 indices worldwide. In the study, it was found that the epidemic affected all stock markets. In addition, it has been revealed that during the epidemic, stock exchanges belonging to Asian countries gained more negative abnormal returns. Griffith et al. (2020) analyzed the effects of the epidemic on sectors in the UK. The study found findings that the impact of the epidemic on industries is changing.

One of the places where the epidemic affected as severely as Europe is the USA. There are also studies evaluating the impact of the epidemic on the US economy. Sharif et al. (2020) investigated the link between oil price volatility, stock market, geopolitical risk, and policy uncertainty and COVID-19. Consistent wavelet tests and wavelet-based Granger causality tests were used in the study. These tests found an unprecedented link between the COVID-19 outbreak and independent variables. Thakur (2020) analyzed the impact of the epidemic on US stock markets. The study found a significant and negative relationship between the Standard & Poor's index and the number of cases. Choi (2020) has found that the contraction in sectors included in the Standard & Poor's 500 index due to COVID-19 is greater than the 2008 financial crisis. Gharib et al. (2021) analyzed the causality relationship between crude oil and spot gold prices during the epidemic period based on West Texas Light. The study found bilateral contagion effects in the oil and gold markets. Mazur et al. (2021) analyzed the impact of COVID-19 on sectors in the S&P1500 index. Their study has found that COVID-19 has a positive return effect in the natural gas, food, health and software sectors, and a negative return effect in the oil, real estate, entertainment and accommodation sectors.

After evaluating the prominent studies in the literature; the studies using the example of Turkey must be evaluated. In their study, Sümer and Özorhon (2020) analyzed the relationship between gold prices and the BIST real estate investment trust index during the epidemic period using the granger causality test. In the study, it was found that index returns can be preferred over gold, except during financial crisis periods. In another study, Kılıç (2020) analyzed the impact of the epidemic on sector indices using the case study method. The study found that the epidemic had negative consequences for most sectors, but found that it provided positive returns in some sectors such as trade. Analyzing the relationship of the epidemic with the net foreign exchange position, Çiğdem (2020) determined a causality relationship between variables. Öztürk et al. (2020) analyzed the relationship between BİST sector indices and the number of cases using the fixed effects model. In the study, it was found that the negative economic effects of the epidemic mostly occurred in the metal products and machinery sector.

When the literature is examined, although studies are examining the relationship between the epidemic and sector indices, it seems that the study addressing the causality relationship between BİST sector indexes and the epidemic is quite rare. It can be determined that there is only one study examining the causality relationship between the epidemic and BİST sector index returns in the literature. In this study by Sümer and Özorhon (2020), the analysis was carried out based on only one index. This study fills the gap in the literature by examining the causality relationship between selected sector indices and the number of cases.

3 Methodology

In the literature, some methods enable the analysis of short and long-term relationships between various financial variables. Among these methods, Engle-Granger (1987) tests are frequently used to examine short-term relationships, and Johansen (1988) cointegration tests are used to examine long-term relationships. To use these tests, variables must not be stationary at level. Therefore, these tests are used only to examine the relationships between variables that are integrated at the same level. The ARDL model proposed by Peseran et al. (2001) can analyze the relationship between variables that are integrated into different levels. Therefore, the fact that the variables to be used in the ARDL model are stable at the level I(0) or stationary at the first difference I(1) does not prevent the analysis. Another advantage of the model is that since it uses the error correction model (ECM), it can establish more statistically significant relationships between short and long-term dynamics. The boundary test equation used in the ARDL method is shown in Formula 1.

$$\Delta Y_t = \Psi_0 + \sum_{i=1}^{m} \Psi_{1i}\Delta Y_{t-i} + \sum_{i=0}^{m} \Psi_{2i}\Delta X_{1t-i} + \ldots + \sum_{i=0}^{m} \Psi_{ki}\Delta X_{kt-i} + \xi_1 Y_{t-1} + \xi_2 X_{1t-1} + \ldots + \xi_k X_{kt-1} + u_t \quad (1)$$

In the ARDL model, first of all, appropriate lag lengths for variables should be determined. The cointegration test in the model is made according to the following hypotheses:

$$H_0 = \xi_1 = \xi_2 = \ldots = \xi_k = 0 \rightarrow \textit{No Cointegration.}$$

$$H_1 = \xi_1 \neq \xi_2 \neq \xi_k \neq 0 \ \rightarrow \textit{Cointegration is available.}$$

The hypotheses created in the ARDL model caspase are tested by the Wald test (F statistics). The F statistics compared with the levels of significance that are to be asymptotically derived by Peseran et al. (2001). The lower and upper limits shown in the findings section of the study are asymptotically derived values. If the F statistic value is less than the lower limit found, the H0 hypothesis is accepted. In other words, there is no cointegration between variables. If the F statistic value is between the lower and upper limits, the cointegration relationship will not be established. This area is called the gray area and represents uncertainty. Finally, if the F statistic value is greater than the upper limit value, there is a cointegration relationship between variables. In this case, the H0 hypothesis is rejected and the H1 hypothesis is accepted. Diagnostic tests should be performed to accept long-term cointegration between variables. These tests can be listed as autocorrelation, heteroscedasticity, normality, ramsey reset, and cusum tests. After determining the long-term relationship between the variables, the error correction model (ECM) shown in Formula 2 should be established.

$$\Delta Y_t = \Psi_0 + \sum_{i=1}^{m} \Psi_{1i}\Delta Y_{t-i} + \sum_{i=0}^{n} \Psi_{2i}\Delta X_{1t-i} + \ldots + \sum_{i=0}^{r} \Psi_{ki}\Delta X_{kt-i} + \mu ecm_{t-1} + u_t \tag{2}$$

The established error correction model is used to analyze the short-term relationship between variables. The coefficient of the ECM variable shown in formula 2 shows how much of the imbalance occurring in the short term is corrected in the long term. The coefficient of this variable must be negative and significant.

4 Findings and Discussion

The study analyzes the relationship between the COVID-19 outbreak and selected indices composed of companies traded on Borsa İstanbul (BİST) using the ARDL model. In this part of the study, the data set, descriptive statistics, and findings related to the variables used in the empirical study are presented. Information on the variables used in the study is shown in Tab. 23.1. When Tab. 23.1 is examined, it is seen that the data set of the variables used in the study was created using different databases. While creating the data set, the sectors thought to be most affected by the COVID-19 pandemic were selected.

In the study, it was used as an independent variable in financial variables that are thought to have a significant effect on COVID-19. These variables are gold prices, oil prices, Turkey's CDS, and the VIX index that is referred to as the fear index. Finally, to measure the effect on sector returns of COVID-19, the number of cases and deaths seen in Turkey and the world is used. In the analysis part, firstly, descriptive statistics of the variables are given in Tab. 23.2.

One of the most important factors when analyzing descriptive statistics is the standard deviation value. The standard deviation value is accepted as a measure expressing risk. When the standard deviation values in Tab. 23.2 are examined, it is seen that the risk of BİST sector indices is higher than the risk of basic financial instruments. It has been determined that the risk related to gold is much less than other variables. When the correlations regarding the variables are evaluated, there is no correlation between the sector returns and the financial variables except the VIX index. Correlation analysis reveals that

Tab. 23.1: Data Set

Code	Explanation	Period	Source
R(XGIDA)	Return of BİST Food Index	01.09–07.10.2020	Borsa İstanbul
R(XTCRT)	Return of BİST Trade Index	01.09–07.10.2020	Borsa İstanbul
R(XTRZM)	Return of BİST Tourism Index	01.09–07.10.2020	Borsa İstanbul
R(XULAS)	Return of BİST Transportation Index	01.09–07.10.2020	Borsa İstanbul
R(XBANK)	Return of BİST Bank Index	01.09–07.10.2020	Borsa İstanbul
R(XBLSM)	Return of BİST Informatics Index	01.09–07.10.2020	Borsa İstanbul
NCTR	Number of Cases of COVID-19 in Turkey	01.09–07.10.2020	covid19.saglik.gov.tr
NCW	Number of Cases of COVID-19 Worldwide	01.09–07.10.2020	covid19.who.int
NDTR	Number of Deaths of COVID-19 in Turkey	01.09–07.10.2020	covid19.saglik.gov.tr
NDW	Numb. of Deaths of COVID-19 Worldwide	01.09–07.10.2020	covid19.who.int
CDS	Turkey CDS	01.09–07.10.2020	investing.com
VIX	VIX Index	01.09–07.10.2020	investing.com
GP	Gold Prices	01.09–07.10.2020	investing.com
BP	Brent Oil Prices	01.09–07.10.2020	investing.com

the significant relationship between the sector returns and the number of cases and deaths in Turkey. Finally, there is a significant relationship between the financial variables and the number of cases and deaths worldwide and Turkey. Established models can be expressed as follows:

Model I = R(XBANK) = β0 + β1LNNCTR + β2LNNDTR + β3LNNCW + β4LNNDW + β5LNBP + β6LNGP + β7LNCDS + β8LNVIX + εi
Model II = R(XBLSM) = β0 + β1LNNCTR + β2LNNDTR + β3LNNCW + β4LNNDW + β5LNBP + β6LNGP + β7LNCDS + β8LNVIX + εi
Model III = R(XGIDA) = β0 + β1LNNCTR + β2LNNDTR + β3LNNCW + β4LNNDW + β5LNBP + β6LNGP + β7LNCDS + β8LNVIX + εi
Model IV = R(XTCRT) = β0 + β1LNNCTR + β2LNNDTR + β3LNNCW + β4LNNDW + β5LNBP + β6LNGP + β7LNCDS + β8LNVIX + εi
Model V = R(XTRZM) = β0 + β1LNNCTR + β2LNNDTR + β3LNNCW + β4LNNDW + β5LNBP + β6LNGP + β7LNCDS + β8LNVIX + εi
Model VI = R(XULAS) = β0 + β1LNNCTR + β2LNNDTR + β3LNNCW + β4LNNDW + β5LNBP + β6LNGP + β7LNCDS + β8LNVIX + εi

Tab. 23.2: Descriptive Statistics

Variables*	Mean	Max.	Min.	Stand. Dev.	Skewness	Kurtosis	J.-Ber.	Probability
R(XGIDA)	0.09	5.05	-9.52	2.12	-1.76	8.44	222.68	0.0000
R(XTCRT)	0.25	7.35	-7.72	2.22	-0.02	5.53	33.94	0.0000
R(XTRZM)	0.34	8.04	-15.74	3.74	-1.06	5.61	60.20	0.0000
R(XULAS)	-0.13	8.95	-12.84	3.29	-0.34	5.24	29.11	0.0000
R(XBANK)	-0.18	7.55	-8.66	2.50	-0.32	5.43	33.58	0.0000
R(XBLSM)	0.34	9.38	-15.36	3.36	-0.94	6.49	83.57	0.0000
LNNCTR	4.48	8.47	0.00	3.55	-0.40	1.27	19.14	0.0000
LNNCW	9.45	12.28	0.00	3.06	-1.67	5.49	92.05	0.0000
LNNDTR	2.10	4.84	0.00	1.84	-0.07	1.34	14.53	0.0006
LNNDW	6.45	9.06	0.00	2.63	-1.07	3.12	24.71	0.0000
LNCDS	6.03	6.47	5.45	0.34	-0.51	1.74	13.85	0.0000
LNVIX	3.38	4.41	2.49	0.49	-0.18	2.32	3.11	0.2109
LNGP	7.41	7.50	7.29	0.04	-0.22	1.96	6.75	0.0347
LNBP	3.65	4.19	2.92	0.34	-0.11	1.91	6.51	0.0384

* The number of observations is 127 for all variables.

Unit root tests of the variables should be done first to be able to analyze with the ARDL method within the framework of the established models. For this purpose, Augmented Dickey Fuller (ADF) (Fuller, 1996), Philips-Perron (PP) (Philips & Perron, 1988) unit root tests, which are frequently used in the literature, were used. Unit root test results for variables are shown in Tab. 23.3.

When Tab. 23.3 is examined, it seems appropriate to use the ARDL test within the scope of the study, since it can be used for different degrees of cointegrated variables. Tab. 23.4 shows the ARDL limit test results for the models.

When Tab. 23.4 is examined, it is seen that models other than Model V provide the assumptions. Model V is rejected because it does not provide the Ramsey Reset test assumption ($p > 0.05$). Therefore, within the scope of the study, a significant relationship could not be established between the tourism sector returns and the pandemic. As other models provide all the assumptions (including the CUSUM test), the analysis of the long-term cointegration relationship between industry returns and COVID-19 has started. Tab. 23.5 shows the cointegration relationships between industry returns and variables.

When Tab. 23.5 is examined, a positive and significant relationship was found between the banking sector returns and oil prices, and VIX index

Tab. 23.3: Unit Root Tests

	Variables	ADF		PP	
		Intercept	Intercept and Trend	Intercept	Intercept and Trend
AT LEVEL	**R(XBANK)**	-12.55*	-12.56*	-12.50*	-12.54*
	R(XBLSM)	-7.68*	-7.65*	-7.85*	-7.82*
	R(XGIDA)	-9.99*	-10.01*	-10.18*	-10.14*
	R(XTCRT)	-10.48*	-10.50*	-10.48*	-10.50*
	R(XTRZM)	-8.92*	-8.98*	-9.42*	-9.42*
	R(XULAS)	-9.78*	-9.81*	-10.20*	-10.19*
	LNNCTR	-1.11	-0.83	-1.13	-1.07
	LNNDTR	-1.14	-0.73	-1.21	-1.05
	LNNCW	-3.61***	-3.28***	-3.58*	-3.12
	LNNDW	-2.90**	-1.70	-2.73***	-1.90
	LNBP	-1.58	-0.86	-1.62	-0.90
	LNGP	-1.21	-2.97	-1.36	-3.16***
	LNCDS	-1.34	-1.34	-1.39	-1.63
	LNVIX	-1.83	-1.39	-1.82	-1.29
AT FIRST DİFFERENT	**R(XBANK)**	-11.43*	-11.38*	-58.98*	-59.64*
	R(XBLSM)	-17.89*	-17.81*	-35.65*	-35.34*
	R(XGIDA)	-13.07*	-13.02*	-44.99*	-43.44*
	R(XTCRT)	-10.55*	-10.51*	-46.21*	-45.98*
	R(XTRZM)	-10.68*	-10.63*	-37.71*	-37.96*
	R(XULAS)	-9.48*	-9.45*	-43.18*	-43.08*
	LNNCTR	-7.69*	-7.71*	-8.14*	-8.16*
	LNNDTR	-8.90*	-8.94*	-9.35*	-9.36*
	LNNCW	-14.23*	-14.59*	-14.33*	-14.88*
	LNNDW	-18.52*	-19.00*	-18.19*	-20.00*
	LNBP	-10.43*	-10.62*	-10.45*	-10.62*
	LNGP	-10.11*	-10.07*	-10.09*	-10.05*
	LNCDS	-14.39*	-14.36*	-14.37*	-14.41*
	LNVIX	-13.00*	-13.17*	-12.86*	-13.04*

It expresses significance at the level of *1 %, ** 5 % and *** 10 %.

during the research period. This situation is that during the pandemic period, increases in oil prices and VIX index increased the banking sector returns. Findings regarding the banking sector can also be evaluated from the perspective of investors. Accordingly, investors should not invest in the banking sector

Tab. 23.4: ARDL Model Estimation Results

	MODEL I		**MODEL II**		**MODEL III**	
F-statistics	9.82(0.0000)		9.03(0.0000)		17.18(0.0000)	
Lag Length	[4,3,1,0,3,1,1,3,2]		[1,1,4,0,0,0,1,4,3,2]		[1,2,0,0,0,0,1,0,1]	
Significance	Critical Value		Critical Value		Critical Value	
	Lower Limit	Upper Limit	Lower Limit	Upper Limit	Lower Limit	Upper Limit
%1	2.79	4.1	2.65	3.97	2.79	4.1
%5	2.22	3.39	2.14	3.30	2.22	3.39
%10	1.95	3.06	1.88	2.99	1.95	3.06
Diagnostic Tests	**Statistics**		**Statistics**		**Statistics**	
R^2	0.54		0.55		0.47	
Adjusted R^2	0.42		0.43		0.41	
F-statistics	4.49(0.0000)		4.80(0.0000)		7.82(0.0000)	
Breus.-Godf. LM	1.22(0.5425)		0.94(0.6236)		2.27(0.3198)	
ARCH LM	3.12(0.0770)		1.03(0.3086)		3.64(0.0561)	
Normality	0.52(0.7686)		4.20(0.1220)		3.61(0.1641)	
Ramsey Reset	1.20(0.2759)		3.42(0.0674)		3.40(0.0768)	
	MODEL IV		**MODEL V**		**MODEL VI**	
F-statistics	17.81(0.0000)		11.12(0.0000)		10.11(0.0000)	
Lag Length	[1,4,1,4,2,4,0,1,0]		[1,2,1,0,0,0,3,3,1,1]		[4,1,0,1,0,0,4,4,4,4]	
Significance	Critical Value		Critical Value		Critical Value	
	Lower Limit	Upper Limit	Lower Limit	Upper Limit	Lower Limit	Upper Limit
1 %	2.79	4.1	2.65	3.97	2.65	3.97
5 %	2.22	3.39	2.14	3.30	2.14	3.30
10 %	1.95	3.06	1.88	2.99	1.88	2.99
Diagnostic Tests	**Statistics**		**Statistics**		**Statistics**	
R^2	0.47		0.48		0.65	
Adjusted R^2	0.34		0.37		0.53	
F-statistics	3.53(0.0000)		4.55(0.0000)		5.49(0.0000)	
Breus.-Godf. LM	2.96(0.2275)		1.69(0.4293)		0.00(0.9979)	
ARCH LM	0.87(0.3500)		0.84(0.3586)		0.12(0.7218)	
Normality	1.46(0.4811)		0.98(0.6101)		5.92(0.0518)	
Ramsey Reset	0.20(0.6548)		6.25(0.0140)		1.86(0.1749)	

Tab. 23.5: ARDL Model Cointegration Results

	MODEL I		MODEL II		MODEL III	
Variables	**Coefficient**	**t-statistics**	**Coefficient**	**t-statistics**	**Coefficient**	**t-statistics**
LNNCTR	0.06	0.33	1.11	2.13**	0.93	4.16*
LNNCW	-0.13	-0.96	0.54	1.14	-0.17	-0.84
LNNDTR	0.52	1.51	-0.99	-1.03	-1.03	-2.26**
LNNDW	0.08	0.39	-1.18	-1.72***	-0.08	-0.26
LNBP	3.09	2.80*	-0.03	0.00	0.37	0.25
LNGP	-9.12	-1.56	-34.50	-1.92***	-16.86	-2.46**
LNCDS	0.12	0.11	6.78	1.66***	-0.23	-0.17
LNVIX	1.01	2.00**	-3.98	-1.94***	0.33	0.47
	MODEL IV		**MODEL V**		**MODEL VI**	
Variables	**Coefficient**	**t-statistics**	**Coefficient**	**t-statistics**	**Coefficient**	**t-statistics**
LNNCTR	-1.29	-3.01*	-	-	-0.12	-0.72
LNNCW	-0.53	-1.16	-	-	-0.14	-0.87
LNNDTR	1.84	2.34**	-	-	1.25	4.01*
LNNDW	0.90	1.16	-	-	0.51	2.13**
LNBP	2.56	1.20	-	-	5.44	4.04*
LNGP	29.08	2.44**	-	-	-34.15	-5.43*
LNCDS	3.44	1.75***	-	-	0.68	0.47
LNVIX	-1.73	-1.98**	-	-	0.49	0.80

It expresses significance at the level of *1 %, ** 5 % and *** 10 %.

index, oil prices and VIX index together in order to diversify their portfolio. Because financial indicators acting together and in the same direction do not allow portfolio diversification.

A positive and significant relationship was found between the IT sector returns and the CDS premiums and the number of cases in Turkey. On the other hand, a negative and significant relationship has been determined between the IT sector returns and the number of deaths in the world, gold prices, and VIX index. Accordingly, the increase in the number of cases in Turkey has a positive effect on the returns of the information sector, while the increase in the number of deaths worldwide has a negative effect.

A positive and significant relationship was found between food industry returns and the number of cases in Turkey. On the other hand, a negative and significant relationship was found between food sector returns, gold prices, and deaths in Turkey. As a result of the measures taken and the first panic, the increase in the number of cases in Turkey led to the increase in demand for food products and increased the food sector returns. Similarly, a negative and significant relationship was found between the trade sector returns and the VIX index and the number of cases in Turkey. A positive and significant relationship was found between the trade sector returns and the number of deaths in Turkey, gold prices, and CDS premiums.

When the returns regarding the transportation sector were evaluated, a positive and significant relationship was found between the number of deaths in Turkey and the worldwide and oil prices. On the other hand, a negative and significant relationship was found between the transportation sector returns and gold prices. The decisions taken at the beginning of the pandemic caused significant declines in transportation sector returns. Considering the relationship between the sector returns and the number of cases, the increase in the number of cases in the long term has a positive effect on the informatics and food sectors. On the other hand, it can be said that its effect on the trade sector is negative. However, the error correction model (ECM) should be established in order to determine the short-term causality relationship in the ARDL model. The results of the model established within the scope of the empirical analysis are shown in Tab. 23.6.

According to the ECM model, the absolute value of the error correction coefficient must be less than 1 and negative to establish short-term relationships between variables. If the number is greater than 1 or positive, it is understood that the error correction model is not working. In addition, the error correction model coefficient is used to balance short-term relationships between variables in the long run. Accordingly, it can be analyzed how long short-term relations reach equilibrium with the formula $1/|ecm|$. Within the framework of these explanations, Model II, III and IV results are seen as meaningful, while other models are statistically insignificant.

In the short term, a negative and significant relationship was found between the IT sector returns and the number of cases in Turkey and the VIX index. A positive and significant relationship was found between the IT sector returns and gold prices. First of all, about 1.5 days is meant by the short term concept in the IT sector. Similarly, a negative and significant relationship was found between the food sector returns and the number of cases in Turkey and the VIX index. On the other hand, a positive and significant relationship was found between food sector returns and gold prices. About 1 day is meant by the concept of short term in the food sector. Finally, a negative and significant relationship was found between the trade sector and the number of cases in Turkey. This situation reveals that the increase in the number of cases negatively affects

Tab. 23.6: Error Correction Model (ECM) Estimation Results

	MODEL I		MODEL II		MODEL III	
Variables	**Coefficient**	**t-statistics**	**Coefficient**	**t-statistics**	**Coefficient**	**t-statistics**
LNNCTR	-1.89	-2.96*	-3.07	-3.69*	-2.43	-4.74*
LNNCW	-	-	-	-	-	-
LNNDTR	-1.58	-1.78***	0.94	0.77	-	-
LNNDW	0.57	1.46	-	-	-	-
LNBP	0.08	0.02	-	-	-	-
LNGP	24.76	1.68***	56.62	2.86*	43.44	3.74*
LNCDS	-4.37	-1.75***	2.60	0.87	-	-
LNVIX	-8.98	-4.81*	-4.88	-2.27**	-5.28	-3.89*
ECM(-1)	-1.88	-9.78*	-0.75	-9.93*	-0.95	-12.87
R^2	0.79		0.64		0.70	
Adj.-R^2	0.76		0.59		0.69	
F-statistics	22.97(0.0000)		12.06(0.0000)		57.00(0.0000)	
	MODEL IV		**MODEL V**		**MODEL VI**	
Variables	**Coefficient**	**t-statistics**	**Coefficient**	**t-statistics**	**Coefficient**	**t-statistics**
LNNCTR	-1.24	-2.04**	-	-	-	-
LNNCW	0.26	0.93	-	-	-	-
LNNDTR	3.92	4.61	-	-	-0.44	-0.44
LNNDW	0.61	1.35	-	-	0.34	0.84
LNBP	2.42	0.86	-	-	-	-
LNGP	-	-	-	-	-29.40	-1.62
LNCDS	-2.18	-1.07	-	-	-3.04	-1.01
LNVIX	-	-	-	-	-10.43	-5.47*
ECM(-1)	-0.99	-13.17*	-	-	-1.94	-10.54*
R^2	0.72		-		0.79	
Adj.-R^2	0.67		-		0.75	
F-statistics	16.03(0.0000)		-		18.01(0.0000)	

It expresses significance at the level of *1 %, ** 5 % and *** 10 %.

the sector returns in the short term. It should be noted here that the short term concept expresses about 1 day.

5 Conclusion

The study aims to determine the short and long-term relationships between selected sector indices on BİST and the COVID-19 outbreak. For this purpose,

BİST sub-sectors such as banking, informatics, food, trade, tourism, and transportation were selected. Within the scope of the research, the number of cases and deaths in Turkey and worldwide were used to measure the effects of the pandemic. Oil and gold prices, Turkey's CDS premium, and VIX fear index variables were used to reveal the relationship between sector indices and financial markets. The period of the research has been determined as 01.09–07.10.2020.

As a result of the study, significant relationships were found between the returns of information, food, and trade indices and the number of cases. In the informatics and food sectors, a negative relationship was found between the short term returns and the number of cases, while a positive relationship was found in the long term. In other words, the investors initially reacted negatively to the number of cases and the sector returns decreased. However, the expectation that the demand for the information and food sectors will increase during the pandemic process had a recovery effect on the market in the long term. Findings regarding the IT sector were also evaluated in terms of investors. In this study, it has been found that the IT sector index and the VIX index can be used for portfolio diversification in the short run and the gold prices and VIX index in the long run. In terms of the food sector, it is considered that investors can diversify their portfolio by using the VIX index in the short term and the gold prices and the food index together in the long term. When the relationship between the number of cases and the trade index was evaluated, it was found that the effect of the number of cases on the trade index was negative in general. It is evaluated that the negative impact of the number of cases on the trade index is due to the negative impact of commercial activities, especially due to the restriction (curfew, etc.) decisions taken under the pandemic.

Similar to the studies conducted by He et al. (2020), Anh and Gan (2020), Mazur et al. (2021) and Griffith et al. (2020) in this study, evidence was obtained that the effects of COVID-19 on sectors differ. Presenting the future studies by differentiating them by sectors and methods may provide useful information. While analyzing the relationships between COVID-19 and sector returns, it should not be overlooked that there is an opportunity for investors to diversify in both increases and decreases.

Bibliography

Al-Awadhi, A. M., Alsaifi, K., Al-Awadhi, A., & Alhammadi, S. (2020). Death and Contagious Infectious Diseases: Impact of the COVID-19 Virus on Stock Market Returns. *Journal of Behavioral and Experimental Finance, 27*(2020), 100326.

Ali, M., Alam, N., & Rizvi, S. A. R. (2020). Coronavirus (COVID-19)-An Epidemic or Pandemic for Financial Markets. *Journal of Behavioral and Experimental Finance, 27*(2020), 100341.

Anh, D. L. T., & Gan, C. (2020). The Impact of the COVID-19 Lockdown on Stock Market Performance: Evidence from Vietnam. *Journal of Economic Studies*, 2020, 1–16.

Choi, S. Y. (2020). Industry Volatility and Economic Uncertainty due to the COVID-19 Pandemic: Evidence from Wavelet Coherence Analysis. *Finance Research Letters, 37*(2020), 101783, 1–8.

Çiğdem, G. (2020). COVID-19 and Net Foreign Exchange Reserve Relationship in Turkey: Evidence from ARDL Bounds Testing Approach. *Journal of Business, Economics and Finance*, *9*(2), 80–96.

Engle, R. F., & Granger, C. W. (1987). Co-integration and Error Correction: Representation, Estimation, and Testing. *Econometrica: Journal of the Econometric Society*, *55*(2), 251–276.

Fuller, W. A. (1996). *Introduction to Statistical Time Series.* 2nd Edition. ABD: John Wiley and Sons Inc.

Gharib, C., Mefteh-Walib, S., & Jabeur, S. B. (2021). The Bubble Contagion Effect of COVID-19 Outbreak: Evidence from Crude Oil and Gold Markets. *Finance Research Letters, 38*(January 2021), 101703, 1–10.

Gherghina, S. C., Armeanu, D. S., & Joldes, C. C. (2020). Stock Market Reactions to COVID-19 Pandemic Outbreak: Quantitative Evidence from ARDL Bounds Tests and Granger Causality Analysis. *International Journal of Environmental Research and Public Health, 17*(18), 6729, 1–35.

Goodell, J. W. (2020). COVID-19 and Finance: Agendas for Future Research. *Finance Research Letters, 35*(July 2020), 101512, 1–5.

Griffith, R., Levell, P., & Stroud, R. (2020). The Impact of COVID-19 on Share Prices in the UK. *Fiscal Studies*, *41*(2), 363–369.

Johansen, S. (1988). Statistical Analysis of Cointegration Vectors. *Journal of Economic Dynamics and Control*, *12*(2–3), 231–254.

Kılıç, Y. (2020). Borsa İstanbul'da COVID-19 (Koronavirüs) Etkisi. *Journal of Emerging Economies and Policy*, *5*(1), 66–77.

Liu, H. Y., Manzoor, A., Wang, C. Y., Zhang, L., & Manzoor, Z. (2020). The COVID-19 Outbreak and Affected Countries Stock Markets Response. *International Journal of Environmental Research and Public Health, 17*(8), 2800, 1–19.

Markowitz, H. M., Hebner, M. T., & Brunson, M. H. (2009). "Does Portfolio Theory Work During Financial Crises?", Working Paper, http://www.

ifaarchive.com/pdf/does%20portfolio%20theory%20work%20hmm%20mbedits%205-19-09.pdf, Accessed Date: 19.09.2020.

Mazur, M., Dang, M., & Vega, M. (2021). COVID-19 and the March 2020 Stock Market Crash. Evidence from S&P1500. *Finance Research Letters*, *38*(January 2021), 101690, 1–8.

Mishra, A. K., Rath, B. N., & Dash, A. K. (2020). Does the Indian Financial Market Nosedive because of the COVID-19 Outbreak, in Comparison to after Demonetisation and the GST? *Emerging Markets Finance and Trade*, *56*(10), 2162–2180.

Öztürk, Ö., Şişman, M. Y., Uslu, H., & Çıtak, F. (2020). Effect of COVID-19 Outbreak on Turkish Stock Market: A Sectoral-level Analysis. *Hitit University Journal of Social Sciences Institute*, *13*(1), 56–68.

Phillips, P. C. B., & Perron, P. (1988). Testing for a Unit Root in Time Series Regressions. *Biometrika*, *75*, 335–346.

Pesaran, M. H., Shin, Y., & Smith, R. J. (2001). Bounds Testing Approaches to the Analysis of Level Relationships. *Journal of Applied Econometrics*, *16*, 289–326.

Pinglin, H., Yulong, S., Ying, Z., & Tao, L. (2020). COVID–19's Impact on Stock Prices Across Different Sectors–An Event Study Based on the Chinese Stock Market. *Emerging Markets Finance and Trade*, *56*(10), 2198–2212.

Reinhart, C. M., & Rogoff, K. S. (2009). The Aftermath of Financial Crises. *American Economic Review*, *99*(2), 466–72.

Sarı, S. S., & Kartal, T. (2020). The Relationship of COVID-19 Pandemic with Gold Prices, Oil Prices and VIX Index. *Erzincan University Journal of Social Sciences Institute*, *13*(1), 93–109.

Sharif, A., Aloui, C., & Yarovaya, L. (2020). COVID-19 Pandemic, Oil Prices, Stock Market, Geopolitical Risk and Policy Uncertainty Nexus in the US Economy: Fresh Evidence from the Waveletbased Approach. *International Review of Financial Analysis*, *70*, 1–9.

Sümer, L., & Özorhon, B. (2020). Investing in Gold or REIT Index in Turkey: Evidence from Global Financial Crisis, 2018 Turkish Currency Crisis and COVID-19 Crisis. *Journal of European Real Estate Research*, EarlyCite, 1–16.

Thakur, S. (2020). Effect of COVID-19 on Capital Market with Reference to S&P 500. *International Journal of Advanced Research*, *8*(06), 1118–1188. Available at SSRN: https://ssrn.com/abstract=3640871.

Asli Kose

The Effect of Covid-19 Pandemic on Solidarity Culture in Turkey

Abstract COVID-19 outbreak has become important problem of the World in 2020. World Health Organization accepted COVID-19 outbreak a pandemic on March 11, 2020. With the pandemic workplaces closed and production decreased. COVID-19 pandemic is affecting Turkey socially and economically as it is affecting many countries in global health. In Turkey, it is determined the first corona virus cases in March 2020. It may have some negative economicial, educational, agricultural and public health effects. This study includes a content that evaluates the adversities of the COVID-19 pandemic affecting social assistance. Social assistances are usually planned by central governments and implemented by local governments. Municipalities, one of the local governments, are one of the important institutions in delivering social assistances to the puclic. Central goverment and local goverments tried to support the public with social benefits by using different resources in COVID-19 pandemic. In this process, the culture of solidarity came to the fore. Turkey is experiencing the most beautiful examples of solidarity culture of the country in location. The world has also contributed positively to its image in addition to creating social benefits with the helth aids provided. The need for social assitances is excepted to increase in the face the consequences of the crisis in the future period. This situation will increase the need of public institutions for governance.

Keywords: Social Policy, COVID-19, Solidarity, Social Aid

1 Introduction

COVID-19 outbreak has become important problem of the World in 2020. World Health Organization accepted COVID-19 outbreak a pandemic on March 11, 2020. With the pandemic workplaces closed and production decreased. COVID-19 pandemic is affecting Turkey socially and economically as it is affecting many countries in global health. Today, countries around the world continue to struggle with the covid-19 pandemic in economic, social and health fields. The results of this national and international struggle will shape the future. The covid-19 epidemic is not only a medical problem, which, instead, can be defined as a public health crisis.In Turkey, it is determined the first corona virus cases in March 2020. It may have some negative economicial, educational, agricultural and public health effects. Social assistance is of significant role in decreasing the social impacts.Social assistance is the focus of social state discussions (Yılmaz, 2015). The place and function of social assistance are shaped depending on the assistance regimes of countries (Gokbayrak, 2017). Social security is both a human right and a policy which is under the responsibility of a state. Social assistance has an important place within social security systems (Bulut, 2011). Social assistance programs are accepted as one of the measures that covers deficits of social security systems (Zengin, Sahin & Ozcan, 2012). Social policies are generally planned by centralized governments and applied by local administrations. States have the most effective position in solving problems among social policy practice fields. Local administrations also have an important position in applying social policies being the closest institutions to public. Although social assistance programs are national in the first place, practice and local interpretation of programs are executed depending on arrangements of local administrations (Toprak & Sataf, 2009). Social assistance is one of the application instruments of social policies. In Turkey, many institutions generate social assistance in order to attain specific aims (Tekindal, 2018). Social assistance and solidarity are important parts of human and society reality. Practices based on needs mostly depend on charity and benevolence. Solidarity in primitive communities, church, benevolence in middle ages and social donation system in Anatolian and Islam communities and mainly in Ottoman have improved during historical process (Dalyan & Bayır, 2019). Today, social assistance that citizens make use of varies according to welfare level of countries. These assistances may vary not only according to welfare but also depending on the scope of effects of economic crises, war, mass migrations, epidemic. Following the first case detected on March 11 in Turkey, measures were taken in phases in order to prevent spread of virus. Due to COVID-19, important structural changes have been experienced in economic and social fields namely monetary and financial market, trade, education and service industry (TUBA COVID-19 Report, 2020). Arrangements made for working and economic process are focused on sustainability of life. Key factors for maintaining the sustainability of life are characterized as accessibility to social assistance.

2 Social Assistance Provided by the Central Administration

The structure that is responsible for providing central social assistance is the Ministry of Family and Social Policy. Below are the sorts of social assistance that the ministry provided during the COVID-19 pandemic.

Within the scope of COVID-19 pandemic Phase 1,2 million 111 thousand houses were assisted with 1.000 TL cash money. Apart from this, periodical share that is sent to social assistance and solidarity foundations was increased from 135 million TL to 180 million TL, and the periodical share was arranged as double considering Ramadan month. Within the scope of Phase 2, social assistance and solidarity foundations were consulted for evaluation of people in need Ministry of Family, Labour and Social Services, 2020.

One of the institutions that provide support for the welfare service is the social welfare foundations. Social Welfare Foundations are one of the institutions that have been reorganized since 2011 for developing social policies of the Ministry of Family and Social Policy (Turkoglu, 2013). These institutions have been filling an important gap in social welfare in Turkey since 1986 (Daslı, 2018). These institutions have an important role in the COVID-19 pandemic as well.

2,3 million houses which were detected with the help of social assistance and solidarity foundations and could not make use of the Phase 1 were assisted with 1,000 TL without any application within the scope of Phase 2. 6 million application were analyzed in Phase 3 and 2,5 million families were assisted with 1.000 TL pandemic social help. Ramadan bonuses of the retirees were paid before Ramadan month (Ministry of Family, Labour and Social Services, 2020). We have each other national solidarity campaign was initiated by the President. Society, public and private sector representatives have contributed to this campaign. (www.bizbizeyeteriz.gov.tr, 2020). Supports of local administrations and fidelity social support groups and also security forces were acquired to meet the needs of elders and handicapped citizens and people living alone due to curfew taken for COVID-19 pandemic (TUBA COVID-19 Report, 2020). Public claims that the private sector would benefit from tax breaks through donations have caused controversy. Confidentiality is the most important characteristics of donations and grants, which have religious, moral, and social aspects with philanthropy at the core. However, it seems contradictory that donations, which should be based on the motive of philanthropy, are subjected to deductions in tax assessments (Ertekin, 2018).

The service sector has been negatively affected at a high level from the measurements preventing mobility of people due to the COVID-19 pandemic (Atay, 2020). Given the prevalence of the outbreak and the extent of the crisis, employers may face significant financial and legal burdens as a result of the COVID-19 outbreak if they do not pay attention to the obligations imposed by the outbreak. On the other hand, when certain practices and advantages defined in the legislation are used, it will be possible to partially compensate for the losses in production as a result of the outbreak (Esen, 2020).

As a part of the struggle against the pandemic, incentives for the private sector, where production and employment were suspended, were implemented through the coordination of the ministries. Certain measures such as short work allowance have been be used by those who have paid 450 days of premium in the last 3 years among those who are subject to a 60-day service contract. This practice means that each insured person receives a short work allowance equivalent to 58 Turkish Liras to 146 Turkish Liras per day (Ministry of Family, Labor and Social Services, 2020). However, certain losses of rights were experienced since the implementation was based on the effective date of the law in the Official Gazette.

In this process, which is successfully managed together with the world acting in concert and creating local solutions, non-governmental organizations should take more active roles (Aslan, 2020). In accordance with the decisions to meet the needs of the elderly, disabled and solitary individuals during the curfew restrictions, certain kinds of support were received from local authorities and organizations such as the *vefa* (*lit.fidelity*) social support groups, especially the security forces (TUBA COVID-19 Report, 2020).

3 Social Assistance Activities of Municipalities as the Local Administrations

Municipalities, known as the closest local administrations to citizens, are the most effective institutions in meeting the needs of the people (Kesgin, 2016). The Turkish municipality understanding has experienced changes in the historical process. Changes in municipal laws and social responsibilities assigned to municipalities have made these institutions important actors in the need to implement social practices (Sezik, 2016). With the Municipal Law No. 5393, municipalities are also assigned important tasks and responsibilities concerning social relief. Although there are municipalities in Turkey that work effectively in terms of social policy functions, applications have not yet reached the desired level (Yıldırım, 2014).

Some of the social assistance implementations offered by local administrations during the COVID-19 pandemic period are presented below (KOSGEB, 2020).

A total of 934.128 people applied for social assistance to Istanbul Metropolitan Municipality, and 613.743 of them were identified as eligible for social assistance. In terms of benevolent bill payment campaign, a total of 6.630.749 TL was paid for the water (ISKI) and natural gas (IGDAS) bills of 52.598 needy people in the city. Apart from these, certain implementations were applied like providing foodstuff boxes, waiving the rental payments for 3 months for

3 thousand tenants using the shops and dwellings of the municipality, free accommodation for medical personnel, and milk assistance for children.

Ankara Metropolitan Municipality provided certain kinds of assistance such as providing shopping cards with cash credits, food aid, hygiene boxes, income support for the private drivers of city transportation, supporting tailors, who were forced to shut down their businesses, by hiring them in production of facial masks in the ateliers of the municipality, fuel support for the 2.850 private city transportation drivers, providing dinners during the Ramadan for the people in need through the "This iftar dinner is for you", paying the debts of individuals in need to the local groceries by the help of philanthropists, paying the water bills of individuals in need and providing financial aid for them through the *6 Million Banding Together for a Happy Feast* campaign.

Izmir Metropolitan Municipality provided food aid boxes and cash assistance for 40.000 households without income, provided support for citizens with disabilities and over 65 years of age, assistance to citizens with chronic illnesses, free service to health workers and discounts on water consumption.

Kocaeli Metropolitan Municipality provided certain types of assistance such as meeting the needs of citizens over 65 years of age and with chronic illnesses, providing food, fuel and hygiene boxes, rent support, water bills support and free transportation to health personnel.

Through the "Shoulder to Shoulder Campaign", Bursa Metropolitan Municipality provided food and basic hygiene boxes within the scope of social solidarity, paid for the water bills of those in need, provided "Card-16" support and assistance for those over 65 years old, psychological support, and provided 2 meals per day for the poor people.

Gaziantep Metropolitan Municipality provided food assistance for 21.000 needy families, paid the debts of needy families to the local grocery stores with a budget of 2 million Turkish Liras through a record book named as *Zimem*, which was also kept as the debt record book in the Ottoman periods. 50,000 soaps and bleach bottles were distributed to citizens in need, food aid boxes were provided for 11.000 households, breakfasts, dry food, and hot food were provided for citizens aged 65 and over, decreased the rental payments of the tenants of the municipality by 50 % and increased the daily wage of its employees by 33 TL.

Adana Metropolitan Municipality provided water bill discount, *Seyhan assistance card*, psychological support line, and assistance to needy people over 65 years of age.

Konya Metropolitan Municipality decided to make a discount in water bills, providing accommodation for homeless people in hotels, waiving the water bills of the unemployed residents for 2 months with an increased social support for citizens in need through the holy month of Ramadan.

Samsun Metropolitan Municipality provided free transportation to health workers with municipal vehicles, accommodation to health workers in hotels, delivery of the needs of citizens over 65 years of age at home, certain needs of 4.618 citizens such as buying drugs or grocery shopping.

Mersin Metropolitan Municipality provided 120.000 food aid, 200.000 health packages, hot meals and free bread to 3500 households per day, and canceled the payments of water bills up to 10 cubic meters for citizens in need.

In the Union of Municipalities of Marmara region, Küçükçekmece municipality provided 5.354 food aid boxes, Maltepe municipality met the grocery, pharmacy, and cleaning needs of 722 families, Balıkesir municipality provided food aid boxes to 20.000 families, Sakarya Metropolitan Municipality distributed basic hygiene boxes, Bursa Mudanya Municipality provided 1500 families with food, vegetables, fruits, and cleaning supplies (Union of Municipalities of Marmara, 2020).

Examining the implementations of social assistance in local governments as part of the struggle against the COVID-19 in Turkey, it seems that the focus is on meeting humanitarian needs. Under the influence of our cultural understanding and with the support of citizens, municipalities with limited resources have contributed to meeting the needs of many needy citizens. Certain conflicts experienced between the central government and local governments in practice did not prevent the continuation of the culture of assistance.

In studies conducted on social assistance in Turkey, it is stated that certain roles of more than one public institution in social assistance (such as ministry, provincial governorship, district governorship) cause coordination problems particularly in the distribution of aid (Gunes, 2012). In this regard, social solidarity and assistance foundations, public institutions operating in this area and municipalities acting together within the framework of governance will reduce management problems and waste of resources in social assistance (Aygen, 2014). Given that the losses that the epidemic will create in the field of production and economy will lead to an increase in unemployment, the need for governance in public institutions will increase particularly in the future. Similarly, in the assessments of TUBA COVID-19 report, it was stated that national approaches rather enclosed than globalized will stand out in management within the pandemic process. According to the new understanding of public administration, governance principles reduce the hierarchical aspects of the public, increasing its rationality (Kalkan & Alparslan, 2009). The most important contribution of the COVID-19 pandemic process to the Turkish public administration culture is that it made the need for governance among the public institutions more visible.

When the cases of social assistance practices of local administrations within the scope of COVID-19 in Turkey are examined, it is seen that assistances are mainly focused on human needs. With the effect of our cultural consciousness, municipalities which have restricted sources have contributed to meeting requirements of citizens in need with the help of citizens. Conflicts of central administration and local administrations in practice could not prevent sustaining the culture of helping each other. Decisions taken for gathering financial assistances under one roof continued as meeting requirements of people in need in different ways instead of cash benefit campaigns of local administrations. Thanks to the campaign of Ankara Metropolitan Municipality which can be regarded as one of the best examples of successful practices, debts of people at local markets were compensated. This practice was taken example by Gaziantep Metropolitan Municipality. Another successful practice is pending billing campaign of Istanbul Metropolitan Municipality which was followed by Ankara, Izmir and Aydın Metropolitan Municipalities. With this campaign, water and natural gas bills of citizens in need were paid by others.

4 Conclusion

The year 2020 will be commemorated with COVID-19 pandemic and losses due to this pandemic. Countries throughout the world are trying to manage this situation with different strategies. Turkey is a country where we experience the most beautiful cases of helping and solidarity culture. Apart from providing social assistance to other countries in the world, Turkey has also brought positive contribution to its general image. By making use of different sources, centralized and local administrations tried to support public with social help. It is expected in the future that people will have more and more social assistance due to the consequences of this crisis. This case will increase the need of public institutions for governance more and more.

Bibliography

Alparslan, A. M., & Kalkan, A. (2009). Şeffaflık, İletişim ve Hesap Verebilirliğin Yerel Yönetim Başarılarına Etkileri. *Sosyal ve Beşeri Bilimler Dergisi, 1*(1), 25–40.

Aslan, R. (2020). Tarihten Günümüze Epidemiler, Pandemiler ve Covid-19. *Göller Bölgesi Aylık Ekonomi ve Kültür Dergisi, 8*(85), 35–41.

Atay, L. (2020). COVID-19 Salgını ve Turizme Etkileri. *Seyahat ve Otel İşletmeciliği Dergisi, 17*(1), 168–172.

Aygen, M. (2014). Sosyal Belediyecilik Üzerine Bir İnceleme: Elazığ Belediyesi Örneği. *Fırat Üniversitesi Harput Araştırmaları Dergisi, 1*(1), 173–192.

Biz Bize Yeteriz. (2020, May 20). Retrived from https://www.bizbizeyeteriz.gov.tr.

Bulut, M. (2011). Sosyal Güvenlik Sistemlerinde Sosyal Yardım ve Türkiye'de Durum. Yardım ve Dayanışma, *2*(3), 57–64.

Dalyan, M. G., & Bayır, Ö. Ö. (2019). 12. Yüzyılda Türk-İslam Toplumuna Sosyal Refah ve Sosyal Hizmetlerin Tarihsel Kökleri-Hayırseverlik Uygulamaları Bakımından Erbil Hakimi Muzafereddin Gökbörü Örneği. *Tarih Okulu Dergisi*, 1682–1695.

Daşlı, Y. (2018). Yoksullukla Mücadele Aracı Olarak Sosyal Yardımlaşma ve Dayanışma Vakıfları. *C.Ü. İktisadi ve İdari Bilimler Dergisi, 19*(2), 526–542.

Ertekin, Ş. (2018). Bağış ve Yardım Kavramının Vergisel Açıdan Analizi. TURAN-SAM Uluslararası Bilimsel Hakemli Dergisi, *10*(37), 222–227.

Esen, B. (2020). Coronavirüs (Covid 19) Salgını Kapmasında Çalışma Yaşamında Dikkat Edilmesi Gereken Yükümlülükler, Haklar ve Alınması Gereken Tedbirler. *Lebib Yalkın Mevzuat Dergisi, 1*(5), 1–9.

Gökbayrak, Ş. (2017). Değişen Refah Devletleri ve Sosyal Yardımlar. *Sosyal Güvenlik Dergisi, 7*(1), 71–90.

Güneş, M. (2012). Yoksullukla Mücalede Sosyal Yardımların Bir Kamu Yönetimi Politikası Olarak Sürdürülebilirliği. *SÜ İİBF Sosyal ve Ekonomik Araştırmalar Dergisi, 12*(4), 149–184.

Kesgin, B. (2016). Sosyal Hizmet ve Sosyal Yardımda Büyükşehir Belediyeleri İle İlçe Belediyeleri Arasında Nasıl Bir Dağılım Yapılabilir?. *Dokuz Eylül Üniversitesi Sosyal Bilimler Enstitüsü Dergisi, 18*(3), 447–462.

Koçak, O., Arslan, H., & Eti, S. (2017). Belediyelerde Sosyal Politika Uygulamaları ve Pendik Belediyesi Örneği. Uluslararası Toplum Araştırmaları Dergisi, *7*(12), 119–144.

KOSGEB. (2020, May 10). Retrived from https://www.kosgeb.gov.tr.

Ministry of Family, Labor and Social Services. (2020, May 20). Retrived from https://www.ailevecalisma.gov.tr.

Sezik, M. (2016). Türkiye'de Sosyal Belediyeciliğin Gelişim Ve Sorun Alanları. İnönü Üniversitesi Uluslararası Sosyal Bilimler Dergisi, *5*(2), 171–186.

Tekindal, M. (2018). Türkiye'de Sosyal Yardımların Yapısal İşlevsel Yaklaşıma Göre Analizi. *Toplum ve Sosyal Hizmet, 29*(2), 335–362.

Toprak, D., & Şataf, C. (2009). Türkiye'de Yerel Yönetimler Reformu Çerçevesinde Sosyal Belediyecilik Yaklaşımı. *Sosyal ve Beşeri Bilimler Dergisi, 1*(1), 11–24.

TUBA COVID-19 Report. (2020, June 10). Retrived from https://www.tuba.gov.tr.

Türkoğlu, İ. (2013). Sosyal Devlet Bağlamında Türkiye'de Sosyal Yardım Ve Sosyal Güvenlik. *Akademik İncelemeler Dergisi, 8*(3), 275–305.

Union of Municipalities of Marmara. (2020, May 25). Retrived from https://www.marmara.gov.tr.

Üstün, Ç., & Özçitçi, S. (2020). COVID- 19 Pandemisinin Sosyal Yaşam Ve Etik Düzlem Üzerine Etkileri: Bir Değerlendirme Çalışması. *Anadolu Kliniği Tıp Bilimleri Dergisi, 25*(1), 142–153.

WHO. (2020, May 30). Retrived from https://www.who.int.

Yıldırım, A. (2014). Belediyelerin Sosyal Politika Uygulamaları Üzerine Bir Değerlendirme: Malatya Belediyesi Örneği. *Adıyaman Üniversitesi Sosyal Bilimler Enstitüsü Dergisi, 7*(17), 485–509.

Yılmaz, B. (2015). Yeni Türkiye, Yeni Refah Rejimi, Yeni Yönet(iş)im ve Yoksulluk: Sosyal Yardımların Anlam ve Ehemmiyetine Dair. *İdealkent, 16*(1), 182–209.

Zengin, E., Şahin, A., & Özcan, S. (2012). Türkiye'de Sosyal Yardım Uygulamaları. *Yönetim ve Ekonomi: Celal Bayar Üniversitesi İktisadi ve İdari Bilimler Fakültesi Dergisi, 19*(2), 133–142.

www.ingramcontent.com/pod-product-compliance
Ingram Content Group UK Ltd.
Pitfield, Milton Keynes, MK11 3LW, UK
UKHW020153290926
15471UKWH00005B/855

9 783631 815939